MUSEUMS, EQUALITY AND SOCIAL JUSTICE

The last two decades have seen concerns for equality, diversity, social justice and human rights move from the margins of museum thinking and practice, to the core. The arguments – both moral and pragmatic – for engaging diverse audiences, creating the conditions for more equitable access to museum resources, and opening up opportunities for participation, now enjoy considerable consensus in many parts of the world. A growing number of institutions are concerned to construct new narratives that represent a plurality of lived experiences, histories and identities which aim to nurture support for more progressive, ethically-informed ways of seeing and to actively inform contemporary public debates on often contested rights-related issues. At the same time it would be misleading to suggest an even and uncontested transition from the museum as an organisation that has been widely understood to marginalise, exclude and oppress to one which is wholly inclusive. Moreover, there are signs that momentum towards making museums more inclusive and equitable is slowing down or, in some contexts, reversing.

Museums, Equality and Social Justice aims to reflect on and, crucially, to inform debates in museum research, policy and practice at this critical time. It brings together new research from academics and practitioners and insights from artists, activists and commentators to explore the ways in which museums, galleries and heritage organisations are engaging with the fast-changing equalities terrain and the shifting politics of identity at global, national and local levels and to investigate their potential to contribute to more equitable, fair and just societies.

Richard Sandell is Professor and Head of the School of Museum Studies at the University of Leicester and his research interests focus on museums, human rights and equality. He is Series Editor, with Christina Kreps, of *Museum Meanings*. His books include *Museums, Society, Inequality* (2002); *Museums, Prejudice and the Reframing of Difference* (2007); *Museum Management and Marketing* with Robert Janes (2007) and, with Jocelyn Dodd and Rosemarie Garland-Thomson, *Re-Presenting Disability: Activism and Agency in the Museum* (2010).

Eithne Nightingale is Head of Equality and Diversity at the V&A and has worked in equal opportunities, education, community development and museums for over 30 years. She has taken a lead on museum-wide equality strategies; collaborated with culturally diverse communities on initiatives encompassing collections research, public programming and partnership development; and has written and lectured extensively on diversity in museums both in the UK and internationally.

MUSEUM MEANINGS
Series Editors
Richard Sandell and Christina Kreps

Museums have undergone enormous changes in recent decades; an ongoing process of renewal and transformation bringing with it changes in priority, practice and role as well as new expectations, philosophies, imperatives and tensions that continue to attract attention from those working in, and drawing upon, wide ranging disciplines.

Museum Meanings presents new research that explores diverse aspects of the shifting social, cultural and political significance of museums and their agency beyond, as well as within, the cultural sphere. Interdisciplinary, cross-cultural and international perspectives and empirical investigation are brought to bear on the exploration of museums' relationships with their various publics (and analysis of the ways in which museums shape – and are shaped by – such interactions).

Theoretical perspectives might be drawn from anthropology, cultural studies, art and art history, learning and communication, media studies, architecture and design and material culture studies amongst others. Museums are understood very broadly – to include art galleries, historic sites and other cultural heritage institutions – as are their relationships with diverse constituencies.

The focus on the relationship of the museum to its publics shifts the emphasis from objects and collections and the study of museums as text, to studies grounded in the analysis of bodies and sites; identities and communities; ethics, moralities and politics.

Also in the series:

Praise for this book

MUSEUMS, EQUALITY AND SOCIAL JUSTICE

Edited by Richard Sandell and
Eithne Nightingale

LONDON AND NEW YORK

First published 2012
by Routledge
2 Park Square, Milton Park, Abingdon, Oxon OX14 4RN

Simultaneously published in the USA and Canada
by Routledge
711 Third Avenue, New York, NY 10017

Routledge is an imprint of the Taylor & Francis Group, an informa business

British Library Cataloguing in Publication Data
A catalogue record for this book is available from the British Library

Library of Congress Cataloging-in-Publication Data
Museums, equality, and social justice / edited by Richard Sandell and Eithne Nightingale.
p. cm. — (Museum meanings)
Includes bibliographical references and index.
1. Museums—Social aspects. 2. Museums—Philosophy. I. Sandell, Richard, 1967–
II. Nightingale, Eithne.
AM7.M8835 2012
069—dc23
2011044793

ISBN: 978–0–415–50468–3 (hbk)
ISBN: 978–0–415–50469–0 (pbk)
ISBN: 978–0–203–12005–7 (ebk)

Typeset in Bembo
by Swales & Willis Ltd, Exeter, Devon

CONTENTS

ILLUSTRATIONS

Front cover

Patricia Cronin, *Memorial to a Marriage*, 2002.

Frontispiece

Tables

Figures

Colour plates

Plates can be found between pp. 168–169.

CONTRIBUTORS

The volume is comprised of chapters written by (and shaped through engagement with) the following academics and researchers, practitioners, activists, artists and commentators:

Musleh Al-Qubati is an archaeologist who received his Master's Degree from Sana'a University in 1998. He is currently working for the General Authority for Antiquities and Museums (GOAM) of Yemen. Mr Al-Qubati has participated in a number of surveys and excavations in Marib. Being a long-standing member of several international excavation teams in Yemen, he has worked as part of the Marib Museum Team, Yemen from the start of the project.

Rajiv Anand is a trained textile artist with a Master's Degree in Art Theory. He has been working in the museums sector for 16 years and has experience of developing projects at a local, regional and national level. His expertise and experience lies in cultural diversity, inclusion, arts education and audience development. Rajiv is a museum consultant who has worked on the national diversity project JAINpedia for the Institute of Jainology. He previously worked for Kirklees Council for six years as the Community Museums Officer working with the hardest to reach audiences on exhibitions and events. He relocated to London to join the Museums, Libraries and Archives Council as the Cultural Diversity Officer advising the local regional agencies on how best to attract diverse groups to museums. Rajiv also worked for the Race Equality think tank the Runnymede Trust before joining the V&A as the South Asian Officer and Diversity Team Leader.

David Anderson is Director General of the National Museum of Wales and formerly Director of Learning and Interpretation at the V&A where he was manager of the museum's learning services, community programmes, and audience research and gallery interpretation. He also had responsibility for cultural policy, diversity and external partnerships across the V&A. He is the author of the influential report, *A Common Wealth: Museums in the Learning* Age (1999), and has published and lectured widely on the educational and social role of museums.

Susan Davis Baldino teaches graduate courses in Museum Studies at Florida State University and is a consultant and advocate for the arts, museums and persons with disabilities. She is a member of the Florida Council on Arts and Culture, board chair for the Center for Autism and Related Disabilities, past president of the Tallahassee Museum and former chair of the Florida Association of Museums Foundation and has worked with 'Keys to Exceptional Youth Success' that provides postsecondary scholarships for students with disabilities. Susan received her PhD from the School of Museum Studies, University of Leicester.

Simona Bodo is an independent researcher with a particular interest in the social agency of museums and their role in the promotion of intercultural dialogue. On these issues she acts as an adviser to public and private institutions (including the Ministry for Cultural Heritage and Activities, Brera Picture Gallery, Fondazione ISMU – Initiatives and Studies on Multiethnicity), and has recently taken part in a number of projects supported by the Lifelong Learning Programme of the European Union. She is co-creator and editor of *Patrimonio e Intercultura*, an online resource devoted to the intercultural potential of heritage education projects.

Janice Cheddie is a researcher, writer and academic whose work focuses on contemporary visual culture, difference, cultural democracy and cultural policy. She is Visiting Lecturer at the Greenwich Business School and Research Affiliate at the Institute of Converging Arts and Sciences (ICAS), University Of Greenwich. She was lead consultant for the Heritage Diversity Task Force, London Mayor's Commission on African and Asian Heritage (2005–2009) and associate editor of *Embedding Shared Heritage* (Greater London Authority, 2009).

Chia-Li Chen is an associate professor at the Graduate Institute of Museum Studies, Taipei National University of the Arts, Taiwan. She is the author of *Museums and Cultural Identities: Learning and Recollection in Local Museums in Taiwan* and *Wound on Exhibition: Notes on Memory and Trauma*. Her research interests focus on three main areas: museums and contemporary social issues, visitor studies and the history of community and literature museums.

Andrew Dewdney is Professor of Educational Development at London South Bank University. His book, *Post Critical Museology: Theory and Practice in the Art Museum* (2012; co-edited with David Dibosa and Victoria Walsh) broadens the Tate Encounters research findings, arguing for a new approach to research in the cultural sector. He is currently writing a new edition of *The New Media Handbook* (2006), co-authored with Peter Ride, which develops a framework for thinking about the emerging academic field of study of new media. He is interested in and concerned with the concept and practical utility of critical reflexivity and really useful knowledge in the service of progressive cultural change.

David Dibosa trained as a curator, after receiving his first degree from Girton College, Cambridge. He was awarded his PhD in Art History from Goldsmiths College, London, for a thesis titled, *Reclaiming Remembrance: Art, Shame and Commemoration*. During the 1990s, David curated public art projects, including a billboard project and a sculpture park in the West Midlands. From 2004 to 2008, he was Senior Lecturer in Fine Art Theory at Wimbledon College of Art, University of the Arts London (UAL). He remains at UAL, where he is now Course Director for MA Art Theory, at Chelsea College of Art and Design.

David Fleming is Director of National Museums Liverpool, where he has worked since 2001. He has a special interest in the social value of museums, and their role in creating social justice. Two recent projects – the International Slavery Museum and the Museum of Liverpool – have been set up consciously to create social justice. He has travelled widely to study museum work around the world and to develop ways to support greater international co-operation between museums.

Christine Gerbich is Research Associate in Visitor Studies at the Technical University, Berlin. She is a social scientist who has worked for several state-funded projects in the educational and health sector in Germany. Since 2007 she has been a staff member of the Marib Museum Team, being responsible for visitor research and exhibition evaluation. Since November 2009 she has been working for the project 'Exhibition Experiment Museology: On Curating Islamic Art and Culture' at the Technical University in Berlin which aims to develop new audiences for the Museum of Islamic Art in Berlin.

Barry Ginley. In 1994, after an eye operation which went wrong, Barry has been visually impaired. In 2001 he studied part time at the University of Reading and has gained the MSc in Inclusive Environments Design and Management. Barry currently works as Head of Disability and Social Inclusion at the V&A and previously worked as a consultant to the RNIB. Building on his expertise on disability, he has recently been appointed as one of 12 Ambassadors for the 'Strengthening Disabled People's User-Led Organisations' project on behalf of the Office for Disability Issues.

Hannah Goodwin is the Manager of Accessibility at the Museum of Fine Arts, Boston, United States, a position she took up following an Artist-in-Residence experience that exposed both inclusive and non-inclusive practices in schools and other venues. As an artist and educator, Hannah is committed to increasing access to cultural experiences for all and, more particularly, furthering accessibility for people with disabilities within her practice, through teaching and advocacy.

Susan Kamel is a curator and Research Associate in Museum Studies at the Technical University Berlin. From November 2009 she was responsible for the research project 'Exhibition Experiment Museology: On Curating Islamic Art and Culture'. The findings of this project will contribute to the refurbishment of the Museum of Islamic Art in Berlin. She is also working for the Marib Museum Project, a cooperative between the German Archaeological Institute, Branch Sanaa and the Yemeni Social Fund for Development. She has edited the book *From Imperial Museum to Communication Centre? On the new Role of Museums as Mediators between Science and Non-Western Societies* (2010) with Lidia Guzy and Rainer Hatoum and written numerous articles on museums of Islamic art and cultures and museums in the Arab world.

Kimberly F. Keith earned her PhD in Sociology at Goldsmiths, University of London, researching how US and UK museum practitioners develop and engage diverse audiences in relation to disparate organisational cultures and strategic policies. For 15 years Kimberly worked in museums developing educational programmes, most specifically for at-risk youth and diverse audiences, at the Children's Museum of Seattle, Washington and the Museum of Glass: International Center for Contemporary Art in Tacoma, Washington. She is a Trustee on the board of the Black Cultural Archives in the Brixton area of south London, and serves on its Raleigh Hall Development Project Board.

Amy K. Levin is Director of Women's Studies and Professor of English at Northern Illinois University, where she has also served as a coordinator of Museum Studies. She received her undergraduate degree from Harvard University and her doctorate from City University of New York. Levin has published four books, including two on museums: *Defining Memory: Local Museums and the Construction of History in America's Changing Communities* (2007) and *Gender, Sexuality, and Museums: A Routledge Reader* (2010). Her current research focuses on narratives of Western humanitarian medical interventions in formerly colonised nations.

Chandan Mahal is Head of Audience Development at The Women's Library, London Metropolitan University, where she is responsible for managing the public events, and the learning and community engagement programmes. She was previously the Diversity and Programme Manager at the Museum of London, where she was responsible for overseeing the implementation of the museum's equality and diversity strategies, with a particular focus on public programmes, audience development and workforce development. She was one of the commissioners for the Mayor's Commission on African and Asian Heritage in 2005 and is currently a board member for engage (the National Association for Gallery Education).

Janet Marstine is Lecturer and Programme Director of Art Museum and Gallery Studies in the School of Museum Studies at the University of Leicester. Her research focuses on museum ethics in theory and practice and on institutional critique and its impact on ethics. Marstine is editor of *The Routledge Companion to Museum Ethics: Redefining Ethics for the Twenty-First Century Museum* (2011) and *New Museum Theory and Practice: An Introduction* (2005). She is the founder and former director of the Institute of Museum Ethics (IME) at Seton Hall University.

Helen Mears is Keeper of World Art at Royal Pavilion and Museums, Brighton and Hove. Previously she was African Diaspora Research Fellow at the V&A, London.

Kylie Message is Associate Professor in the School of Archaeology and Anthropology and Associate Dean (Research Training) for the College of Arts and Social Sciences at the Australian National University. She is author of *New Museums and the Making of Culture* (2006) and co-editor of volumes on cultural politics, collections, and material culture that include *Compelling Cultures: Representing Cultural Diversity and Cohesion in Multicultural Australia* (with A. Edmundson and U. Frederick, 2009) and *Museum Theory: An Expanded Field* (with A. Witcomb, forthcoming). She is a Managing Editor for the journals *Museum and Society* and *Museum Worlds (Advances in Research)* and review editor for *Australian Historical Studies*.

Wayne Modest is currently head of the Curatorial Department of the Tropenmuseum in Amsterdam, the Netherlands. He previously held positions as Keeper of Anthropology at the Horniman Museum in London and Director of the Museums of History and Ethnography at the Institute of Jamaica. He also held visiting research affiliations at Yale Centre for British Art, and New York University's programme in Museum Studies. With a regional focus on the Caribbean, his research interests include material and visual culture; slavery;

museum anthropology and the histories of collecting and exhibitionary practices. His publications include catalogue contributions, book chapters and the forthcoming book *The Collaborative Museum: Curators, Communities and Collections* (co-edited with Viv Golding). He is
also working on an edited volume with Tim Barringer entitled *Victorian Jamaica*.

Eithne Nightingale is Head of Equality and Diversity at the V&A and initiated the major
Heritage Lottery Funded project, 'Capacity Building and Cultural Ownership – Working
with Culturally Diverse Communities' which encompassed collections research, public programming and partnership development. She has written and lectured on diversity in museums in the UK and internationally and is currently carrying out research for a PhD on Children, Migration and Diasporas, linked to the Museum of Childhood in London's East End.
Eithne has worked in race relations, education, community development and museums for
over 30 years. She is also a photographer and a travel/fiction writer.

Mark O'Neill. Since moving to Glasgow in 1985 Mark O'Neill has led the creation of two new
museums, including the UK's only museum of world religions, and the renewal of two Victorian
institutions, notably that of Kelvingrove Art Gallery and Museum, which received 3.2 million
visits in its first year after reopening in 2006. He was Head of Glasgow Museums from 1998 to
2005 and Head of Arts and Museums from 2005 to 2010. In his current role as Director of Policy
& Research, Glasgow Life, he aims to apply visitor centred approaches developed in museums to
libraries, arts and sport. He has published and lectured widely on museum philosophy.

Irna Qureshi is a writer, anthropologist and oral historian specialising in British Asian heritage. She has curated several exhibitions on this theme and has worked with museums including the V&A to implement strategies to develop South Asian audiences. She has written
about the public perception of Muslim actresses working in the Pakistani film industry and is
currently writing about being British, Pakistani and female in Bradford, against the backdrop
of classic Indian films.

Clifford Pereira FRGS is a freelance history researcher, one of two world authorities on the
Bombay Africans and recognised in East Africa and East Asia for his work on Africa and the
early Ming Dynasty. Cliff is a consultant to the British heritage sector, with considerable experience of partnership working with the Royal Geographical Society and numerous community
engagement projects with diverse funding bodies. A former Chairman of the Black and Asian
Studies Association (BASA) and a long time member of the Anglo–Portuguese Society, Cliff was
recently awarded Honorary Assistant Researcher by Royal Holloway, University of London.

John Reeve teaches on the Museums and Galleries in Education MA at the Institute of Education, London University, and was previously Head of Education at the British Museum. He
is editor of the *Journal of Education in Museums* and was chair of GEM (Group for Education in
Museums) until September 2011. He is a trustee of Strawberry Hill House, and an adviser to
museums and galleries including Sir John Soane's Museum and the National Gallery. He has
also worked with museums and heritage organisations abroad especially in India. He was co-
editor of *The Responsive Museum* (with Caroline Lang and Vicky Woollard, 2006). He edited
the catalogue for the *Sacred* exhibition at the British Library (2007) and wrote *A Visitor's Guide
to World Religions* for the British Museum Press (2006).

Richard Sandell is Professor and Head of the School of Museum Studies at the University of Leicester. He has been awarded research fellowships at the Smithsonian Institution (2004/2005) and the Humanities Research Center of the Australian National University (2008) to pursue his research interests which focus on museums, human rights and equality. He is the editor of *Museums, Society, Inequality* (2002), author of *Museums, Prejudice and the Reframing of Difference* (2007); co-editor (with Robert R. Janes) of *Museum Management and Marketing* (2008) and co-editor (with Jocelyn Dodd and Rosemarie Garland-Thomson of *Re-Presenting Disability: Activism and Agency in the Museum* (2010)).

Atul Shah is founder and CEO of Diverse Ethics, a consultancy advising organisations on ways of understanding and embracing cultural intelligence in the workplace. He is author of *Celebrating Diversity and Social Cohesion – A Jain Perspective*. He was on the Board of the Museums, Libraries & Archives Council and is an active writer and broadcaster.

Lois H. Silverman is an independent scholar, museum studies specialist and consultant to museums and social agencies worldwide. She is widely known for her publications, lectures and seminars on visitor meaning-making and her innovative projects exploring the therapeutic potential of museums. Drawing on her PhD from the Annenberg School for Communication and a Master's of Social Work from Indiana University, Lois works on a variety of collaborative projects between museums, social service agencies and communities. She is the author of the groundbreaking book, *The Social Work of Museums* (Routledge, 2010) and the co-editor of *Transforming Practice* (Museum Education Roundtable, 2000).

Harbinder Singh is the founding Director of the Maharajah Duleep Singh Centenary Trust – Britain's first Sikh heritage based organisation. He has led all of MDSCT's major projects over the past 18 years. These include collaborating with the V&A on the 1999 *Arts of the Sikh Kingdoms* exhibition and with English Heritage on initiating and touring the *Jawans to Generals* exhibition. He is responsible for conceiving and spearheading the launch of the Anglo Sikh Heritage Trail which works in conjunction with a wide range of arts and heritage based institutions throughout the UK.

Heather J. L. Smith is the Equality Specialist for the National Trust for England, Wales and Northern Ireland. She has worked at the Trust for eight years, holding positions responsible for advising on access for disabled people, and integrating equality and diversity into the National Trust's strategy and planning. Prior to this, Heather lived in Scotland where she worked in a contemporary art centre and completed her PhD. Her subject of research was the provisions in museums and art galleries for blind and partially sighted people, something of great personal interest following a series of major eye operations in her early years.

Marzia Varutti is based at the School of Museum Studies, University of Leicester. Expanding on her doctoral dissertation investigating museums in the People's Republic of China, Dr Varutti has subsequently conducted research on the relations between museums and indigenous groups in Taiwan (funded by the British Academy and the Ministry of Foreign Affairs, R.O.C.), and the representation of ethnic minorities in the museums of Norway (funded by the Research Council of Norway). She has published on a wide range of themes including cultural representation, museums and social inclusion, nationalism, and heritage and memory – in China, Taiwan and Norway.

Victoria Walsh is a freelance curator, project manager and research consultant and was Head of Public Programmes at Tate Britain (2005–2011) during which time she was co-investigator of the major research project 'Tate Encounters: Britishness and Visual Culture'. She is also co-investigator of the Tate research project 'Art School Educated: Curriculum Development and Institutional Change in UK Art Schools 1960–2000'. She holds an MA in Art History (Courtauld) in Curating (RCA 1995) and a doctorate on the artist J. A. M. Whistler (Oxford Brookes 1996) and has published on post-war British artists Nigel Henderson, Francis Bacon, Gilbert & George and architects Alison and Peter Smithson.

Fred Wilson is a conceptual and installation artist whose work explores the relationship between museums, individual works of art, and collections of other kinds. Wilson's work has been featured in over 100 group exhibitions, including the 50th Venice Biennale (2003) as the American representative, the Whitney Museum of American Art Biennial Exhibition (1993), and the 4th International Cairo Biennale (1992). He has had over 25 solo museum exhibitions internationally, and has been the recipient of numerous honours and awards, among them, the John D. and Catherine T. MacArthur Foundation Award (the 'Genius Grant'), Chicago (1999). Fred Wilson is represented by The Pace Gallery, New York, and currently lives and works in New York City.

Oliver Winchester is Project Curator at the Wellcome Collection in London. He was Assistant Curator of the 2011 V&A exhibition *Postmodernism: Style & Subversion 1970–1990* and Head of the V&A LGBTQ Network having previously worked as Assistant Curator of Contemporary Programmes where he managed the V&A 'Friday Late' series. Specialising in subcultural, queer and politically engaged visual culture, Oliver has worked at Christie's auction house and the Barbican Art Gallery and has worked on exhibitions that include *Helen Chadwick: A Retrospective* and *Araki. Self: Life: Death* and has written for various publications including *Queering the Museum* at Birmingham Museums & Art Gallery, most recently contributing to the exhibition catalogue *Diaghilev and the Golden Age of the Ballet Russes*. Oliver sits on the Kensington & Chelsea Arts Grants Board.

Amelia Wong manages social media outreach and develops web content for the United States Holocaust Memorial Museum. She holds a BA in History/Art History from UCLA and a PhD in American Studies from the University of Maryland, College Park, where her dissertation interrogated how museums are constructing community through social media in the interest of democratic reform. She has also held several positions in humanities research in Los Angeles and in the mid-Atlantic United States.

Gary Younge is an author, broadcaster and award-winning columnist for the *Guardian*, based in Chicago. He also writes a monthly column, Beneath the Radar, for the *Nation* magazine and is the Alfred Knobler Fellow for The Nation Institute. He has written three books: *Who Are We?*, *Stranger in a Strange Land* and *No Place Like Home*. Raised in Stevenage by his Barbadian-born mother, Gary studied French and Russian at Heriot-Watt University in Edinburgh and Newspaper Journalism at City University in London. He has reported extensively from all over Europe, Africa the United States and the Caribbean and written for a variety of publications including *The Los Angeles Times, GQ Style, The New Statesman, Hello!, Gay Times, The Scotsman* and *Cosmopolitan*.

FOREWORD

In the past 30 years, museums have faced waves of powerful external forces which have made change inevitable. This book is about the choices some museums have made in response to these pressures and the opportunities to which they gave rise. The accelerated growth of consumer culture has forced museums to function in a highly market-driven economy, with unprecedented competition for people's time and attention. Museums responded, some unwillingly, others enthusiastically, with blockbuster exhibitions, a focus on sponsorship and philanthropy, and grandiose buildings which aspire to be 'iconic'. More than ever before, museums have become part of the world's largest industry: tourism. At the same time, museums have struggled to keep up with the need for new forms of engagement arising from the explosive popularity of social media and virtual experience. Under increasing scrutiny, museums and their staff have been critiqued for complicity with structures of power, oppression and exclusion, attacked for their political agendas, and regularly subjected to the more mundane but intrusive demands of democratic accountability through the policies of state and foundation funders. Groups whose histories and identities have been ignored or denigrated by museums have demanded representation in displays and programmes. Underlying these demands have been the principles of human rights which have inspired the struggle for justice across the planet since the Second World War. Many museum staff have sought to embrace these ideas and, working with communities, artists and academics, to use them to change museums from within. This book is a record of how some museums responded to the rights revolution which has taken place since the Universal Declaration was signed in 1948.

The 'global awakening' in which people of all walks of life are recognising their power to claim and exercise their human rights may seem sudden, but it is a consequence of these longer-run developments. As this volume demonstrates, those who work in and value museums have been part of this revolution. While museums' awareness of and passion for their potential to foster social change have far outpaced our understanding of how to harness and implement it, the chapters in this book take an essential step towards closing that gap. Museums themselves are experiencing a global awakening to their power and practice as agents of cultural activism. *Museums, Equality and Social Justice* is a clear testament to the process.

What comes across vividly in this volume is that museums and the people who work in and with them are deep in the throes of profound, difficult and exciting *learning* that belies any sense of easy progress. The kind of organisational learning required to engage with the rights revolution poses a fundamental challenge for all expert institutions, including museums, perhaps because it is both collective and highly personal. The museum's imagined audiences can no longer be limited by our own assumptions and blind spots and those of the culture within which we grew up and were trained. All museum visitors, all citizens, and all the people who created the museum objects must now be seen as fully human. This requires seeing the world within new and unfamiliar frames, and has to be carried on, not about, but with people who have been represented as somehow 'other'. Few of us reach adulthood without absorbing stereotypes and prejudices, whether based on class, ethnicity, race, gender or sexuality. Confronting and overcoming the resulting blind spots can be emotionally demanding work, with many consequent opportunities for insensitivity, embarrassment and failings of insight. It requires humility and a courage which is not usually part of the culture of prestigious institutions. Yet as this volume records, many museums and people who work in and with them are rising to these challenges. Their learning is inspiring.

Many of the chapters in this collection reflect not only the desire of individuals to humanise museums, but also offer the much-needed articulation of and reflection upon evolving best practices and policy that is critically important at this juncture. With a welcome diversity of authors, the editors fruitfully move the field-wide conversation from questions of *whether or not*, to questions of *how*. These chapters reflect the on-going development of practice and policy from tentative first steps – often dismissed as tokenistic and reflecting unreconstructed stereotypes, to more equal and respectful engagement, to attempts to embed equality and diversity in the heart of museums. The frustration and anger of those who responded to invitations by museums or who demanded representation and participation in museum displays and decision-making processes are apparent here. So is the willingness and insight of citizens, artists and activists to help museums move towards practices and policies that suit the complexities and opportunities of diversity, social justice and human rights. The approaches to implementation and action illuminated in these pages create an empowering guide for practice.

Perhaps the most positive response to the rights revolution is a generosity of spirit and an expression of solidarity with the human condition and, in particular, with those who are marginalised. As the chapters make clear, however, good intentions and generosity are not enough to sustain positive social change. The contribution of any social institution is only as good as its analysis of society and as the role it chooses to play in response. Thus, the rights revolution also confronts museums with a series of intellectual, political and ethical tasks as well as cultural and emotional learning. The tasks go beyond the functions of curatorship, conservation, management and education, to defining the museum in relation to the needs of society, and embodying its role as well and fully as possible. As some of the contributors venture to suggest, museums have unique contributions to make as agents of cultural activism, as leaders, and as revolutionaries. This book is therefore a clarion call for museums to imagine and embrace their full potential.

No matter what a museum's legal structure, whether publicly funded, or authorised by society to function as a charity, it is expected to contribute to the common good. If its basic values do not include solidarity with the excluded, then the museum is reinforcing that exclusion. While the most radical analysis will always find museums' progressivism falling short, it is also important not to make the 'perfect revolution' the enemy of the 'good enough' reform.

Any review of the state of the world and of museums would however suggest that, while good foundations have been laid, and some promising work carried out, the task of realising the potential of museums to contribute to creating a society where everyone is treated as fully human has only just begun. The chapters in this remarkable collection are at once a record of profound organisational learning, a critical guide for practice, and a stirring call for museums to understand and realise their full potential in contributing to the creation of a richer, fairer society.

Mark O'Neill and Lois H. Silverman

ACKNOWLEDGEMENTS

We are grateful to many individuals and organisations that have shaped our approach to this book and enriched our thinking with their expertise, practice and insights, including Rajiv Anand, Jocelyn Dodd, Nancy Fuller, James Gardner, Victoria Hollows, Eilean Hooper-Greenhill, Robert Janes, Christina Kreps, Kylie Message, Kris Morrissey, Sarah Ogilvie, Mark O'Neill, Cliff Pereira, Irna Qureshi, Atul Shah, Marjorie Schwarzer, Lois Silverman, Harbinder Singh and the late Stephen Weil.

We are especially indebted to Chandan Mahal, Makeda Coastan, Christopher Breward, David Anderson, Debbie Sibley and Sarah Ames who formed a steering group for a major international conference – *Margins to the Core? – Exploring the Shifting Roles and Increasing Significance of Diversity and Equality in Contemporary Museum and Heritage Policy and Practice* – held at the V&A in 2010 that subsequently provided the impetus for this book.

Collaboration and dialogue with a range of organisations has enriched our understanding of the themes and topics explored in the book including The Black Cultural Archives, Anglo Sikh Heritage Trail, Black and Asian Studies Association, Institute of Jainology, Scottish Transgender Alliance, The Mayor's Commission on African and Asian Heritage (Greater London Authority) and the Diversity in Heritage Group.

Eithne Nightingale would like to thank colleagues at the V&A especially Mark Jones, Damien Whitmore, Beth McKillop, Teresa Hare-Duke, Liz Miller, Barry Ginley, Oliver Winchester, Janet Browne, Helen Woodfield, Marilyn Greene and Amanda Bruce. She would also like to thank the V&A for sponsoring research conducted for this book in the United States and UK.

Richard Sandell is grateful to students and colleagues in the School of Museum Studies, University of Leicester for their generosity, collegiality and support over the past 14 years and to the Research School of Humanities, Australian National University, for the award of a research fellowship in 2008 that supported his research into museums and human rights.

Finally the editors would like to thank Suzana Skrbic, Barbara Lloyd and John James for their invaluable assistance in sourcing images and Matt Gibbons, Amy Davis Poynter, Ilaria Parodi and Nicola Imrie for their support, advice and encouragement throughout the process of bringing this volume to fruition.

Maud Sulter, *Terpsichore*, 1992. V&A Museum. Museum no. E. 1795–1991, © Maud Sulter.

INTRODUCTION

Eithne Nightingale and Richard Sandell

The last two decades have seen concerns for equality, diversity, social justice and human rights move from the margins of museum thinking and practice, to the core. The arguments – both moral and pragmatic – for engaging diverse audiences; creating the conditions for more equitable access to museum resources; and opening up opportunities to participate in (and benefit from) museum experiences, now enjoy considerable consensus (Silverman 2010; Marstine 2011). Their influence can be detected in the practices, programmes, policies and structures of museums and galleries throughout many parts of the world. Moreover, attempts to construct new narratives that reflect demographic, social and cultural diversity and represent a plurality of lived experiences, histories and identities – once the preserve of a few pioneering institutions – are increasingly widespread. These trends in democratic representation and display practice (and the controversies they have sometimes generated) have attracted considerable academic interest (Macdonald 1998; Anico and Peralta 2009; O'Neill 2011). Moreover, a growing number of museums, galleries and heritage organisations have become increasingly confident in articulating their purpose and value in social terms and claiming a role as agents of progressive social change (Sandell 2002, 2007). In particular, there is increasing professional and scholarly interest in the potential for museums to take up an explicitly activist moral standpoint on human rights issues – one that aims to actively shape the conversations that society has about difference – and to engage visitors in (frequently challenging) debates pertaining to social justice (Sandell 2007; Sandell *et al.* 2010).

At the same time it would be naïve and misleading to suggest an even and uncontested transition from the museum as an organisation that has, for many years, been widely understood to marginalise, exclude and oppress to one which is wholly inclusive and committed to fairness and equity in all areas of practice. Indeed, some have questioned the extent to which heightened attention to diversity and equality has brought about real change in institutions – their values, policies and practices with regards to all areas of activity – as well as changes in the demographic profile of those who visit, work within, collaborate with and benefit from museums (O'Neill 2002). Moreover, whilst recent years have seen more widespread and mainstream adoption of practices that respond to and engage with issues of diversity and equality (and a welcome marginalisation of a minority of staunch opponents to this work)

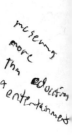

museums more than education & entertainment

there are also worrying signs that momentum towards making museums more inclusive, equitable and socially engaged is slowing down or even – in the present political, social and economic climate – reversing (Janes 2009).

Within this context we argue that there is a pressing need to explore the museum's relationship to (and potential to act upon) inequality and injustice; to investigate, better understand and evidence the ways in which museums, heritage and culture not only reflect but also shape normative conceptions of fairness and power relations between groups; as well as impact individuals' lived experiences. The increasing influence of morally-based human rights discourses globally, alongside growing support for the argument that levels of inequality and deprivation within society negatively impact social mobility and cohesion; crime levels; economic viability; and the mental and physical wellbeing of all citizens (Wilkinson and Pickett 2009), lend further support to the need for this investigative work. We therefore aim to explore the unique role that museums might play in countering inequalities and engendering support for social justice on both the local and global stage; a potential that, despite significant shifts in policy and practice, remains largely untapped.

The book then is conceived to reflect on and inform debates in museum research, policy and practice at this critical time by bringing together original, provocative, scholarly and accessible contributions that explore the shifting roles and increasing significance of diversity, equality and social justice in international, contemporary museum policy and practice. Whilst comprehensive coverage of the numerous and complex issues involved in this field is not possible in a project of this kind, we have nevertheless sought to include diverse perspectives and to be mindful of the importance of exploring both group-specific equality issues as well as the themes that cut across the experiences of different communities. Taken together, contributions address different strands of equality – race, religion and belief, disability, sexual orientation, socio-economic status, age, gender – exploring common ground and strand-specific issues as well as interconnections and tensions between them whilst, at the same time, critiquing these bounded classifications and recognising the shifting, sometimes arbitrary and hybrid, nature of identity. The book is intended to complement other important studies dedicated to specific social groups and equality issues.[1] Equality discourses are considered alongside those pertaining to human, legal and cultural rights, reflecting the ways in which these are increasingly intertwined at both local and international levels. Collectively, the contributions to this volume reflect on past practices and, crucially, seek to inform future debate and practice.

Whilst museums have increasingly experimented with more democratic forms of engagement – creating enhanced opportunities for different perspectives, experiences and forms of expertise to inform their work – less progress has been made towards the opening up of opportunities to engage in academic debate. Publication, in particular, is often restricted to a relatively narrow group of academics and researchers. We have therefore purposefully attempted to draw upon a richer mix of perspectives in this collection. The volume is comprised of (and has been shaped by input from) academics and researchers (both established and emerging), artists, activists, journalists and practitioners working at different levels in wide ranging national, local and community based organisations and with experience of diverse collections from contemporary art to natural science; from ethnic- or religious-specific museums to those dedicated to human rights issues.

The volume grows out of a major international conference – *From the Margins to the Core – Exploring the Shifting Roles and Increasing Significance of Diversity and Equality in Contemporary Museum and Heritage Policy and Practice* – held at the Victoria & Albert Museum in 2010 and organised in partnership with the University of Leicester. The event, which featured more than 100 speakers and attracted delegates from many parts of the world, was the culmination of more than two years of discussions with key figures in the field of diversity and equality. A number of contributors to this volume participated in the conference (and have subsequently developed their arguments in chapter form) appearing alongside specially commissioned work from additional contributors.

The concepts with which this book is centrally concerned – equality, diversity and social justice – are closely linked and interdependent. However, recognising that understanding and applicability of the terms varies according to the context and country in which they are used, we deploy the terms in relatively distinctive ways.

Equality refers to the elimination of discrimination on the grounds of group membership (for example, linked to race, gender, disability and so on) and is widely used in such areas as employment, education, leisure and health services. Attempts to secure equality of opportunity in these different arenas have been at the heart of many struggles for formally constituted and legally recognised civil and human rights by different groups.

Diversity policies and practices generally embody measures intended to celebrate, promote respect for, and enhance understanding of difference and – in terms of workforce – to harness the benefits of diverse staff. Diversity encompasses visible and non-visible differences and can include culture, socio-economic status, values and so on. Equality and diversity are closely linked; there can be no equality of opportunity if difference is not understood, taken account of, valued and harnessed.

Understand differences & embrace to reach equality

We use the term social justice to refer to the ways in which museums, galleries and heritage organisations might acknowledge and act upon inequalities within and outside of the cultural domain. This usage is underpinned by a belief in the constitutive, generative character of museums; their capacity to shape as well as reflect social and political relations and to positively impact lived experiences of those who experience discrimination and prejudice. Whilst museums have often operated in ways which exclude, marginalise and oppress, there is growing support (and evidence) for the idea that museums can contribute towards more just, equitable and fair societies.

We have purposefully omitted a detailed justification of the merits of a commitment to equality and a concern for diversity and social justice within museums – an argument which was necessary only a decade ago when growing interest in these issues provoked an often fierce backlash from opponents arguing that museums should operate outside of these social and political concerns and focus on the 'core business' of collecting, researching and interpreting material to the public (O'Neill 2002; Sandell 2002). This position is possible because of a burgeoning body of empirical research (both within the museum studies literature and amongst the many visitor studies carried out by museums around the world) that now evidences the long-held view that museums have social value; that audiences gain learning and therapeutic benefits from participation (Silverman 2002, 2010; Hooper-Greenhill 2007; O'Neill 2010); that the narratives they construct and the moral standpoints they adopt have social effects and consequences (Sandell 2007; Dodd *et al.* 2008) and that museums are highly valued public forums for encountering and negotiating contested social issues (Message 2006; Cameron and Kelly 2010; Barrett 2011). We therefore start from a position that reaffirms the fundamental importance of issues of equality and diversity to the work of museums and the centrality of this work to their future development, relevance and effectiveness. This enables us to open up and address timely issues for further exploration and to develop ideas that can help to inform

Interpret includes social justice

future innovation, developments and debates in museum thinking and practice. Crucially, the volume seeks to examine issues of equality, diversity and human rights across all areas of the museum's organisation and activity and their actual and potential transformative impact on leadership and management, governance, employment, collections development, public programming, marketing and so on.

Contributors draw on a productive range of disciplines and theoretical perspectives to address questions and concerns fundamental to contemporary practice and policy including critical legal studies, social anthropology, social movement studies, change management, philosophy, cultural studies, disability studies, politics and international relations to locate specific arguments and case studies within a broader context.

Contributions have been grouped according to three primary themes, although many individual chapters speak to issues that cut across these broad, closely interlinked parts.

Margins to the core?

The chapters in this part examine the challenges encountered in effecting long-term change in museum policies and practices across key areas such as governance, leadership, organisational values and structure, workforce, collections and programming.

Whilst the authors explore very different contexts and approach the theme of organisational change from markedly different professional, scholarly and personal backgrounds, there is nevertheless a degree of consensus around the need for an embedded and sustained commitment to the principles of equality and social justice. Whilst some examine how factors within and outside the museum shape decisions, others examine the potentially transformative effects of specific strategies such as collaboration and partnership with external organisations; co-creative practice with excluded communities; and institutional critique through engagement with artists.

Eithne Nightingale and Chandan Mahal explore how far different institutions have integrated diversity and equality imperatives into their strategic planning and core business. Drawing on examples from the United States and UK, they discuss issues of leadership and ownership; the role of individual staff; decision-making processes, consultation and collaboration with external individuals and organisations. In reviewing how different equalities are prioritised, and interconnect, they examine the relative merits of initiatives that address specific community experiences (such as the Museum of African American History and Culture due to open on the Mall in Washington, DC in 2015) and approaches that favour the threading of diversity throughout broader museum narratives. Informed by research in the UK and United States, they envisage what a fully equitable, diverse and inclusive museum might look like.

Fred Wilson, in his interview with Janet Marstine, reviews the development of more socially just and engaged museums and galleries over recent decades. His insights – generated through experience of working within institutions as a trustee, and as an artist and curator brought in to develop specific projects – highlight the need for leadership, greater relevance, risk taking and experimentation and for a more diverse workforce, a change which, he argues, is a prerequisite for long-term transformation. Whilst acknowledging progress in how museums and galleries 'reflect change' he believes their potential for 'driving change' has yet to be realised.

Several authors touch on the theme of collaboration, an important and growing trend in professional practice. Kimberly Keith interviews leaders from culturally specific community heritage organisations to inform discussion of the opportunities and pitfalls bound up in collaboration between mainstream museums and community agencies. Her analysis highlights the significance of genuine commitment, dialogue, respect and the establishment of common values in establishing mutually beneficial and equitable partnerships.

Heather Smith, Barry Ginley and Hannah Goodwin identify the barriers within museums, galleries and heritage organisations, which have hindered attempts to extend access for disabled visitors. Their analysis reveals both the importance and the limitations of formal mechanisms for instigating change (such as the law) and highlights the impact on policy and practice of individuals with specialist expertise in (and responsibility for) access and disability. To create genuine and sustained change – that can transform both the culture of an organisation and the quality of experience it offers to visitors – they call for ongoing dialogue and co-creative practices with disabled audiences.

David Fleming offers a candid account of his experiences of leading two major museum services (operating in very deprived cities in England) through a long-term, sometimes painful process of organisational change, a prerequisite for surviving changing political, social and economic contexts. His reflections on the interrelated aspects of museum policy, practice and culture (vision and shared values, strategic planning, programming, finance and so on) offer an holistic understanding of the need for (and challenges involved in) transforming organisations.

Janet Marstine's chapter helpfully locates museums' attempts to evolve in response to diversity and social justice imperatives within a broader trend of heightened concern for ethical issues across a range of professions. More particularly, her in-depth empirical analysis of the impact of Fred Wilson's 'compassionate form of institutional critique' – that has often interrogated collections through a post-colonial lens – offers new insights for museum leaders of how organisations change and are changed and highlights the importance of alignment between the values of the individual, the sector, the organisation and the global context within which they operate.

Connecting/competing equalities

The chapters in this part examine not only specific equality strands – gender, disability, race, age, sexual orientation, religion and belief, socio-economic status and so on – but also the common ground that they share as well as the tensions between them. Contributors explore how museums are responding to the fast-changing equalities terrain and shifting politics of identity at global, national and local levels and highlight the ways in which the universalising discourse of human rights intersects with the contingent character of particular equality struggles in different international contexts.

In the opening chapter Gary Younge reveals how familiar categories – race, gender and so on – are necessary and valuable for progressing equality and, at the same time, flawed; incapable of expressing the dynamic and shifting character of identity. Drawing upon the lived experiences of diverse individuals he makes a powerful case for recognising and respecting difference in all its forms. Economic difference, he argues, is key but has been largely ignored with the white working class often 'stranded without a sponsor'. His analysis highlights the struggle between those who occupy the 'core' (with greater access to power and resources) and those at the 'margins' who help define the mainstream. Recognising their interdependence, Younge argues that such a struggle can be both creative and transformative as long as people respect and meet each other halfway. museums do feel elitist

Presenting the findings from a major research project that examined the ways in which young people perceived and engaged with art at Tate Britain, Andrew Dewdney, David Dibosa and Victoria Walsh similarly highlight the limitations of fixed identity categories. They critique policies that measure success on the basis that museum audiences, staff or collections are more 'diverse', drawing on Fanon's concept of epidermalization to argue that categorisation according to skin colour masks issues of power. Asserting that politics has been replaced by government policies that seem to have failed, they argue instead for new, alternative ways of engaging with inequality.

John Reeve argues that museums have been largely neglectful of issues of religion and belief, often deploying interpretive frames that emphasise the aesthetic qualities of objects at the expense of their spiritual significance. Drawing on examples from across the globe he questions this approach arguing for the importance of context for all audiences. As 'secular guardian[s] of religious artefacts' (Chin 2010) he asks that museums enter into more meaningful collaborations with faith communities, are multi-voiced in their interpretations and take up more active roles in contemporary public debates around religion.

Oliver Winchester considers attempts by museums to develop more inclusive narratives of sexual identity and problematises the 'restrictive trans-historical essentialism' that has underpinned many initiatives to date. Drawing on the collections of the V&A and interrogating very different objects, their biographies and possible meanings, his analysis urges us to go beyond presenting a series of discovered identities and hidden histories, proposing approaches to interpretation that can accommodate the variety and complexity of lesbian, gay, bisexual, transgender and queer (LGBTQ) lived experience.

Amy Levin employs queer and feminist theory and analyses the representational strategies in contemporary exhibitions to assess the extent to which museums might resist and move beyond limiting and reductive binary classifications with regards to gender and sexuality. Her discussion helpfully explores ways in which gender and sexual identities intersect with issues of class, race, ethnicity and colonialism and also addresses, head on, the tensions that can arise between LGBT communities and some religious groups.

Susan Baldino sheds light on the needs of a growing but poorly understood audience and one largely neglected and under served by museums. Her groundbreaking study, capturing the outcomes of an action research project involving museums, schools and young people, offers compelling evidence that museums hold enormous potential to develop transformative learning experiences for people on the autism spectrum.

In the final chapter in this part, Simona Bodo explores the potential for museums to support intercultural understanding and respect in societies characterised by increasing diversity and tensions between communities. Critiquing recent museum and heritage practices, she calls for an approach which goes beyond targeting according to racial origin and ethnicity in favour of the opening up of a third space; one which is transformative for all parties – the institution as well as those participants who, in Gary Younge's words, live in both the 'core' as well as the 'margins'.

Museums and the good society

What roles might museums play in promoting social justice and engendering support for human rights? More particularly, how are museums engaging with and responding to claims to cultural access and demands for more equitable forms of representation by diverse communities? The chapters in this part address these questions, interrogating and problematising the part that museums might play in nurturing more equitable, fair and just societies. Whilst grounded in analysis of very different settings, chapters by Sandell, Varutti and Message, share a concern to understand the agency of museums in relation to broader rights claims and struggles.

Richard Sandell draws on debates and theoretical perspectives from a range of disciplines to examine museums' increasing engagement with human rights issues, exploring their potential to function as 'sites of persuasion' (Morphy 2006) that engender support for often controversial rights claims. Gathering evidence from museum practitioners, news media, audiences and transgender rights activists he shows how museums not only reflect but potentially reconfigure normative moral codes and conventions at both a local and global level.

Marzia Varutti focuses attention on Taiwan, offering a fascinating account of how national, local and newly created museums have engaged with human rights issues since the fall of the military dictatorship in 1987 and become increasingly involved in contemporary social issues. Her analysis focuses, in particular, on the ways in which museums have been caught up in indigenous rights movements and the challenges that persist as the country has increasingly sought to recognise, rather than suppress, differences.

Opening up a dialogue between critical legal studies and museum studies, Kylie Message further examines the potential for museums to progress a social justice agenda. Exploring the clash between 'constituted' power – as reflected in the Museum of Australian Democracy – and 'constituent' power exemplified by the Aboriginal Tent Embassy and the Yirrkala bark petitions, both signifiers of aboriginal struggles over land reform, Message presents new ways of understanding the relationship between culture and the legal processes through which rights are commonly formalised.

David Anderson shows how cultural rights – enshrined in international legislation – are frequently misunderstood by the public and media and widely ignored by governments and museums. Drawing on research into creativity and synthesising concepts from the fields of human rights, politics and international relations, Anderson posits a framework within which everyone has the right to have their culture recognised; freedom of expression; opportunities to engage with other cultures, to participate in cultural activities and be creative. Through a focus on obligations towards (and claims made by) faith communities, he considers how a commitment to cultural rights for all might be negotiated by museums and galleries.

Susan Kamel and Christine Gerbich offer an honest and reflective account of the challenges of applying new approaches to museum thinking and practice to their work in supporting the construction of a new archaeological museum in Yemen and where many museums have followed in the imperialist 'orientalist' tradition. They show how awareness of the local context and 'appropriate' museology's (Kreps 2008) concern for inclusion holds considerable potential for supporting both progressive museum practice and a re-examination of issues that are sometimes taken for granted in Western museums.

Janice Cheddie reflects on her involvement with the Mayor's Commission on African and Asian Heritage in London which brought together Black and Asian scholars and community practitioners on the one hand and museum and heritage practitioners on the other. Drawing on this experience she shows how human rights can be deployed to articulate the case for cultural diversity; emphasises the need to consider how knowledge is acquired, negotiated and disseminated; underlines the importance of class and gender and the need for the sector to focus on structural difference and inequality rather than racial or ethnic identity.

Amelia Wong draws on innovative practice across the world, from both within and beyond the museum field, to show how social media can radically alter the ways in which museums engage with their audiences and pursue their social goals in more ethical, transparent and impactful ways. At the same time, her nuanced critique cautions against overly celebratory claims regarding the role that social media can play in support of equality and social justice and points to how museums can most effectively harness their promising potential.

In the final chapter, Helen Mears and Wayne Modest address the potential for African collections in Western museums – created out of colonialism – to be redirected towards social justice endeavours claiming that such collections offer unique entry points into developing understanding of our historic and contemporary diversity. Their powerful critique of discriminatory museum practices and their call for radical change and ongoing reflection speaks back to the need, highlighted by contributors to Part I, to dismantle those internal structures that serve to exclude to bring about fundamental changes within museum thinking and practice.

A project such as this is bound to be selective and there are, inevitably, omissions. Yet by bringing together consideration of diverse equality concerns and exploring the relationships between them, we hope to have created a volume that makes a unique contribution to the field; one which complements and enriches important work that focuses on the museum's engagement with particular communities' experiences of marginalisation and exclusion. Our aim has been to produce a volume that is both reflective and challenging, that can critique some cherished and long-held assumptions, inform future practice and research and ultimately assist museums in realising their untapped potential to contribute to a more equal society.

Note

1   See, for example, Smith *et al.*'s volume on heritage and issues of class (2011); recent work by Nightingale (2010) on museums and cultural diversity; Sandell *et al.*'s (2010) focus on disability representation; and Levin's collection of writings on gender and sexual identity in the museum (2010).

References

Anico, M. and Peralta, E. (eds) (2009) *Heritage and Identity: Engagement and Demission in the Contemporary World*, London and New York: Routledge.

Barrett, J. (2011) *Museums and the Public Sphere*, Malden and Oxford: Wiley-Blackwell.

Cameron, F. and Kelly, L. (eds) (2010) *Hot Topics, Public Culture, Museums*, Newcastle upon Tyne: Cambridge Scholars.

Chin, K. (2010) 'Seeing Religion with New Eyes at the Asian Civilizations Museum', *Material Religion*, 6 (2): 192–216.

Dodd, J., Sandell, R., Jolly, D. and Jones, C. (2008) *Rethinking Disability Representation in Museums and Galleries*, Leicester: Research Centre for Museums and Galleries, University of Leicester.

Hooper-Greenhill, E. (2007) *Museums and Education: Purpose, Pedagogy, Performance*, London and New York: Routledge.

Janes, R. R. (2009) *Museums in a Troubled World: Renewal, Irrelevance or Collapse?*, London and New York: Routledge.

Kreps, C. F. (2008) 'Appropriate Museology in Theory and Practice', *Museum Management and Curatorship*, 23 (1): 23–41.

Levin, A. K. (ed.) (2010) *Gender, Sexuality, and Museums: A Routledge Reader*, London and New York: Routledge.

Macdonald, S. (1998) 'Exhibitions of Power and Powers of Exhibition: An Introduction to the Politics of Display', in S. Macdonald (ed.) *The Politics of Display: Museums, Science, Culture*, London and New York: Routledge: 1–21.

Marstine, J. (ed.) (2011) *Redefining Ethics for the Twenty First Century Museum: The Routledge Companion to Museum Ethics*, London and New York: Routledge.

Message, K. (2006) *New Museums and the Making of Culture*, Oxford: Berg.

Morphy, H. (2006) 'Sites of Persuasion: Yingapungapu at the National Museum of Australia', in I. Karp, C. A. Kratz, L. Szwaja and T. Ybarra-Frausto (eds) *Museum Frictions: Public Cultures/Global Transformations*, Durham, NC and London: Duke University Press: 469–499.

Nightingale, E. (ed.) (2010) *Capacity Building and Cultural Ownership – Working with Culturally Diverse Communities*, London: V&A.

O'Neill, M. (2002) 'The Good Enough Visitor', in R. Sandell (ed.) *Museums, Society, Inequality*, London and New York: Routledge: 24–40.

O'Neill, M. (2010) 'Cultural Attendance and Public Mental Health – From Research to Practice', *Journal of Public Mental Health*, 9 (4): 22–29.

O'Neill, M. (2011) 'Religion and Cultural Policy: Two Museum Case Studies', *International Journal of Cultural Policy*, 17 (2): 225–243.

Sandell, R. (ed.) (2002) 'Museums and the Combating of Social Inequality: Roles, Responsibilities, Resistance', in R. Sandell (ed.) *Museums, Society, Inequality*, London and New York: Routledge: 3–23.

Sandell, R. (2007) *Museum, Prejudice and the Reframing of Difference*, London and New York: Routledge.

Sandell, R., Dodd, J. and Garland-Thomson, R. (eds) (2010) *Re-Presenting Disability: Activism and Agency in the Museum*, London and New York: Routledge.

Silverman, L. (2002) 'The Therapeutic Potential of Museums as Pathways to Inclusion', in R. Sandell (ed.) *Museums, Society, Inequality*, London and New York: Routledge: 69–83.

Silverman, L. H. (2010) *The Social Work of Museums*, London and New York: Routledge.

Smith, L., Shackel, P. and Campbell, G. (eds) (2011) *Heritage, Labour and the Working Classes*, London and New York: Routledge.

Wilkinson, R. and Pickett, K. (2009) *The Spirit Level: Why Equality is Better for Everyone*, London: Penguin.

PART I

Margins to the core?

1

THE HEART OF THE MATTER

Integrating equality and diversity into the policy and practice of museums and galleries

Eithne Nightingale and Chandan Mahal

For too long equality and diversity considerations have been relegated to the margins of the business of museums and galleries (Sandell 2002) with many institutions interpreting their responsibilities in this area as being limited to one area of activity (for example, collections or staffing) or restricted to specific equality issues (such as race, gender or disability) with a corresponding disregard for the interconnections or tensions between them. Ignoring the changing nature of our society and the multi-faceted and shifting nature of people's identities they have often been limited (or at worst, insensitive or inappropriate) in their response to diversity and equality issues.

At the same time, there have been examples of outstanding work at institutional, departmental or individual levels. Some organisations have genuinely tried to embed diversity and equality across their organisation; to engage staff at all levels; to draw on the expertise of stakeholders outside the institution in order to respond to changes within society (Janes 2009; Silverman 2010); and to adopt approaches which advance opportunity across a range of equalities or foster relations between groups of people (Bruce and Hollows 2007).

This chapter draws on good practice to explore the challenges inherent in this work as experienced in a range of museums in both the United Kingdom and United States. It explores how far museums and galleries have integrated diversity and equality into mainstream policy; the importance and nature of leadership; the role of staff across the organisation and the significance of internal and external networks, consultation and partnerships. It assesses whether some institutions have focussed on particular equality strands more than others (and for what reasons) and considers whether sufficient attention has been given to exploring the interconnections and tensions between equality issues. It attempts to identify both barriers to, and effective drivers for, change in order to inform future practice in both developing and sustaining this work, recognising the different political, social and economic contexts in which people work. Lastly, drawing on this evidence, it endeavours to envision what a truly equitable, diverse and inclusive museum might look like.

We have based much of the discussion on an analysis of museum policies and on interviews conducted with staff occupying different roles in a range of national, local and regional museums in the UK and the United States.[1] We have also drawn on our own experience of holding roles with a specific brief on developing equality and diversity policies and practices in museums based in London. Eithne Nightingale is Head of Equality and Diversity at the Victoria & Albert Museum (V&A) in London, a national museum that holds world-class collections in art and design. Chandan Mahal, formerly Diversity Manager at the Museum of London, is Head of Audience Development at the Women's Library, also based in London.

Strategic planning and policy formulation

During the interviews we were concerned to establish the role of strategic planning and policy formulation in advancing equality. Are such processes a prerequisite for the mainstreaming of diversity and equality issues or are they viewed simply as time-consuming, ineffective and overly bureaucratic? Do policies and plans instigate genuine change and nurture consensus and commitment amongst staff or do they encourage complacency and remain largely ignored?

The Museum of London was one of the early pioneers in approaching issues of equality and diversity strategically. In 2003 a Cultural Diversity Audit was carried out which covered four areas: leadership; communication; service delivery; and employment. This led to the appointment of a Diversity Manager, Chandan Mahal, who drove forward the recommendations of the audit and oversaw the development of the Museum's Race Equality Scheme partly in response to the requirements of the UK Race Relations (Amendment) Act 2000.[2] This was followed by the setting up of an Equality and Diversity Strategy Group in 2005, composed of members of senior management, heads of department and staff from across the Museum. Within the Directorate, individual members of senior management took a lead on different aspects of diversity – race, disability, LGBT and so on. There was also a Disability Working Group. In response to equality legislation, equality impact assessments were introduced to identify both positive and negative impacts on all new major policies and functions in relation to specific equality strands. The two Diversity Managers[3] worked with colleagues in Human Resources and, with the active support of senior management, organised professional development training delivered by external consultants. During this period the main focus was on policy and developing diversity action plans for different departments, which the Diversity Managers had a role in monitoring and reviewing. The Diversity Managers subsequently went on to work on gallery projects as part of the Community and Audiences department, which has since become the Public Programmes department. There are no longer dedicated Diversity Managers, the Equality and Diversity Steering Group no longer exists nor does the practice of each director championing some aspect of diversity. This is not to suggest, however, that issues of equality and diversity are deemed less important. Indeed Cathy Ross, Director of Collections and Learning at the Museum of London asserts that:

> It has got translated incredibly well in terms of the broader understanding within the organisation. Everybody knows that it is terribly important and it's something that's been internalised in terms of people's thinking particularly in terms of exhibitions. It's no longer something just on the outside so that has been good.

Yet she expresses reservations as to whether the museum is 'actually knuckling down and getting some proper planned documents and strategies to move us forward on this'.

Annette Day, Head of Programmes, points to the need to review progress: 'It would be good to have a way of measuring change. What does not happen is the review and measuring of diversity . . . the Diversity Manager role did more of that'.

Rita McLean, Director of Birmingham Museums and Art Gallery in the Midlands, UK, reinforces the importance of monitoring impact: 'Consistency is quite hard . . . it is really useful to check what you're doing regularly to make sure it does not slip off the agenda'.

Of all the museums interviewed, it was Birmingham Museums and Art Gallery that showed the most consistent approach to integrating equality and diversity into their annual strategic planning. This included carrying out equality impact assessments on all new major policies and functions such as the collecting policy, lifelong learning and audience development strategies. Such a practice forces the organisation to consider both negative and positive impacts in relation to the multiple equality strands that have now been subsumed into the Equality Act 2010 (race, disability, gender, LGBT, marital status, age and religion and belief).[4] For example the equality impact assessment of the museum's Collecting Policy 2009–2013 outlines specific positive impacts such as strengthening the representation of work by black, Asian and disabled artists; increasing the representation of Muslim cultures and other faith groups. Overall impacts include improving the quality of life through celebrating diversity and contributing to community cohesion, thus directly linking the core activity of the museum to equality and social issues (Plate 1.1). The equality impact assessment identifies no potential negative impacts of the collecting policy.

The Horniman Museum in south London, a 'free, family-friendly museum with exhibits from around the world', takes a rather different approach. Assistant Director, Finbarr Whooley, states that the Museum is 'policy light', adding that 'we don't even have an audience development policy'. However the Museum does follow the general line of direction from the Trustees who set out an aspiration that the visitor profile, which is measured through an annual survey, matches that of the local community. Indeed the Horniman has been very successful in diversifying its audience with the percentage of black, Asian and minority ethnic audiences (BAME) increasing from 8–9 per cent in 2000 to 34 per cent in 2010.

Rebecca McGinnis, Access Coordinator and Museum Educator at the Metropolitan Museum of Art in New York, who previously worked in London, remarked on the difference between the two environments in which she has worked: 'Coming here [to the United States] I was all ready to have a policy but it doesn't quite pan out that way although I think we're moving more in that direction'.

Lonnie Bunch, Director of the National Museum of African and American History and Culture (NMAAHC), believes that there is more of an emphasis on policy in the UK largely because of the role of the Government's Department of Culture, Media and Sport, there being no equivalent body in the United States. The fact that most of the funding for US museums, apart from the Smithsonian, is from private rather than public sources may also be a contributing factor although certain businesses (both in the UK and United States) have been very active in the areas of diversity and equality incorporating this into their mission and strategic plans.

The V&A has had an Access, Inclusion and Diversity Strategy, approved by the Museum's Trustees, since 2003. In addition there have been related action plans and, as required by law, both Disability and Gender Equality Schemes. All of these have now been integrated into one policy in line with the Equality Act 2010. In addition, the V&A's annual strategic plan makes clear reference to issues of access and equality and has as one of its four objectives: 'To provide optimum access to collections and services for diverse audiences, now and in the future'. All staff members have equality and diversity included as one of their corporate objectives in their annual performance management plans.

However, whilst the V&A has pioneered many equality and diversity initiatives, the Museum has been resistant to introducing equality impact assessments except in the area of employment, despite the benefits of having an audit trail in the event of a discrimination case. There is concern that such assessments are overly bureaucratic and indeed the present UK Equality Act 2010 is unclear as to the requirement of such assessments. It was the former gender, race and disability legislation, now subsumed under the UK Equality Act 2010, that led to the introduction of equality impact assessments in the UK and, whilst many local authorities and health services complied, the arts and cultural sector has been more reticent. The fact that Birmingham Museums and Art Gallery is funded by the local council undoubtedly contributed to their more consistent compliance.

The V&A's Equality and Diversity Strategy Group (formerly the Access, Inclusion and Diversity Strategy Group), chaired by an Equality and Diversity Champion who is a senior manager, is a formally constituted sub-committee of the Museum's Management Board. There are, or have been, other short- or long-term working parties around specific issues such as socio-economic class; religion and belief; LGBTQ and a Staff Disability Forum. Some of these, initiated by staff around common interests, have undoubtedly contributed to significant change within the V&A.

However a recent evaluation of a major project in the Museum – *Capacity Building and Cultural Ownership – Working with Culturally Diverse Communities* – funded by the Heritage Lottery Fund, questioned the effectiveness of the former Access, Inclusion and Diversity Strategy Group. A Social Network Analysis – that examined the relationships that existed between individuals in the organisation – showed that few of the Group's members were on other committees in the Museum and concluded that the Group therefore had limited influence. Steps have since been taken to recruit more members who are in a better position to influence change but the effect of this has yet to be seen.

The potential for inertia and limited influence of committees is well expressed by Magdalena Mieri, Director of the Smithsonian's Latino History and Culture Program at the National Museum of American History: 'I don't think committees work. They suggest things are changing and let people feel good about themselves . . . but often committee members aren't empowered or willing to make real changes'.

So where does the future lie? Does the fact that Horniman Museum has significantly diversified its visitor profile, despite its lack of detailed policy, support the view that this is not a prerequisite for change? Is the V&A right to resist implementing a more rigorous equality assessment in relation to all its policies and plans, preferring a less bureaucratic response? Does the case of the Museum of London, where there is no longer an emphasis on policies or meetings, mean that such an approach is now outdated given that diversity and equality have become more central to people's thinking? Does the size, location, funding or remit of a museum determine the need for a more or less formal approach?

It seems clear that policies that are not consulted upon or consistently applied in practice are unhelpful as are procedures that are so bureaucratic that either they are not implemented or they alienate people. The existence of strategy groups or committees – unless focussed and with an influential, well-networked membership – may encourage complacency. If policy-making is to affect change there needs to be a set of specific objectives that can be measured, based on the particular context of the museum, and integrated into strategic planning. Some equality impact assessments may have become too onerous and therefore counter-productive but we would argue that there needs to be some mechanism, however basic, where staff are prompted to consider the potential impact on equality concerns, both positive and negative, at the initial conception of any major policy or plan and for this to be recorded. This could be in relation to audience development, employment or collecting policies or the development of a gallery, public programme or exhibition. The role of dedicated posts (see also Chapter 4, this volume) is further explored in the next section but it is clear that there needs to be someone with a clear responsibility for coordinating policy across the institution, ensuring consistency and, importantly, reviewing and reporting progress against set objectives.

Interestingly discussions around the implementation of the Equality Act in the UK also point to the need to undertake an Equality Analysis and set specific, measurable and realistic objectives and for these to be transparent, monitored and made public.

Ownership and leadership

Leadership is often cited as a critical factor in driving forward change, and was frequently referred to in our interviews, but such a claim poses interesting questions. How far is any individual leader able to move forward without broader support from across the organisation (Chapter 5, this volume)? What happens when directors, senior managers and others in positions of authority constitute a barrier to change through limited interest in (or commitment to) equality issues? Since progress is often initiated by highly committed staff lower down in the organisation or working on the edges of the museum and in response to external factors, how might this commitment be harnessed to achieve change in core values and practices?

Cathy Ross believes that leadership has been a key driver for change at the Museum of London: 'It has been driven by the top in that the Director has always been incredibly aware of diversity and keen that the Museum should be a model of good practice for diversity'. Yet she also expresses concerns about key people leaving:

> Things have changed for the better. I think diversity has been mainstreamed into our thinking but sometimes I worry if those key people leave, whether it's sufficiently embedded to carry on . . . If the Director left, this may have an impact. He has been a key driver and it's a Director's prerogative, to steer things in a particular way . . . but I think it has been embedded.

Camille Akeju, the Director of the Smithsonian's Anacostia Community Museum, believes that leadership, per se, is not enough:

> It's one thing for a leader to go in and say 'this is what we're doing'. It's another thing for a leader to go in and help staff identify the changes that need to happen across the organisation and to ensure individuals take ownership and responsibility for those changes.

At Birmingham Museums and Art Gallery, it is the Planning and Support Manager who, at present, has overall responsibility for overseeing and driving forward equality and diversity issues but as the head of service, Rita McLean, asserts: 'leadership is not just at my level but right through the organisation. Progress is impossible without this'.

Clearly, a concern for diversity and equality should be part of everyone's responsibility but, at the same time, progress will only be made when individual staff members have the knowledge and skills, the confidence and commitment, to integrate this into their work.

What has been striking during this research is the difference that individuals can make, sometimes (but by no means always) irrespective of their ethnic or social background, their experience, role or position within the hierarchy.

Rosie Miles, a curator of Prints and Drawings at the V&A from the 1970s until 2007, collected work by black artists from Britain, the United States, the Caribbean and Africa even though, at the time, the V&A did not officially collect from Africa or the African Diaspora. It was also a few interested V&A curators, supported by educators, who started to identify overlooked collections of relevance to the African Diaspora, an initiative that, with later funding from the Heritage Lottery Fund, has led to the uncovering of over 4,300 objects, a revision of the Collecting Policy and active consideration of an 'Africa' gallery (Chapter 21, this volume).

At the Museum of London, Alex Werner (Head of History Collections Department) became an enthusiastic collector of works of African or Caribbean material, a gap that, in this case, had been identified by the Museum. It was he who acquired the French edition of Quobna Ottobah Cugoano's *Thoughts and Sentiments on the Evil and Wicked Traffic of the Slavery and Commerce of the Human Species Humbly Submitted to the Inhabitants of Great Britain*, showing how such texts were circulating in Europe. Vincent Carretta, Professor of English at the University of Maryland, United States, called Cugoano 'the first Anglophone-African historian of slavery and the slave trade, and the first African to criticize European imperialism in the Americas'.[5] The French introduction also includes information about Cugoano's life and character that had not been recorded before.

There are many more examples of curators at the Museum of London actively collecting material relating to all aspects of diversity, one of the priority areas identified in the contemporary collecting plan. In 2008, for example, the Museum acquired significant material relating to the Sri Lankan Minister, Kamal Chunchie, an important figure who set up the Coloured Men's Institute in 1926 to support black and Asian sailors living in poor conditions in London's East End.

We found other instances of individual staff members who have made distinctive contributions, sometimes beyond their job responsibilities. Cedric Yeh is a curator working with the Armed Forces collections at the Smithsonian's National Museum of American History (NMAH). Twelve years ago Cedric Yeh began to take a personal interest in museum-wide collections that related to Asian Pacific American history, the Museum later supporting what became his 'official, unofficial position'. His motivation was to ensure that the Asian Pacific American community, of which he himself is a member, should see their own heritage reflected in the NMAH:

> The objects I identified weren't collected for their significance in terms of diversity. They're labelled as 'machinery' or 'fabrics' and things like that and we would have to do a lot of research to uncover what exactly we had . . . We found remarkable pieces that no one had known about.

The first piece displayed at the NMAH was a porcelain figure of a white man pushing out a Chinese labourer from the safety of a nest, referring to the Exclusion Act of 1882, the only law that ever targeted a specific ethnic group. Inside the nest are whites, African Americans and other ethnic groups.

We did a little research and found out more about the maker of this mass product . . . and we were wondering, 'who was he selling these to and where would you put this'? On a mantle piece, on top of a fireplace, on your office desk?

Fath Davis Ruffins, curator of African American History and Culture at the NMAH, believes that no substantial change will happen until the staff composition is more diverse and, indeed, the example of Cedric Yeh lends support to this view:

> If you don't diversify the staff then you don't have people who have some of these concerns . . . historically what has been collected in the Smithsonian has been because a person was really interested in that particular thing.

It is interesting that Fath Davis Ruffins, an African American, was one of three people who were employed under an affirmative action programme over 20 years ago. One of the others was Spencer Crew, who made his way up to be Director of NMAH, a clear vindication of such approaches to staff diversity. In the UK, Birmingham Museums and Art Gallery has been an enthusiastic supporter of positive (affirmative) action traineeships targeted at black and ethnic minorities, with a high percentage of trainees moving onto full-time positions and being promoted within the sector although, not as yet, at director level (Davies and Shaw 2010). There have been other positive action programmes targeted at people with disabilities and, at the Smithsonian, a foundation pays stipends for interns with disabilities.

Positive action programmes, however, should not replace a more thorough critique of employment policies. As Sandell (2000: 217) has argued:

> Some organisations, which may not necessarily operate direct racial discrimination, nevertheless may develop corporate cultures that reflect the norms, attitudes and values of the dominant majority and can serve indirectly to exclude ethnic minorities. Within such organisations can exist a tendency to recruit to an implicit model, one that reflects the existing demographics of the profession.

Magdalena Mieri, Director of the Latino History and Culture Program at the NMAH, identifies this tendency to recruit 'in one's own image' as a significant barrier to organisational change: 'There have been a number of openings for junior positions and it's always the same people . . . It's not taking the risk to hire someone that might look a little different'.

In 2010 there was an executive order from the US President to increase the number of people employed with severe disabilities. However, as Beth Ziebarth, Director of the Accessibility Program, points out, executive orders do not address internal reticence: 'There is a real attitude issue with the supervisors and the managers as to the perceived difficulty in having a person with a disability working with you, the additional expense'. Similar concerns have been expressed at the V&A where, nevertheless, there has been an increase in disabled staff from 2 per cent to 6 per cent over a period of eight years.[6]

Diversifying staff is clearly an important issue; one that works in tandem with measures to encourage all staff to take on responsibility for equality and diversity issues. Yet how does one engage those individuals who resist change; who may not see the relevance of equality considerations to their area of work; or lack the skills or confidence to contribute? The challenge of encouraging colleagues to 'get on board', is well expressed by Magdalena Mieri:

> It's truly a challenge to convince my colleagues that Latinos have been here a long time, that they are part of this society. It's the largest minority in this country – a reality that the Smithsonian needs to embrace in terms of the collections . . . I try to do programmes that I think could be really good for this institution, to help us to think broader, but some colleagues don't come to the programmes. Everyone is too busy, so I don't know how to deal with that . . . internally. I don't know how to break in, how to make inroads.

Several institutions, both in the UK and United States, employ staff with a specific remit to help embed diversity and equality across the organisation and who face the same challenges as Magdalena Mieri. They may have a generic role to develop policy across all equalities and across all functions, as previously at the Museum of London, or a more specific role in relation to one area of responsibility, for example, employment or reaching new audiences. Alternatively they may have a remit to address a specific strand of equality (for example, in relation to disability or to work with communities generally under-represented in most museums' visitor profiles, such as the Latino, African Caribbean or Asian communities). Such staff may be located in different parts of the institution and operate at different levels within the hierarchy thereby influencing their ability to effect change across the organisation.

Often posts with a specific responsibility for outreach or to broaden audiences sit within education or public facing departments. Whilst these posts are key to excellent work such a model, if interpreted as the sole or major focus for the museum's diversity and equality work, can undermine the position that issues of diversity and equality are just as relevant to employment practices, for example, or to collections. This contradiction was pointed out by some senior managers when interviewed by the evaluator of the V&A programme, *Capacity Building and Cultural Ownership – Working with Culturally Diverse Communities*. Although a cross-museum initiative, the project was managed by the Head of Diversity placed within the Learning and Interpretation Department. The project evaluator, Professor Simon Roodhouse, concluded in his report to the Museum: 'A whole museum, centrally driven, networked system approach, generating new knowledge, may deliver the next stage of development. It does point to consideration being given to integrating diversity into policy priorities'.

This need for a centrally driven approach was recognised early on by the Museum of London with the Diversity Manager reporting directly to the Director. At English Heritage, the Head of Social Inclusion & Diversity and the Social Inclusion & Diversity Adviser work in the Government Advice department in the Directorate of National Advice and Information. Their role is to ensure legal compliance and co-ordination of corporate policy on all aspects of equality and diversity as well as to support English Heritage's aim to broaden engagement with the historic environment. The National Trust, too, has a central strategic role, working across the organisation in relation to all equalities. The staff member with a role to drive forward equality and diversity policy at the Tate is placed in the Directorate, confirming the importance of a central strategic position.

At the Smithsonian in Washington there are central units concerned with different strands of cultural diversity that work across the departments and across the museums. There is also a centrally placed disability post in the Directorate, again with a wide-ranging role, as Beth Ziebarth, Director of the Accessibility Program states:

> We work on guidelines to help enforce or implement the policy, we do staff training, we plan direct accessibility services like signing interpreters, real time captioning,

getting direct feedback

alternative formats of publications etc. I'm responsible for reviewing and advising on facility and exhibition designs. We do outreach to the disability community ... we're always cooking up ways that we can integrate more about the history of people with disabilities into what is happening at this museum.

However, Beth Ziebarth does not underestimate the internal barriers that hinder attempts to embed a concern for greater access across *all* activities of the Museum:

> Most of our administration would view people with disabilities just in terms of accessibility issues – facility access – not even thinking about access to the programs . . . and never getting into the idea of content and the idea of reflecting people with disabilities in our displays and exhibitions.

The effectiveness of such 'diversity or equality' posts in supporting change or influencing all areas of the organisation may not only depend on where they are located but also their position in the hierarchy. The Social Network Analysis that identified the relative lack of influence of the V&A's earlier Access, Inclusion and Diversity Strategy Group, also showed that the staff who were most consulted about diversity by people from across the Museum (in particular, the Head of Diversity and the Manager of the project, *Capacity Building and Cultural Ownership – Working with Culturally Diverse Communities*) had little access to most senior managers and the Director. Such posts, however effective in building networks across and beyond the museum, are ultimately dependent on the support they receive from the leadership and the access they have to decision-making processes.

Consultation, collaboration and partnerships

Another major factor in driving forward change can be the degree of openness to external influence. As Lonnie Bunch, Director of the National Museum of African American History and Culture (NMAAHC), states: 'Change seems to me to often start outside . . . then that begins to play out in the museums'.

Some museums are particularly active in recognising and harnessing expertise beyond their walls. The Museum of London used external advisors in the development of the London Sugar Slavery Gallery in Docklands (Figure 1.1) and it was the Museum's collaboration with members of London's LGBT communities that was a catalyst for research into existing collections and a collecting policy around LGBT history.[7] Drawing on this experience, the Museum of London established a Community Collaboration Committee made up of senior managers and staff. An additional Review Group meets before the Collaboration Committee to review the 50 or so proposals they receive a year. As Annette Day, Head of Programmes, explains:

> If the Review Group feels it is a proposal that the Museum can take further, someone is assigned to work with the partner to develop it further. The aim of this is to be more transparent, and more equitable about how we deal with external partnerships.

The recommendations of the Collaboration Committee also feed into the Exhibitions Committee. Interestingly neither the membership of the Community Collaboration Committee nor the Review Group include any external representatives.

FIGURE 1.1 Entrance to *Sugar and Slavery* exhibition, Museum of London. With permission of the Museum of London.

Birmingham Museums and Art Gallery has a Community Action Panel with significant external representation. This meets monthly and has advised on a wide range of issues – from the exhibitions policy to gallery redisplays, from the website to sale of goods in the shop. Birmingham Museum also has a Community Gallery that encourages staff to work alongside community groups turning participatory arts projects into high quality exhibitions.

Katherine Ott, a curator in the Division of Medicine and Science at the Smithsonian's NMAH, who is planning an exhibition about the history of disability in the United States and who has previously organised exhibitions about the Disability Rights Movement, considers that the active involvement of people with disabilities is key. Drawing on the familiar slogan of the disability rights movement in the United States, she stated: '"Nothing about us without us". You can't do it if you don't have the people you are representing as part of the team'.

Yet such community collaborations are often fraught with tensions with external partners feeling that the partnership may be far from equitable (see Chapter 3, this volume). The more powerful and prestigious the institution, the less likely they may be prepared to listen to external advice or to share power. It is therefore impressive to read in the introductory text of the National Museum of the American Indian (NMAI) on the Mall in Washington that, 'The Museum rests on a foundation of consultation, collaboration and co-operation with natives. It has shared the power museums usually keep'.

However the media and other commentators have criticised the NMAI for its lack of coherence and scholarship even though it has attracted large, diverse audiences. The NMAI itself has learned much since opening their two facilities in New York City (1994) and Washington, DC (2004) and has re-organized to have more emphasis on research and scholarship, both internally and externally, engaging a broader group of scholars in planning exhibitions and major programmes. Many complex factors come into play, as noted by John Haworth, NMAI's New York Director:

> For NMAI, we engage native communities, with both native and non-native scholars informing our work . . . An indigenous perspective is primary to everything we do and we want to make certain that the design, the lighting, the presentation is expertly rendered, beautifully designed.

Lonnie Bunch makes a similar point but identifies an important difference between American-Indian and African-American communities:

> The Indian museum argued rightly, from their point of view, that they have been victims of some of this scholarship and therefore they wanted to err on the side of community. What I argued is the African American experience is further along when it comes to interpretation. There is fifty years of scholarship and I've argued that the African American story is more important than just to be in the hands of the community so what I wanted was . . . a tension between scholarship and community.

The Social Network Analysis carried out for the *Capacity Building and Cultural Ownership* project at the V&A identified over 80 black, Asian and minority ethnic organisations with which the project had worked but found that most of these relationships did not extend beyond the project staff members, many of whom have subsequently left. This points to the need for a 'whole museum approach' to ensure the Museum both sustains, and benefits more broadly from, such relationships and, conversely, that such external partners feel able to network, influence and forge relationships with people across and through the organisation including at senior level (see Chapter 3, this volume). Organisations who have worked collaboratively with museums and galleries may often feel 'dropped' when the specific exhibition or programme is over. The importance of such 'cultural flows' – both at a formal and informal level and between individuals and organisations (see Chapter 8, this volume) – in either serving as a barrier or contributing to change, should not be underestimated.

What is clear is that leadership from trustees, directors and senior managers is important. But more importantly, it is the nature of that leadership which is most significant; leadership that allows others to contribute and supports them to take ownership of diversity and equality initiatives is what is needed. Individuals and groups (both formally and informally constituted) can affect change and particularly so when managers are responsive to ideas and concerns of staff at all levels and from across the institution. Diversity of staffing is central but the additional challenge is in engaging everyone, even the most reluctant, ensuring coherence across organisations and identifying and removing barriers to change. For senior managers and those with a specific remit on diversity and equality this can be a daunting task but one best achieved when channels of communication are open, networks of influence are sustained and when the 'core' listens to, and takes account of, those at the margins, recognising that such positions often change and are in flux. Museums and galleries need to consult, collaborate or form partnerships with external stakeholders thus benefitting from the rich resources that lie outside their organisations.

Connecting and competing equalities

Museums are faced with a range of challenges with regard to different equality strands that they may or may not address consciously in developing strategic priorities. It is clearly a challenge to address all strands simultaneously and yet, do institutions risk emphasising concern for one group at the expense of another? In an increasingly fluid and globalised world are distinctions on the basis of disability, gender, race, sexual and gender identity, age, socio-economic status, religion or belief less relevant or are they increasingly intertwined? Are identity politics passé and issues of poverty more pertinent? How are strategic priorities arrived at and what is the impact of the different political, social, cultural, local, national and international contexts in which we operate?

It was clear from the interviews we conducted that much of the emphasis, both in the UK and United States, in relation to collections, programming and audience development has been on issues of race and ethnicity. This is certainly the case at the V&A which has a long tradition of working with UK based South Asian and Chinese communities, spearheaded by the Asia department and supported by staff in the Education department. In addition, over the last decade, the V&A has developed programmes and initiatives to engage people from diverse cultural backgrounds including black British African Caribbean communities. Such programmes and initiatives have included gallery developments, exhibitions, public, learning and community programmes.

Making assumptions about specific audiences' areas of interest based on race or ethnicity is problematic (see Chapter 3, this volume) and yet, whilst the V&A has not solely focussed on culturally specific content as a means to attract diverse visitors, this is an approach that has yielded results. Such temporary exhibitions as *Arts of the Sikh Kingdom* (1999) and *Black British*

Style (2004/2005) or festivals such as Chinese New Year and programmes and events around the 200th anniversary of parliamentary abolition of slavery in 2007, for example, have brought in a significantly larger proportion of visitors from black, Asian and minority ethnic communities (between 25 per cent and 90 per cent) compared with the regular V&A visitorship (Figures 1.2 and 1.3). It is difficult to track whether such programmes have had an effect on overall visitor figures but the percentage of black, Asian and minority ethnic audiences at the South Kensington site increased from 8 per cent in 2001 to 14 per cent in 2010/2011. This is, however, not to maintain that numbers are the only criteria for success.

Other UK museums too have given considerable emphasis to cultural diversity. Birmingham Museums and Art Gallery, located in a city with one of the highest percentages of black, Asian and minority ethnic residents in the UK, is keen to make sure that, as Rita McLean states, 'our collections are representative and to make connections between our collections and communities'.

There has been no specific research carried out into the reasons for the dramatic increase in black, Asian and minority ethnic visitors at the Horniman Museum (from 8/9 per cent in 2010 to 34 per cent in 2010). Finbarr Whooley suggests that key drivers for change have been the development of the *African Worlds* Gallery, the focus on customer care and the growth in family audiences as a result of a strong multi-cultural learning programme.

At the Museum of London, race and ethnicity has always been an important focus given the history and ethnic diversity of the city. As Cathy Ross stated,

> I remember thinking that class was more important than race to put it crudely, particularly as I had come from Newcastle. It took me about three years to understand that London is a different ball game, that race is incredibly important and that, ethnicity, belonging and identity are actually things of the moment.

The situation in the United States is even more pronounced due partly to two central aspects of the nation's history; slavery and the genocide of American Indians. Indeed, the very foundations of the country are based on people emigrating to the United States from across the world.

One response to this situation has been the growth of ethnic-specific museums – Latino, Asian Pacific American and African American. Although some are local community museums in specific cities, towns or neighbourhoods – such as the Chinese Museum in New York – others occupy more prominent positions at a national level. The National Museum of the American Indian (NMAI) opened in 2004 on the Mall opposite Capitol Hill in Washington, DC. The new National Museum of African American History and Culture (NMAAHC), scheduled to open in 2015, is also planned for the Mall. An equivalent, but perhaps less high profile, development in the UK is the new premises of the Black Cultural Archives to be opened in 2013 in Brixton, south London.

Camille Akeju, Director of the Anacostia Community Museum, voices her concerns about the NMAAHC:

> I don't think we do ourselves justice by having a stand-alone identity. It will always make you vulnerable. I think the charge should have been to make the National Museum of American History relevant and equitable in its interpretation of history.

Fath Davis Ruffins, curator at the NMAH, suggests that ethnically specific museums may be less relevant for younger people:

FIGURE 1.2 Africa Fashion Day, 1 October 2005, V&A Museum. With permission of the Victoria and Albert Museum, London.

FIGURE 1.3 Chinese New Year celebrations, 30 January 2011, V&A Museum. With permission of the Victoria and Albert Museum, London.

Some people actually opposed having an African American Museum because it potentially takes African American history and culture out of American History and Culture ... A lot of younger people in the US don't see race and ethnicity in the way that people who are baby boomers and older see it ... so, to some degree, we may end up with institutions on the Mall that reflect an older way of thinking ... it will be interesting to see what younger people do with the American Indian Museum, African American Museum, maybe Latino Museum.

[handwritten margin note: new generations = new ways of thinking]

Spencer Crew, the first black Director of the NMAH, makes a similar point whilst also believing that ethnic museums will continue to have a role:

I'm not sure if it will resonate in the same way for the younger generations ... because I think they're a much more multi-racial group ... The spectrum of people dating other people of different backgrounds is just becoming more and more the norm.

James Gardner, then Senior Scholar at the Smithsonian Institution, also supports the contribution of ethnic specific museums whilst recognising the challenge of making the NMAH 'relevant and equitable':

The argument I would make is there are two different dynamics. One is about breadth and integration – which is what the American History Museum is about and the other is about breadth, which relates to the African American Museum ... The voice of the American History Museum is an old white guy, you know, that's the voice, that's the default voice.

He makes an additional point:

There's an assumption that only people of colour have race ... it's a conceptual issue, a real obstacle ... One of the interesting developments in the US is the growing interest, and no museum has dealt with this yet, in whiteness studies.

Lonnie Bunch, Director, is all too aware of these dichotomies but sees the NMAAHC as a potential space that will allow Americans to confront the issue of race, something he believes they rarely do:

Let's take African American culture and use it as a lens to understand what it means to be an American, the mainstream story of America shaped by race. A museum that's separate really allows us to illuminate America in a way that we couldn't if we only had a gallery and a half in the Museum of American history.

The tension between focusing separate attention on a specific group or embedding that group's experiences and perspectives into mainstream narratives and practices is one which resonates across different equality concerns. In fact Charles Desmarais, previously Deputy Director for Art, Brooklyn Museum, in supporting the rationale for the Centre for Feminist Art at the Museum, makes the case for both approaches:

I don't think that we want to pigeonhole all women into the Feminist Art Centre or require that every examination of work by men or women is looked at through that lens, but that lens is useful as a part of the whole view of the subject.

The Centre for Feminist Art was developed as the result of the intervention of Elizabeth Sackler, a board member who offered to acquire Judy Chicago's *Dinner Party* if the Museum could display it (Plates 1.2a and 1.2b). Interestingly, one of the biggest categories of books and gifts that are bought in the museum store relate to the Centre for Feminist Art, arguably lending support to the business case for such an initiative, alongside any social, moral or political case.

Other equality issues might also benefit from being considered from a business case perspective. Charles Desmarais believes that the Museum misses opportunities, for example, by neglecting to emphasise the religious dimension of their collections, recognising that the biggest sales in the museum shop are of a series of New Testament watercolour illustrations by the French artist, James Tissot, of the *Life of Christ* (Plate 1.3).

We did this exhibition on Tissot but I don't think we were very successful. In the late 19th century, early 20th century, people would fall on their knees in front of these pictures. I would have really played up the religious aspect and yet, institutionally, that's not something we would do.

Brooklyn Museum is not unusual in playing down the religious dimension in its galleries or exhibitions. Museums in both UK and United States, whilst holding objects of spiritual and cultural significance to diverse communities, often see issues of religious and belief as problematic, wishing to assert their secular or aesthetic role (see Chapters 9 and 15, this volume). Yet, it might be argued that museums are not only missing out on opportunities to engage new audiences but also to utilise such collections to increase interfaith understanding. The intercultural tours at the V&A, run by guides who are themselves from different faiths, point to the potential for this wider social and educational role. As Rashida Hunzai, one of the Intercultural Tour Guides, comments:

My first tour was to show a group of ministers of various Christian churches and imams of mosques from a Lancashire town whose motivation was to build bridges to overcome religious and racial tensions in their community . . . When we examined the Safavid church vestment woven for Armenian priests to conduct mass, both the Christian and Muslim members of the group began to understand that there was greater mutual understanding and cultural appreciation several hundred years ago between the followers [of these two] religions.

Nightingale 2010: 50

Other drivers for change stem from legal imperatives bound up in equality and anti-discrimination laws (see also Chapter 4, this volume). In both the United States and UK the law has been instrumental in requiring museums and galleries to address issues of access. Yet, as Rebecca McGinnis of the Metropolitan Museum of Art (Figure 1.4) points out, institutions may need a prompt to not only comply but to recognise that good practice necessitates going beyond the legal requirements:

FIGURE 1.4 A visit to the Metropolitan Museum of Art, February 2011. Photo: Eithne Nightingale.

So the Council's office, the lawyers can say 'we are breaking the law' and that's the first point. That's when people listen and then we can say 'and here are some guidelines for exhibition design that incorporate the legal compliance issues but also include best practice'.

Whilst the UK's Equality Act 2010 offers specific protection on the basis of a number of characteristics (age, disability, gender reassignment, marriage and civil partnership, pregnancy and maternity, religion and belief, sex and sexual orientation) there are no legal requirements to specifically address socio-economic class and museums (in both the UK and United States) seem to place less emphasis on this issue than on race and ethnicity for example. Tyne and Wear Museums in the UK provides a rare example of an organisation that set out to achieve a sustained shift in the proportion of visitors it attracted from lower socio-economic groups, a task that took many years and a holistic approach to managing organisational change (Fleming 2002).

Social class or socio-economic background poses other pragmatic challenges for museums. Damien Whitmore, Director of Public Affairs and Programming at the V&A, when discussing how the museum might enhance its appeal to visitors from a broader socio-economic class, asked an interesting question, 'What would the programme look like?'. If you look at the V&A programme at South Kensington at any point in time there are several exhibitions which focus on or incorporate aspects of cultural diversity – *India Design Now*, *Fictions and Figures – South African Photography*; *Chinese Watercolours* and so on. Exhibitions that attract a higher proportion of visitors from a broader social class are rather less easy to identify.

Fath Davis Ruffins from the NMAH points to other difficulties: 'If you ask most people they will say they're middle class regardless of where they are on the income spectrum'. At the Horniman Museum in south London it is the aquarium, the only free one in the area, which appeals most to lower income families. It would seem self-evident that charging would be a significant barrier but the lifting of entrance fees at the V&A has not substantially led to a broader socio-economic visitor profile. Clearly barriers to participation other than financial ones continue to deter some visitors from working-class backgrounds.

Of course issues of socio-economic class dovetail with other equality strands and the V&A at South Kensington, having struggled to formulate a strategy to attract a broader social class per se, has decided to address socio-economic status through other audience priorities – for example, race and ethnicity; disability and young people – and where they have more of an understanding of how to attract such audiences. The Museum was more successful in attracting a broader social class of the Sikh community, for example, during the exhibition the *Arts of the Sikh Kingdoms* through extensive networking with Sikh organisations across the UK and outreach to gurdwaras (temples). Over 60 per cent of the 119,000 visitors were Sikh; of these, 70 per cent had never visited the V&A before and over 30 per cent had never visited any museum or gallery (Nightingale and Swallow 2003). The V&A Museum of Childhood, on the borders of two of the most deprived boroughs in the UK and with a strong community, family and schools programme, is far more effective than the V&A at South Kensington in attracting visitors from a broader social class.[8]

Clearly no equality issue operates in isolation. In the United States, for example, the largest proportion of people with disabilities is American Indian. In the UK people from black and minority ethnic communities remain three times more likely than average to be detained under the Mental Health Act.[9] Identities shift and are multi-faceted (Younge 2010, and

Chapter 7, this volume). Someone can be bisexual, Asian Caribbean and Hindu; or white, disabled and Muslim. Any one of those aspects of identity may take on greater or lesser significance for the individual at different times and in different contexts (Modood 2010).

An important and effective way of addressing multiple equality issues simultaneously and exploring how they intersect is through more universal themes that cut across diverse identity categories and group experiences. The Museum of London's new Galleries of Modern London (Plate 1.4), for example, gave the staff an opportunity to take such an approach. As Annette Day commented:

> We wanted to include voices of women, voices of soldiers from other parts of the Empire, people talking about the mother country, people who came as Jewish refugees, people from different classes. In the Portraits exhibition . . . we tried to juxtapose interesting portraits against those from the 60s so they do talk about race, class and gender or sexuality quite explicitly.

Similarly, Cathy Ross stated:

> The other things in that period that we wanted to cover and that we were also aware of were more recent issues around diversity, for example around religion and focus on Islam. We picked some films to reflect this. For example there is an early film of when the Regents Park mosque was being built.

The Smithsonian American Art Museum and the National Portrait Gallery all show evidence of diversity having been considered in the development of interpretive themes, selection of objects and interpretation. Paintings of American Indians by George Caitlin remind us of the tragic eclipse of the native way of life; studio portraits of women posing for the African-American photographer, James Van Der Zee, evoke the vibrancy and glamour of Harlem; and a sculpture of Rosa Parks (Plate 1.5), arrested for daring to sit in the white part of the bus, recall the struggle for civil rights.

Camille Akeju emphasises the need to show how histories interact, citing an exhibition at the National Geographic Museum in Washington about African-American contributions to American history and culture:

> One of the things I liked best about that exhibit is that they tell the white American story and African American story in parallel streams of thought and then they intersect – in and out – you can't tell one without the other.

Interestingly, with the setting up of the new African American Museum on the Mall, the Anacostia Community Museum – set up as a satellite of the Smithsonian in the 1960s in a part of Washington where the community was 99 per cent African American – is changing to become an urban issues-focused museum.

Museums may encounter difficulties when they are perceived to focus on one or more groups at the expense of others. In response to the criticism that, in focusing on other faiths, the Birmingham Museums and Art Gallery had ignored Christianity, the Museum used the Papal visit in 2011 to display objects related to Cardinal Newman who was beatified during the Pope's visit. Aware of tensions in the local area, the V&A Museum of Childhood in the East End of London has developed programmes and initiatives to attract and sustain local white audiences whilst, at the same time, attracting new black, Asian and minority ethnic audiences (Figure 1.5). There are very often new challenges created through dealing with issues simultaneously but sometimes

FIGURE 1.5 Children watching a Punch and Judy show during a St George's Day celebration at the V&A Museum of Childhood, 23 April 2011 (in partnership with Tower Hamlets Council). With permission of the Museum of Childhood, Victoria and Albert Museum, London.

museums underestimate the preparedness of audiences to engage with such complexities. The V&A's Museum of Childhood for example, as part of the *World in the East End* project, integrated the story of a relationship between a Jehovah's Witness mother and her lesbian daughter into the Families Gallery and with no adverse reaction. In fact this part of the galleries, which draws on both tangible and intangible material collected from and by diverse communities, is popular with all audiences. Museums need to be both braver in addressing such complexity and also more transparent on how (and why) they are addressing such issues.

At the same time, there may be valid reasons for placing more emphasis on one group rather than another. Certain local, regional or national audiences may be under-represented; the museum collections or expertise may offer specific opportunities. There may be a political, social, moral, legal or business case for strategic decisions, all of which should be considered. Yet given the increasingly fluid and hybrid nature of our societies there seem to be important reasons for developing approaches which consider equality issues and strands simultaneously, which show how they intertwine, that identify opportunities for bridging relationships or exploring tensions between groups. Lastly, given the increasing gap between rich and poor – in the United States and the UK where the richest 20 per cent earn nine times as much as the poorest in comparison to Japan and Scandinavia where the figures is less than four times as much (Wilkinson and Pickett 2010) – there is an imperative that socio-economic class becomes more of a priority.

It is no easy task for museums to make decisions given finite resources and particularly in a time of economic restraint. Institutions may well be vulnerable to criticism that they are not doing enough in one area or focusing on one equality at the expense of another. Their audiences may reduce over time if they do not address changes in demographics; they may even face a legal challenge or a reduction in specific funding depending on decisions they take. These are just some of the reasons why a clear and transparent policy, with an explicit rationale as to how decisions have been arrived and what has been achieved against set objectives, is so important.

The equitable, diverse and inclusive museum

What might this ideal equitable, inclusive institution – which reflects and embraces all aspects of diversity – look like? Clearly no one size fits all but the interviews we conducted have highlighted insights and examples of good practice that can help contribute to this utopian vision.

Policies that gather dust or are merely a 'tick box exercise' are inadequate. A broad understanding of the issues, shared across the staff of the museum, though important, is also not enough. Diversity and equality need to be incorporated into strategic planning with the setting of specific objectives that are regularly reviewed whilst, at the same time, avoiding overly bureaucratic and time-consuming procedures. When devising a policy or major project or programme there needs to be a requirement or prompt, however light touch, for staff members to consider diversity and equality from both a positive and negative standpoint, recording this and any consequent action. Someone in a senior enough position to effect change, and/or with full support from the chief executive and access to decision-making, needs to oversee and coordinate such processes.

Committee structures can be effective but only where they have influence. Both formal and informal networks and consortia are important for the generation and pursuit of cross-departmental ideas and initiatives. An organisation that supports staff to be collaborative and to take up an active role in advancing equality, that involves staff at all levels and listens to their concerns and ideas, is a healthy one.

Leadership, practised at all levels of the organisation, is a key issue but equally ownership – through which everyone can contribute to a vision that can be translated into practical realities – is also important. Posts with a dedicated responsibility for equality and diversity, whether that is with a strategic or operational brief or having a focus on one equality issue or more, can be influential in driving change but need active support of senior managers and such posts should not undermine the notion that diversity and equality are everyone's responsibility. Given the difference that individuals can make, organisations need to utilise and support those with specific experience and interest as well as the less confident or reticent, whether that is through staff development, mentoring or line management direction and support. Directors, senior managers and line managers could also benefit from staff development whether that is in understanding their legal responsibilities, incorporating equality into strategic planning or dealing with change.

The diversifying of both staff and internships is important but this process cannot rely solely on positive/affirmative action schemes, important as these are. Institutions need to move away from a model of employing 'like for like' and, as in other professions and in the corporate sector, recognise the strength in having a diverse workforce. They need to develop practical ways to achieve this, whether that is through training in equal employment practice, using different mechanisms and channels to attract candidates, varying the composition of interview panels or using positive action clauses as allowed by law. An holistic approach to diversity management is needed for long-term, sustainable change.

Strategic priorities will change according to the nature of the institution, the resources available and the political, socio-economic and geographical context in which it operates. Beyond ensuring legal compliance across all equality concerns it is evident there is no one model. There may be a rationale at one time for focusing on a specific aspect of diversity and equality; there may be another for working more broadly.

Clearly there needs to be some understanding and knowledge of the strengths and resources of the organisation, what is and is not being achieved. This could be in the areas of diversifying the workforce or audiences, fostering relations between communities, contributing to social cohesion or highlighting the contribution of a particular culture or individuals from specific backgrounds.

Specific equalities may throw up particular or similar challenges. Museums need to be aware of changing demographics, hybrid notions of identity and belonging, to understand whether a specific ethnic museum, exhibition or programme is appropriate. Race and ethnicity do not exclude white. Museums seem to have paid less attention to socio-economic status and some serious debate, rethinking and leadership needs to occur in relation to this issue, taking into account that fewer people now consider themselves 'working class'. The fact remains, however, that our national galleries and museums in both the United States and UK attract a significantly higher percentage of the wealthy and the more educated and that both countries are amongst the most unequal societies in the world.

Museums seem wary of addressing issues of religion and belief, perhaps missing opportunities to engage people for whom the collections are of both spiritual and cultural significance. We restrict our thinking on gender issues if we don't include men or transgender people; if we think of only who visits and not of how we interpret collections; if we look simply at the numbers of men and women staff employed and ignore barriers for progression to senior level positions. We restrict our thinking on disability if we only think of making our buildings physically accessible rather than exploring how disabled people are portrayed in our collections, the number of disabled staff we employ, of targeted rather than inclusive programming. Developing programmes for previously excluded communities makes market sense, an issue that is often ignored. There is value in examining the business case for diversity and equality alongside moral, social, ethical and legal considerations.

Institutions need to be more brave, less afraid of conflict or of tackling sensitive issues within society such as the tension between some LGBT and faith communities. They need to pursue experimental and innovative ways of interweaving histories and bringing communities together.

Lastly museums and galleries need to be more nimble-footed: to predict and be at the forefront of change rather than trying (often failing) to catch up. A more diverse staff is a prerequisite for this, as is the development of external networks and partnerships of those who can support the museum in becoming more inclusive. Relationships need to be developed as genuine collaborations where the museums draws on the richness and diversity of expertise of different stakeholders whether they be funders, sponsors, visitors and non-visitors, academics or communities. A museum or gallery that is responsive, creative and not afraid of risk taking; that listens to those at the margins to determine priorities; enlists support and reviews where it is going, is one which is moving towards becoming a more diverse, inclusive and equitable museum.

Notes

1   We would like to thank and acknowledge the contributions of all interviewees including Rita McLean, Director of Birmingham Museums and Art Gallery, Birmingham, UK; Annette Day, Head of Programmes, and Cathy Ross, Director of Collections and Learning, at the Museum of London, UK; Finbarr Whooley, Assistant Director, Horniman Museum, London; Amelia Wong, Production Coordinator, Division of Outreach Technology, United States Holocaust Memorial Museum, Washington, DC; staff of the Smithsonian Institution including Lonnie Bunch, Director, National Museum of African and American History and Culture; Magdalena Mieri, Director of the Latino History and Culture Program, National Museum of American History (NMAH); Cedric Yeh, Deputy Chair, Armed Forces History, NMAH; Fath Davis Ruffins, Curator of African American History and Culture, Division of Home and Community Life, NMAH; Camille Akeju, Director of the Anacostia Community Museum; Katherine Ott, Curator, Division of Medicine and Science, NMAH; Beth Ziebarth, Director, Accessibility Program, Eduardo Diaz, Executive Director, Latino Centre; Stephen Velasquez, Associate Curator, Division of Home and Community Life, NMAH; James Gardner, then Senior Scholar, National Museum of American History and National Portrait Gallery; Spencer Crew, African-American historian, formerly Director of the NMAH; John Haworth, Director, National Museum of the American Indian; Charles Desmarais, then Deputy Director for Art, and Kevin Stayton, Chief Curator, Brooklyn Museum, New York, United States; Rebecca McGinnis, Access Coordinator and Museum Educator, Metropolitan Museum of Art, New York.

2   The Race Relations Amendment Act 2000 placed a duty on most public authorities in the UK to eliminate race discrimination, promote equality of opportunity and good relations between all racial groups. It has now been subsumed into the Equality Act 2010 (England, Wales and Scotland).

3   A second Diversity Manager, June Bam Hutchison, was appointed on a short-term contract from 2006 to 2008. Chandan Mahal left her post as Diversity Manager at the Museum of London at the end of 2007.

4   The Equality Act came into force on 1 October 2010 and covers England, Scotland and Wales. The Act applies to all employers and organisations that provide a service to the public or a section of the public (service providers). It also applies to anyone who sells goods or provides facilities. The

grounds on which discrimination will be deemed unlawful are now called 'protected characteristics'. They are: Age; Disability; Gender Reassignment; Marriage and Civil Partnership; Pregnancy and Maternity; Race; Religion or Belief; Sex; Sexual Orientation.

   Public authorities are subject to the equality duty, in the exercise of their functions, have due regard to the need to: i) Eliminate unlawful discrimination, harassment and victimisation and other conduct prohibited by the Act; ii) Advance equality of opportunity between people who share a protected characteristic and those who do not; iii) Foster good relations between people who share a protected characteristic and those who do not. See www.equalities.gov.uk.

5   Cited in Jackson (2009: 192).
6   The number of staff with disabilities employed in 2009/2010 was 6 per cent.
7   Interestingly it was an internal working group of staff that was the stimulus for a parallel initiative at the V&A. See Chapter 10, this volume.
8   The Museum of Childhood attracts a higher percentage of people from Level 5 (unskilled) to Level 8 (never worked or long-term unemployed) groups (based on National Statistics Socio-Economic Classification) in comparison with the V&A at South Kensington (18 per cent as compared to 9 per cent in 2010/2011).
9   For further details see MIND (2010).

References

Bruce, K. and Hollows, V. (2007) *Towards an Engaged Gallery. Contemporary Art and Human Rights: GoMA's Social Justice Programmes*, Glasgow: Glasgow Museums.

Davies, M. and Shaw, L. (2010) 'Measuring the ethnic diversity of the museum workforce and the impact and cost of positive-action training, with particular reference to the Diversify scheme', *Cultural Trends*, 19(3): 147–179.

Fleming, D. (2002) 'Positioning the museum for social inclusion', in R. Sandell (ed.), *Museums, Society, Inequality*, London and New York: Routledge: 213–224.

Jackson, M. (2009) *Let this Voice be Heard: Anthony Benezet, Father of Atlantic Abolitionism*, Philadelphia: University of Pennsylvania Press.

Janes, R. R. (2009) *Museums in a Troubled World: Renewal, Irrelevance or Collapse*, London and New York: Routledge.

MIND (2010) 'Racial equality in mental health stuck at a standstill', report Online. Available at: www.mind.org.uk/news/2785_racial_equality_in_mental_health_stuck_at_a_standstill (accessed 12 October 2011).

Modood, T. (2010) *Still Not Easy Being British: Struggles for a Multicultural Citizenship*, London: Trentham Books.

Nightingale, E. (ed.) (2010) *Capacity Building and Cultural Ownership – Working with Culturally Diverse Communities*, London: V&A.

Nightingale, E. and Swallow, D. (2003) 'The arts of the Sikh kingdoms; collaborating with a community', in L. Peers and A. Brown (eds), *Museums and Source Communities: A Routledge Reader*, London and New York: Routledge: 55–71.

Sandell, R. (2000) 'The strategic significance of workforce diversity in museums', *International Journal of Heritage Studies*, 6(3): 213–230.

Sandell, R. (2002) 'Museums and the combating of social inequality: roles, responsibilities, resistance', in R. Sandell (ed.), *Museums, Society, Inequality*, London and New York: Routledge: 3–23.

Silverman, L. (2010) *The Social Work of Museums,* London: Routledge.

Wilkinson, R. and Pickett, K. (2010) *The Spirit Level: Why Equality is Better for Everyone*, London: Penguin Books.

Younge, G. (2010) *Who Are We? And Should it Matter in the 21st Century?* London: Penguin Books.

2

MUSEOLOGICALLY SPEAKING

An interview with Fred Wilson

Janet Marstine

Marstine: Do you think art museums in the US have become more socially just over the course of your career?

Wilson: I think museums are more socially just in the way that the rest of the country is more socially just because, since the 1970s, the popular media has expanded people's awareness. The core audience, for art museums at least, remains white, upper middle-class and well educated. There's still lots that has to happen in the United States around equity and social justice. But, in my lifetime, I've seen a great change in that museums are now realizing that there are people not in the room that should be there. *That* issue of social inclusivity is now discussed all the way to the board level. I am on the board of trustees at several major institutions. Diversifying the board has become a part of the discussions of nominating committees. *That* is a huge change. When I first came into the art world, even those people who really were do-gooders, who wanted change, were just wringing their hands, asking – how do we make 'them' happy? You know, the language being used – 'them' – showed that not only were these museum professionals clueless, but they had no connection or access to anybody other than people like themselves. They didn't know *how* to make that leap. Others didn't want to make that leap, but they were masking it. But, over the course of thirty years, there has been enough agitation in some circles, and enough education in others, that staff members now see a need for a socially equitable museum structure. Staff members also understand that they can gain from it, not only financially, but intellectually. And I see this development not only in museums but also in nonprofit art organizations and commercial art galleries.

Marstine: You emphasize the way that museums have been impacted by society at large. Do you also think that museums have the power to impact society?

Wilson: They do, but they haven't taken full reign of that. At this point, the majority of museums are just trying to keep up. They're not leading; they're just where everyone else is. I'm talking about mainstream, large institutions that people look to as models. They're not risk-takers. Risk-taking tends to take place at smaller, more marginalized institutions.

Marstine: What are some of the biggest factors that impede museums' social engagement?

Wilson: Institutions change very slowly. The rate of change is so slow, in large part, because of money but also because the desire for change has to come not only from the staff but also from the trustees. In the art museum, while boards have grasped the significance of diversity, they differ in opinion on what social justice is, and I imagine many would not see its relevance for art museums if asked flatly. In fact, in my capacity as a museum board member, I've never been involved in a conversation like that. However, while the words 'social justice' might not be uttered in the boardroom, it is nevertheless possible to gain agreement from the board for an idea that may just help to move the institution in that direction. Art museum boards are not monolithic; the variety and complexity of the individuals, given their economic clout, might surprise people. Boards do have to agree on things to move forward. Everybody is aware of this balance of power, so the pace of change is slow.

Art museums in the United States are in a really funny position. They need to court the elite for financial support but, at the same time, they also try to speak to 'the street', as museums also rely on the average visitor for support – not to mention the large amounts they get from foundations and corporations that look at audience numbers before they give money. And so art museums have this dual personality.

Marstine: What does it mean to substantively embed diversity in a museum?

Wilson: Awareness is the first step. And, for many museums, there *is* awareness. Once you have awareness, you can no longer deny the reality. Current museum scholarship often shows that awareness. For example, many exhibition catalogue essays today discuss artists of color with great sensitivity. But sometimes the scholarship overshadows what museums could *do* to create change. The next layer is embedding diversity in the staffing across all departments of these institutions, from marketing and development to registration, curation and education, so that the conversations about diversity become more insightful, not simplistic readings of artists' works or token exhibitions for Black History Month. But, at the same time, just 'looking the part' is, in itself, not creating change. A museum's staff has to be committed to pushing forward the dialogue on inclusivity, and follow the dialogue with systemic action.

A lot of museum education departments are doing really interesting things with marginalized communities. I think the future of embedding diversity is to further integrate what museum educators are doing with curatorial conversations.

In the end, embedding diversity and social justice through mission and vision statements, strategic plans and promotional materials is perhaps most effective, with the museum structure existing today, as it is proactive; it keeps the agenda on the forefront for all to see and holds the institution accountable over the long term.

Marstine: What innovative models come to mind when you imagine a more socially responsible museum?

Wilson: Well, the Pulitzer Foundation for the Arts in St. Louis has three full-time social workers on staff, working side-by-side with the curators to create themes for exhibitions and programs for the most vulnerable, impoverished and ignored communities. I don't think there's any one model, though. I think there are specific aspects of practice, particularly in the area of risk-taking, that museums could emulate. The bigger museums get, the more they lose their nimbleness. For whatever reason, museums seem to lose a lot of this flexibility when they 'professionalize' and go through the accreditation process. This is why I am the 'fly in the ointment'; I am not 'accredited' or 'professionalized'. I bring my experience, passion and creativity to the museum, and my projects reflect that. I try to establish a relaxed relationship with various departments within the museum. I can do nothing else – it is who I am. In this regard, perhaps I embody the spontaneity of the street, and bring it into the museum. I'm not streetwise or anything like that, necessarily, but I try to bring the outside in, be it popular culture or current scholarship from other fields, so that museum people can, for a moment, not follow the rules the way they normally would.

Marstine: What are the unique challenges that art museums face, as distinct from other kinds of museums?

Wilson: I believe the future of the museum lies in accepting its holistic, interdisciplinary nature, as it originates from the Wunderkammer, where diverse subjects were mixed together and existed in a dialogue. Of course it would be a twenty-first century museum, not the Wunderkammer of the past. Art museums, in particular, are too rarefied today, as if to deny the interdisciplinary, contextual aspects of their collections – for example, the anthropological, the historical, and the sociological. That's a problem. Of course other types of museums need to be open to other scholarship as well, but the art museum prides itself on the lack of context more than the others.

Marstine: What special role can university museums play in creating a more socially just institution?

Wilson: University museums have the opportunity to foster life-long learning. Typically, however, students experience the university museum – if they do go in at all – the way they would experience any other museum anywhere, as something apart from their lives, and not particularly relevant to their developing skills in visual, creative, and critical thinking; they understand museum-going as a leisure activity, rather than a learning experience, and this perception remains with them when they go out into the world. Currently, many university museums define their audience as their city or town's inhabitants. Too often they mimic and see themselves in dialogue with more high profile museums around the country. I think university museums should focus on students and the campus community as their primary audience. The museum should focus on programming that engages student audiences through teaching basic museological literacy: how to read and use a museum. Universities should support these efforts. All the university's departments have collections of one sort or another; they can enhance all that the students learn.

In terms of promoting social justice, because university museums exist within a specific, academic community and don't typically have the same systems of governance as other kinds of museums, they can do a lot of things that these other museums can't do. They have the ability to be nimble and address challenging themes. The university is a place for scholarship, debate and the development of ideas and the university museum can play a leading role if it is embedded physically and intellectually in campus life.

Marstine: What is the role of the culturally specific museum in the United States?

Wilson: In regions of the Anglophonic world with significant indigenous populations – the United States, Canada, Australia and New Zealand – museums and source communities have begun a dialogue on what constitutes culturally sensitive modes of research, display, interpretation and promotion. Communities have their own viewpoints on what is the right thing to do and the right way to think about it and this is how culturally specific museums have emerged. In a way, it is important that the culturally specific museum ignores mainstream museum culture. The dialogue is within a cultural community. For culturally specific audiences, the museum is a relief from the onslaught of imagery and point-of-view of the mainstream. It is a safe place to reassess and assert one's identity, and see it in 'museum' terms. Within any particular community, however, you have a diversity of opinions about identity. I think it's important to push the outer edges of what it means to be in any particular community, to challenge stereotypes and to explore issues that might not immediately seem relevant to the community in question but that engage identity from multiple perspectives. Another significant aspect of culturally specific museums is that they are training grounds for people within underrepresented communities to gain museological experience in a supportive environment where their opinions are respected and talents are nurtured. Emerging from the environment of the culturally specific museum are not only new themes and new ways of looking but also new concepts of what the 'museum' means within particular communities. And *that* may also be useful to 'mainstream' museums.

The National Museum of the American Indian is doing this. Mainstream circles have leveled some heavy criticism at NMAI's architecture, design and interpretation. But, in my mind, when the mainstream doesn't get it, yet the point is very clear to people of color or specific cultural, ethnic, or economic groups, that often indicates that something really radical is taking place. From my observation, I believe NMAI is not overly concerned with explaining the cultural significance of every object in the collection; the conversation is: we are all around you; we look like you, we don't look like you, we are what you imagine we are, and we are mostly not what you imagine we are, but we're here. The whole museum is political. If you want to know this other stuff, you go to some other museum.

Marstine: Do you think that diversity and equality in the museum are dependent on public funding and that private funding is a contradiction in terms with social justice?

Wilson: Hell no. Not in this country! Look at the censorship of the Smithsonian during the *Enola Gay* and *The West as America* exhibitions. In the US, public funding of cultural institutions makes them vulnerable to the agendas and whims of politicians; a healthy balance between private and public funding is most likely to encourage diversity initiatives. What we have in our favor in the United States is that politicians don't really care about art so they are not really looking. When we have a national pavilion at the Venice Biennale, we really can do whatever we want.

Marstine: In your opinion, what is the relationship between social justice and activism in museums?

Wilson: Museums need to be politically engaged but the danger of activism is that it can be seen as a brand. That's not how I, personally, approach things because when you present yourself as an activist, people who are interested in that agenda go towards you but a whole lot of other people walk away. Also, activist agendas can become too fixed. It's important to have clear goals but as people gather around the idea of something and it picks up steam, it can veer off and become something no longer creative but instead static and didactic.

Political significance can emerge from many different avenues in the museum, including the aesthetic. For example, in its temporary exhibitions, the Metropolitan Museum brings together all kinds of objects from diverse communities around a common aesthetic or art historical moment. That's a major feat. For a show on Byzantium, the Met was able to negotiate with countries that have a long history of warring with each another. And the Met does this over and over and over again to create the exhibitions that they do.

Marstine: Are you suggesting that we don't want to underestimate the power of aesthetics in promoting a kind of social justice which may go under the radar?

Wilson: Right. It's very important not to be reductive in our thinking about institutions. For instance, the Museum of Modern Art, in its early days, was engaged in all sorts of socially responsible programs and exhibitions. Social justice is not a new thing to museums; it is part of the complex history of museums. Some institutions might be surprised by what they find on social justice in their archives.

Marstine: What has the artist's role been in creating a more diverse and socially responsible museum?

Wilson: In the 1960s, 1970s and 1980s, artists worked hard to agitate for change in the museum. In New York, the Art Workers' Coalition was responsible for creating a free day at MoMA. The Guerrilla Girls and PESTS, an organization of artists of color, organized various types of guerrilla activities at various museums and galleries for lack of inclusion. Artists were the majority on the funding panels of the state and federal arts councils. Many artists of color were on these panels, too. They actively forced change through funding or de-funding institutions. Because of them, an artist of color can now walk into a gallery and the receptionist at the front desk won't assume that they are a delivery person or cleaner.

Marstine: What role has institutional critique played in advancing issues of ethics and social justice?

Wilson: Institutional critique has helped move the dialogue forward. Institutional critique remains under the radar for collectors and their ilk, however, as it's not valued by the art market. I had a fire in my belly around issues of social justice because they directly affected me and because, as an outsider, I was able to see the rhetoric of the museum and the profession's complete denial of the codes in place, codes that exclude, stereotype, and reinforce hegemonic power structures. I wanted to explore how museums were talking about culture and what wasn't being talked about.

Marstine: How do you situate your own work in terms of the insider/outsider dichotomy?

Wilson: I started out as someone who understood museums but was not an insider. I wasn't *of* that country, but I understood how to *act within* that country and pretend. I'd been a tourist, so to speak, so I knew a few words, and I knew how to behave, which is a big deal if you are in another country. If you know a few words, and you know how to act, people get relaxed around you. My being the outsider inadvertently made museum staff become a bit dislocated and unstable, but ultimately it was mutual respect, friendship, and trust which enabled them to take risks. People were very frank with me about themselves, even if a bit guarded about how they felt about my project. But now I'm a total insider; I can't get any more inside. Now that I know a lot more, I have the opportunity to dig deeper to find new avenues to explore.

Marstine: You are on the Board of Trustees at the Whitney Museum of American

Art, the Sculpture Center, the American Academy in Rome, and Creative Capital. How do you define your position as a trustee?

Wilson: I'm still trying to figure this out which, I think, is healthy. What others think my role is, and how much do I create the role, as opposed to what they want me for, are questions I still have. All these boards are as varied as the institutions they represent. They have different strengths and weaknesses. I am the president of the Sculpture Center board, and have been a trustee for many years, so my role there is somewhat different from the others, as the director and I maintain a close working relationship. But in general, I am the artists' voice, and I speak for the artist community. I also speak for the museum community because I have this breadth of understanding about museums, and I am typically the only trustee like that. Diversity and other specific social issues don't come up much in the meetings with the full board unless I bring it up; it's mostly the brass tacks. The interesting stuff happens in the committee meetings. However, I have noticed over the years that, every so often, there's an assumption among a few members on these boards that those with the money have the real decision-making power. But in my experience, when it comes right down to it, my voice and my vote count.

[*handwritten: he has title though...*]

At the Whitney I'm on the education and collections committees and I do a bit of writing and speaking for them to support the fund-raising effort. I'm there to support the director and the staff, because I understand what their needs and issues are. But just as I do with my museum interventions, at the board meetings I sit back and absorb what's happening before I insert my ideas, so that my actions are well thought-out, decisive, and will make a difference. I'm thinking for the long term.

Marstine: Do you think that a less hierarchical and more collaborative organizational model helps museums to instill social responsibility?

Wilson: Ha! I really don't know about this. I don't know of any museum that is run exactly in this way. A non-hierarchical model in art museums sounds like it makes more sense because many artists are non-hierarchical. The corporate model in which whoever is at the top decides what is important and then middle managers blindly carry out orders is anathema to how I personally work or think. In the art museum, if departments become fiefdoms, shoe-horning artists and their work into that hierarchical system impedes the museum visitor's understanding of how art jumps across boundaries. I imagine a non-hierarchical, collaborative model allows for fluidity and cross dialogue. But as far as social justice is concerned – as with any business, government, or organization – success also depends on how you hire and why you hire, and on who are the people involved. A collaborative model does not preclude individuals that don't listen or unfairly dominate the group and, conversely, a really strong leader in a corporate model, who has a visionary way of thinking, can be a catalyst for change.

[*handwritten: top down mentality ↓ need bottom to reach top first*]

Marstine: How can museums better recognize the contributions and voices of support staff?

Wilson: With major initiatives such as defining mission and imagining new construction or simply understanding the public's reaction to exhibitions or programs, everyone should be invited to give their opinions and ideas; when museum administration brings support staff in after the decisions have been made the institution loses out on significant insights and exceptionally high interest in the museum and their jobs. However, if we're talking about diversity, museums cannot simply look to support staff if underrepresented groups happen to be in those positions. Because those staff members may be protecting their jobs, it's not fair or effective to expect them to represent perspectives on inclusivity. It is very important that underrepresented groups are hired in all departments and at all levels. That said, for institutions to be open to risk-taking, staff members across departments need to talk together in order to question their assumptions. For example, the Pulitzer Foundation for the Arts developed a project, in conjunction with its staff social workers, in which they hired ex-offenders to be guards in their galleries; as part of their training, the guards learned about the art works from the curators. What the curators didn't realize beforehand was how much they'd get back from the new guards. Such collaborative efforts melt away personal and museological assumptions.

 I love this

3

MOVING BEYOND THE MAINSTREAM

Insight into the relationship between community-based heritage organizations and the museum

Kimberly F. Keith

This chapter explores the nature of collaborative relationships between community-based heritage organizations and museums and their potential to progress social justice, understood for the purposes of this chapter to refer to attempts to establish equality, equity and parity where it is currently lacking. The particular aspect of the museum that will be examined is its position as truth-teller, authority and keeper of what is sacred in society, a role that was established at its inception and is linked to its colonial and empirical past (Duncan and Wallach 1978; Bennett 1995). Once established, this position became ingrained in the public's imagination and the museum's narrative came to be accepted as the 'mainstream' account of arts and culture which went largely unchallenged until the later part of the twentieth century (Sandell 2002, 2007; Crooke 2007; Pollock and Zemans 2007). In recent years the narrative of the museum has been challenged both from inside and outside of the institution. Key external drivers for change include government agendas to promote access, inclusion and diversity through audience development and exhibition content. Moreover academic discourse, arising from cultural politics and feminist critiques, has recognized that the interpretation of objects and artifacts held in museums must be considered from multiple perspectives, particularly related to the cultures, religions and societies from which the objects are derived (Jordan and Weedon 1995; Lidchi 1997; Hall 2001). Internal drivers for change include the response to such external influences by individual practitioners and the consequent implementation of organizational change management in accordance with social, cultural and financial trends beyond the museum's walls.

Context

In the United Kingdom, the Department for Culture, Media and Sport (DCMS) and agencies such as the Heritage Lottery Fund (HLF) and Arts Council England (ACE) foster the promotion of access, inclusion and diversity through policy initiatives that are often tied to special funding. These policies are specifically designed to address unequal access to the arts and culture, often incorporating broader social aims to encourage community cohesion and promote cross-cultural awareness and understanding. One means to advance the engagement and portrayal of diverse peoples and cultures has been through the support of collaborative projects between museums and community-based heritage organizations. Such collaborations can help further access and inclusion with regards to diversifying audiences of the 'mainstream' museum, and at the same time they can also interrogate the museum's narrative which supports and perpetuates its position of authority.

Community-based heritage organizations engage in a range of activities from establishing community archives to providing access to cultural and creative expression, the aim of which is to help shape the identity, and both preserve and promote the social and cultural history, of diverse groups. In terms of social justice, collaboration between museums and heritage organizations can begin to address issues of equity through questioning the partiality of the museum's traditional narrative and expanding this through the inclusion of external, different, and potentially oppositional, voices. Collaborations can also serve to create parity between organizations of differing sizes, scale and scope.

However, as the museum and the community-based heritage organization are distinctly and differently situated in the social and cultural landscape, variations in their mission and approach can create tensions during the collaborative process. This chapter will examine these tensions whilst questioning the potential and actual influence of community-based heritage organizations (often working in the 'margins') on museums (that operate largely in the 'mainstream'). The benefits and drawbacks to partnership, and the challenges of working with the 'mainstream', will be interrogated through testimony drawn from discussion between four heritage sector practitioners who have worked collaboratively with museums. Although distinct positions are offered, drawn from individuals' personal experiences, this chapter aims to offer a collective account of the present relationship between the 'margins' and the 'mainstream'.

Community heritage sector practitioners

The four practitioners whose experiences inform this chapter are Harbinder Singh, Cliff Pereira, Rajiv Anand and Kimberly Keith. Harbinder Singh is the Honorary Director of the Anglo-Sikh Heritage Trail (ASHT), a national initiative that draws together relevant UK locations, institutions and artifacts to create virtual and actual trails pertaining to Sikh heritage and culture. The main aim of ASHT is to promote greater awareness of the shared heritage between Sikhs and mainstream Britons. The material content at the center of its initiatives are the many Sikh or Sikh-related artifacts held in national, regional and local museums in the UK (Plate 3.1a).

Cliff Pereira is the former Chair of the Black and Asian Studies Association (BASA), the aim of which is to foster research and disseminate information on the history of Black peoples in Britain. BASA publishes a newsletter three times a year and holds an annual conference. BASA has taken up issues with government departments and agencies such as English Heritage (with regard to the blue plaque scheme that functions to commemorate the link between notable figures of the past and the buildings with which they are associated) and the Museums, Libraries and Archives Council regarding material held in archives, libraries and museums in Britain. Additionally, Cliff has had extensive involvement with exhibitions and community engagement initiatives with the Royal Geographical Society.

Rajiv Anand is the museum consultant for the Institute of Jainology, which espouses that 'compassion and non-violence towards all living beings are the fundamental principles of Jain philosophy'. The Institute's mission is 'to propagate Jainism and its values through art, culture and education' (Institute of Jainology 2011). The mission is met through objectives such as: providing a platform for interaction between different Jain communities and organizations; creating an awareness of the history, art, philosophy and practices of Jain faith, including its relevance to today's world; and undertaking the cataloging and digitization of Jain manuscripts and artifacts.

Kimberly Keith, the author of this chapter and chair of the discussions on which this chapter draws, is a trustee for the Black Cultural Archives (BCA). This is a 'national institution dedicated to collecting, preserving and celebrating the histories of people of African descent in the UK. Using its unique collection, the BCA promotes the teaching, learning and understanding of the African peoples' contribution to the society and culture of Britain' (Black Cultural Archives 2011). Its public programs and partnership initiatives with organizations such as the Victoria & Albert Museum and the British Film Institute enable a variety of communities to learn and connect with this often hidden history.

Expanding the museum's narrative

The efficacy of collaborative work between the 'mainstream' and the 'margins' was interrogated through a discussion that queried the role of community-based organizations in influencing museums and the effectiveness of 'mainstream' organizations in recognizing and utilizing external expertise. One recurring theme throughout the discussion was the desire to enhance and expand upon the museum's narrative of specific objects and/or particular cultures. In relation to this, concerns were raised about the power and authority of the curator who is often perceived as difficult to access and holding tight control over the museum's narrative.

Rajiv: I worked at the V&A [Victoria and Albert Museum] as the South Asian Education Officer for three years from 2005 until 2008 and then straight after that I came into consultancy work. So, in a way, I've got an almost 'insider-outsider' approach because I've worked very closely with the curatorial staff in the Asia Department and the educators in the Learning and Interpretation Department, which I was part of, to bring the collections and the objects 'alive' through relevant sorts of cultural interpretations that can be understood by everybody. And I think contextualization is really important and also issues of access, intellectual access as well, because the curators can write as much as they want, or as little as they want, but you need to be a specialist to understand what they're saying.

[handwritten margin note: how much to say]

Rajiv was able to influence the V&A's narrative on South Asian objects and artifacts because he was employed by the V&A as an expert on South Asian culture. However, he faced challenges in making his voice heard as, at the V&A, the educational and curatorial functions operate as separate silos and do not work together on a regular basis. This was felt to be the case in many museums rather than an issue specific to the V&A. As Rajiv was in the Learning and Interpretation Department and was not in a curatorial position he had to purposefully instigate cross-departmental dialogue in order to bring about change in the museum's narrative. Later, when he was employed by the Institute of Jainology to work on the V&A's *JAINpedia* exhibitions, utilizing fifteenth- to nineteenth-century artifacts in the V&A's collection, he was in a position as a community heritage representative to contribute to the cultural interpretation of the material and to influence the curatorial voice (Plate 3.1b and Figure 3.1). Rajiv was uniquely placed to do this but many community heritage organizations

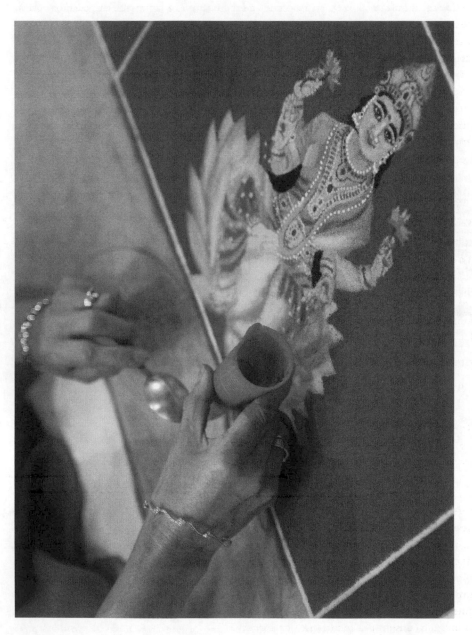

FIGURE 3.1 Jain Rangoli, made during Jainpedia Diwali Weekend, 13–14 November 2010 at the V&A. Event organized in partnership with the Institute of Jainology. With permission of the Victoria and Albert Museum, London.

lack the resources, contacts and relationships needed to access museums in a significant way. His comments raise two points. First, the curatorial voice can be highly specialized and difficult to engage with by non-specialists and, second, the need to modify the curator's voice may be evident to an outsider but is perhaps hard to disentangle or address as an insider. This indicates that it may take an outsider's perception with an insider's access to create change in the museum's narrative, a point which highlights the necessity for organizations on the 'margins' to collaborate with the 'mainstream'.

Ideally, information regarding the social and cultural significance of specific objects would augment or change the museum's narrative. This enhanced narrative could affect both the repositioning of objects in the museum's catalog or gallery, and the engagement of diverse audiences. However the assumed connection between visitors and material representations of particular social and cultural traditions can be problematic. This is well illustrated by a further point raised by Rajiv that 'identity is so fluid, everyone has their own different facets. You could be an Asian migrant and gay, and be disabled at the same time'. This complexity of the individual's identity is in accordance with layered, stratified, nuanced, fluid and non-fixed notions of race and ethnicity (Gilroy 1993; Hall and Du Gay 1996; Back and Solomos 2000) but is rarely observed by museum practice. *how to show multiple identities at same time?*

Harbinder: There is a sort of perverse inconsistency in the position of museums which is that it's okay for a white middle class lady to come here because she has a fascination for Italian sculpture although she's never been to Italy. But if I'm Asian and I come here, then *assuming* the expectation is that the only thing I'm going to be interested in is the Sikh objects. *minorities* And that, to me, totally throws the *raison d'être* for the whole existence of the museum. *only* So when I came here for that exhibition it wasn't because they had the chair of Ranjit *care* Singh. It was because this is a world collection and I'm here to enjoy it! Why should our *about* enjoyment be assumed to be limited to only those objects in which we have an historical *their* interest? *history*

Cliff: It's also a very narrow-minded approach to who the public actually is. The museums have this approach, as you said, that we, as minorities, are only interested in our own narrative. But then if the majority is not aware that another narrative exists – or in some cases maybe they are aware – then they're not actually engaging with it, so maybe it's a question of getting away from 'boxing the narrative' into these ethnicities.

Often museums contact minority communities when they have a project presumed to be representative of that particular community. However identity is complex and deeply personal and when groups or individuals are approached as part of a 'target audience', based upon conjecture about an aspect of their being, there may be antipathy encountered in the exchange. This is one reason to avoid 'boxing the narrative' in relation to ethnicities and difference as it is important not to assume that membership to a specific community equates to an interest in learning about that culture, especially from an organization outside of that community. At the same time it is imperative for the museum to collaborate with representatives of specific communities to ensure the accuracy of its narrative. This all points to the complexity of collaboration as difference and diversity must simultaneously be negotiated in relation to the object, the museum's narrative, its audience and the personal and professional positions of individual practitioners.

Keepers of the museum's narrative

The challenges of working with curators who are keepers of the museum's narrative and the staffing dynamics of the museum were topics that repeatedly arose throughout our discussions.

Harbinder: One of the biggest issues I've found is capacity and that they [curators] tend to be very transient in what they do, and the amount of time that we [heritage organizations] have of their attention is pretty small . . . But the bigger problem, I think, is continuity; when staff move on from one project to another or they move between museums and disciplines then it's very difficult to pick up the baton again and not to drop it and to have that continuity. That staff evolution or rotation to me is one of the biggest frustrating factors. It's bad enough engaging with curators when they're not moving – that is a challenge in itself – but when they move on, or they – or we – get new people coming in, then we're sometimes having to re-establish our credentials afresh. So I would call it the transient nature of museum work that is a problem to us.

Kimberly: Yes, often the relationships with community representatives reside with the individual that is facilitating the program and when they move on that's a problem. But when the institution – as opposed to an individual practitioner – takes ownership of a project and states that it is between them and say, the Institute of Jainology or the Anglo Sikh Heritage Trail, that it's a partnership, but then conversely the museum does not have the capacity to continue the relationship, I see this as being tokenistic and instrumentalist.

Cliff: I think, from BASA's perspective, the real problem is this embedded, or I would say constitutional, agenda that's missing – that there is no mission statement by the Museums Association or by any single museum to address the sensitivities and the accessibility to these [culturally specific] collections . . . But doesn't that mean that now, having recognized these objects as existing, there should be some sort of mission statement to acknowledge that? We don't find any movement by the museum sector to actually do that. And I think that's something that needs to be addressed. Because once you've got the statement, you then have a back-up for the lack of continuity that you were talking about, because a mission statement stays even though the people involved can move on.

This exchange raises many interesting points. When the 'margins' and the 'mainstream' collaborate it is often individual practitioners who establish organizational relationships. Continuity and transience affect individuals and organizations significantly and even when measures are taken to track the activity of the partnership (written documentation and rigorous verbal and written fact sharing) there is still the potential for information loss, misinterpretation and/or a relationship breakdown when individuals move on. This is because collaborations are developed, in part, through the convergence of the personal and professional characteristics of individual practitioners in addition to their roles within both the partnership and their particular organizations, which are all aspects of their respective social, cultural and symbolic capital (Bourdieu 1984, 1985). It seems impossible for organizations to capture and absorb the nuanced details involved in these interpersonal encounters which build and sustain relationships so that when an individual leaves a partnership, part of the relationship is lost. In order to mitigate against this it is necessary to recognize the significance of the role of the individual, to be aware of the challenges inherent in sharing information across departments and between organizations, and to take measures to ensure that communication is consistently reviewed and assessed.

If the museum has not taken measures to enfold the relationship into its organizational and operational culture, the museum's capacity to continue the relationship is compromised when the practitioner leaves, leading to the development of tokenistic and instrumentalist practices and projects. This is because the 'why' and the 'how' of partnerships is often carried out by an individual (and is established during the process of collaboration); remove the individual and the collaborative effort could be reduced to an objectified quantitative output, and the museum's narrative may continue to be drawn from its traditional position of authority, steeped in colonial and empirical tropes. Cliff suggested that this circumstance could be alleviated through the development of a mission statement specifically designed to address culturally-specific collections. However, a mission statement may not necessarily counter the potential for instrumentalist practices as it would require enforcement by individuals who may or may not be disposed to engage in collaborative efforts to expand the museum's narrative.

Challenges to affecting the museum's narrative

Cliff believes that minority narratives, and particularly feminist narratives, are lacking in the national museums that he has worked with. In his view the museum's 'imperialistic terms have not moved on to the twenty-first century. In fact, they haven't moved to the post-colonial, let alone into the post-post-colonial twenty-first century'. He also mentioned that museums he has visited in both Canada and Australia are moving forward using terms such as 'a world collection'. These international museums are recontextualizing objects through an examination of their provenance and the settings in which they are displayed, incorporating multiple cultural interpretations throughout this process. Cliff mentioned that community input was integral to this approach and that its implementation can have the two-fold result of empowering the community, through allowing its voice to be heard on a national platform, and expanding the museum's narrative, which may in turn increase the museum's accessibility. Cliff added that such changes in language and context were in response to pressure applied by individuals within heritage institutions who acted as brokers with the museum and who had vested interests in the outcomes. In many cases these brokers were ethnic minorities themselves. Cliff likened this process to one which he experienced at the Royal Geographical Society (RGS) in the UK where the permanent inclusion of working-class and ethnic minority staff and the addition of cultural advisory groups for specific projects promoted the development of multi-strand narratives which have expanded the social and cultural context of the RGS collection.

Such examples of good practice by museums both abroad and in the UK led to the group reflecting on exhibitions and projects that took place across Britain in 2007 and which marked the bicentenary of the parliamentary abolition of the slave trade. Many such events were created in response to government initiatives and linked to time-bound funding. Negative views about these projects included the fact that they were time-limited, that ethnic minority staff were employed on short-term contracts for project-specific activities and changes in the museum's material content and narrative was on a temporary rather than long-term basis. Museums returned to their 'normal' operating procedures after the 2007 season of events.

When a project is time-limited and funding and other resources are restricted, the opportunity to develop shared values is also limited and without shared values it is difficult to build a sustainable collaboration. For example, if the distinct positions of the museum and heritage organization outlined at the outset of this chapter are considered – i.e. that the museum is the authority and keeper of what is sacred in society and that the heritage organization promotes the social and cultural significance of the heritage of particular minority groups – then it is possible to infer that the values for each organization stem from distinct positions. The museum is concerned with the conservation, display and narrative of the object. The community heritage organization is concerned with the purpose, significance and meaning of the object. This could be interpreted as the museum being 'object' oriented and the heritage organization being 'people' oriented with the values behind these positions being significantly different. If there are no shared values around project objectives, such as determining the primary significance of the object within the collaboration, then the partnership may be solely a 'tick-box exercise'. Such an instrumentalist approach to conducting a partnership would be unlikely to produce evidence of sustainable outcomes based on a shared ethos and purpose.

The temporary appointment of ethnic minority staff for time-bound, project-based initiatives is tokenistic and problematic, leading to unsustainable relationships with both visitors and community heritage organizations. Museums may be able to fulfill short-term funding objectives and pay lip service by hiring ethnic minorities, but if such staff are not retained on a permanent basis then there can be no systemic change in the museum's narrative or ability to increase accessibility to museum collections. Ethnic minorities, according to the practitioners whose experiences inform this chapter, merge professional interests with personal interests and ethnic, religious, cultural, sexual and gender characteristics. The permanent placement of individuals with these characteristics could begin to inform change in the museum's organizational and operational practices (Chapters 1 and 2, this volume). Without the sentiment and interest which stems from both a personal and professional investment in the state of museum practices, organizational change may be slow to occur, if at all.

Change in the museum's narrative or content as a result of engagement in temporary exhibitions or activities is often short-lived. The resources attached to these projects are often unsustainable and it may not be possible to continue relationships with audiences and organizations beyond the scope of the project. As the museum moves on to its next initiative focus will shift to another topic, resources will be directed towards the next group, and the museum will most likely not include previous stakeholders in these new developments. Once considered necessary and important, audiences and organizations can feel abandoned and used. This is problematic as a project may be of central significance to the community group but may be just one of many for the museum and perhaps of less significance than other projects. If the community group allocates a significant amount of resources towards a collaborative project, expectations for both the project and the partnership are elevated. Unless the temporary nature of the project and the finite boundaries of the partnership are explicitly communicated, feelings of resentment may arise within the community group, leaving the impression that the collaboration between the 'margins' and the 'mainstream' is both tokenistic, instrumentalist and poorly valued.

Although these points were raised particularly in relation to the season of events in 2007 they were also considered to be applicable to the regular operations of the museum which often include time-bound activities such as 'special' and 'temporary' exhibitions and programs frequently tied to specific funding. The museum continues to seek funding to work with community-heritage groups yet, for the most part, this funding is for supplementary projects that lie outside of its general operating budget, thus supporting the notion that these projects are not of primary concern as they are, quite literally, at the 'margins' of the museum's operations. This issue of priority and centrality must be addressed in order to minimize tensions between the 'margins' and the 'mainstream' and create sustainable relationships which would genuinely progress social justice in the museum.

In order to address these tensions and to implement change it is first necessary for someone within the museum to recognize the obligation to do so, which in itself can be quite a challenge. Individuals tend to work within the confines of their specialism, inhabiting a specific position within the organizational structure and culture of their particular museum. This situation raises two key concerns. First, an individual practitioner may not recognize the need to incorporate or explore diverse perspectives and, second, gaining access to and influencing museum practitioners can be difficult. The museum's position will not move if individuals in the 'mainstream' are not motivated to do so and if individuals from the 'margins' are not able to influence the process. Harbinder suggested that this particular dilemma stems from the fact that heritage organizations often do not have the resources or capacity to engage with museums; that the time required to influence the 'mainstream' is considerable and, as a result, entire communities, including their representative organizations, have abrogated responsibility for changing the museum's narrative. If the 'margins' cannot access the 'mainstream' and if the 'mainstream' is entrenched in its position and cannot look outwards, then the initial steps towards achieving social justice through collaboration cannot be taken.

Benefits of (and obstacles to) effective partnerships

There are benefits to be gained through collaboration between the 'mainstream' and the 'margins' despite the challenges that need to be negotiated. Harbinder suggested that one of the greatest benefits was access to collections and the availability of complementary resources, such as technical knowledge in terms of conservation and display practices. Access prevents isolation and he felt that, when access was granted, the opportunity to 'alter the perspective of those objects or even simply to expand the description that there was of those objects' was possible. In this sense Harbinder felt that collaboration was useful because it helped to redress certain issues that may have otherwise been overlooked. Yet issues of access and the opportunity to contribute diverse perspectives raised the concern that, when information flows one way – from the 'margins' to the 'mainstream' – a collaborative effort can be reduced simply to a process of consultation which can undermine the equality, equity and parity aspects of any partnership.

Harbinder: I did not necessarily always expect there would be reciprocity in our partnership with the museum because I thought that we were the lead partner; we didn't need anything back sometimes. So I look at it from that angle. That it was *they* – the museum – who needed to be corrected and we didn't need any correcting from that side.

Kimberly: Right; I understand and I share your position. I'm still thinking about this word 'collaboration', and I think of partnership and then I also think 'we're the little heritage guys and they're the big "mainstream" guys', and if we're collaborating with them, I see that as doing something *together*, or something that's circular and reciprocal; but I don't see partnerships as working that way. I certainly don't see ours as working that way; I see it as consultation. Honestly, [in the V&A/BCA partnership project, *Staying Power*[1]] the museum's curators could purchase photographs that were produced by Black British photographers or that have Black people in them and they could say that they are about Black British identity and that could be the end of it (Figure 3.2). But, by having the BCA

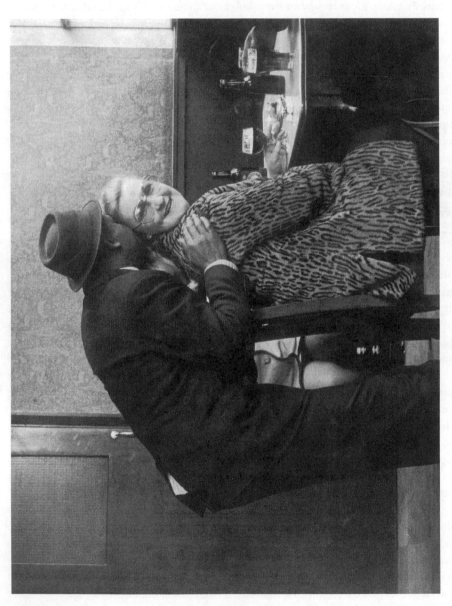

FIGURE 3.2 Charlie Phillips, *Customers at the 'Piss House' pub on the Portobello Road*, Notting Hill, London, 1 January 1969. Photo by Charlie Phillips/Getty Images. Collection: Hulton Archive, one of the photographs purchased through the *Staying Power* project.

at the table, we actually talk about the subject matter and the content and the rationale of purchasing one artist's work over another, and what it means to the Black community to do that – we have a dialogue about that. However, the communication and advice seem to be going one way.

Harbinder felt that ASHT was the lead partner in its collaboration with the museum and that his organization did not need anything other than access to collections and the potential to correct the narrative of the museum. I countered with my perception of the dynamic between the 'margins' and the 'mainstream' as being between small and large organizations, in terms of size, scale and scope; with the implication being that small heritage organizations are often the secondary partner in collaborative efforts. The terms 'lead' and 'secondary', used to describe the relative positions of partner organizations, highlight various aspects of inequality. Factors such as age of the organization; collection size or content; subject specialism; geographic location; membership numbers and scale of operating budgets, all contribute to the actual and perceived position of an organization and its relative status in the partnership. In Harbinder's case his organization's social and cultural capital was of paramount importance, leading him to determine ASHT to be the lead partner. The perception of the position of ASHT by the museum is unknown. However, in my view, it is unlikely that the museum would have considered ASHT to be the lead partner. The relative positions of the partner organizations, either actual or perceived and either spoken or unspoken, influence how individuals interact during the collaborative process – from how they speak to one another to which organization retains the tangible outputs of the collaboration. Not addressing and discussing the relative positions of the organizations involved in partnerships and implications therein can undermine the collaborative effort.

When differing organizations collaborate, equity and equality concerns often focus on the use or allocation of resources or, more specifically, the (unequal) distribution of resources. In the example of the *Staying Power* project, the V&A was awarded funds to acquire objects for its collection which it could have done without the input of the BCA in terms of the technical aspects of acquisition, determining the type and quality of print, the provenance of the artist or the object's significance in relation to its existing collection. The V&A partnered with the BCA in order to ensure that the social and cultural significance of the subject matter of the images reflected Black British identity. As the BCA did not receive remuneration for its input and will not retain the photographs in its archive collection, this could support the notion that the relationship built around *Staying Power* is primarily consultative in nature.

All practitioners cited examples where their organizations contributed significant amounts of professional subject expertise to museums for no remuneration or material benefit. This was seen as problematic on two accounts. First, many practitioners from community heritage organizations, and arguably from most charitable/non-profit organizations, work on 'a budget of love', meaning that they contribute time and resources beyond the stated parameters of their job descriptions and hours of employment in order to fulfill tasks and meet objectives that they feel passionate about and without additional compensation. Second, in Cliff's words, 'some institutions expect community collaboration to be free because they don't consider communities to have a receipt stamp on them'. These conditions create often unrealistic expectations which, in turn, create a vicious cycle: museums expect community expertise for free; free expertise is given because community experts feel strongly about expanding the museum's narrative. Museums expect to pay for the expertise of academics and scholars who contribute to their catalog and exhibition content yet the same expectation is not held for community-heritage expertise. Heritage experts are accustomed to being on the margins and to giving away their knowledge without remuneration. In *Staying Power* the classification, documentation and accompanying narrative of the photographs in the V&A catalog is of the utmost importance to the BCA because it may affect how visitors view and interact with the objects. For the BCA, it is important that the narrative is representative of Black people and the Black experience; providing a significant motivating factor for the BCA to partner with the V&A. But the BCA's engagement is also partially instrumentalist in that, whilst it may work on a 'budget of love', it is also working with the world's premier museum of art and design thus deriving a certain amount of cachet and kudos from funders and heritage sector peers.

The struggle to focus on social responsibility

The practitioners suggested that issues of equity and social responsibility should be addressed by both the museum and the funder and that efforts should go beyond the bare minimum required by the UK Equality Act 2010. There was concern that funders rarely require museums to address the practical issues of enabling access to specific audiences, such as taking objects or exhibitions into specific communities or providing transportation for targeted communities to come to the museum. Without the funder obliging the museum to embed access and inclusion considerations into grant applications and subsequent project planning, the museum may not address these issues at all.

The practitioners expressed a desire for funders to be more proactive in the collaborations that they support but recognized that many funders, whilst setting parameters for the museum's engagement with Black, Asian and minority ethnic (BAME) communities, do not themselves have a deep understanding of BAME needs or interests. Any understanding of minority ethnic communities should be developed through an exploration of the positional nature of difference and multiculturalism. Ideally, this would be combined with a consideration of the varied nature of both audiences and material objects when working with the museum. Operating without this knowledge is a symptom of what contemporary theorist Stanley Fish refers to as 'boutique multiculturalism'. This he describes as 'the multiculturalism of ethnic restaurants . . . weekend festivals . . . [which] is characterized by its superficial or cosmetic relationship to the objects of its affection' (1997: 378) and which is conducted without actually engaging with difference at a deeper level.

It is particularly problematic when funders stick to the superficial safety-zone of 'boutique multiculturalism' as museums and their community heritage partners feel pressure, as suggested by Cliff, to 'tailor programs and engagements to fit a funder's criteria, rather than start with what the community wants and then seek support to fund the community-based initiative'. If a program for a specific community stems from a tenuous understanding of, and a lack of consultation with, said community, the resulting program may be irrelevant to the community yet fulfill the objectives of the initial policy and funding remit, rendering the program a tick-box exercise.

Conclusion

The various tensions inherent in the collaborative process between the museum and the community heritage organization have been explored throughout this chapter. Creating change in the museum's narrative, negotiating organizational and individual positions, generating social justice in partnerships and operating in the face of policy and funding agendas were issues that evoked tensions during collaboration. By examining the tensions, particularly those that may go unsaid during the process, specific areas of concern can be recognized and addressed in future partnerships. This can be best achieved through developing shared values and clear objectives and through open dialogue employed in a reciprocal partnership. If social justice is to be achieved through collaboration, the delicate balance of power in the precarious relationship between the 'margins' and the 'mainstream' must be addressed and negotiated by individual practitioners and implemented throughout their respective organizations.

Through the convergence of the 'margins' and the 'mainstream', exhibitions can enlighten, programs and projects may engage, and awareness and understanding can be fostered. Although effective collaboration is often measured in terms of tangible or measurable outputs rather than outcomes such as shifts in organizational and operational practices, the success of collaborations can be evidenced in their ability to endure despite the tensions that are involved.

continual change

Note

1 *Staying Power* is a five-year partnership between the V&A and the Black Cultural Archives, supported by the National Lottery through the Heritage Lottery Fund. The primary aim of the project is to collect photographs relating to the Black British experience from the 1950s to the 1990s.

References

Back, L. and Solomos, J. (2000) *Theories of Race and Racism: A Reader*, London and New York: Routledge.

Bennett, T. (1995) *The Birth of the Museum: History, Theory, Politics*, London and New York: Routledge.

Black Cultural Archives (2011) Online. Available at: www.bcaheritage.org.uk (accessed 12 October 2011).

Bourdieu, P. (1984) *Distinction: A Social Critique of the Judgement of Taste*, Cambridge, MA: Harvard University Press.

Bourdieu, P. (1985) 'The Social Space and the Genesis of Groups', *Social Science Information*, 24, September: 195–220.

Crooke, E. (2007) *Museums and Community: Ideas, Issues and Challenges*, London and New York: Routledge.

Duncan, C. and Wallach, A. (1978) 'The Museum of Modern Art as Late Capitalist Ritual: An Iconographic Analysis', *Marxist Perspectives*, 1(4): 28–51.

Fish, S. (1997) 'Boutique Multiculturalism or Why Liberals are Incapable of Hate Speech', *Critical Inquiry*, 23(2): 378–396.

Gilroy, P. (1993) *The Black Atlantic: Modernity and Double Consciousness*, London: Verso.

Hall, S. (2001) 'Museums of Modern Art and the End of History', in S. Hall and S. Maharaj, *Modernity and Difference, Annotations 6,* United Kingdom: Institute of International Visual Arts (inIVA): 8–23.

Hall, S. and Du Gay P. (eds) (1996) *Questions of Cultural Identity*, London, Thousand Oaks and New Delhi: Sage.

Institute of Jainology (2011) Online. Available at: www.jainology.org (accessed 12 October 2011).

Jordan, G. and Weedon, C. (1995) *Cultural Politics: Class, Gender, Race and the Postmodern World*, Oxford: Blackwell.

Lidchi, H. (1997) 'The Poetics and Politics of Exhibiting Other Cultures', in S. Hall (ed.) *Representation: Cultural Representations and Signifying Practices*, London: Sage/Open University: 151–222.

Pollock, G. and Zemans, J. (eds) (2007) *Museums After Modernism: Strategies of Engagement*, Malden and Oxford: Carlton Blackwell Publishing.

Sandell, R. (ed.) (2002) *Museums, Society, Inequality*, London and New York: Routledge.

Sandell, R. (2007) *Museums, Prejudice and the Reframing of Difference*, London and New York: Routledge.

4

BEYOND COMPLIANCE?

Museums, disability and the law

Heather J. L. Smith, Barry Ginley and Hannah Goodwin

Access should be formally established as a right and not a benevolent demonstration of being reasonable.

Prideaux 2006: 62

The second half of the twentieth century saw the emergence and increasing influence of the disability rights movement in the United States and UK. Disability activists played a key role in increasing the visibility of disabled people, making a powerful case for equality and high-lighting widespread social, political, economic and cultural discrimination. Alongside battles for equal access to education, employment opportunities, participation in political processes and so on, activists also sought to challenge dominant cultural representations of disability (the disabled person as freak, outsider, recipient of charity) that underpinned deeply entrenched negative attitudes (including fear, repulsion and pity) amongst the non-disabled population (Gartner and Joe 1987; Hevey 1992; Oliver 1996).

The separation of disabled people from the mainstream and their exclusion from many institutions and settings within the public sphere was challenged alongside the assumption that the 'solution' to the 'problem' of disability was to be found in medical knowledge. As disability scholars Barnes *et al.* (1999: 27) explained:

> In developing what became known as a social approach to disability, disabled people . . . argued that it is society which disabled people with impairments, and therefore any meaningful solution must be directed at social change rather than individual adjustment and rehabilitation.

Disability activists made the cause they championed impossible to ignore at a political level and the need for a legislative response that would tackle discrimination became increasingly inevitable. In the United States, the Americans with Disabilities Act (ADA) was passed in 1990, followed some years later by the Disability Discrimination Act (DDA) in the UK in 1995.

These landmark acts and subject revisions and additions to the bodies of anti-discrimination legislation that exist in the UK and United States (as well as their counterparts in many other parts of the world), have undoubtedly played a key role in enhancing access to cultural organisations for disabled people. However, despite some important advances in the sector and impressive examples of innovation, the experiences of visitors suggest that there is a considerable distance to go before equality for disabled people is fully embedded in museum thinking, practice and organisational values. As Marcus Weisen (2010: 54) argues:

> Billions have been spent in recent years on new museums, major extensions and refurbishments across the globe, with little or no regard paid to providing a shared experience of the collections for disabled people. The cumulative effect is discrimination on a grand scale against disabled people.

To understand this situation – in which some organisations have made significant advances whilst others appear to have neglected their legal obligations and, more fundamentally, demonstrated a lack of concern for the needs of their audiences – we consider the strengths and weaknesses of legislation as a driver for change and the additional strategies that might be pursued to create truly accessible, inclusive and welcoming cultural organisations.

Legislation is usually introduced to enforce behaviour; either to make something happen or to make something stop. It is the place of recourse when nothing else has, or is deemed likely, to work. In the world of disability discrimination, legislation therefore constitutes a powerful driver for change, one that can be brought to bear on institutions – like museums and heritage organisations – that might otherwise be slow to tackle entrenched discriminatory practices. At the same time, however, the law has often been perceived as a blunt instrument, determining a prescribed course which does not always allow for the peculiarities of particular circumstances to be fully recognised. More significantly, there is a danger that a reliance on the law to achieve change can focus too much attention on what (minimum) changes are deemed necessary to meet legal requirements, rather than fostering a climate in which a genuine concern for (and commitment to achieving) full equality of rights is embedded.

 (handwritten note: law doesn't change culture)

In this chapter we draw on our experience as practitioners concerned with enhancing access to culture for disabled people and reflect on progress in our own organisations – the National Trust and the Victoria and Albert Museum (V&A) in the UK, and the Museum of Fine Arts (MFA), Boston in the United States – to explore how greater equality might be achieved within the cultural sector. We do not intend to assess one organisation against the other or to provide a detailed, direct comparison of UK and US discrimination legislation. Rather our goal is to explore the impact of this legislation in general and highlight other ways in which progress might be made. When reviewing the work of the V&A, MFA and the National Trust, particular attention will be played to the role legislation plays in motivating accessibility improvements at these organisations, the progress made since the inception of the ADA (1990) and the DDA (1995), changing staff structures and responsibilities, and the involvement of disabled people in the development of solutions to accessibility.

The organisations within which we work share some common aims but are inevitably shaped in different ways by variable levels of resource to effect change, their different locations and their operation under two different legislative structures. All three organisations welcome the public to their spaces and acknowledge a responsibility for making their collections, facilities and services accessible to the present day public, as well as preserving them for future generations. The V&A, 'the world's greatest museum of art and design' in London, receives a significant proportion of its funding from the UK government and holds collections unrivalled in their scope and diversity. The MFA in Boston, Massachusetts, is an independent museum and benefits substantially from both corporate and public donations. Since it was established in the late nineteenth century, its collection has grown to over 450,000 works of art. The National Trust is a charity and part of the UK voluntary sector, relying heavily on membership subscriptions and other fundraising to continue to care for over 350 historic places including 140 registered museums in England, Wales and Northern Ireland.

Developing legislation

In the UK, the development of legislation to increase the rights of disabled people began towards the end of the Second World War, with the introduction of The Disabled Persons (Employment) Act 1944. Whilst the act, intended to support disabled people in finding employment, was motivated in large part by the needs of the economy and the effect of the war on workforce availability (rather than a wholehearted recognition of the rights of disabled people) it nevertheless spurred disability campaigners on.

It was not until the 1970s that the Chronically Sick and Disabled Persons Act (CSDPA 1970) introduced, through a code of practice, responsibilities for providing access to public buildings. The CSDPA 1970 code of practice stated:

> Any person undertaking the provision of any building or premises to which the public are to be admitted, whether on payment or otherwise, shall, in the means of access both to and within the building or premises, and in the parking facilities and sanitary conveniences to be available (if any), make provision, in so far as it is in the circumstances both practicable and reasonable, for the needs of members of the public visiting the building or premises who are disabled.

The CSDPA 1970 also ensured, for the first time, the appointment of a Minister for Disabled People. The original appointee, Alf Morris, was vociferous in his views on the importance of advancing access for disabled people:

> We must all insist that it is an affront to civilised values, in a country claiming to respect human rights, for a citizen with a past or present disability to suffer prejudice, exclusion and both demeaning and hurtful discrimination for no other reason than her or his disability. It is an utter disgrace that to the restrictions that disability imposes there are added the gratuitous extra handicaps that attitudinal and physical barriers create. Let no one imagine that such discrimination is a thing of the past.[1]

In the years that followed, the changing international climate and growing global support for human rights drove UK disability activists on to campaign for a yet more robust law. The Disability Discrimination Act was eventually introduced in 1995.

Activists in the United States had campaigned for legislation that aimed to establish complete prohibition of discrimination on the grounds of disability with a defined timeline for action. The ADA 1990 followed the 1973 Rehabilitation Act which, as with the initial UK legislation, had focused primarily on employment issues. Under the ADA, no individual may be discriminated against on the basis of disability with regard to equal enjoyment of goods and services in places of public accommodation (including museums). The legislation provides similar protections against discrimination for disabled people as the Civil Rights Act of 1964, which made discrimination based on race, religion, sex, national origin and other characteristics illegal.

A perceived key difference between the ADA in the United States and the DDA in the United Kingdom was the inclusion in the former of 'titles' which include technical specifications for precisely how premises should be made accessible for disabled people. The CSDPA 1970 and the DDA 1995 had kept such specific information outside of the legislation itself, arguably making the US legislation stronger than that in the UK.

Reasonable adjustment

Closer analysis of the titles of the ADA 1990, however, suggests that they were not quite the 'sticks' to drive forward improvements that they had initially been perceived to be. Although technical detail is contained in the legislation, its use (just as with the code of practice, regulations and recommendations that followed the introduction of the DDA in the UK), is nevertheless built around the concept of 'reasonable adjustment'.

The term 'reasonable adjustment' (also known as 'reasonable accommodation') places obligations on employers and service providers to take steps to remove barriers that exclude or discriminate against disabled people. On the one hand, reasonable adjustment has been understood to be critical for advancing accessibility for disabled people (Lawson 2008), not least because it places a duty on service providers to take an active approach to the dismantling of barriers to participation. On the other hand, however, it has been criticised for being too vague and too dependent on wide ranging factors to be a powerful means of enforcing change.

In 2006, the Centre for Disability Studies at the University of Leeds published the findings from a major research project analysing the legislative structures and technical expressions of discrimination and disability in the context of the built environment in six European states (the UK, Malta, Ireland, France, Italy and Sweden) and compared these with approaches in the United States and Australia. In the report, Simon Prideaux (2006: 38) highlights the inherent weaknesses in the reliance, within UK legislation, on the concept of reasonable adjustment to effectively tackle discriminatory barriers to access:

> Significantly, the use of the provisos 'reasonable', 'practical' and 'impractical' throughout the majority of UK legislation serves to dilute the true extent of the requirements laid down by the DDA. Numerous permutations merge together so that businesses are relieved of the obligation to make substantial improvement to both their services and their properties. Alterations may be deemed to be ineffective, too costly or too disruptive.

The report raises similar concerns in relation to US legislation alongside a discussion of the practical challenges associated with enforcing compliance with the ADA (ibid.).

For many disabled people, the concept of 'reasonable adjustment' and the degree of flexibility it affords to organisations has permitted too many public service providers and employers to sidestep their duty to dismantle barriers to access and participation. Disabled people remain poorly consulted on improvements and temporary, ill-thought-through (and often ineffective) attempts to overcome poor access are often introduced in place of long-term solutions. Organisations can tend to view reasonable adjustments in terms of the minimum changes that will ensure legal compliance, demonstrating limited understanding of (or commitment to) the moral imperatives that underpin the legislation.

Given the limitations of legislative responses to discrimination, what else might be done to promote equal access for disabled people? In this next section, we turn to the museum context to consider the progress made against the backdrop of anti-discrimination legislation in the United States and UK and, more particularly, to consider what other strategies might be pursued to develop more effective and sustainable solutions to equal access.

Progress in cultural organisations

Janice Majewski and Lonnie Bunch (1998) describe three distinct tiers of access that museums should address to meet the needs of disabled visitors; access to the *physical environment*, access to *content*, and access to *history and culture*. Their analysis offers a productive way for reviewing the progress that museums have made towards greater access and helps to highlight ways in which further gains might be secured.

The first tier they identify concerns provision of access to the physical environment of the museum, enabling disabled visitors to enter the building and move freely around it. It is this area which cultural organisations have tended to focus most attention on, in part because physical barriers (and the solutions developed to address them, such as ramps and handrails) are more readily visible and more widely understood than other means of exclusion. This process of improving physical access in organisations has often begun with the development of policies and procedures, the identification of objectives as well as a prioritised list of adaptations which require investment. Policies can help to demonstrate an understanding of the imperatives presented by anti-discrimination laws; they can evidence an organisation's commitment to the principle of working towards equal access and they can hold staff to account for a particular way of working. However, words on a page do not, in themselves, effect change. Moreover, there is a danger that access solutions developed without the full involvement of disabled people will fail to satisfactorily address the physical barriers faced by visitors with wide ranging impairments.

The V&A, Museum of Fine Arts and the National Trust, in common with many other cultural organisations, have developed policies and strategies to promote inclusion and to clarify the implications of (and obligations posed by) anti-discrimination legislation. The V&A, which receives funding directly from central government (the Department of Culture Media and Sport), is required to meet a number of key performance indicators including those which directly relate to improvements in access and broadening audiences. These performance measures are identified in the museum's strategic plan which senior managers are tasked to deliver, helping to embed a responsibility for access within the organisation. Moreover, a concern for access is embodied within the museum's *Future Plan*, an overarching ten-year redevelopment scheme designed to open up the V&A to more people, ensuring that all construction and refurbishment projects must comply with relevant building regulations and standards. At a more detailed level, the V&A has implemented a Disability Action Plan to support the museum in achieving equality in terms of employment, service provision as well as access to premises and to ensure the consistent availability of support whenever disabled people visit the site.

The second tier Majewski and Bunch (ibid.: 156) identify concerns the provision of access to content. In exhibitions, they argue;

museums must give consideration to issues that range from label legibility to label text comprehension; from video captions and audio description to multiple levels of understanding and enjoyment of the exhibition's themes and content. Accessibility to content means accessibility to the written word, the objects, the media presentations, and the interactives.

Whilst a number of organisations have made considerable progress towards improving access to content, many more have consistently overlooked this issue. Marcus Weisen highlights good practice in gallery refurbishment and re-display at both the British Museum and the V&A which both consider intellectual access for blind people in every new gallery redevelopment. He further highlights the Cité des Sciences et de L'Industrie in Paris that has committed to building a level of intellectual access for visually impaired and Deaf people into every temporary exhibition since 1986. However, Weisen also highlights the highly uneven quality of practice in this area, citing a list of new, high profile museum developments internationally that have wholly neglected access for people with sensory impairments (sometimes in spite of legal duties to promote access). The best intellectual access, he concludes, is developed by museums that work to develop 'a living culture of best practice' (2010: 57), one which goes beyond a reductive and narrow focus on legal requirements.

Similarly, Catherine Kudlick's personal account (2005: 78) of her experiences as a visually impaired person attempting to visit museums and galleries in the United States with a blind companion, prompts her to reflect on the persistence of multiple barriers to access, the impact of disability legislation and the need for further change:

> Why is it that when America seems eager to open its civic places to the broadest possible audience, certain public institutions appear so ill-informed about people who require alternative ways to fully participate? Here we are, at a time when the [Americans with Disabilities Act] has been in effect for over a decade, people with disabilities have seen the promise of increased social awareness and powerful technology, and a generation of people . . . have grown up in large urban centers pouring money into their civic places. And yet in the early twenty-first century, two people still couldn't visit this museum on the spur of the moment or at the very least encounter employees sensitized enough to treat them with anything but contempt. Why is it that some people view visitors like us as problems rather than as opportunities to present exhibitions in new and interesting ways?

There is growing awareness in museums that providing a variety of ways for visitors to access information can facilitate a range of learning experiences and opportunities as well as improve access for more people. Indeed, information in large print, Braille or audio, for example, is increasingly available in the more committed organisations. The Disability Discrimination Act included audio guides as an example of an 'auxiliary aid' which might be considered 'reasonable' to provide so it is perhaps not surprising that this provision is more prevalent than others. For people who are Deaf or hard of hearing, the availability of induction loops at reception desks, in cafés and in shops is also increasing. However, these types of intervention do not meet all the needs of people with wide ranging hearing or sight impairments and a wider variety of interpretation options would significantly improve the visitor experience for more people.

Whilst the V&A, MFA and the National Trust offer interpretation in many of these stand-ard 'alternative' formats there have also been attempts to develop more creative approaches to access that begin to challenge the accustomed boundaries of 'reasonable adjustment'. At the MFA, for example, a commitment to making its programmes accessible to disabled visitors has included increasing provisions for people who are Deaf or hard of hearing and increasing the availability of audio interpretation for blind and partially sighted people. New technologies have supported experimentation with FM assistive-listening devices available for events and drop-in guided tours as well as the introduction of an iPod touch guide, with multiple acces-sible features. These facilities are offered free for Deaf, blind and partially sighted visitors. Key to the MFA's approach is providing choice, and consequently the Museum is looking at new ways to support visitors with disabilities who may need additional assistance once they get to the Museum. Similarly, the V&A has improved provision of its talks programme for people with sight or hearing impairments (Figure 4. 1 and 4.2) and devised a workshop programme specifically tailored for the needs of mental health service users. Scanning pens are available to convert text into speech. At the National Trust, some sites are now training their staff and volunteers in audio descriptive skills to support blind and partially sighted visitors and to improve the experience for visitors generally. Some properties are trialling assistive listening devices during their guided tours to further enhance accessibility.

The third tier of access that Majewski and Bunch highlight concerns the representation of disabled people and the inclusion of disability-related narratives and interpretation within exhibitions. This, they argue, has been almost entirely overlooked. Whilst recent years have seen an increase in experimentation in this area,[2] many organisations (even those with an established track record in developing exhibitions exploring issues related to other minority and excluded groups) continue to neglect the stories, lives and experiences of disabled peo-ple. Many museum staff remain anxious about this area of work and unsure how to proceed although recent initiatives have highlighted the significance of collaborative and participatory practices that can ensure disabled people are empowered to play a leading role in presenting their own histories and experiences (Dodd *et al.* 2008). Much more needs to be done to ensure that exhibitions, displays and events that include the experiences of disabled people become an established feature of cultural organisations' programmes.

Moving forward

How then might access and equality for disabled people – at all of the tiers proposed by Majewski and Bunch – be advanced within cultural organisations to become an embedded feature of good practice? In this last section, we focus two critical issues; the internal arrange-ments within organisations and the relationships that museums, galleries and heritage organisa-tions can build with external communities.

Staffing structures and responsibilities

As cultural organisations face difficult financial times and the need to achieve more with fewer resources, there is a danger that specialist expertise in the field of access is lost. As organisa-tions accrue greater experience in enhancing access and recognise the value of making this work part of everyone's responsibility, there may be a temptation to move away from a model which relies on specialist individuals or units to both manage legal compliance and to

FIGURE 4.1 British Sign Language (BSL) Tour; Programmes for deaf and hard of hearing visitors. V&A Museum. With permission of the Victoria and Albert Museum, London.

FIGURE 4.2   Touch Tour; Programmes for blind and partially-sighted visitors. V&A Museum. With permission of the Victoria and Albert Museum, London.

drive forward more creative approaches to equality. Indeed, in recent months we have seen a number of organisations in both the UK and United States make cuts along these lines. It is perhaps unsurprising, given our own professional backgrounds and responsibilities, that we would argue that there is a continuing need for staff with specialist expertise but our experiences of initiating change, nurturing shared values and embedding a commitment to greater access for disabled people within our own large organisations attests to the importance of these roles.

Whilst a truly inclusive and accessible organisation requires the commitment and input of staff in all areas and at all levels, policies and procedures do not write themselves and, to be effective, they rely on in-depth knowledge of the needs of audiences, as well as the requirements of the law. In our own organisations, strategies to coordinate responses to legislation and enhance awareness of the value and significance of broadening access per se have been driven forward by individuals with particular responsibility for this.

Following on from the use of external access consultants on specific new gallery developments, the V&A appointed its first Disability and Access Officer in 2002 to guide the museum through the implications of the DDA. This appointment provided opportunities to work more broadly across the museum (rather than confining activity to specific projects); to develop a Disability Action Plan; and to build relationships between the museum and a range of external disability organisations. The postholder chairs an Access Group where representatives from leading disability organisations provide guidance and advice on best practice and how this can be utilised by the museum. There is also a Staff Disability Forum, where V&A staff can get involved in the development of policy and practices which will provide a more inclusive environment and service to disabled people. The forum is also used to consult with disabled employees on their experience of working for the organisation.

The National Trust developed a post in the early 1990s when the DDA was being developed but before the act was passed. This post grew out of increasing awareness within the Trust that access provision at the historic properties that the Trust cares for was insufficient to meet the needs of diverse audiences. As well as leading on new initiatives, the postholder (originally titled Access for All Adviser) was able to make connections with disability organisations and local access groups and, in doing so, support individual sites to increase their capacity for trying new ideas. Crucially, sites were supported and encouraged to involve disabled visitors in developing ideas for enhancing access. The Trust is divided into a number of regions across England, Wales and Northern Ireland and each area has a member of staff who works with the Equality Specialist at a national level, to develop improvements to individual sites. Some sites have taken this a step further and asked a member of their staff or volunteer teams to take a lead role in co-ordinating their own access initiatives. These initiatives have proved to be an effective way of increasing ownership of (and commitment to) the accessibility agenda at a local level.

At the MFA, the specialist access post was created well before the introduction of the ADA and has been a part of the organisation for around 30 years. As such, it is the longest standing post from the three organisations discussed here. Although the position has had different titles over the past three decades, it has remained an integral part of the MFA. The post reflects the organisation's long-standing aspiration to become a truly accessible organisation in every facet of its activity, with all departments sharing responsibility for achieving this goal. While the MFA's initial commitment to accessibility predates the ADA, the legislation has clearly played a role in moving the organisation forward. In order to become a museum that welcomes people of all abilities, the MFA has needed to expand the number of people within the organisation that are thinking about access. This has not happened through increased hours or new positions, but rather through a broader acknowledgement of where accessibility intersects with existing responsibilities; a broader range of staff have been encouraged and supported to take responsibility for increased accessibility within their own work. Frontline staff training has also become a priority, with recognition that policies and practices behind the scenes are wholly undermined if someone is treated inappropriately at the front door.

Dialogue and collaboration

Having specialist staff with expertise in the field of access has enabled many museums, galleries and heritage bodies (including our own) to nurture an organisation-wide commitment to greater equality of opportunity for all visitors; to facilitate the involvement of disabled people in decision-making processes; and to push the boundaries of 'reasonable adjustment' beyond a narrow and reductive focus on the details of specific legal requirements. Anti-discrimination legislation has been an important driver for change, although those changes have been largely technical in nature – the introduction of access solutions (ramps, handrails, audio guides and so on). These changes are hugely significant – they permit a greater range of people the opportunity to participate in cultural activities – but they do not, in themselves, deliver full equality of opportunity for disabled people. More effective and sustained change, we would argue, requires a change in organisational culture and individual behaviours and practices to ensure all staff can develop a genuine understanding of the moral (as well as legal) responsibilities to enhance access for all. In our experience, this step-change can only be achieved by opening up dialogue between the institutions and the communities and audiences they aim to serve. This process of dialogue and engagement nurtures respect for everyone's life experiences and histories and creates opportunities to share these with others. Working with and engaging people with lived experience of discrimination breaks down the barriers that lack of knowledge and understanding can create.

In our own professional experience, the most effective and transformative of initiatives have come about through co-creative practice (Govier 2009) – when disabled people have been actively involved in working with staff to identify and dismantle barriers to participation. In the National Trust, for example, there has been increasing emphasis on working closely with local communities. As a result of growing recognition amongst senior managers that there is more work to be done to broaden the Trust's appeal, a new strategy was launched in 2010, to improve the knowledge of the work of the Trust amongst diverse constituencies and to encourage more people to get involved with our activities. When individual sites and properties have taken this collaborative approach with local groups of disabled people, there has been a marked difference not only in the quality of provision for disabled visitors but in the depth of understanding amongst Trust staff of what disabled people expect and want from cultural organisations.

Conclusion

It is our view that the achievement of equality of access for disabled people in museums should not be reduced to a response to legal imperatives. If, as many professionals increasingly claim, museums are important because they promote understanding and respect between diverse communities then, we would argue, they are well placed to embed a commitment to accessibility and inclusion for disabled people at their core, playing a leading role in identifying and dismantling physical, intellectual and emotional barriers to culture. Creative responses to ensuring full access for all visitors and developing a nuanced understanding of the political and social significance of disability representation, history and culture should come naturally to organisations that claim a unique role in helping visitors understand their place in the world around them.

A legal mandate can be used to convince sceptics of the need for change but, in the end, legislation alone is not enough to foster the comprehensive and sustained change in thinking and practice that is needed in most cultural institutions. Working collaboratively and on an equal footing with disabled people is crucial to helping practitioners approach accessibility in the same creative and knowledgeable way that they tackle other aspects of their work. Establishing honest dialogue and exploring the potential of this co-creative practice can potentially transform an organisation – and the experiences it offers to visitors.

Notes

1 These comments were made during a debate in the House of Commons, Friday 26 February 1993, following the presentation by Alf Morris MP of a petition 'urging this House to make unjustifiable discrimination against people with actual or perceived disabilities unlawful'. The full text is available online: www.publications.parliament.uk/pa/cm199293/cmhansrd/1993-02-26/Debate-2.html (accessed 13 September 2011).
2 See, for example, Sandell *et al.* (2010) which discusses examples of newly developed approaches to re-presenting disability history and culture from countries including Taiwan, Zambia, Canada, the UK, United States and Norway.

References

Barnes, C., Mercer, G. and Shakespeare, T. (1999) *Exploring Disability: A Sociological Introduction*, Cambridge and Malden, MA: Polity Press.

Dodd, J., Sandell, R., Jolly, D. and Jones, C. (2008) *Rethinking Disability Representation in Museums and Galleries*, Leicester: Research Centre for Museums and Galleries, University of Leicester.

Gartner, A. and Joe, T. (eds) (1987) *Images of the Disabled, Disabling Images*, New York: Praeger.

Govier, L. (2009) *Leaders in Co-creation? Why and How Museums could Develop their Co-creative Practice with the Public, Building on Ideas from the Performing Arts and Other Non-museum Organisations*, Leicester: RCMG. Online. Available at: www2.le.ac.uk/departments/museumstudies/rcmg/publications (accessed 15 September 2011).

Hevey, D. (1992) *The Creatures That Time Forgot: Photography and Disability Imagery*, London: Routledge.

Kudlick, C. J. (2005) 'The Local History Museum, So Near and yet so Far', *The Public Historian*, 27(2): 75–81.

Lawson, A. (2008) *Disability and Equality Law in Britain: The Role of Reasonable Adjustment*, Oxford and Portland: Hart Publishing.

Majewski, J. and Bunch, L. (1998) 'The Expanding Definition of Diversity: Accessibility and Disability Culture Issues in Museum Exhibitions', *Curator*, 41(3): 153–161.

Oliver, M. (1996) *Understanding Disability: From Theory to Practice*, Basingstoke: Palgrave.

Prideaux, S. (2006) *Good Practice for Providing Reasonable Access to the Physical Built Environment for Disabled People*, Leeds: The Disability Press.

Sandell, R., Dodd, J. and Garland-Thomson, R. (eds) (2010) *Re-Presenting Disability, Activism and Agency in the Museum*, London and New York: Routledge.

Weisen, M. (2010) 'Disability Discrimination in Museums is Systemic – the Case for National Strategic Approaches in the UK and Worldwide', in *Papers and Notes from The Margins to the Core, Sackler Conference for Arts Education*, London: Victoria and Albert Museum. Online. Available at: http://media.vam.ac.uk/media/documents/conferences/2010/margins-to-the-core/v&a-fromthemargin-stothecore-compiledpapers&notes.pdf (accessed 15 September 2011).

5

MUSEUMS FOR SOCIAL JUSTICE

Managing organisational change

David Fleming

Creating a cultural organisation that avoids appealing only to a narrow elite is a major task, one that can take years to complete. There are many pitfalls and a host of pressures that militate against achieving this. Museums, in particular, are often passive and insular by nature, and frequently they are hidebound by regressive practices and attitudes that prevent them from fulfilling an active role in society. In this chapter I will explore how museums can work to remove obstacles that stand in the way of becoming more inclusive, focusing on such issues as leadership, mission and vision, governance, organisational personality, staff structures, finances, programming and promotion.

I will draw principally upon my experiences as a museum director over the past twenty years in both Tyne and Wear and Liverpool – two areas in the UK that suffer multiple socio-economic deprivation – and contextualise my arguments, where appropriate, by drawing on examples of museums around the world. In seeking to create museums that work for social justice I have encountered prejudice, ignorance, hostility and wilful opposition and, at the same time, I have also had the benefit of working with supportive colleagues, politicians, trustees, civil servants and others. At the present time in National Museums Liverpool (NML), just as we are confronted by a massive, damaging squeeze on public finances, we are showing what can be achieved over a period of time. We are an organisation that has sloughed off many practices and attitudes that prevented us from moving forwards in a way that includes rather than excludes; that hindered us in responding to public need in return for our public funding; that put us at risk of irrelevance and indifference. I intend to analyse how we have achieved this.

The notion of a museum being active in seeking to fulfil a social justice agenda remains a radical one. This is despite the very real progress that has been made in recent years in terms of the museum profession's growing acceptance of a number of fundamental principles relating to our role in society.[1] The need to define (or redefine) the museum's social role lies at the heart of the management challenge in creating museums that seek to achieve wide relevance and public value. What we have to embed is a corporate commitment to a particular set of roles; roles that are different from those that museums played for most of the twentieth century. This demands the engagement of all parts of the organisation, most urgently and critically at leadership and governance levels, where the new commitment can be achieved fairly rapidly, even if it takes longer to persuade everyone else to sign up. It is these levels that I shall examine first.

Leadership

Without effective leadership, no museum can hope to change into one that is accessible and democratic, with a broad appeal and a broad impact (Fleming 2002; Janes 2009).

Happily, it is becoming increasingly difficult to find examples of museum leaders who are anti-democratic, who abide openly by the traditional code that museums are the preserve of an educated elite. This kind of attitude tends no longer to be tolerated by politicians who are intimidated by the vested interests that attach themselves to museums; or even by politicians who, in their nature, are themselves anti-democratic.

There are still, though, examples in most countries – especially in museums that cater primarily for a tourist market – where the desire for tourist income can take precedence over a commitment to social justice. And, there are still museums (most commonly, though not exclusively, art museums, university museums and national museums) run by people who are genuine throwbacks to an era when the needs of the public were subordinate to the capriciousness of the museum Director. I have visited a number of different countries around the world and have found a worrying constant: many younger museum people clearly want to modernise, but they do not carry the authority to do so, and they believe they are being held back by their Directors. This tends to be a generational issue and, as time goes by, finding this kind of 'dinosaur leadership' will become more difficult. This, at least, is what we have to hope.

Leadership, of course, is not solely about Directors. Other members of a museum's senior team (and, indeed, colleagues at all levels of the organisation) may have a strong influence on the museum's values and principles. I have encountered dysfunctional senior teams where a commitment to access and democracy was a low priority. Equally, it may be that it is the combined strength of purpose of the senior team that brings about change, reform and modernisation. This was certainly the case at Tyne & Wear Museums (TWM) where, as the new Assistant Director in 1990, then the Director from 1991, I was under constant pressure from my senior staff to ensure that reform was undertaken, and not to be too slow in going about it!

It is also true, however, that sometimes dictatorial behaviour is necessary to instigate the process of change. Anyone who has studied leadership knows about the advantages (and drawbacks) of dictatorial or 'heroic' leadership on the one hand, and consensual and consultative leadership on the other (Fleming 1999). My own view is that strong, determined leadership at the outset of a process of major change in museums is likely to be needed, but once the change process is under way, then the style of leadership can evolve into something more involving and consensual. In any event, we should not underestimate the capacity for elements within the organisation to resist democratisation, and therefore underestimate the need for determined (perhaps uncompromising) leadership, to ensure change continues and is embedded into the museum's thinking and practice.

In circumstances where the museum leadership is in favour of democratising reform, then it needs to lead by example and behaviour and it needs to articulate the organisation's role and purpose very clearly; generally through the device of the Strategic Plan which, in turn, will carry the museum's mission and statement of values.

Mission, values, vision

Museum missions, values and visions – important elements of a museum's make up – play a critical role where change is being introduced. At both TWM and NML, mission, values and vision were essential devices not only for helping transmit a new sense of purpose and a new way of doing things, both internally and externally; but for involving different staff and governing bodies in the process of re-envisioning the organisations. A great deal of effort in both of these museum services was expended in drafting, redrafting and refining these documents, over a period of years. The documents evolved as time passed, as the two museum services generated bigger and more diverse audiences, thus confirming the legitimacy of what we were doing, reinforcing our confidence and commitment, and confounding sceptics and critics.

At NML in 2003 (National Museums and Galleries on Merseyside as it was then), managers described the existing Mission Statement as 'uninspiring' and 'pompous', among other things and, crucially, criticised it for being 'more about things than people'. We have just updated our mission and values at NML and the latest text, still in draft form, reads:

Our mission

We change lives, and enable millions of people, from all backgrounds, to engage with our world-class museums.

Our values

- We believe that museums are fundamentally educational in purpose.
- We believe that museums are places for ideas and dialogue that use collections to inspire people.
- We are a democratic museum service and we believe in the concept of social justice: we are funded by the whole of the public and in return we strive to provide an excellent service to the whole of the public.
- We believe in the power of museums to help promote good and active citizenship, and to act as agents of social change.
- We believe in seeking out new opportunities and innovative ways of working, so as to keep our public offer fresh, relevant, challenging and competitive.

This text is supported by a Strategy Statement that explores the socio-economic context in which NML works, pointing out that the Liverpool area is the most deprived in the UK, and stressing the responsibility of NML to deliver first class museums in order to 'help mitigate the social consequences of adverse economic conditions' (National Museums Liverpool 2011). This explicit concern to take account of – and act upon – social disadvantage is one which opponents of democratic reform in museums are appalled by (Appleton 2001).

Importantly, the Strategy Statement should use language that motivates staff and trustees, and effectively convinces them that our mission and values are both genuine and worthy of passionate, unconditional support.

Governance

The support of the governors of a museum is essential in managing for social justice; if the governors waiver, the entire process can be undermined.

TWM is a local authority museum service where, in the 1990s, the staff had the growing, enthusiastic support of our elected councillors, who comprised the TWM Joint Museums Committee, our governing body. Most of the members of this committee were Labour councillors, who were politically predisposed towards opportunity for cultural activity being available to everyone in the local community. As the majority political group, they were the ones the museum staff had to have onside in our drive to be socially inclusive.

This we had achieved, although when a group of left-wing Newcastle councillors began to exert influence over our Committee in the mid-1990s, we had to persuade them all over again of TWM's commitment to social justice, so ingrained was their belief that the cultural sector at large was run by elitists who had no interest in the needs or wishes of the majority of the population. One faction styled itself proudly 'Philistines for Labour', and demanded to be persuaded that museums had any relevance whatsoever in a world full of social tensions, inequality of opportunity and poverty.

It is worth remembering that, at that time, we had a Conservative-run central government in England, and one that appeared to have little commitment to social inclusion or social justice. In TWM, and elsewhere in the local authority museum sector, a socially active strategy was generated entirely without central government encouragement. Contrary to what some commentators have written, museums working for social justice predated the election of a Labour government in 1997.[2]

This is an important point because, despite the demise of the New Labour movement and the election of a Conservative-led coalition government, there should be no reason to suppose that those museums with a genuine commitment to social justice will lose motivation, though they may well lose momentum as budget cuts restrict their capacity to pursue socially inclusive programming.

The real risk, then, is that museums which have merely been paying lip service to social justice while the political climate was favourable, will go back to their socially regressive ways, especially when the museum sector is facing the reality of severe budget cuts. This could be manifested in a number of ways, such as the abandonment of education and outreach programming; the end of the targeting of excluded and marginalised groups; the recruitment of trustees and directors with elitist views; or the introduction of prohibitive admission fees. Regrettably, we have already seen some signs of this kind of reaction amongst UK museums, including the targeted withdrawal of funding for socially progressive initiatives.

In fact, it was a far simpler task to gain the support of the councillors at TWM than it was to win over the government-appointed trustees at NML. At TWM we were dealing with politicians, who behave within certain parameters, depending upon which political party they belong to. Their views and motivations can, to a degree, be predicted. Trustees, on the other hand, are individuals who hold a very disparate range of beliefs and do not need to keep to a 'party line'. They have, usually, no declared political allegiance.

What trustees have in common with local authority councillors is that they will tend to follow the lead of the chairman of the governing body. Councillors of the chairman's political party will follow his or her lead quite slavishly, because that's how politics works; councillors from a different political party may or may not take their cue from the chairman, but their views will in any case usually be predictable, and will conform to their own political ideology. Trustees, however, have no political ideology to constrain them, and there is far more scope for individual opinions to be expressed.

At NML, in the early days of my tenure as Director, my priority was to revitalise the organisation. Notwithstanding the many outstanding successes of my predecessor, Sir Richard Foster, NML in 2001 was in need of modernisation and refreshment. Audiences were low and in decline, and were not diverse. We had to recognise this as a major failing, and do something about it. This meant introducing an enormous raft of changes, including a new mission and values.

Up to a point, the need for radical change was accepted by the trustees; but only up to a point. After an initial 'honeymoon period' for me as the new Director, there grew a lack of congruence between senior management and trustees, which went through two phases. The first phase was when the trustee body that was in place when I became Director seemed to become nervous about a reform programme. This kind of reaction is not uncommon. While the trustees had signed up to an explicit programme of reform in appointing me, some individuals became a little sensitive about the way in which the implementation of reform might be interpreted as critical of their prior performance. There is, of course, quite a complex psychology in play here but it will be familiar to many people who have introduced reform and modernisation, in any context.

This nervousness and sensitivity was manifested in a number of ways: one trustee declared that museums were not primarily educational; there was a reluctance to change the name of the organisation to something shorter and more motivational; a dismissiveness of (and lack of enthusiasm for) a new mission and values; a tendency to dilute some of our more passionate language and to be unhelpfully pedantic; a tardiness in accepting major structural change; a degree of reverence for other national museums which senior staff found craven and pathetic. At the point where I was described sarcastically by a senior trustee as having 'arrived on a white charger to save NMGM', I knew that I did not have the full support of the trustee body in my reform programme. Nonetheless, the programme of reform proceeded, through the sheer determination of the senior staff, and with the support of some trustees (though not as quickly as they, or I, would have liked).

The second phase was when relations between senior management and the trustee body, under a new chairman, deteriorated still further to the point where the senior team openly discussed how we could best manage the organisation in the face of a trustee body which exhibited some behaviours which we found intolerable. I have no doubt that underlying the strained relationship between staff and trustees were fundamental differences over the degree to which NML should act as an agent for social justice. Some of our trustees (though by no means all) could not have been less interested in building diverse audiences, and considered our efforts to popularise the museum service as banal. What they seemed to want instead was a traditional, elitist museum service that was not relevant to the majority of the population. One example of this was the reaction of one senior trustee to our Annual Review for 2006/7 (NML 2007) which was illustrated throughout with children's drawings and comments based on their museum visits. 'I'm afraid that I find it embarrassing' he wrote. 'We are a national museum and not a primary school'.

This view contrasted markedly with those of senior members of our staff: 'it's a quality publication that does an excellent job of advocating a lively and increasingly successful museum service to a varied stakeholder base'; 'it's colourful and fun. Including visitor comments, especially ones from children, shows we are providing a service our audience wants and enjoys'; 'Its energetic feel and inclusion of diverse views give a strong message about the organisation I hope we are becoming'.

NML staff (and many other people) valued our 2006/7 Annual Review because it recognised that as an organisation we were increasingly in touch with our audiences. Imagine
our reaction when we discovered that the trustee who disliked it was 'soliciting disapproval'
from other trustees of the Annual Review – typical behaviour, but a campaign that, happily,
achieved little, and was stopped when other trustees voiced their approval of the Review at
a Board meeting.

Today we have a tremendously supportive chairman and Board. They are every bit as
committed as the staff in pursuing a social justice agenda. This removes any fear of failure,
which is so inhibiting when management is trying to reinvent an organisation. It provides a
source of encouragement and validation, which is what you have to have from your governors
if you are to effect all the actions necessary to bring about sustainable change.

Organisational personality and change

Herein lies the essence of managing a museum for social justice. What has to be created is an
organisational culture, or personality, that actively nourishes the social justice agenda. This
involves a great deal of analysis, some of which can be painful.

At TWM in the 1990s we were acutely aware that we were undergoing personality change,
as we set out to shrug off the trappings of elitism that had given us a poor reputation with local
politicians and press. It was reported to me, not long after I arrived at TWM, that the then
Leader of Newcastle City Council, Jeremy Beecham, had recently said that the best thing to
do with TWM was to 'put a bomb under it'. This was hardly a ringing endorsement, though
Beecham was to become a strong supporter of TWM, once he had seen that we were capable
of providing a quality service to a wide public.

We knew that we had to raise energy levels, become more extrovert and approachable,
demonstrate our capabilities more clearly, show that we cared about what we did. We tracked
these changes in a series of meetings throughout the decade, at which staff continually analysed our achievements and compared them with former days. This self-analysis is critically
important in bringing about lasting reform (Janes 2009).

For example, at a staff meeting in September 1996 we considered how we had changed
since 1991, concluding that we were now politically strong, with bigger, broader audiences;
that we enjoyed significant private sector support; that our professional reputation had grown,
that partnership with TWM was now something other organisations sought. We knew that we
had changed, and that underlying this change was a culture that today we would say was based
upon a dedication to social justice, but which then we described as being 'people-oriented'.

By 1998 staff were saying that TWM needed to be 'witty', 'young', 'sexy', 'friendly', 'car-
ing', 'visionary' and 'honest'. We had become an organisation that the employees thought of
in personality terms.

At NML between 2001–2, we undertook a series of sessions, involving staff and trustees,
to create a personality profile of the organisation. This did not make happy reading. We concluded that we were:

> slow-moving, fragmented, bureaucratic, risk averse, traditional, derivative, old fash-
> ioned, paranoid, hierarchical, isolated within Liverpool; with low levels of trust, no
> shared vision, divided loyalties, power obsessions, a blame culture, no team culture, an
> anti-management culture.

Whereas we wanted to be:

> exciting, lively, humorous, welcoming, quirky, daring, colourful, extrovert, eccentric, wicked, generous, glamorous, risqué, inspirational, beautiful, amazing . . . and popular.

The great thing was that we knew we had problems, and that there was a will to resolve them. The sobering thing is that not everyone could quite find it within themselves to do anything about it.

At a 'visioning workshop' in February 2003, a group of about 30 senior NML managers concluded that the organisation was still 'fragmented, bureaucratic, hypocritical, old fashioned, unfocused, hierarchical, secretive, inflexible, territorial, frustrating, tribal, paranoid and boring'. We undertook a 'characterisation' exercise and imagined that, if NML was a person, who would we be? The answers gave rise to a great deal of hilarity, but in truth they were rather alarming. We decided that we were like four people: romance novelist Barbara Cartland ('seen better days'); politicians John Major ('risk averse, comfortable, old fashioned, past his best') and Iain Duncan Smith ('safe and respected, but boring and unambitious'); and, worst of all, long-standing soap opera character Ken Barlow ('respectable, principled and educated, but stuffy and staid, with high ideals that are never realised, and a bit embittered').

A year later, early in 2004, I wrote a paper for trustees entitled 'Picking up Speed'. In this paper I wrote:

> One of the hardest things to change in a complex organisation is its culture. What I found when I came to NML was a culture of rivalry and finger pointing, compliance and deference, with a bureaucratic overlay which made decision-making and prioritisation difficult . . . I sense widespread support for our new Aims and Beliefs which, while imperfect, does a decent job for now of outlining what we need to do – and with what attitude – in order for us to move onward successfully, i.e. to be a people- and service-minded organisation rather than an insular and procedurally-minded one. We have gone some way towards freeing up the collective mindset of NML, enabling us to be less risk averse and more creative, more confident in sharing information, more relaxed, easier to engage with.

In a meeting of about 20 senior NML managers in March 2011, we revisited the 'characterisation' exercise of seven years earlier. The results were encouraging: instead of being like Ken Barlow, we perceive ourselves to be like Clint Eastwood ('a maverick with depth and longevity, who operates successfully in different spheres'). We also see ourselves as 'someone heading in the right direction' like Shami Chakrabarti ('strong-willed, raw edged, maturing, with an increasing profile . . . and a bit annoying'). These newer characterisations are clearly a big improvement on what we had in 2003, and they indicate a change in attitude at NML. The risk aversion, lack of ambition, stuffiness and bitterness of 2003 have been replaced by other attributes, ones that have enabled NML to pursue a social justice agenda. This has led to audiences diversifying and growing by several hundred percent.

It is worth mentioning here that we have developed other behaviours that have enabled the pursuit of social justice: we have encouraged respect for all disciplines and functions within NML: there are no elites. We have encouraged supportive management styles. We have introduced free admission to everything we do. We have integrated ourselves as far as possible with communities and interest groups in and around Liverpool that share our belief in social justice. We have invested in training and development of staff to help ensure they do not indulge in discriminatory behaviour. We have shown zero tolerance to behaviour such as racism, or discrimination against people with disabilities. We have given high priority to initiatives such as our Refugees and Asylum Seekers project, and to the development of the International Slavery Museum. To me, these actions and approaches create the right conditions for pursuing a social justice agenda.

Staff structures

I am no great believer in there being a single, ideal organisational structure for museums – circumstances differ too much for there to be a uniform solution to the age-old problem of structure – but there are certain constants needed for museums to be able to manage for social justice, and it is possible to create staff structures to help do this.

At TWM in 1990 and at NML in 2001, there were peculiarities embedded within the staff structures that helped prevent either museum service from achieving its proper role. In both services, for example, we needed to channel resources into the education function, to give that function a prominent place within the structure, and to charge our education staff with leading on social inclusion and diversity initiatives. In both services we needed to create inclusion-minded marketing, and again to give the function sufficient seniority and encouragement within our structures to be able operate effectively: at NML in 2001 our marketing staff were line-managed by an accountant, for example, as part of a mélange of 'central services'. This was not a sign that marketing was regarded as a creative, dynamic force within NML, crucial to the achievement of social justice.

Because of the importance of a varied exhibition programme to cater for the diversity of demand among the public, both TWM and NML needed an empowered exhibitions function, free from the crippling bureaucracy that plagues many museums, and which can easily prevent an alignment of programme and policy. At NML in particular, the bureaucracy surrounding the initiation of exhibitions in 2001 was of mythical proportions.

The point is, there needs to be an organisational mindset which embraces the principle that meeting public needs and expectations is the core purpose of museums. The way that museums are structured is a powerful indicator of this mindset. Structures which indicate that functions such as education, marketing and exhibitions are less important than mainstream collections management functions are likely to be found only in museums that do not take the achievement of social justice too seriously.

In 2004, when NML commissioned a report on organisational structures, in order to help identify what reforms were needed, it became clear that some trustees found the report threatening to the status quo. They became defensive to an almost comical degree. Clearly, in their minds the organisational structure of NML was representative of a particular way of behaving that they were reluctant to change.

Finances

Like organisational structures, the organisation and allocation of finances need to reflect priorities. If a museum is determined to work to a social justice agenda, this will almost certainly mean moving money out of some budget headings in order to increase others. There will always be resistance to this from staff whose budgets are left diminished. Furthermore, restructuring budgets always carries with it risk, because it means allocating resources to areas of work that have not yet justified the new investment.

But there is no alternative. Over time, the results will ease the pain, as increasing budgets for education and community work and marketing results in bigger, more diverse audiences. Clear policy and determined leadership are required to effect changes like this.

Programming

Programming to achieve social justice is varied and accessible, with the needs of the family paramount. There must always be room for experimentation and programming for niche audiences, but managing for social justice means prioritising the needs of the many over the needs of the few, and it means taking our educational responsibilities very seriously.

Our overriding aim is to communicate, not to confuse. Our core audience is the general public – not our peers, not art critics, not academics, not politicians, not vested interests. It takes a certain kind of humility to sign up to this aim, and humility has not always been in great supply in the museum profession. It is only by implementing a range of programmes and over a period of time that a museum will be able to make a genuine impact. There is little value in doing one-off events or one-off projects. Working towards social justice takes time and effort, which is why it requires commitment, determination and belief.

In TWM a successful project, which formed part of a whole raft of actions at the Laing Art Gallery that were designed to turn it into a family-friendly institution, was the creation of the *Procter & Gamble's Children's Gallery*. The launch of this new space had the effect of opening up the Laing to a whole new generation of young users with their families. A similar impact was had at NML's Walker Art Gallery, which we used routinely to describe as a 'child-free zone', but whose audience changed remarkably when we opened *Big Art for Little Artists*, a children's art activity area. A gallery in the new Museum of Liverpool – *Little Liverpool* – is also designed to ensure that the very young feel as welcome in the museum as older people.

It does not all have to be about children, of course. At the International Slavery Museum (ISM) we deal with some extremely serious adult issues, though this has not prevented large numbers of young people from visiting the Museum. We deal with issues such as human trafficking, domestic slavery, apartheid, racism and other human rights abuses. This has led NML into all sorts of uncharted territory for a museum service, including active campaigning against human rights abuses. Recently, we have even opened up a *Campaign Zone*, to encourage visitors to take up human rights causes. In many ways, our work at ISM is focussed entirely upon fighting for social justice, but it has required an approach that has broken many museum taboos.

We have, through ISM, created an international network of museums that fight for human rights – the Federation of International Human Rights Museums (FIHRM),[3] which has linked together Holocaust museums, genocide museums and a host of others. Most of these museums exist to advance social justice, and the creation of a global network serves to validate the work they do.

This leads me to touch upon the 'stories or objects' debate. The point is, the FIHRM network is made up of museums that have real collections. It's just that they choose to use them in non-traditional ways, and not rely completely on what they have in their collections. In so doing, they help break the notion that museums can only, or should only, communicate through their collections – an idea that I find so absurd that I am always amazed whenever I hear someone making this claim; it is rather like listening to someone insisting that the Earth is flat.

There are two more notions I want to mention in connection with programming for social justice. One is that the modern museum is more likely to involve the public in creating museum content than its traditional predecessor and this is itself a socially inclusive device that helps bring about social justice. This is, of course, most likely to be found in the social history museum although there are no valid reasons why co-creative practices cannot help to transform other kinds of museum too (Govier 2009).

Second is the need for museum content to be in a constant state of change and renewal. Gone are the days when a museum could relax after a capital programme of works has delivered new displays that need not change for another generation. The modern museum has to work much harder to cover more ground, so that it may maximise the opportunities for attracting a diverse audience.

Research and promotion

The museum has to know its audience – and its target audience – so it can identify needs, and so that it can make contact. For promotion to be effective, the museum must put serious effort into learning the socio-economic detail of its catchment area. Market research is terrifically important; how else would we at NML know that the three most popular newspapers among our existing visitors are the *Daily Mail*, the *Mirror* and the *Liverpool Echo*? Or that our existing visitors listen mostly to Radio 4, Radio 2 and Radio Merseyside? Or that National Museums Liverpool operates in a city which remains the most deprived in the UK. Employment rates, educational attainment and skills levels are well below the national average; the welfare cost per capita is the highest in the UK (National Museums Liverpool 2011). How a museum promotes itself to audiences is a key part of managing for social justice. This includes the language deployed in press releases and publications, print styles, the placing of advertising and editorial, an attitude that is respectful towards local media, and sceptical of much of the national media.

The global sector

There is also, of course, a global dimension to managing for social justice. Many of the worries that some of us have about museums in the UK remaining socially exclusive are shared in other countries, some more than others. I have found that in countries like Australia and New Zealand, Canada, the United States, and some north European countries, there is a growing awareness of the value of museums as agents for social justice. What is common to all countries, though, is a grip on the sector held by people who think in traditional terms, whose energies are devoted to museum *process* rather than *outcomes*.

There is growing support for the idea that museums should lend their support to a range of rights-based social issues (Sandell and Dodd 2010; Chapters 14, 16 and 17, this volume) and, crucially, there are agencies supporting and encouraging museums to take up a socially responsible role. One of these is INTERCOM, the ICOM international committee for management, and another is the Federation of International Human Rights Museums (FIHRM).

INTERCOM held its annual meeting in 2009 in the Mexican city of Torreon. A gathering of 150 delegates from more than 20 nations, mostly young people working in museums, decided to make a public declaration about the responsibility of museums to promote human rights:

> INTERCOM Declaration of Museum Responsibility to Promote Human Rights:
>
> INTERCOM believes that it is a fundamental responsibility of museums, wherever possible, to be active in promoting diversity and human rights, respect and equality for people of all origins, beliefs and background.
>
> *International Committee on Management 2009*

This is a remarkable statement that advocates a totally new role for museums, one which not only brings with it a host of responsibilities, but which flies in the face of the prevailing belief that museums should remain neutral in their work.

FIHRM is an affiliation of museums from around the world that share a belief that museums which operate within the sphere of human rights will be more effective if they work together. There are a surprising number of museums of this type, ranging from small institutions in developing countries to large national museums in Western Europe, North America and Australasia. At FIHRM's inaugural conference, held in Liverpool in September 2010, I stated that:

> The Federation will enable museums which deal with sensitive and thought provoking subjects such as transatlantic slavery, the Holocaust and human rights issues to work together and share new thinking and initiatives in a supportive environment.
>
> The Federation is about sharing and working together, but it is also about being proactive – looking at the ways institutions challenge contemporary forms of racism, discrimination and human rights abuses. We believe that these issues are best confronted collectively rather than individually.

In a letter to me concerning the FIHRM conference, the President and CEO of the Canadian Museum for Human Rights, Stuart Murray, wrote: 'It is our fervent hope, that when we all work together, we will, indeed, be agents of change throughout the world – laying a foundation of respect for people everywhere through learning, dialogue and, most importantly, action'. I think this gets to the core of managing for social justice – it is through collaborative working that museums will make genuine progress.

I conclude with a brief word about motivation. Working towards social justice is a long-term commitment; it requires determination and bloody-mindedness. It needs to be driven by passion, by a belief that everyone deserves equal access to what we do in museums and not just because government (or anyone else) tells us that this is what we should do, but because *it's the right thing to do.*

Notes

1   See, for example, Janes and Conaty 2005; Sandell 2002; Silverman 2010.
2   For more on this issue, see Fleming (2001) and Sandell (2002).
3   For further information, see www.fihrm.org.

References

Appleton, J. (ed.) (2001) *Museums for 'The People': Conversations in Print*, London: Institute of Ideas.

Fleming, D. (1999) 'Leadership', in K. Moore (ed.) *Management in Museums*, London and New Brunswick: Athlone: 93–107.

Fleming, D. (2001) 'The Politics of Social Inclusion', in J. Dodd and R. Sandell (eds) *Including Museums: Perspectives on Museums, Galleries and Social Inclusion*, Leicester: Research Centre for Museums and Galleries: 16–19.

Fleming, D. (2002) 'Positioning the Museum for Social Inclusion', in R. Sandell (ed.) *Museums, Society, Inequality*, London and New York: Routledge: 213–224.

Govier, L. (2009) *Leaders in Co-creation? Why and How Museums could Develop their Co-creative Practice with the Public, Building on Ideas from the Performing Arts and other Non-museum Organisations*, Leicester: RCMG. Online. Available at: www2.le.ac.uk/departments/museumstudies/rcmg/publications (accessed 15 September 2011).

International Committee on Management (2009) 'INTERCOM Declaration of Museum Responsibility to Promote Human Rights'. Online. Available at: www.intercom.museum/TorreonDeclaration.html (accessed 15 September 2011).

Janes, R. R. (2009) *Museums in a Troubled World: Renewal, Irrelevance or Collapse?*, London and New York: Routledge.

Janes, R. R. and Conaty, G. T. (eds) (2005) *Looking Reality in the Eye: Museums and Social Responsibility*, Calgary: University of Calgary Press/Museums Association of Saskatchewan.

National Museums Liverpool (2007) *Annual Review, April 2006–March 2007*, Liverpool: National Museums Liverpool.

National Museums Liverpool (2011) *Strategic Plan 2011–15*, Liverpool: National Museums Liverpool.

Sandell, R. (2002) 'Museums and the Combating of Social Inequality: Roles, Responsibilities, Resistance', in R. Sandell (ed.) *Museums, Society, Inequality*, London and New York: Routledge: 3–23.

Sandell, R. and Dodd, J. (2010) 'Activist Practice', in R. Sandell, J. Dodd and R. Garland-Thomson (eds) *Re-Presenting Disability: Activism and Agency in the Museum*, London and New York: Routledge: 3–22.

Silverman, L. H. (2010) *The Social Work of Museums*, London and New York: Routledge.

6

FRED WILSON, GOOD WORK AND THE PHENOMENON OF FREUD'S MYSTIC WRITING PAD

Janet Marstine

'What is the long-term impact of your work on museums?' This question is asked of Fred Wilson almost every time he lectures on his museum projects (Wilson 2008). It is a line of inquiry that suggests audiences recognize that Wilson has introduced significant change to the museum sector – but they want to know 'what happens next'.

Wilson is widely known for his installations that challenge assumptions about the dynamics of race, ethnicity, class and gender in museums and in hegemonic culture. His formally stunning and politically revealing juxtapositions of objects help us to envision a more socially responsible museum and society. But to address 'what happens next', we must also consider Wilson's collaborative process during his interventions, for which he typically spends months on site, familiarizing himself with institutional histories, policies, collections and engaging with a broad range of personnel. What is the long-term impact of this performative process on individual staff, departments, institutions and the museum sector more broadly? What role might artists like Wilson play in supporting institutional change and nurturing a more socially engaged and responsible museum practice?

This chapter explores the ways in which artists, through the language and practice of institutional critique, can be powerful drivers for change in the museum. By analyzing data from interviews[1] I have conducted with Wilson and with security staff, educators, docents, preparators, registrars, designers, curators and directors who worked with the artist on two different projects, I will examine how Wilson's collaborations have helped a workforce to embrace new practices in order to transform the core values of institution. The institutions selected as case studies – The Seattle Art Museum (SAM) and the Hood Museum of Art, Dartmouth College, in Hanover, New Hampshire – provide an opportunity to explore the impact of Wilson's work over time; *The Museum: Mixed Metaphors* opened at SAM in 1993 and *SO MUCH TROUBLE IN THE WORLD – Believe it or Not!* was staged at the Hood in 2005. Together, the case studies demonstrate the potential of the artist's voice to offer important ethical insights through which museum policies and practices concerning social inclusion can be evaluated and revised.

As consummate insiders/outsiders at the museum, artists have the potential to take risks and function as the museum's conscience. In analyzing the subversive impact of Wilson's early, groundbreaking intervention, *Mining the Museum*, museum evaluator Randi Korn stated,

Wilson 'was able to do it because he is an artist' (Yellis 2009: 341). Wilson describes his mode of institutional critique through exhibition making as the '*trompe l'oeil* of curating' (Wilson and Berger 2001: 33); he creates illusions of truth that reveal deeper realities than do appearances themselves.

Miwon Kwon has argued that these kinds of institutional critique 'can easily become extensions of the museum's own self-promotional apparatus' (Kwon 2000: 47). But whilst museums do commission Wilson's projects to diversify audiences and, in the words of Jennifer González, 'perhaps to assuage some historical guilt' (González 2008: 100), this does not preclude their deeply transformative potential. Wilson engages in what might be described as a compassionate form of institutional critique; one that shows his love of museums and his belief in their capacity to change. He argues:

> I think there are many curators and, interestingly, more and more directors, who on one level or another want things to change. There are many curators who know there are problems in their institutions around race, class, and community. And there are many museum professionals who, for various reasons, want to bring in a different demographic to their institution. They want their museums to be more sensitive and inclusive. I'm brought in because there's a genuine desire to self-reflect and even to change attitudes and policies.
>
> *Wilson and Berger 2001: 34*

Wilson's form of institutional critique undoubtedly serves the museum but I would argue that this does not constitute a weakness; rather Wilson's installations help make museums more ethical in ways that benefit a much broader range of constituencies.

Ethics and good work in the museum

Using the theoretical model of the GoodWork Project at Harvard University, this chapter explores how Wilson's process contributes to museum ethics by shaping individual values, impacting the domain of work and transforming the sector. Most well-known for his 1983 theory of multiple intelligences (Gardner 1983), Howard Gardner is a principal investigator of the GoodWork Project, along with psychologists Mihaly Csikszentmihalyi and William Damon. Together, they initiated this ambitious undertaking in 1995 to consider how leaders in diverse professions perform 'good work'. As Gardner and his associates define it, ethics is a central component of good work. Through 1,200 interviews in the United States over a ten-year period with representatives of professions ranging from journalism to genetics to higher education, the project identified three elements that characterize good work: '1) It is technically Excellent; 2) It is personally meaningful or Engaging; 3) it is carried out in an Ethical way' (GoodWork Project 2010: 5). Whilst the original project did not query museum professionals, Gardner and Celka Straughn, a former GoodWork researcher, have subsequently applied their theories to the museum profession (Straughn and Gardner 2011). Their application of the GoodWork model is a useful tool by which to analyze the long-term impact of Fred Wilson's interventions.

The GoodWork Project asserts that good work transpires when four forces align: 'The individual beliefs and values of the worker; the domain of work (long standing values of the profession); the current professional field (comprised of organizations, gatekeepers, etc.);

and the wider societal reward system' (GoodWork Project 2010: 19). Contextualized for museums, these forces include, respectively: the value system of an individual staff member; long-held principles of the sector such as preservation, learning and public good; the particular museum, professional associations, along with donors and critics; and, finally, current national and global priorities. What defines good work is continuously negotiated among these arenas (Straughn and Gardner 2011).

Reflecting these four forces are four elements that shape good work, according to the Project: 'Individual standards; cultural controls of a domain (such as mission statements and strategic plans); social controls (for example, trust and community needs; and external or out-come controls (or extrinsic benefits)' (GoodWork Project 2010: 19–22).

According to the model, creating an environment for good work to thrive requires a strong support system that clearly articulates professional needs and expectations, commu-nicates effectively to the public the nature of the profession and embraces free expression of individual values (Gardner 1998: 9). Good work is dependent equally upon a set of core values such as integrity established by the profession and on the ability to create change (Gardner 2007: 12–13). The project team ascertained that ethical work occurs when:

> workers attempt to operate according to the longstanding values of their domain, even if these values clash with self-interest, and; workers recognize issues of moral complex-ity, take the time to think them through, seek advice and guidance, and reflect on past actions and future consequences.
>
> *Ibid.: 13*

For good work to flourish, typically, all of these forces must be aligned: 'In alignment, all of the various interest groups basically call for the same kinds of performance; in contrast, when a profession is misaligned, the various interest groups emerge as being at cross-purposes with one another' (GoodWork Project 2010: 28). The 'what happens next' in museums in which Wilson performs interventions is dependent on these issues of alignment. Wilson recognizes that the values of the various interest groups that impact museums – individual staff members, the sector as a whole, particular museums, professional associations and global culture – can be aligned to address social inclusion. But he also understands that museum practice, steeped in convention, is often misaligned with these trends. Wilson's interventions address this mis-alignment to promote good work (ethical work as the GoodWork Project defines it) and to embed a concern for diversity and equality at the heart of the institution.

Capturing and assessing the impact of Wilson's projects is a complex endeavour. Museums in which he works typically maintain and preserve copious documentation of his finished projects but little of the all-important process of engagement with staff. The high turnover rate of staff that museums sustain often amounts to short institutional memory (Updike 1996). Also, clearly, Wilson is not operating in a vacuum; his projects are among many political, social and cultural forces that influence museum workers. But whilst there may be many methodological challenges bound up in analyzing the impact of Wilson's institutional critique, there is nevertheless a consensus amongst those with whom he has worked that his projects have functioned as a catalyst to drive ethics forward. Derrick Cartwright, current director of the Seattle Art Museum and former director of the Hood when Wilson received his com-mission there, likened this effect to Freud's concept of the mystic writing pad (Cartwright 2010), as defined in a 1925 essay. The mystic writing pad is a child's toy, a wax-covered board over which a thin piece of plastic is laid and upon which one can draw with a sharp instrument. When the plastic sheet is lifted from the surface of the board, the writing disappears, thus its 'mystic' quality. However, a faint trace of the drawing remains on the wax. Freud saw this process as similar to the way that the psyche itself processes experience into memory. For Freud, 'the appearance and disappearance of the writing' is like 'the flickering-up and passing-away of consciousness in the process of perception' (Freud 1961: 230–231). Though Wilson's installations have disappeared, Cartwright sees traces of the artist's ideas etched deep in the memory of the institutions where he has worked and the staff that moves on to other institutions. Barbara Thompson, former Curator of African, Oceanic and Native American Collections at the Hood, put it this way:

what does he do?

> Without sounding too much like a die-hard Wilson devotee, there is not a single project that I work on that I do not ask myself, 'how would Fred . . . approach this.' And while it is easy for me to think this way, given my collections area (which is full of loaded and challenging histories), I have seen my colleagues in American and European art do the same and more often now than ten years ago; we are working together, collaborating and crossing territories; challenging our tried and true methods for more exciting avenues. Is this a result of Fred Wilson? Maybe. Is it a result of our changing times and the breakdown of ivory towers? Yes. Is it a 'natural' progression in the development of museum practice and theory? Probably. In other words, many factors are at play and Wilson's work . . . is one of these factors.
>
> *Thompson 2010*

As Thompson's comments suggests, the phenomenon of the mystic writing tablet, as applied to Wilson's project, implies that some alignment of values and intents at individual, institutional and sectoral level have occurred. Wilson's institutional critique buoys Thompson's individual beliefs as well as values and developments in the museum sector and in society more broadly, to put theory into practice. To look more deeply at this dynamic between Wilson's projects and the good work they inspire we must examine Wilson's installations, their larger context and his process for creating the interventions.

The interventions: context and process for good work

Wilson's projects for SAM and the Hood share certain core values that impact how good work might be done there. Both are situated in institutions with encyclopedic art collections and offer new solutions to the problems of exclusivity, hierarchy and canonicity endemic to the art museum. Both challenge the injustices of racial prejudice in a mode that is simultaneously serious and ironic but Wilson's larger aim at SAM and the Hood is to encourage viewers to think critically about visual perception. He explains:

> I produce projects around the issue of race when the issue jumps out at me. I don't go looking for it. If it is not there, as in some foreign or culturally specific museums, other issues rise to the surface, such as ecological issues, sexual and cultural difference, gender, class, politics, and even aesthetics. The underlying connection between all the works is my interest in perception.
>
> *Wilson and Berger 2001: 34*

Wilson links visual perception in museums to discrimination in a way that taps into his own personal experience with racism. He recounts:

> As a child, I felt misunderstood in all the contexts, outside the family, that I was in. People would see me and make up their own minds about who I was based on what I looked like. They created a history for me, based solely on my appearance. I relate this to museums. They are the ultimate environment where people mark objects and make up stories about them in their own minds, based on how they look. Art museums particularly privilege the visual above all else. The fact that an object has or had a use is secondary to how it looks, even if the visual tells you next to nothing about its intrinsic nature.
>
> *Ibid.: 37*

To that effect, Wilson's projects at SAM and the Hood are never reductive or rooted in binary oppositions. He uses juxtaposition as a tool to open up a line of questioning for viewers. He remarks, 'If I have two images or objects side by side, a third thought is revealed. It . . . allows the viewer to enter my thinking a bit, but come up with conclusions for themselves, as well' (Wilson and Appiah 2006: 9). This eliciting of critical thinking is what led the De Young Museum director, Harry Parker, to declare, after working with the artist, 'Once you see one of his shows you have some Fred Wilson in you' (Newkirk 2000: 159).

Both *Mixed Metaphors* and *SO MUCH TROUBLE IN THE WORLD* were commissioned at auspicious moments when SAM and the Hood were looking introspectively into their past and future. The Seattle Art Museum invited Wilson to do a project in the first few months after its new downtown building by Venturi and Rausch had opened. The Hood asked him to create an installation to mark the twentieth anniversary of its Charles Moore building. In both cases, the curators who conceived the idea of the commission understood that Wilson's brand of institutional critique offered an opportunity to do more than celebrate; it instead opened a pathway to assess practice and to respond to new conversations in the sector about diversity and equity. As Hood Associate Director Juliette Bianco remarked:

> We spent quite some time thinking about how we wanted to present ourselves on the occasion of our museum building's twentieth anniversary . . . While it was a year for celebration, we did not want it to be purely 'show and tell'. And that led us to the idea of Fred Wilson . . . We thought that the opportunity to have Fred interrogate our collections, present them in a new light, and perhaps critique the institution and our museological practices, would be a more meaningful way to launch the future.
>
> *Bianco 2009*

Bianco's sentiments represent the motivation of individuals and institutions working with Wilson to align theory and practice in order to have good work flourish.

Wilson's projects respond not only to internal factors but also to external trends, particularly those highlighted by post-colonial theory and the call for social inclusion emerging from critical museum studies and related fields and, from a larger perspective, diversifying populations and developing globalism. The American Association of Museum's 1992 report, *Excellence and Equity: Education and the Public Dimensions of Museums* (American Association of Museums 1992), which called for museums to become more responsive to diverse communities, encapsulates an alignment between the principles of professional associations and national and global priorities towards the kind of good work that Wilson aims to inspire. Wilson refers to his underlying themes as 'unspoken, not unknown, things' (Wilson and Berger 2001: 38). In both commissions, Wilson and the museum came together to address a situation in which the environment was changing more rapidly than the cultural institutions within it. Thus, among many staff members, there was an urgency to create change that aligned with the goals of Wilson and of these interest groups.

Wilson's gentle and insightful demeanor facilitated an atmosphere of trust between artist and staff; as Phil Stoiber, Associate Registrar at SAM, described, 'Fred's legacy was modeling trust, diplomacy, integrity and discretion and the importance of language and communication to take us through difficult issues' (Stoiber 2009). This was intentional on Wilson's part; 'My projects are only as good as the relationships I build', he stated (Wilson and Berger 2001: 34). Wilson's non-hierarchical approach to interventions at SAM and the Hood created a climate in which all staff members had a voice in the project – again, helping to shape an alignment to make good work happen. Central to Wilson's working process is that he not only challenges the 'high-low' hierarchies of museum objects, he also questions the traditional organizational hierarchies of museum employment. Patterson Sims, former Associate Director for Art and Exhibitions and Curator of Modern Art at SAM, described Wilson's approach to staff:

> He was no less interested in the security staff's ideas than in the curators', no less curious about the responses of the development department than the docents. He was a master of role-switching, of letting the guard be the docent, of having the artist give the gallery lecture, and having his own functions encompass those of curator and exhibition designer.
>
> *Sims 1993: 10–11*

At Seattle, Wilson arranged for security to give public tours of the exhibition; at the Hood the preparators and exhibition designer became *ipso facto* co-curators as he solicited their advice on juxtapositions, Wilson's all-important language for deconstructing power relationships.

The Seattle Art Museum/The Museum: Mixed Metaphors

Still, the institutions have significant differences that shaped the dynamic of alignment in each project. The Seattle Art Museum, founded in 1931, is a large public institution in which new-moneyed elite and progressive thinking built collections with strengths in non-western and contemporary art. Its mission statement at the time of Wilson's tenure there stated: 'Forward-looking and ambitious, the Seattle Art Museum is dedicated to engaging a broad public in an open dialogue about the visual arts by collecting, preserving, presenting and interpreting works of art of the highest quality'.[2] But whilst this relatively young institution had no 'big secrets' to be unearthed and professed a commitment to access, it nevertheless maintained conventional museological practices about canonicity and authority that became the focus of Wilson's attention.

This focus on hierarchy of collections provoked a young and somewhat angry Fred Wilson, as he later described himself, to declare in a 1994 interview, 'This museum, like the Metropolitan, and all museums that have general collections of art from around the world, have all jumped into saying they're multicultural. And to me, they're about as multicultural as the British Empire' (Wilson and Buskirk 2009: 352). A lack of transparency in the way the museum displayed and interpreted artworks prompted Wilson to assert, 'Museums are not static institutions, they only seem to be. Their display techniques and vague labeling deliberately mask the changes that represent a society in flux' (Wilson 1996). At Seattle exposing these museological conventions became his pedagogical imperative.

As one of Wilson's earliest museum interventions, the Seattle installation was cause for consternation among some staff members. Then Museum Director, Jay Gates, asserted, 'Making connections between different cultures and breaking down resistance to accepted hierarchies and reinterpretation proved challenging to some of us' (Gates 1993: 1). Gates was referring not only to his employees but also to himself. In a 2009 interview, he candidly admitted that, sixteen years before, he did not fully grasp the implications of Wilson's interventions for museums. In 1993, when Wilson was in residence at SAM, Gates was concerned that Wilson was messing with the new building and with its state-of-the-art details such as expensive mounts to protect against potential seismic activity, for which the director had worked so hard to raise funds. Rod Slemmons, SAM Associate Curator of Photography and Prints at the time, stated, 'Some of what Fred did was not particularly appreciated or even condoned by a few of our trustees and staff members. But the good news is that it was tolerated' (Slemmons 1993: 44). At a time when Wilson's approach was still so new, tolerance towards his experimentation was, in itself, an attitude suggesting a degree of alignment; the consensus even among those with reservations was that Wilson's agenda would inevitably gather momentum.

SAM commissioned Wilson to integrate his project within the existing permanent collection displays. Though tags labeled 'MM' (for *Mixed Metaphors*) and a map of Wilson's work helped guide audiences through the intervention, viewers really had to look hard to discern which elements of an exhibit were Wilson's work and how their interjection transformed the meanings of the objects around it and the museum itself. A strong element of surprise facilitated critical engagement and a self-reflective understanding of perception, for Wilson the key to combating prejudice.

Support of *Mixed Metaphors* through the Anne Gerber Fund freed Wilson to make the political statement he saw fit. Gerber was a community activist who had fought to end segregated housing in Seattle, championed the American Civil Liberties Union and took the initiative to repatriate First Nations materials from her personal art collections (Bouchegnies 2000). Gerber established the Fund at SAM to support 'risk taking art that would normally not get funded' and her sense of purpose aligned effectively with Wilson's (Farr 2005).

The Hood Museum of Art/SO MUCH TROUBLE IN THE WORLD – Believe it or Not!

At Dartmouth, which began collecting as early as 1772, the Hood boasts holdings of 65,000 works, twice the size of SAM's, in a more intimate and elitist setting. Its mission when Wilson was in residence there (and now) centers on object-based learning. It aims 'to inspire, educate, and collaborate with our academic and broader communities about creativity and imagination through a direct engagement with works of art of historic and cultural significance by making effective use of our collections and staff' (Hood Museum of Art, Statement of Purpose). Having had the benefit of more than a decade of sector-wide conversations on access and equity, staff members at the Hood were fully committed to collaborating with Wilson despite, or perhaps because of, Dartmouth's long history of exclusivity. In the proposal for *SO MUCH TROUBLE IN THE WORLD*, curator Barbara Thompson wrote:

It would be the first [Fred Wilson installation] at an Ivy League institution and would therefore reveal not just the nature of the Hood Museum of Art but would define also broader issues and problems associated with Ivy League and similar traditionally elitist institutions that take pride in their historical longevity, the conservation of their heritage (whose traditions are they conserving? Wilson would surely ask) and in their intellectual excellence (at whose cost/exclusion, he would continue). As a doubly charged 'elitist' institution (Ivy League *and* an art museum), the Hood Museum of Art would surely provide an especially rich source for Wilson's scrutiny and representation.

Thompson 2005

According to Brian Kennedy, director of the Hood from 2005 to 2010, Wilson was the first African-American artist to do a major project at the museum (Kennedy 2009).

Wilson used the Hood's temporary exhibition space which he transformed to produce emotionally saturating environments that comment upon racial tensions in the collections and the college. In the process he introduced a personal voice common to his more recent projects, in this case lamenting the trauma of war and violence. Despite the differences in focus and approach, Wilson's projects for Seattle and Dartmouth are equally concerned with issues of diversity and equity.

The interventions: products of good work

At Seattle, *The Museum: Mixed Metaphors*, as the title suggests, is a refutation of the fetishism of quality and a means to embrace new conversations among objects, cultures and peoples. Wilson stated:

While general art museums house and interpret collections from around the globe, I find the interpretation rather narrowly focused on meanings that support a Western view of relationships between cultures. I view museums as mixed metaphors and my installation [as] another way to mix them up.

Wilson 1996

One of his most politically significant sites for these new conversations at SAM was among the African and Egyptian collections which he juxtaposed to make pertinent connections. For example, in the ancient Greek, Roman and Egyptian gallery, he displayed Somali, Turkana, Pokot and Tellum wooden headrests radiating around an Egyptian Old Kingdom alabaster example. Relating to this juxtaposition that was concerned with reclaiming Egypt's African identity, Wilson (ibid.) asserted:

Egypt is now and always was on the continent of Africa. Museums have a hard time placing it in Africa when organizing permanent exhibitions or arranging floor plans. For museums, Egypt in ancient times was afloat somewhere in the Mediterranean until it attached itself to North Africa sometime in the nineteenth century.

In the African galleries, Wilson injected elements of contemporary culture into the groupings, adding objects of little monetary value when it fit his needs. For instance, he inserted a grey flannel business suit alongside examples of traditional African robes intended to demonstrate how dress communicates rank. Television monitors with videos of contemporary African music and soap operas further interrupted associations of Africa with a dead past, as did a knock-off Rolex watch, borrowed from the director of SAM security, in a display of gold weights nearby (Plate 6.1). Examples of African architecture, including photographs of a tennis court in Lagos, Nigeria; a tree-lined street in Abidjan, Ivory Coast; a major monument in Lomé, Togo; and a model of an international style project by a Nigerian architect, had some viewers insisting the buildings must be from downtown Seattle or Los Angeles (Sims 1993: 34). A pseudo-taxonomic explanatory panel including an illustration with numerical codes and an associated list of works, recalled the utter absurdity of conventional taxonomies in archeological and natural history exhibits.

Wilson mimicked installation techniques commonly used for the display of indigenous culture in the early twentieth-century Euro-American galleries. On jungle dark blue-green walls (the same colour as those in the African galleries), Wilson piled early modernist works, one on top of the other, without the requisite space usually accorded to these objects to create the so-called 'transformative' or liminal experience (Staniszewski 1998). As Wilson described it, this installation:

> was perhaps the most disturbing to visitors, or the most engaging . . . While the clustering created a visually exciting and frenetic arrangement no one work could be seen by itself. The individual works seemed to be struggling to breathe. When viewers asked what the reason for this was, it had to be explained by museum staff that this is the way African and Native American collections were displayed on the floor below.
>
> *Wilson 1996*

At Dartmouth, Wilson helped staff to 'change the habits of the place and make it less risk averse', in the words of former director Derrick Cartwright (Cartwright 2010). The first part of the title, *SO MUCH TROUBLE IN THE WORLD*, comes from a Bob Marley song which spoke to Wilson of both recent and past political violence and injustice:

> When I first came up with the 'SO MUCH TROUBLE IN THE WORLD' title, the (July 2005) bombings in London had just happened. So they were on my mind and just pulled for me the experience of September 11, my experience with bombings when I was in Egypt, and a coup in Nigeria when I was there, and then my own childhood experiences with racism.
>
> *Wilson et al. 2006: 49*

The second part of the title, *Believe it or Not!*, refers to Robert Ripley who, through a Dartmouth connection, was awarded an honorary doctorate from the college when he donated over 100 objects from his collection of curiosities. Wilson chose not to exhibit anything from Ripley's collection except a sign and some photographs as he did not want to perpetuate Ripley's concept of exploitation for spectacle, as seen in the Ripley's *Believe it or Not!* franchises. But he found useful the tension between truth and fiction brought by introducing Ripley as a concept into the museum. He explained:

> I was really interested in the relationship between real museum and pseudo-museums like Ripley's . . . If you look back over time often museums begin to look like *Ripley's*

> *Believe it or Not!* Although they may be using the best [methods] at that time, they may have biases and misinformation that they are not aware of.
>
> *Thompson 2006: 14*

Together the two parts of Wilson's title blur the boundaries between the real and the fictive. They convey a sense of incredulity towards both the museological conventions that construct and reinforce hegemonic power and the horrors of war that this hegemony produce.

Through a display of portraits representing Daniel Webster, Wilson hoped to expose for staff and visitors the limiting and patriarchal nature of Dartmouth's collecting habits (Plate 6.2). When Wilson was exploring the Hood's collections he was surprised to find over a hundred images of Webster, the nineteenth-century American orator, lawyer, statesman and Dartmouth graduate. Webster was beloved (and his portraits collected) by Dartmouth alumni not only because he was a prominent abolitionist but also as he argued successfully before the Supreme Court in 1818–19 the college's right to remain a private institution. Wilson, however, was troubled by Webster's support of the Compromise of 1850 which supported stronger legal avenues for the recovery of fugitive slaves in order to pacify southern states to prevent secession; as Secretary of State from 1850 to 1852, Webster had to oversee enforcement of the Fugitive Slave Act (ibid.: 16). Wilson's installation problematizes Webster's image by displaying over fifty portraits, salon style, in a small area, not unlike his display of early modernism at SAM. Music from the Mbuti people of the Democratic Republic of Congo played in the background in a strategy similar to that of his installation of post-war art at Seattle with its soundtrack of African percussion.

As Wilson gently parodies the legacy of Daniel Webster and his unexamined treatment in the hands of the Museum, he questions how Dartmouth has appropriated Webster imagery to ennoble their own cause. He also asks what is missing from Dartmouth's historical narrative through a sole row of portraits above the Webster display depicting people of color (and women) associated with the college. Significant historical figures such as Charles Eastman, a Dakota Sioux who became a physician and attended to the victims at the Massacre of Wounded Knee, and one of only twenty Native Americans to graduate from Dartmouth in its first 200 years (ibid.: 17), looked down at visitors as if to ask: where is our history represented?

In juxtaposition to the Webster installation is a series of busts, titled *The Races of Man,* that Wilson found, chipped from benign neglect, in off-site storage. More than one staff member became choked with emotion as they recounted to me the groundswell of feeling that Wilson's reifying treatment of these objects inspired. The busts are copies of casts produced by the American Museum of Natural History for the St. Louis World's Fair of 1904 intended to substantiate theories of racial hierarchy and inequality and to justify colonization. The casts were taken directly from individuals who were taken to the fair to be put on display as representative of the 'primitive'.

For example, Ota Benga, a member of the Bachichiri people in the Democratic Republic of the Congo (who have been commonly referred to in the west as Pygmies), was presented as 'a missing link' – or an intermediary form of life to illustrate the evolutionary transition from primate to early humans (Delsahut 2008: 298). He was treated with such disdain that, after the fair, Ota Benga was transferred by the American Museum of Natural History to the primate house of the Bronx Zoo where he shared a cage with an orangutan. After the ministers of several African American churches protested, Ota Benga was sent to a tobacco factory in the South where he committed suicide (Bradford and Blume 1992).

Wilson was disturbed by the anguished expressions on the faces of the busts. 'You can see in their faces that they are not happy with their situation', he exclaimed (Wilson and Appiah 2006: 20). In response, he animated the busts, gave them back their dignity, in a way that requires emotional engagement from viewers (Plate 6.3). He masked with white tulle the labels inscribed on the casts identifying each by ethnicity. And he created inscriptions of his own with the sensibility of the language-based interrogation of conceptual art. 'I have a name'; 'I have a purpose'; 'Someone knows me – but not you', they whispered through red lettering barely discernible from the maroon of the walls and pedestals, as if to assert their identities. Wilson lined up the casts in a row at eye level so that the viewer could not avoid them. Only Ota Benga, of short stature, is positioned lower than, and aloof from, the others, re-presenting his sad story. The installation stands in sharp contrast to that of the Daniel Webster grouping; in a historical corrective, the busts now appear as unique individuals whilst the Webster portraits seem merely types.

Cause and effect: evaluating the impact of Fred Wilson's interventions

How has Wilson sparked an alignment between 'best practice', what museums do, and the values of social inclusion that individuals, the sector and global trends espouse? How is Wilson a driver for change in the museum to foster the kind of alignment that makes good work flourish? Do these one-off projects contribute to the shaping of mission statements, do they inform strategic planning and the approach and activities of staff across institutions? Fundamentally, can institutional critique change an organization's culture and its practices?

Interviews with staff many years after their initial engagement with Wilson suggests that the artist's 'writing' is still legible on that Freudian mystic tablet of museum memory. Whilst it is important to recognize that many other factors are at work in effecting transformation at SAM and the Hood, through my research I found evidence that Wilson's process influenced staff across the spectrum of museum activity, helping reshape mission and strategic planning; and inform approaches to acquisitions, collections management, exhibitions, design, learning and personnel issues through a heightened concern for greater diversity and equity. Wilson's institutional critique is a catalyst for good work by aligning museum theory and practice.

Institutional purpose and direction

Mission statements and strategic plans are key indicators of organizational change and revised documents at SAM and the Hood evidence new commitment to social engagement and inclusion after Wilson's residency. For example, at SAM, a new mission statement, approved by the Board of Trustees in 2002, prioritizes relevance:

> SAM provides a welcoming place for people to connect with art and to consider its relationship to their lives . . . SAM collects and exhibits objects from across time and across cultures, exploring the dynamic connections between past and present.[3]

This new mission, 'connecting art to life', as SAM staff refer to it, developed out of a 1999 four-year project, *Deepening the Dialogue: Art and Audience*, intended to 'diversify its [SAM's] audience and foster a deeper and ongoing community involvement in the daily life of the museum' (Seattle Art Museum 2004: 3). A key goal of the project, funded by a Wallace Foundation grant, was to diversify the museum holistically, from staff to volunteers, board to audiences, in a mode much like Goodwin Willson had envisioned (Goodwin Willson 2005: 44–45). This process has continued.

At the Hood, Director Brian Kennedy's top priority when he arrived midway through Wilson's tenure there was to devise with staff and administrators a new four-year strategic plan. Wilson's institutional critique became an important tool to assess the past as the group considered its future. A primary objective, as a result of Wilson's project, was to make the museum more accessible and transparent to diverse campus and community audiences. Associate Director Bianco asserted:

> It was our twentieth anniversary and our new director was starting. And so we had the serendipity of a number of significant occasions . . . We had a director who was really interested in strategic planning, and thinking about how to take an academic museum and connect it even more with the campus and community . . . The museum had the opportunity to open up, invite people in, and listen to people, respond to them with the work that we do, and even create a dialogue . . . The Fred Wilson project sparked this way of thinking. We invited groups for tours from different departments on campus that had maybe not spent much time at the Hood. We used Fred's show as a teaching opportunity across disciplines . . . to teach people what we do with the museum in addition to teaching content.
>
> *Bianco 2009*

In meetings to generate ideas for the new strategic plan, *SO MUCH TROUBLE IN THE WORLD* was repeatedly upheld to exemplify the potential relevance and commitment to institutional diversity and equity that the Hood could sustain. In these efforts, administrators expressed support for risk-taking; for provocative projects with learning at their core.

Strategic planning meetings identified a host of activities to build and diversify audiences. And so, as Bianco states, 'That became a part of our strategic plan, this connecting with campus groups and bringing different groups in for all our exhibitions. And it's become relatively routine' (Bianco 2009). Two key campus groups with which the Hood partnered for the first time for Fred's installation but, as a result of the strategic plan, strengthened relations are OPAL – the Office of Pluralism and Leadership – an umbrella group under which the African-American, Asian, Native American, Latino and GLBT student groups organized and ID and E – the Office of Institutional Diversity and Equity (ibid.).

Collections practice

At the Hood, Wilson's intervention has also impacted acquisitions and the Museum's position on deaccessioning. Kennedy aggressively built up the Hood's Native American and non-western collections to attract new audiences, in part, as a result of the biases Wilson revealed in the collections. Kennedy added public art on campus to grow relations with the community and took on the difficult ethical issue of whether to show or censor some racially insensitive murals on campus that had been hidden from view with moveable panels. After years of controversy among the campus community without any action taken, Kennedy moved forward with a committee to articulate a plan in which the murals will be shown only under

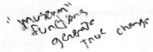

' museum" functions generate true change

specific conditions and after gaps in the Hood collections are addressed to provide context and counter-narrative to these problematic works. In short, as Dartmouth art historian Mary Coffey asserted, 'Kennedy has established trust within factions historically mistrustful of Hood Museum of Art resources' (Coffey 2010).

Concerning collections management, the Hood has recently felt pressure from an external review to deaccession works deemed without aesthetic merit; but as former Hood registrar, Kellen Haak, remarked, 'Fred showed us that there is more to the collection than meets the eye' (Haak 2009). To Wilson, collections represent the thoughts and ideas of people, insights into the human condition. 'Behind objects are people that should be considered', he later remarked, when asked about deaccession (Wilson 2009). Through *SO MUCH TROUBLE IN THE WORLD*, he exposed the vulnerabilities and expressive power of works created by non-canonical artists and cultures, laying bare some of the ethical issues inherent in deaccessioning decisions. Dartmouth Associate Provost, Mary Gorman, made clear that Wilson's installation at the Hood, in effect, protected marginalized works from deaccession (Gorman 2010). They have gained a second life as they told an (inconvenient) story about institutional history.

Display, public programs, education

Wilson likewise has shaped the approaches to exhibitions at SAM and the Hood. At SAM it is in display choices for the permanent collection that transformation is most evident, particularly given opportunities for change with a 2007 expansion of the museum. And from the moment Wilson's project opened at Seattle, curators recognized that the one-off project carried implications for the display of permanent collections. Rod Slemmons asserted:

> When his installations are removed, we will still have permanent collections displayed according to the Western Tradition of art history and along racial, geographic, and chronological hierarchies, much like other large museums in the country . . . If his art is truly successful – and it will be quickly tested when it disappears – we will continue to explore the questions he has raised.
>
> *Slemmons 1993: 44*

Slemmons imagined select spaces in the Museum where diverse objects would speak to one another to make connections across cultures and time, as Wilson had modeled in *Mixed Metaphors*. 'Following Fred's lead, we could mount small comparative displays in the galleries, punctuating for a moment the chronological sequence that would place religious, social, economic, and aesthetic considerations of several works from different cultures side by side' (ibid.: 43).

SAM, in fact, put these ideas into practice in its expansion. In the 1991 downtown building the third floor displayed African, Asian and Northwest Coast collections and the fourth floor exhibited American, European and Ancient Art. The 2007 installation rejects this segregation of objects into western/non-western binaries. Instead, as Pam McClusky explains, 'the revised order of the world is rooted in cultures overlapping – Egypt is next to Africa, Africa is next to Europe, Native American is adjacent to American' (McClusky 2010). Also, in the reinstallation, curators have used transitional or 'crossroads' gallery spaces to stage objects from diverse cultures in complex conversations. These cross-cultural connections, in turn, require new collaborations among departments. I would argue that they also set an ethical model for the way people should behave as well.

For Pam McClusky, Wilson's intervention 'provided artistic license to put directly into practice ideas that she had long been flirting with' (Sims 2008). It allowed her the freedom to take risks by crossing (and transgressing) all kinds of boundaries, from the geographic to the aesthetic to the chronological; often, like Wilson, including works less 'valuable' or canonical, for example, to express an idea. Wilson's example also helped her to make the galleries more performative and to introduce greater transparency through displays that engage viewers in museological issues.

McClusky's new African galleries are deeply performative. Visitors emerge from the escalator to a cacophony of mannequins in diverse positions; standing, crouching, seated, enacting a Nigerian Afikpo masquerade, a clear corrective of the standard technique of exhibiting African masks devoid of their function and context and in line with western sculptural traditions. Masquerade video as well as contemporary African art video, for instance by William Kentridge, further enliven the space, as does a soundsuit by American artist Nick Cave in which Cave performed and which resembles African ceremonial costume. Sound and movement create a multisensory theatrical experience for visitors – who are more than just 'viewers'.

At SAM it was not only curators who rethought their approaches to display. Michael McCafferty, SAM's exhibition designer, told me that, as a result of Wilson's installation of early modernism with its dark blue-green walls that mimicked those of the African galleries, he vowed never to paint the walls of galleries exhibiting non-western materials in earth tones again (McCafferty 2009). McCafferty designed the 2007 African galleries with white walls and clear transparent shelving so that visitors could not only view all sides of an object and see from one gallery into the next but also literally and metaphorically experience museological transparency (Figure 6.1).

The boldness and transparency with which Wilson selected and interpreted objects from the collections, engaging issues of questionable attribution and provenance, gave McClusky the license to continue in this direction (McClusky 2010). For example, in *The Untold Story*, she selected objects from the permanent collection,

> based on the often perplexing manner in which they were collected. Stories that are usually left behind in object files, as part of the records that the public doesn't see, became the focus. Every label was treated as if it were a short story, with a title to match.
>
> *McClusky 2011: 306*

She included, for instance, a rat trap made by the Giriama people of Kenya with the title 'Death on Display'. McClusky divulges in the label:

> No one here quite knows how this works or if it has ever been used . . . Never on view at this museum before, whether the trap actually belongs in an art museum is a valid question that has no absolute answer.

McClusky explains, '*The Untold Story* texts exposed the choices that collectors make, some of which are not exactly in the realm of professional practice, and how the museum works with their legacy' (ibid.: 308).

At the Hood temporary exhibitions since Wilson's tenure have examined the politics of representation and other museological issues. These shows include *Collectanea: The Museum as Hunter and Gatherer; No Laughing Matter: Visual Humor in Ideas of Race, Nationality and*

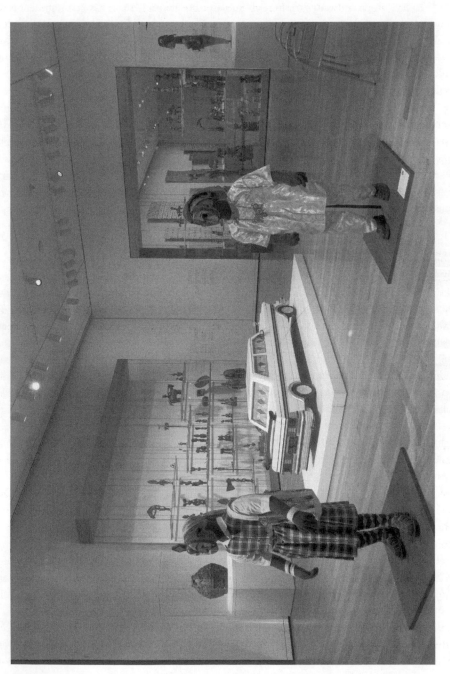

FIGURE 6.1 *A Noble Tension* Gallery. Seattle Art Museum, Seattle, WA. Photograph, Susan Cole. Courtesy, Seattle Art Museum

Ethnicity; and *Black Womanhood: Images, Icons and Ideologies of the Black African Body*, among others. And whilst there have been conflicts – for example, students interpreted the Museum's use of the word 'Hood' in publicity as a double entendre also to connote slang for neighborhood during the *Black Womanhood* exhibit – a perceived slight for which the Museum apologized – the institution and its communities are engaged in the kind of substantive discourse that indicates a growing sensitivity to the concerns of diverse stakeholders (Bianco 2009).

Fred's intervention also created changes in the Hood's educational programming. Whilst Lesley Wellman, Assistant Director and Curator of Education, had already introduced Hood docents to discussion-based learning and small group work with audiences in temporary exhibitions, with *SO MUCH TROUBLE IN THE WORLD* she began the process of applying this dialogic approach to the permanent collection; this now occurs on a regular basis. Also, inspired by Wilson's installation, the Hood initiated museologically-based general tours that engage visitors in the institution's reflective practice. These tours examine how the museum works and the value systems behind the choices that it makes (Wellman 2009).

Workplace culture and staff relations

Wilson impacted personnel issues at both institutions by giving support staff key roles that brandished their skills in critical thinking. Wilson, who had worked as a guard whilst at university, was particularly concerned about the status and invisibility of museum security. To this effect, in 1991, he created *Guarded View* (Whitney Museum of American Art, New York) in which four headless mannequins of color, each in a different New York museum security uniform, stand anonymously before the white walls of a nameless gallery. The only clue to the races of these gloved figures is their necks, indicated through shades of brown. At SAM, he developed a friendship with the guards, some of whom were also actors. Wilson had studied performance himself so they had much in common. Professing faith in their abilities, Wilson asked security to give tours of the installation. Wilson approached them, as former SAM guard Paul Klein recounted, by exclaiming, 'I want you guys to do it. You know what you're talking about' (Klein 2009). Their experience as guides not only gave new confidence to those in visitor services, it also increased their status at the institution.

Phil Stoiber, Associate Registrar of SAM, explained that Wilson's modelling of 'a culture of inclusivity' towards museum security compelled him to understand that visitor services personnel, in their support of risk management, are as critical to object care as are registrars and conservators; Stoiber states that Wilson's example continues to inspire him to challenge the invisibility with which guards are traditionally perceived (Stoiber 2009). Wilson's recognition and integration of museum security in his projects has played an important role in the transition from guard to gallery attendant in museums across the United States over the last fifteen years.[4]

At the Hood, Wilson gave new voice to the preparators and exhibition designer by tapping their artistic talents to help create his juxtapositions. Typically, 'our involvement is to help winnow it [the objects selected] down to what we can actually fit into the gallery', said preparator John Reynolds (Reynolds 2009). In contrast, Wilson made them feel like curators with real decision-making capacity; it changed forever the way the three think about the collections and the space. In working with the Hood's images of war, for example, Wilson sparked in them the responsibility of representation. The three told me that they feel ethically torn when they hang images of war and disaster now, without a larger context to mitigate the potential of gazing as spectacle (Dunfey *et al.* 2009).

Conclusions

Thus, through a delicate dance, Wilson shapes the overlapping threads of individual and institutional ethics. By collaborating with Wilson, museum staff learn a new language of practice from the margins that empowers them to redefine the core. Wilson's interventions may be just one of many drivers for change in the museum but, as these case studies attest, this form of compassionate institutional critique can help provide alignment of museum practice with individual, sector and global values to foster good work; as Gardner and Straughn define it, work that has ethics at its heart. Good work is also supported by Wilson's fostering of free expression and trust, his ability to demonstrate that staff can indeed effect change and his insistence on moral complexity, as conceptualized by the GoodWork Project; his interventions present for museum workers rich opportunities to think through practice and its relationship to theory, to seek from him and from each other advice and guidance, and to reflect on past actions and future consequences.

Wilson is not the only artist to practice this form of compassionate institutional critique. One can see similar strategies of aligning practice and theory to create a more socially inclusive institution in the museum performance pieces about mourning and loss by Ernesto Pujol and about destabilizing space by Anthony Shrag. Clearly, there are many aspects of diversity and equity that SAM and the Hood have yet to address – this is, of course, an ongoing work – but Wilson's engagement with museums provides a useful model of reflexive practice that continues to be read from the mystic writing pad of museum consciousness.

Notes

1 I am grateful to former and current staff at the Seattle Museum of Art and the Hood Museum of Art, Dartmouth College, for allowing me to interview them for this project, and to Fred Wilson for his generosity and trust. I also thank Richard Sandell, Jürgen Heinrichs and Celka Straughn for their insights at many stages of this research.
2 Information provided by Seattle Art Museum Librarian, Traci Timmons.
3 Approved by the Seattle Art Museum Board of Trustees Executive Committee 11 February 2002; information provided by SAM Librarian T. Timmons.
4 Nonetheless, security at museums across the United States remain among the most undervalued and poorly paid staff members, despite attempts to address the issue.

References

American Association of Museums (1992) *Excellence and Equity: Education and the Public Dimensions of Museums*, Washington, DC: American Association of Museums.

Bianco, J. (2009) Interview by author, 22 July.

Bouchegnies, D. (2000) 'Anne Gerber (1910–2005): A Life in Art', *Historylink.org – The Free Online Encyclopedia of Washington State History*. Online. Available at: www.historylink.org/index. cfm?DisplayPage=output.cfm&file_id=2852 (accessed 11 April 2010).

Bradford, P. V. and Blume, H. (1992) *Ota Benga – The Pygmy in the Zoo*, New York: St. Martin's Press.

Cartwright, D. (2010) Interview by author, 16 February.

Coffey, M. (2010) Interview by author, 8 March.

Delsahut, F. (2008) 'The 1904 St. Louis Anthropological Games', in P. Blanchard, N. Bancel,

G. Boetsch, E. Deroo, S. Lemaire and C. Forsdick (eds) *Human Zoos: Science and Spectacle in the Age of Colonial Empires*, trans. T. Bridgeman, Liverpool: Liverpool University Press, pp. 294–306.

Dunfey, P., Reynolds, J. and Zayatz, M. (2009) Interview by author, 21 July.

Farr, S. (2005) 'Art, Social Causes Inspired Anne Gerber, 94', *Seattle Times*, 25 January. Online. Available at: http://seattletimes.nwsource.com/html/localnews/2002159773_gerber25.html (accessed 11 April 2010).

Freud, S. (1961) 'A Note Upon the Mystic Writing Pad', in J. Strachey (ed. and trans.) *The Standard Edition of the Complete Psychological Works of Sigmund Freud*, 24 vols. London: Hogarth, vol. 1 9, pp. 227–232, first published 1925.

Gardner, H. (1983) *Frames of Mind: The Theory of Multiple Intelligences*, New York: Basic Books.

Gardner, H. (1998) *The Ethical Responsibilities of Professionals*, GoodWork Project Report Series, No. 2, July (updated February 2001). Online. Available at: pzweb.harvard.edu/eBookstore/PDFs/GoodWork2.pdf (accessed 10 April 2010).

Gardner, H. (2007) 'Introduction: Who is Responsible for Good Work?', in H. Gardner (ed.) *Responsibility at Work: How Leading Professionals Act (or Don't Act) Responsibly*, San Francisco: Jossey-Bass, pp. 1–18.

Gates, J. (1993) 'Foreword', in *The Museum: Mixed Metaphors, Fred Wilson*, ex. cat. Seattle: Seattle Art Museum, pp. 1–2.

González, J. A. (2008) *Subject to Display: Reframing Race in Contemporary Installation Art*, Cambridge, MA and London: MIT Press.

Goodwin Willson, J. L. (2005) 'Expanding Multicultural Discourse: Art Museums and Cultural Diversity', MA Thesis, University of Oregon.

GoodWork Project Team (2010) *The GoodWork Project: Overview*. Online. Available at: www.goodworkproject.org/docs/papers/GW%20Overview%204_08.pdf (accessed 9 April 2010).

Gorman, M. (2010) Interview by author, 10 March.

Haak, K. (2009) Interview by author, 5 August.

Hood Museum of Art, Statement of Purpose, Online. Available at: http://hoodmuseum.dartmouth.edu/about/museum/index.html (accessed 11 April 2010).

Kennedy, B. (2009) Interview by author, 22 July.

Klein, P. (2009) Interview by author, 11 March.

Kwon, M. (2000) *One Place After Another: Site-Specific Art and Locational Identity*, Cambridge, MA and London: MIT Press.

McCafferty, M. (2009) Interview by author, 11 March.

McClusky, P. (2010) to author. E-mail (13 May).

McClusky, P. (2011) '"Why is this here?:" Art Museum Texts as Ethical Guides', in J. Marstine (ed.) *Routledge Companion to Museum Ethics: Redefining Ethics for the Twenty-First Century Museum*, London and New York: Routledge, pp. 298–315.

Newkirk, P. (2000) 'Object Lessons: Fred Wilson Reinstalls Museum Collections to Highlight Sins of Omission', *Art News*, January, pp. 156–160.

Reynolds, J. (2009) Interview by author, 21 July.

Seattle Art Museum (2004) *Annual Report*, Seattle: Seattle Art Museum.

Sims, P. (1993) 'Metamorphosing Art/Mixing the Museum', in *The Museum: Mixed Metaphors, Fred Wilson*, ex. cat. Seattle: Seattle Art Museum, pp. 3–39.

Sims, P. (2008) Interview by author, 1 December.

Slemmons, R. (1993) 'Afterwords', in *The Museum: Mixed Metaphors, Fred Wilson*, ex. cat. Seattle: Seattle Art Museum, pp. 40–44.

Staniszewski, M. A. (1998) *The Power of Display: A History of Exhibition Installations at the Museum of Modern Art*, Cambridge, MA and London: MIT Press.

Stoiber, P. (2009) Interview by author, 6 March.

Straughn, C. and Gardner, H. (2011) 'GoodWork in Museums Today . . . and Tomorrow', in J. Marstine (ed.) *Routledge Companion to Museum Ethics: Redefining Ethics for the Twenty-First Century Museum*, London and New York: Routledge, pp. 41–53.

Thompson, B. (2005) 'Project Proposal, Fred Wilson, "SO MUCH TROUBLE IN THE WORLD – Believe it or Not!"', Hood Museum of Art Archives, Dartmouth College.

Thompson, B. (2006) 'Making "SO MUCH TROUBLE IN THE WORLD"', in *Fred Wilson: SO MUCH TROUBLE IN THE WORLD – Believe it or Not!*, ex. cat. Hood Museum of Art, Dartmouth College.

Thompson, B. (2010) Online posting, Museum Ethics Listserv, Institute of Museum Ethics, Seton Hall University (5 February).

Updike, R. (1996) 'What About Those Changes At SAM? – Is It An Art Museum Adrift? – Staffing Turnovers Have Raised Eyebrows, Even As Its Financial Picture Brightens', *Seattle Times*, 10 March. Online. Available at: http://community.seattletimes.nwsource.com/archive/?date=19960310&slug=2318129 (accessed 25 February 2010).

Wellman, L. (2009) Interview by author, 22 July.

Wilson, F. (1996) 'The Silent Message of the Museum', keynote paper, *Power and Empowerment: Preparing for the New Millennium*, Museums Australia, 1 November.

Wilson, F. (2008) Interview by author, 6 April.

Wilson, F. (2009) Interview by author, 13 October.

Wilson, F. and Appiah, A. (2006) 'Fragments of a Conversation: Fred Wilson and K. Anthony Appiah', in *Fred Wilson: A Conversation with K. Anthony Appiah*, ex. cat. New York: Pace Wildenstein.

Wilson, F. and Berger, M. (2001) 'Collaboration, Museums, and the Politics of Display: Conversation with Fred Wilson, 25 January 2001', in M. Berger (ed.) *Fred Wilson: Objects and Installations, 1979–2000*, University of Maryland, Baltimore County: ex. cat. Center for Art and Visual Culture, pp. 32–39.

Wilson, F. and Buskirk, M. (2009) 'Fred Wilson, A Conversation with Martha Buskirk', in A. Alberro and B. Stimson (eds) *Institutional Critique: An Anthology of Artists' Writings*, Cambridge, MA and London: MIT Press, pp. 350–353, first published in *October* 70, Fall 1994.

Wilson, F., Lusaka, J. and Strand, J. (2006) 'Fred Wilson: Learning to Speak Museum: Interview by Jane Lusaka and John Strand', *Museum News*, January/February, pp. 44–50.

Yellis, K. (2009) 'Fred Wilson, PTSD, and Me: Reflections on the History Wars', *Curator: The Museum Journal*, October: 52 (4), pp. 333–348.

PART II
Connecting/competing equalities

7

THE MARGINS AND THE MAINSTREAM

Gary Younge

I want to start with a tale of two white girls – Sandra Laing from Mpumulanga in South Africa and Bliss Broyard who was raised in the blue-blood world of Connecticut's twee suburbs and private schools. Broyard's racial identity was ensconced in the comfort of insular whiteness that had always known there were 'others' but never really considered them. In her book, *One Drop*, she confesses:

> I'd never had a conversation about race. In the world I was raised in, it was considered an impolite subject . . . Although I grew up within an hour's drive of three of the poorest black communities in the United States . . . those neighbourhoods seemed as distant as a foreign country.
>
> *2007: 42*

But in early adulthood Broyard would discover that, on one level, she had a greater connection to those neighbourhoods than she imagined, for on his deathbed her father, Anatole, confessed that he was in fact a black man who had been passing as white throughout most of his adult life. Initially she was thrilled at the news and wrote: 'It was as though I'd been reading a fascinating history book and then discovered my own name in the index. I felt like I mattered in a way that I hadn't before.'

But then came the heavy lifting. The family her father had left behind, many of whom lived in the South, and her relationship to those poor black communities that she had *known of* but never actually *known*, forced her to reassess everything she had once thought about herself: 'I felt unsettled: I'd already experimented with describing myself as black on a few occasions and it hadn't gone over well.'

The other white girl, Laing, was born to two white Apartheid-supporting Afrikaaner parents in the small town of Piet Retief near the Swazi border. Her grandparents were also white. Blood tests proved she was her father's daughter. Yet Sandra emerged dark-skinned with afro hair – a black girl. And, under the strict segregationist laws of Apartheid, the fact that she had two white parents could only mean so much. Sandra was removed from her whites–only school and reclassified as 'coloured'.

Sandra's parents fought the reclassification hard as was apparent in her father's explanation in the *Rand Daily Mail*:

> Sandra has been brought up as a white. She is darker than we are, but in every way she has always been a white person. If her appearance is due to some 'coloured blood' in either of us, then it must be very far back among our forebears, and neither of us is aware of it. If this is, in fact, so, does it make our family any different from so many others in South Africa?

Eventually Sandra would be reclassified as white. But in a country where segregation was rigid and nobody accepted her as white, this legalistic change was more than a technicality but less than an objective reality. Eventually she decided that since black people were prepared to accept her literally on face value while whites were not, that she would reclassify herself back to coloured.

Two white girls in two nations founded in no small part on racial classification and segregation, discover that they are both in different ways black. These might be considered as isolated cases but both are instructive in that they shine considerable light on how the relationship between the margins and the core is understood, misunderstood, assumed, accepted and all too often unacknowledged. There are four specific ways in which this plays out in society in general.

First, the margins in no small part define the core. They establish the boundaries within which the core can be understood. Without the margins there can be no core, just as without borders there can be no nation. The two concepts are not only inextricably linked – they are logically symbiotic. A lot was riding on Sandra Laing's classification. Far from being a personal matter, her race becomes an affair of state. If she's white who isn't; if she's black whose family could be next? In a system founded on racial separation there has to be some clear distinction about where one 'race' starts and another one ends. Without it the entire social fabric starts to fray. Those distinctions, by definition, take place at the margins.

The second way in which this is played out is that the categories we are working with, when we talk about what constitutes the marginal as opposed to the core, are almost never definite or often even definable. Both of these girls are both white and black. In ordinary conversation we assume we know what these terms mean. But since race has no basis in biology, genealogy, science or performance, this assumption is mistaken. As soon as we start to define most of the terms we commonly use in identity and culture things fall apart. South Africa's Population Registration Act in 1950 defines a white person as: 'Any person who in appearance obviously is or who is generally accepted as a white person, other than a person who, although in appearance obviously a white person, is generally accepted as a coloured person.'

Far from being watertight such categorisations are in fact incredibly porous. So while we have to work with the categories that exist, we should never be under the illusion that they are not open to challenge.

The third way in which this scenario plays out is that what is categorised as marginal and what is understood to be core has, at its root, nothing to do with numbers and everything to do with power. There is a reason why Bliss Broyard's father decided to cross the colour line or why the Laings wanted Sandra to remain on their side of it. The lines in question divided society into a life with or without resources, privilege and power – decisions are made at the core, consequences are felt at the margins. So, en route from the margins to the mainstream are many gatekeepers – some official, others self-appointed – keen to stamp their imprimatur of authenticity and exact a price for entry. Often the line is determined in court and somebody has to draw it. All too often what we insist is marginal has in fact simply been marginalised.

The fourth and final way that this is played out is that the relationship between the margins and the core is never settled but in constant flux. The categories we work with are not only not watertight, they are positively fluid. Identities and cultures are in a state of constant evolution, both within themselves and in relation to other things. They change, not just as a result of time and tide, but as a result of struggles either within the margins and the core, between the margins and the core or usually both. In a post-Apartheid South Africa, Sandra Laing could have harnessed her racial identity for affirmative action; while Anatole Broyard, who was raised in the segregated South, ran away from his blackness, his daughter, in a post-civil rights America, could run towards it. What is marginal today could well be core tomorrow and vice versa.

The manner in which the core is defined by its margins is best illustrated by events in the last few years in Israel where, with the stroke of a pen, more than 40,000 people were told they were no longer Jewish. The story starts on the margins. In 2008 a woman known as 'Rachel', an immigrant, who had been converted by Rabbi Chaim Drukman, went to file for divorce. The rabbinical judge asked her a few questions about her conversion and, evidently unimpressed, then probed her on her observance. Left with the impression that she did not observe the Sabbath or otherwise meet the standards he believed worthy of a Jewish convert, he ruled her conversion invalid. This also meant her marriage of the last 15 years had never been valid and that her children were no longer Jewish in the eyes of the Rabbinate either.

Rachel had been converted by Drukman who became the head of the Israeli conversion court. When a three-judge panel heard her appeal they decided not only to uphold her disqualification but to disqualify *all* the conversions performed by Drukman since 1999. In one fell swoop 40,000 people who thought they were Jewish were told they were no longer Jewish.

This is no small thing. Israel is a Jewish state. That is not just an incidental description but its deliberate intention. The express aim of its political class and popular culture is to keep it that way. So the question of who is deemed to be Jewish, by whom and on what basis is central to the nature of Israel's existence. Indeed it is an affair of state. And how that question is defined in turn defines the state and its relationship to international Jewry. That definition takes place at the margins – the point at which someone may be included or excluded. But it is of the utmost importance to the core. For what it means to be let inside is shaped to a large degree by what it takes to be left outside.

The truth is that relatively few Jews would have passed the tests for observance set down by the Rabbinate. In 2007, a poll by the Israeli Democracy Institute found that only 27 per cent of Israeli Jews kept the Sabbath, while 53 per cent said they did not keep it at all.

But if the core makes little sense without the margins, also the efforts to definitively establish where those margins lie all too often produce nonsensical results.

The Rabbinate's stiffer criteria for recognising conversions and acknowledging Jewish heritage would, according to one campaigner, exclude 80 per cent of the American Jewish Federation. So, the overwhelming majority of the pillars of US Jewry, those who run the religion's principal philanthropic and cultural organisations, would not qualify. Rabbi Shaul Farber, whose organisation helps Jews navigate the demands of the Rabbinate, explains: 'The problem I have is not proving that people are Jewish. The problem is certifying that they are Jewish to a certain threshold. The trouble is the threshold keeps changing.'

This brings us to the second point that what constitutes inclusion in the margins as opposed to the core is invariably highly subjective and problematic. The lines we draw to categorise human difference are never straight and always blurred. Trying to make sense of human difference is a valiant and important effort. But, as John Berger in *Ways of Seeing* points out, just because we find words for things doesn't necessarily mean we have found meaning for them: 'The relation between what we see and what we know is never settled . . . The way we see things is affected by what we know or what we believe' (1972: 8).

The French government's efforts to combat Islamic extremism by banning headscarves in schools were not triggered by girls whose fundamentalist parents made them cover up. They were triggered instead by a case of two converts to Islam, whose father is a Sephardic Jew, and who did not want them to wear the veil but respected their right to do so. Even those categories with which we are most familiar and most comfortable can prove less certain than most thought. The 800m women's world champion, South African Caster Semenya, had to undergo gender verification tests in 2009 to prove she was actually a woman. As Nick Davies (cited in Kessler 2009), a spokesman for the International Association of Athletics Federations explained: 'If it's a natural thing and the athlete has always thought she's a woman or been a woman, it's not exactly cheating.'

Take Barack Obama. The son of a black immigrant from Kenya and a white woman from Kansas, raised by his white grandparents in Hawaii, he is commonly acknowledged to be the first African-American president. But is he? True, his father is from Africa but that would make him Kenyan American, as others are Italian American or Polish American, with the notion of their forebears as the descriptor. African-American refers to the ethnicity of people who were taken from Africa as slaves. The reason they get a continent and everyone else gets a country – Italian-American, Japanese-American, Irish-American – is because African-Americans cannot say with any certainty where their ancestors came from. During his 2004 Democratic convention speech that launched him to prominence he said his father came to America, 'a magical place'. Few African Americans thought America was magical in 1959.

But he's black right? Well, it depends who you ask. A poll in 2008 showed that, after being told his parents' race and nationality, 75 per cent of whites and 61 per cent of Hispanics classified Obama as biracial, while 66 per cent of blacks regarded him as black.

And these definitions matter. In the past we have referred to Asian where we meant Muslim, Muslim where we meant Pakistani, urban where we meant black, black where we meant youth, Western where we meant European, British where we meant European or alternative where we meant gay – to name but a few.

A few years ago there was an intense debate over the fact that two-thirds of the black students admitted to Harvard – some of whom were beneficiaries of affirmative action – were the descendants of Caribbean or African immigrants as opposed to African-American slaves. Mary Waters, Harvard sociologist (cited in Rimer and Arenson 2004), identifies the problem:

> You need a philosophical discussion about what are the aims of affirmative action. If it's about getting black faces at Harvard, then you're doing fine. If it's about making up for 200 to 500 years of slavery in this country and its aftermath, then you're not doing well. And if it's about having diversity that includes African-Americans from the South or from inner-city high schools, then you're not doing well, either.

We should also recognise that we have multiple identities. We are many things at once and, at all times, we are also the same thing – ourselves. A black man, a white woman, a straight

Sikh, a gay millionaire – in all sorts of ways it is possible for us to occupy the core and the margins simultaneously.

One of the problems with diversity, as currently understood, is that it can often take precious little account of economic difference – an omission that leaves the while working class stranded without a sponsor. In the world of multi-culturalism, as it is often portrayed, they are assumed to have no culture. They are told their whiteness is a mark of power they have never felt and a signifier for potential bigotry they may not harbour. Caught in a pincer between the battle for scarce resources and the battle for equality, the white working class might then feel concerned – forced to argue not for more resources but against 'others' getting their cut. Under those conditions they experience their race and class not as interlocking identities but as a besieged grievance which the Right are only too happy to leverage for political gain.

The fact that people have a multitude of affiliations does not mean certain identities might not come to the fore at certain moments. But any attempt to diminish that multiplicity, or rank identities into some preordained or definitive hierarchy will inevitably end in distortion. As wrote the late American novelist Kurt Vonnegut: 'We are the sum of the things we pretend to be. So we must be careful what we pretend to be' (1961: v).

These complexities should neither paralyse nor petrify us, but simply make us aware that any attempt to categorise the diversity of human experience is inevitably flawed even when it is necessary.

Two of the many principles that might help navigate this complexity are first that everyone has the right to call themselves whatever they want and that second, with this right comes at least one responsibility – that if you want your identity to have any broader relevance beyond yourself it must at least make sense. In the words of philosopher, Anthony Appiah: 'It must be an identity constructed in response to facts outside oneself, things that are beyond one's own choices' (2005: 18).

Far from being neutral, these facts are rooted in material conditions that confer power and privilege in relation to one another. This brings us to the third point. The means by which things are categorised as core or marginal is shaped by who has the resources and capacity to frame that discussion with all the limitations inherent and implied in that state of affairs. What masquerades as core is all too often simply 'powerful'. Any push for diversity that refuses to challenge that power structure is really not worthy of the name. We don't need institutions that look different and behave the same. To create them is to mistake 'equal opportunities' for 'photo opportunities'.

There are two main problems with this. First, like most marketing ploys, it leaves many people cynical and paves the way for a backlash. It exposes the few beneficiaries to charges of tokenism and its lack of integrity lends succour to those opponents of equal opportunities. Second, it is of absolutely no use to those who are underrepresented to have the underlying reasons why some groups are not recruited, promoted or retained, left intact, while a few identifiable faces are moved to more prominent places. Such institutional cosmetics ill-disguise a social and pervasive mindset in which the margins are subject to relentless examination while the core coasts by with eternal presumption. Nobody ever asks: 'when did you first realise you were straight?' or 'how do you balance fatherhood and work?'. As the African proverb states: 'Only when the lions write history, will the hunters cease to be the heroes.'

The hunters are still out there. Nowhere has this been more evident than in discussions about the position of Islam and Muslims both in Britain in particular and Europe in general. In Britain, the emergence of 'home-grown bombers' from the Muslim community has been mentioned as though this is a new development, when in fact Britain has been growing its own bombers for years. Indeed, there is a whole evening dedicated to burning one – it's called Guy Fawkes Night. Meanwhile the government has frowned upon Pakistani arranged marriages to foreigners while somehow forgetting that arranged marriage forms the basis for many British literary classics and that, of the six British monarchs of the last century, five married foreigners and most of those unions were arranged.

Following rioting by black and French-Arab youth in France in 2007, Jacques Myard, a nationalist deputy, explained the disturbances thus: 'The problem is not economic. The reality is not economic. The reality is that an anti-French ethno-cultural bias from a foreign society has taken root on French soil' (cited in Younge 2007: 26).

The French may need to import many things – from trashy popular films to fast food – but the one thing they have long produced themselves is a culture of riotous assembly. There is nothing foreign about rioting in France – the country was built on a riot.

All of which is to say that, for better and for worse, Muslims in Europe are far more European than many of their fellow Europeans care to admit. Given the colonial links, the prevalence of Western culture in the global arena and the power of the Western economy this should really come as no surprise. For many it is the only place they know. And yet in Britain each time a terror cell is found the media gasp at the discovery that the bombers or potential bombers played cricket, worked in chip shops and supported Manchester United.

So those who exist at the margins have little option but to be aware of their marginality; those who occupy the centre have the luxury of assuming that if people are not aware of their experiences, at the very least they should be. As Cady Roth, the protagonist of restricted growth, from Armistead Maupin's novel, *Maybe the Moon* wisely remarks:

> When you're my size and not being tormented by elevator buttons, water fountains and ATMs you spend your life accommodating the sensibilities of 'normal' people. You learn to bury your own feelings and honour theirs in the hope that they'll meet you halfway. It becomes your job, and yours alone, to explain, to ignore, to forgive – over and over again. There's no way you can get around this. You do it if you want to have a life and not spend it being corroded by your own anger. You do it if you want to belong to the human race.
>
> *1992: 111*

But all too often those at the core do not see the need to meet people halfway and thereby fail to recognise that everyone else is doing all the travelling. For them, being at the core is an objective position in itself. It lends them not a perspective but an orthodoxy in which every food with which they are unfamiliar is 'ethnic food' and every month is their history month. As noted historian E. H. Carr (1961: 36–37) argued:

> Every human being at every stage of history or pre-history is born into a society and from his earliest years is moulded by that society . . . Both language and environment help to determine the character of his thought; his earliest ideas come to him from others . . . the individual apart from society would be both speechless and mindless.

Denial in this regard raises two crucial problems. First, that those at the core are likely to remain cripplingly unaware of their bias and second that the inability to recognise and interrogate one's own perspective paves the way for their experiences to be evoked, not as an identity, but as a grievance. The only political force prepared to talk about whiteness in Britain is the BNP; similarly it is left to the fox hunters to defend the countryside; and the *Daily Mail* to talk about Middle England. Each, in their way, will evoke the threat of marginalisation as a pretext to build a fortress around the core.

This sense of siege usually demands a bespoke reality. Every victim needs an aggressor; every aggressor has a tool of oppression. And in the event that these do not exist they must be invented. In this case the aggressor is usually the 'liberal establishment' and their instrument of social control is 'political correctness'.

Given the rightward shift in politics and economics over the last 30 years it is difficult to work out quite where this establishment resides. Finding a working definition of political correctness is not easy, which gives it the added benefit of meaning anything people want it to mean.

In the space of one month in 2006 'political correctness' was used in the British press on average ten times a day – twice as frequently as 'Islamophobia', three times as often as 'homophobia' and four times as often as 'sexism'. During that period it referred to the ill-treatment of rabbits; the teaching of Gaelic; Mozart's opera, *La Clemenza di Tito*; a flower show in Paris and the naming of the Mazda3 MPS.

Place of Power

But what they are generally complaining about are constraints on their rights to be offensive and insensitive without conseqeunce. In the past racially offensive remarks, comments about your female colleague's breasts or 'spastic' jokes were considered part and parcel of daily banter both in and outside the workplace. Now they are not. We have abandoned them for the same reason we no longer burn witches at the stake or stick orphaned children in the poor house. We have moved on. Values change, societies develop and their language and behaviour evolves with them. That's not political correctness but social and political progress. It was not imposed by liberal diktat, but established by civic consensus.

This brings me to my final point, that the relationship between the margins and the core are in constant flux. And while specific changes have to be assessed on their merits, opposition to the very idea of change is untenable since it would be contingent on peoples' lives, capacities and aspirations standing still. As Stuart Hall argues: 'Cultural identities come from somewhere, have histories but, like everything which is historical, they undergo constant transformation. Far from being eternally fixed in some essentialised past, they are subject to the continuous play of history, culture and power.'

Precisely when and how these shifts in people and societies happen is often difficult to fathom. It could be a century, a generation or – if we think about how America changed after 9/11 – a day. But even those single events do not appear out of a clear blue sky. More often than not, when identities change, they are the product of organic processes that shift the plates of ingrained prejudice, institutional power, popular presumption, orthodoxy and common sense over time and at such a glacial pace that we barely notice them until they have changed form entirely.

While time may facilitate change it cannot do it by itself. The principal reason why the relationship between the core and the margins changes, is because people make it change. There will always be those who are resistant to these changes, not on their merits but in principle. But in order to enforce their worldview they must perform three solipsistic manoeuvres.

First they must distort history. For if something is essentially unchanging then it must be the same now as it ever was. Second, they must quash all speculation about their future – for if it is essentially unchanging then it can never be different. Both of these stances come together in arguments against gay marriage. As Andrew Sullivan (2008) argued in *The New Republic*:

> If marriage were the same today as it has been for 2,000 years, it would be possible to marry a 12-year-old you had never met, to own a wife as property and dispose of her at will or to imprison a person who married someone of a different race. And it would be impossible to get a divorce.

Third they must ignore all the other changes that happen around them. One of the reasons that opinions about gay lifestyles have changed is because views on straight lifestyles have undergone a radical shift. Between the 1950s and today, divorce rates more than doubled in the United States and the age at which people got married is now nearer 30 than 20. Meanwhile, between the 1960s and 2005, the percentage of births to unmarried women increased seven-fold. In a world where people do not stay married, feel the need to get married, to have children and/or have children when they are married, the link between marriage and procreation and sanctity and fidelity are at least tenuous and, for the most part, completely broken. Such is the defence of 'tradition'; not to make an argument but simply repeat a fact.

So to conclude, there is an inherent tension in the relationship between the margins and the core. How could there not be? It is a tension, in part, shaped by a battle for definition and, in part, by a struggle for resources – a strain between who we are and what we need. Power, resources and opportunity are in play in how we choose to understand (or misunderstand) the value of ourselves and others.

There is little to be gained by fetishising that tension. First of all, if managed in the right way, it can be extremely creative. Insensitivity never achieved much. Baiting, ridiculing and humiliating are poor substitutes for satire, irony and humour although they often masquerade as such. When they are employed by the powerful against the powerless it is not clever but cowardly.

But oversensitivity never achieved much either. Not every nuance, challenge, wordplay and ignorance is a slight; not every slight is worthy of escalating into an incident; not every provocation need be indulged. Just because someone claims marginality does not mean they have to be believed or that they cannot also have power at the core. Identity is a crucial place to start. It is a terrible place to finish.

But there is little to be gained by ignoring the tension either. The relationship between the two is not only symbiotic but unresolved. Pretending that power relationships are not there does not make them go away; it simply means a refusal to see them. I have a three-year-old. When his friends' parents tell me that their child doesn't see skin colour I usually tell them to get their kid's eyes tested. In all sorts of ways our differences make a difference; and in any case it is not the difference that is a problem. It's what people choose to make of that difference.

The journey between the margins and the core is one that most of humanity makes every day – be it geographically, culturally, linguistically or politically. Whether it's a white middle-class kid listening to hip hop or an immigrant worker coming into central London to clean offices, the best we can do is travel from A to B safely and intelligently, with due regard for our fellow passengers, in the knowledge that without A there would be no B and that neither A nor B will necessarily be in the same place when we come to make the return trip.

References

Appiah, K. A. (2005) *The Ethics of Identity*, Princeton: Princeton University Press.

Berger, J. (1972) *Ways of Seeing*, London: Penguin.

Broyard, B. (2007) *One Drop*, New York: Little, Brown and Company.

Carr, E. H. (1961) *What is History?* New York: Random House.

Kessler, A. (2009) 'Gold Medal Athlete Caster Semenya Told to Prove She is a Woman', *Guardian*, 20 August: 5.

Maupin, A. (1992) *Maybe the Moon*, New York: HarperCollins.

Rimer, S. and Arenson, K. W. (2004) Editorial, *The New York Times*, 24 June.

Sullivan, A. (2008) 'State of the Union', *The New Republic,* 28 May.

Vonnegut, K. (1961) *Mother Night*, New York: Dell Publishing.

Younge, G. (2007) 'To Believe in a European Utopia before Muslims Arrived is Delusional', *Guardian*: 26.

8

CULTURAL DIVERSITY

Politics, policy and practices. The case of Tate Encounters

Andrew Dewdney, David Dibosa and Victoria Walsh

Prologue

What happens when politics become policies, which, in turn, become practices in a museum? Such a question was posed at the Whitechapel Art Gallery in November 2010, in a debate organised by Third Text and Arts Council England, one of a number that have taken place in the aftermath of the defeat of the New Labour government in Britain. Indeed, over the past two years, issues surrounding cultural politics and their relationship to institutional practices have been articulated as a contestation of the effectiveness of cultural diversity policy in the arts. In such a contest, one can point to the gains that have been accrued through the translation of progressivist thinking into cultural equity programmes and social justice agendas. Legitimate claims, for example, can be made that advances in employment and programming have taken place. On the other hand, one can point to institutional manoeuvres – containment strategies – that have ensured that demands for change are neutralised in order to protect the integrity of long-held views around 'core mission' and objects bearing 'real cultural value'. Such a framing of the ongoing argument may be a little stark for everyday tastes but politics, after all, is a messy business. The following account hopes to make some sense of the entangled positions, the disrupted careers, the frustrated hopes and broken visions of professional stakeholders seeking change by highlighting what has been lost as well as gained in the slippage from politics to policy and practice.

From the politics of representation to the practices of difference

A focus on the relationship between cultural diversity policy and institutional practice was a key strand of 'Tate Encounters', a three-year research project examining the relationship between art museum practice and the formation of national identity. The examination was conducted through the lens of a study of Tate Britain – particularly, its remit to display the National Collection of British Art from 1500 to the present day. Formally titled, 'Tate Encounters: Britishness and Visual Culture', the project was led by Professor Andrew Dewdney (London South Bank University) in collaboration with Dr Victoria Walsh (Tate Britain) and Dr David Dibosa (University of the Arts London). It was funded by the Arts and Humanities Research Council (AHRC) as part of its first strategic funding programme, 'Diasporas, Migration and Identities'. With a team of six researchers and a two-year period of fieldwork, engaging over thirty-four members of Tate Britain staff as well as more than 600 undergraduate students from London South Bank University, Tate Encounters was a major project. It produced a range of outputs, including as many as forty recordings of individuals and groups discussing issues that arose from the research. Much of this material can be accessed on the project's archive website.[1]

Among the material collected on the website is a contribution by the Director of the National Portrait Gallery in London, Sandy Nairne,[2] to a recorded panel discussion on the history of cultural diversity policy in the UK. In this discussion, Nairne presented a series of arguments, outlining the development of the political context in the 1980s that brought artists face-to-face with curators and museum directors in debates around culture, representation, equality and access. Artists, such as Lubaina Himid, Maud Sulter and Keith Piper, were cited as key participants in such discussions. One of the main observations Nairne made about their work was the way in which it foregrounded politics as well as arts practice. Lubaina Himid, for instance, curated a groundbreaking show, *The Thin Black Line* (1985), at the ICA London. The exhibition featured, for one of the first times in Britain, work exclusively by black women artists including Sonia Boyce (Plate 8.1), Chila Burman and Ingrid Pollard. In her comments about the show, Himid gave voice to some of the concerns surrounding 'visibility' and 'representation' that had begun to characterise various aspects of the cultural politics of the time.

> All eleven artists in this exhibition are concerned with the politics and realities of being Black Women. We will debate upon how and why we differ in our creative expression of these realities. Our methods vary individually from satire to storytelling, from timely vengeance to careful analysis, from calls to arms to the smashing of stereotypes. We are claiming what is ours and making ourselves visible. We are eleven of the hundreds of creative Black Women in Britain. We are here to stay.
>
> *Himid n.d.*

The issues at stake in current debates revolve less around black women artists' interventions but rather more around the changes in institutional practices as a result of the politics in which the work of artists and institutions were seen as embedded. If such politics were made meaningful by artists what was the work that institutions had to do to make sense of the politics that positioned them as institutions that had to change? Tate Encounters addressed such a question by looking at New Labour's cultural diversity policy as a re-formulation and re-positioning of the critique of cultural institutions that had been advanced by cultural practitioners during Labour's years in Opposition. By recourse to policy formation, one can address institutional practice as a response to demands positioned as *coming from outside*. Through careful attention to the emerging institutional environment during New Labour's term in office, one can see demands for change as being repositioned from *political* engagement, using terms such as visibility and representation, to *policy* engagement, relying on terms like inclusion, increased cultural engagement and social justice.

This emergence of cultural diversity as a governmental discourse bridging both cultural and social policy, can be seen in the espousal of cultural diversity policy by David Lammy MP. In May 2005, Lammy was appointed Minister of State at the Department of Culture,

Media and Sport under Tessa Jowell's Secretariat. During a speech titled, 'Where Now for Britain's Shared Heritage?' given at the British Museum in an event hosted by the National Lottery Fund on Tuesday 25 October 2005, Lammy underlined the operational implications for museums of policies focusing on diversity:

> If it is to play the role I am articulating for it, as custodians not just of national assets but of national ideas, then the sector itself must do more to reflect Britain today. Our cultural institutions have made positive progress in diversifying their audiences, and as we are in the British Museum, I would give credit to programs like *Africa 05* and other projects, which have had a measurable impact on reaching a wider cross-section of society. Others are doing likewise – I have seen at first hand the V&A and the National Portrait Gallery's commitment to diversity.
>
> *Lammy 2005*

Diversity became rendered then in terms of aiming to 'reflect Britain today'. Such a call for reflection can be seen as a modulation of a more radical position, not so much to 'reflect' the society but to transform it. A politics of visibility and representation, set out by Lubaina Himid as a 'call to arms and a smashing of stereotypes' became re-formulated as cultural diversity policy. The recognition of a visible difference in institutions through the differentialisation of power became rendered as recognisable (read 'auditable') diversity in staff, exhibitions and audiences. Blackness as a political position from which to critique power (black as subaltern), was thereby re-read as blackness as skin-colour. Moves towards promoting the importance of skin-colour are what Frantz Fanon referred to as 'epidermalization' – the reading of identity through skin-colour (Fanon 1967). It is by such sleights of hand that political visibility becomes rendered as no more than noting the visible markers of diversity. Such a shift has been remarked upon by cultural commentator Kobena Mercer as a detachment from the radicalism of 'difference' in order to attain the de-radicalised aims of diversity (Mercer 1994). Instead of critiques of racialised power structures emerging from groups such as Black Women artists, policy formulation became based on a problematisation of how far those structures offered visible markers of diversity. The structures themselves remained firmly intact.

Himid's statement 'Black women . . . are here to stay' could be seen as having been made meaningful not so much in terms of making a difference to the way that power structures were organised but much more in terms of a measure of how effective those power structures were in delivering specified policy aims. As such, the political formulation was turned on its head – not black women as *subjects* wielding power but black women as the *objects* of policy instruments. As such, the presence of black women, as well as others figured to inhabit the Black Asian Minority and Ethnic (BAME) category, became reflected in institutional policy development areas.

The case in point in cultural diversity policy is that the classification of people by race and/or ethnicity through demographic census, when correlated against other behavioural quantitative measures, such as museum attendance, shifts the problem from the museum to the targeted group as if something in the culture of the non-attendees stops them valuing the cultural offer in British institutions. In the most blatant case the problem is assumed to be something to do with their skin colour. The rendering of race as a problem in societal terms is then responded to culturally by the development of policies which direct the museum to target BAME audiences. Such a common-sense view of who is at the centre and the margins of cultural participation misses out on the all important (analytic and political) stages of who is

" help conflict race

defining the initial quantitative demographic correlation as a problem, in what terms and for what purposes. Thus the translation of politics into policies and practices gets short-circuited by a racialised demographic concealing the real and lived politics of difference and sameness. In the view of the Tate Encounters research, racialised forms of classification that attempt to define the life experience of individuals and the social life of associative and interest groups in terms of the culture of imagined or existing communities have to be viewed with a high degree of scepticism. From the Tate Encounters point of view, it is more fruitful to begin with accounts of difference which recognise the subjectively authored view of both the embodied voice of the museum and that of any potential audience. Such a position, as Raymond Williams (1965) and Stuart Hall (2006) have acknowledged in their differing ways, is a necessary but slow process of building new shared descriptions and insisting upon multiple histories through a process of new offerings, contestations and adjustments.

Cultural diversity policies of the last decade in Britain have notably been translated into the practice of targeting individuals and groups according to BAME categories in the belief that this produces a more inclusive and equal society. Targeting, coupled with monitoring and auditing practices, represents a form of cultural instrumentalism, which was championed by the British New Labour government (1997–2010) as a means of achieving greater social cohesion. Whilst the intentions that lie behind such targeting strategies reflected a democratic impulse – equality in access and participation in culture – the outcomes and effects were limiting precisely because the policy further reproduced the division between BAME and everything that it is not. Thus cultural diversity policy, framed within a multicultural view of society, may produce no lasting transformation of knowledge, imagination or creative practice within the social body. This policy of targeting had, and continues to have, another limiting consequence when coupled with the museum's adoption of commercial marketing practices reliant on segmentation models of consumption which were, over the same period, aggressively imported into cultural organisational thinking. The problem with the concept of a segmented market for culture is that it reduces the relationship of active creative communication to that of product and consumer: the market decides and divides according to the principle of exchange. Over the last two decades, museums in Britain have experienced a marked rise in attendance and media popularity, and in relationship to the now eclipsed New Labour cultural policy emphasis upon social inclusion, the growth in visitor numbers could be enlisted to support the view that the historical division between elite and popular culture was being overcome. From the point of view of trying to get closer to understanding visitor experience and the museum's engagement with its publics, the consumer-led museum produces and measures the audience in terms of the segmented market. In the commodified museum, cultural diversity is primarily understood as the process of achieving greater market reach at the margins of the market.

Cultural policy and institutional structures

Analytical models from Science and Technology studies, in particular Actor Network Theory (Latour 2007), became influential in the final synthesis of the three strands of the Tate Encounters analysis[3] which attempted to describe the movement of cultural diversity from politics, to policy and to the practices of Tate Britain. In this analytic synthesis the conclusion was reached that to understand Tate Britain as a single institution, with a transparent organisational structure, capable of a direct translation of policy into operational practices, would not explain the research data and more specifically would not explain Tate's 'diversity practices'. The research had shown that notions of cultural diversity, in politics, in policy and in practice, were constituted within networks of differing type and reach. Such networks within the organisation had variable connections between them, both inside and beyond Tate Britain.

It was significant to note that the transmission of cultural diversity 'messages', most clearly those closest to an official political source, travelled very quickly and directly from government through to all of Tate Britain's internal networks, while other translations of diversity policy in the dedicated practices of gallery education, for example, circulated in smaller, local and ultimately closed networks. The research framing of organisational operations in terms of knowledge practices and local networks is, in part, a revised way of talking about conventional departmental organisation and the 'normal' divisions of specialist knowledge and practice. However, such a framing also opens out the way to thinking about public museums in terms of both local and distributed networks. It is to think about the museum, in Britain, as others have (Grenfell and Hardy 2007) as extending beyond its walls to include: the permanent civil service, art markets, the professional art world, cultural practitioners, dimensions of broadcast and publishing media and others. In these networks, people and things, such as the objects of collection, ideas and policies, are all active elements, with varying degrees of agency in determining what a particular network does and doesn't do.

The organisational structure of Tate Britain and other museums reflects, and remains largely based upon, a hierarchy of expertise in taste and viewing, which travels within such networks as described. At Tate Britain, the main outline of the curatorial network largely remains based upon the intellectual legacy of European Modernism, although such a position is increasingly under strain from globalising processes within and beyond art practice and art markets. In the European-founded version of International Modernism, the established route or flow of value remains defined by the production of art (the supply side of value), expressed in terms of the vision of the artist, the intermediaries of gallery owners, dealers and collectors, together with the authority of public curators and academics. The art museum is, however, part of both supply and demand, the production and consumption of art, and, because of this, it performs a complex set of mediation tasks in relaying cultural value. What is demonstrable from the organisational study are the separations and breaks between the supply and demand sides of cultural value in which the manufacture of audience through marketing, publicity, media and education belongs to a subordinate set of network processes. The managed separation of the museum's participation in the creation of the value of the work of art, from its participation in the construction of audience, serves to mask the private exchange value of art through the naturalisation of the figure of the artist.

Maintaining the myth of the artist remains a puzzle given contemporary interest in the constructedness and transparency of all things and brings forth the question of why the art museum does not do more to develop practices which reveal its own part in the construction of cultural value. In continuing the curatorial dominance of European Modernism, Tate Britain continues to relay the one-way flow of the cultural message to a recurrent audience imagined as the universal viewer, whilst at the same time segmenting its audience as so many consuming social categories such as 'art lovers' or 'mums and children'. In this audience typology, caught in a contradiction between the market and an older public mission, those who do not attend the museum as art lovers or consumers are deemed to be in the margins and this, unfortunately, is where people classified as black, Asian, minority or ethnic are consigned. This process is so profoundly naturalised, because the majority of museum professionals share the same cultural myth and practice logic of the one-way direction of the cultural message.

Post-identity practices of viewing

In the first report of the project to the AHRC in January 2008, Tate Encounters acknowledged that its original thinking about one of the key subject groups in the study had dramatically changed. After a three-month pilot project the subtitle of the original research application, 'Black and Asian Identities', was dropped and the project title shortened to 'Tate Encounters: Britishness and Visual Culture'. This did not represent a retreat from an identification with what has historically been termed black and Asian British cultural politics, nor a change of heart about investigating migration and Diaspora as a means of understanding Tate Britain. What it did represent was a direct response to the practical engagement with voluntary undergraduate participants from London South Bank University (LSBU) who demonstrated a clear resistance to any engagement with the art museum and the research project based upon an identification cast in terms of race or ethnicity. This was overwhelmingly borne out in subsequent sustained participation. The two criteria for voluntary participation had been that participants or their families had migrated to Britain and that they were the first in their immediate family to enter higher education. The criteria produced a wide set of Diasporic journeys from the twelve students who subsequently sustained a two-year engagement with the project. This group had family ties and roots in China, Malaysia, Bangladesh, Finland, Latvia, Ukraine, Poland, Eire, Spain, Nigeria, Ghana, Barbados and St. Lucia. Everything about participant engagement in the research indicated that the social categories and thinking that had been established through patterns of post-war migration to Britain from the Caribbean and South Asia no longer reflected the present realities of an aspirational student group attending a university in which over 51 per cent of 22,000 students completing ethnic monitoring forms on entry identified themselves as non-white (LSBU). Most of LSBU students come from the Greater London area in which 42 per cent of its population is classified as non-white and from the published data of 2008, London received 180,000 international migrants amounting to 2 per cent of its population (Greater London Authority 2011).

Both the large surveyed group of students and the smaller group who sustained engagement in the study resisted being 'hailed' or 'interpellated' by the project on the basis of an identity characterised by race or ethnicity. This rejection became the reflexive starting point for the exploration of an alternative to, as well as a re-formulation of, an established cultural politics of identity based upon the conjunctural moment of post-war and post-colonial British migration. The evidence from the research data suggested that identity was not the operative first term of a first encounter with the art museum, but more that identities were entailed and negotiated through the subject viewing positions on offer. There was a greater sense of curiosity and interest in the art museum's practices of the control of viewing than there was a common response to feelings of exclusion by virtue of any racialised or nationalistic discourse. This did not mean that participants did not recognise strong elements of racialised and nationalistic discourses in the construction of viewing positions, but rather that such positions did not provoke a counter-racialised or nationalistic set of responses. In short it did not lead participants to feel they had to reinforce identities based upon, for example, their 'blackness' or 'Irishness', but more that such markers of identity were as much a part of the constructedness of the subject as of the constructedness of the museum's own discourse.

All of the student participants in the study, who sustained an engagement over the two-year fieldwork period, produced their own responses to their encounter with Tate Britain in the form of either a photo-text essay or video narrative. A reading across all of these productions reveals a uniform interest in getting 'behind the scenes' at Tate in what can be understood as the effort to articulate questions of Britishness and identity. These essays are disinterested from the point of view of art appreciation. The perspectives generated by the sustained encounter were not aimed at seeking membership of an art community but rather the opposite, to demonstrate a detachment from the terms of the offer made to them by the art museum. They did this through an insistence upon the everyday practices of the museum in relationship to their own lives. One project will serve as an example here. *Whirlwind at Millbank*[4] is a fifteen-minute video, shot as an improvised fictional story of a Nigerian student's part-time job as a catering assistant at Tate Britain, who meets and goes out on a date with a young female curator.

The script and *mise-en-scène* of *Whirlwind at Millbank* is in the style of a Nollywood film, with its low-budget, single fixed camera and naturalistic, soap-opera story told using non-actors. The film was written and directed by Adekunle Detokunbo Bello[5] and involved members of the research team and co-researchers. The video develops an upstairs/downstairs narrative of working at Tate Britain in which the main character's fear of meeting racism is confirmed by the white workers in the kitchens, whom he experiences as hostile. In contrast, the white female curator, played by Louise Donaghy,[6] is depicted as sympathetic and tolerant. Her role hints at romance, in her suggestion that the kitchen worker should join her in a tour of the galleries at the weekend. In a final scene, Louise Donaghy ad-libs a spontaneous and tongue-in-cheek performance of an art expert in which the curator 'explains' the depiction of a young black figure in Dante Gabriel Rossetti's painting, *The Beloved* (1865–6). The scene serves to underline the distance between the world of art and the world of everyday life, which the drama presents and magically resolves in a fairy-tale style ending by the power of love. The video raises both the issue of racism and representation obliquely by bringing the discourses of popular film, research and art appreciation together as an encounter with the art museum.

The politics of difference and the practices of audiences

Tate Encounters took the museum's engagement of audiences as one of its abiding strands, cutting across the three key themes of cultural policy, the national collection of British art and visual cultures. Working towards an ever-closer inter-disciplinarity between sociology, visual cultures and museum practices, sociological methods, such as surveys, offered the research what might be termed 'negative evidence': evidence of refusals to 'swallow the medicine' of increased cultural engagement; indications that the museum's re-interpretation of inclusive strategy had turned open-door access into a labyrinth. A survey of over 200 students showed that, on a surface reading of responses, non-museum attenders (the 'dis-audience') found Tate Britain a place of regulation and control, which prohibited rather than gave permission to express identity, and they associated it with political discourses of heritage and nationalism, which the contemporary diluted but did not conceal. Again, such a perspective might be deemed as painting too stark a picture in order to facilitate a clear framing of counter-debates. However, the complex terrain of audiences, curators, artists, policy-makers, politicians and activists can only make sense if it is *topographised* – brought together by an act of (political) will. The tracing of relations between these spheres of activity can be given effect through various methods, whether historical, sociological or museological. The question of non-relation, though, of what can not or, rather, *will* not be positioned as open to inclusion, remains of vital interest. One claim for such a body of knowledge might be that it reproduces a reminder that something must fall out of the solution when one attempts to resolve political difference through policy with the hope of realising it in practice.

Terms such as 'dis-audience' rely on the proposition that there are a range of coherent discourses concerning visual experience among non-museum attenders (the dis-audience knows what the willing audience does not know). Such a position acts as refusal of both subject classificatory models and of 'deficit culture' thinking. Tate Encounters has largely been an experience of attempting to generate a new set of understandings about the relationship between an art museum and its (dis-)audiences in order to glimpse the possibility of moving beyond the historical stalemate contained by a singular and binary discourse of race and culture. The analysis of the data from the Tate Encounters research suggests that Tate Britain, like many other museums, carries within itself a double burden, which on the one hand is shackled to the need to make manifest art's transformative potential for the universal individual and on the other is weighed down by the stubborn fact that its best efforts to transform itself into an inclusive institution through widening participation programmes have failed by the measures set by cultural diversity policy. In the concluding phase of the Tate Encounters research, this double burden was understood as an unrecognised contradiction within the reproduction of knowledge practices across the academy and the museum.

Public policy minority targeting combined with segmented market targeting should have produced something for everyone, but, only as separated segments, reproduced according to the existing social divisions of means and values. There is no coming together here, no new mingling of cultures, nothing of the social and cultural body is transformed. At Tate Britain, cultural diversity was rendered across the networks as a problem to be solved. Such problematisation involved an interpretation of diversity as being characterised through visual markers of racialised difference. Fanon's term 'epidermalization' helps again in the analysis here because it points towards the ways in which the work of difference becomes confused with variegation of skin colour. In this way, the real work of difference becomes obscured. Differentiating between the concept of difference and racialised categorisation opens up the potential for recognising models of power and the institutionally normalised practice which support them and thus creates the space for revision and innovation. However, such potential gets lost in the masquerade of what Kobena Mercer has termed 'multicultural normalisation': 'Cultural difference was acknowledged and made highly visible as the sign of a "progressive" disposition, but radical difference was gradually detached from the political or moral claims made in its name' (Mercer 1999–2000: 54).

Within a cultural organisation on the scale of Tate Britain, it is difficult to pinpoint how detachment works. What we can suggest is that the separation of the issue of power from that of cultural difference takes place through the process of substitution of politics for policy and a naturalisation of difference in terms of the products of multicultural variegation. Thus, in marketing and education, difference becomes redesignated as diversity, in terms of missing BAME audience numbers. In acquisitions, difference becomes reassigned as cultural diversity in terms of the problem of the missing artworks by black British artists in the collection. In staff development, it becomes seen as the problem of the missing black and minority ethnic employees in the upper levels of expertise and management. Cultural diversity became a way of avoiding *political* discussions about the need to differentialise power or the possibility of changing the direction of cultural flow. A discussion of the networks that keep cultural flow moving in one direction was displaced by ever more complex arguments about the demographics of people and objects. Viewed in this way, efforts to solve the problem are directed towards getting 'the right mix', backed up by statistics; the right numbers of appropriate people in correct alignment with the right amount and kind of objects to, presumably, produce the picture of cultural diversity for which everyone has been looking.

Here, the case is once more overstated in order to emphasise the limits of a discourse relying on a narrow rendition of the representational claims articulated in some versions of cultural politics. As discussed earlier, the proposition that equality of opportunity might be demonstrable in action belongs to the discursive transformation from the politics of cultural difference towards the formulation of cultural diversity policies. In this way of looking at things, cultural diversity policy in practice at Tate Britain became operationalised as the management of risk to its central historical purposes.

Cultural value and risk management

Analysing the organisational study carried out at Tate Britain in terms of local and extended networks led to the overarching conclusion that cultural diversity, as both policy and practice, became an actor within the networks which manage risk to the institution. Primarily, the museum's educational and outreach work with targeted groups met a policy obligation to engage those defined as socially and culturally excluded. In this respect the museum managed the risk of doing nothing to meet policy imperatives and potentially risk external criticism and/or the reduction of public subsidy.

The analysis of cultural diversity in terms of networks is intended to demonstrate that it is practically possible to avoid the assimilationist closure (multicultural normalisation) and intrinsic failure that comes with the moral and reforming museum, just as much as it is possible to avoid the reproduction of cultural elitism which comes with attempts to shore up aesthetic modernism. The demonstration of the management of risk does not provide evidence of the immutability of established networks. Network practices accrue their effects and affects over time depend upon the conduct of individual practices, which become subject to modification and change. Modification can move towards a more thorough differentialisation of institutional power and away from the uni-directional flow of the dissemination of cultural value.

Tate Encounters research attempted to illuminate the interactions between politics and culture as a nexus of lived relationships within one institution, in which an unsettled politics of cultural diversity was constituted and through which it travelled from policy to practice. The account of the research given here was prefaced by a discussion of certain cultural and artistic practices, which directly informed the politics of multiculturalism and subsequently cultural diversity policies. In the introduction, the first couplet of the movement from politics to policy to practice was laid out and it was suggested that the direct cultural challenge to the institutional racism met by black, Asian and ethnic minorities in Britain in the 1980s, expressed in demands for equality and social justice, was adapted and changed in the formation of New Labour policy in ways which ultimately reduced the original demands to that of widening access and, more damagingly, recast those making the demand as a series of minorities seeking participation in an existing and established culture. In the account of the organisational study and that of the co-researcher's encounters with Tate Britain, the second part of the couplet, from policy to practice, was explored and it was suggested that the research demonstrated how, in detail the politics coded in policy met with an accommodation to the core practices of the museum and how a 'felt and lived politics' became contained. This was achieved by confining questions of diversity within closed networks of professionals, predominantly in learning and education, who were tasked with bringing into the museum those counted by demographic modeling to be not present, those who were deemed by the same typological reckoning to be culturally different. Difference here was not understood as a relational term, but by what has already been termed as the fixed markers of difference, of which skin colour is the paradigm. In this static reduction, people classified as 'black, Asian, minority ethnic' were deemed not to share the cultural values of the museum and hence, from a certain reading of the politics of inclusion and widening participation, to be in cultural deficit.

In detail, the research shows that Tate Britain was both open to promoting cultural diversity initiatives within its organisation, in welcoming and giving a home to the research for example, but also and more substantially involved in the management of the risks posed by cultural diversity imperatives to the core values of the museum. The research shows that risk was managed precisely through diversity policy in routine practices of experts and departmental divisions within the overall specialist division of knowledge. More positively, the research also shows how diversity practices, which address and seek to represent individuals and groups by virtue of the visual markers of difference and hence cultural deficit, were rejected by participants who encountered the museum and saw all too clearly the politics of such modes of address. In contrast, participants sought a disclosure of value systems that operated in the museum and found greatest relevance when enabled to expand a continuity of the value systems of the everyday and their life worlds.

The interest in and knowingness towards questions of cultural power, displayed by the participants of Tate Encounters, is possibly a much more widespread knowledge position amongst those the museum seeks to target. What is needed here is for museums to shift their distribution of values – giving more value to the experience of those who come into contact with them whether through work, study or leisure. A broader range of values can thereby contribute to the knowledge and experience of highly complex objects assigned the status of 'art'. Forms of knowledge that emerge from these varied sources, distributed across networks in and outside the museum, now press for attention and – by taking the possibilities they pose seriously – the museum could open its networks beyond the existing scholars, experts, educators and collectors that currently dominate. Publics that the museum has not thought possible might thereby be recognised as already within its reach.

Notes

1 See Tate (n.d.).
2 Nairne took part in a recorded panel discussion, *Art and Politics: Uncertain Practices, the Changing Status of Difference*, with Baroness Lola Young and Munira Mirza. 13 March 2009, Tate Britain.
3 The research investigated cultural policy, viewing experiences and British visual culture in three parallel studies.
4 *Whirlwind at Millbank* can be seen at www.tateencounters.org.
5 Adekunle Detokunbo Bello was a co-researcher for Tate Encounters. He studied part-time at London South Bank University while also working part-time there as a security assistant.
6 Louise Donaghy was a co-researcher for Tate Encounters and was studying for a BA (Hons) Arts Management at London South Bank University.

References

Fanon, F. (1967) *Black Skin, White Masks*, New York: Grove Press.

Greater London Authority (2011) *Focus on London*. Online. Available at: www.london.gov.uk (accessed 20 September 2011).

Grenfell, M. and Hardy, C. (2007) *Art Rules: Pierre Bourdieu and the Visual Arts*, London: Macmillan.

Hall, S. (2006) *Black British Art: the Revolt of the Artist*. Online. Available at: http://channel.tate.org.uk/media/27535869001 (accessed 11 September 2011).

Himid, L. (n.d.) cited in M. Meskimmon (1996) *The Art of Reflection: Women Artists' Self-portraiture in the Twentieth Century*, New York and Chichester, West Sussex: Columbia University Press.

Lammy, D. (2005) *Where Now for Britain's Shared Heritage?* Speech hosted by the Heritage Lottery Fund at the British Museum, London. Online. Available at: www.davidlammy.co.uk/da/24528 (accessed 11 September 2011).

Latour, B. (2007) *Reassembling the Social*, Oxford: Oxford University Press.

Mercer, K. (1994) *Welcome to the Jungle*, London: Routledge.

Mercer, K. (1999–2000) 'Ethnicity and Internationality: New British Art and Diaspora based Blackness', *Third Text*, 49: 51–62.

Tate (n.d.) *Tate Encounters: Britishness and Visual Culture*, London: Tate. Online. Available at: www.tateencounters.org (accessed 11 September 2011).

Williams, R. (1965) *The Long Revolution*, London and Harmondsworth: Penguin.

9

A QUESTION OF FAITH

The museum as a spiritual or secular space

John Reeve

Contexts: religion in contemporary cultures and museums

'Religion' and 'beliefs' are complex and revealing strands of diversity in museums and galleries and now the focus for programmes and research after a strangely long silence. There are, however, few museums that prioritise presenting and interpreting religions, yet religious beliefs are now, more than ever, a major area of public discussion, controversy and media attention, prejudice and misunderstanding. Most museums and galleries have material that relates to religions and other beliefs, but usually without any consistent approach to it. As a profession, we are still cautious about entering this particular secret garden.

This chapter asks why this is and what successful practice there is in museums and galleries. I am grateful to both Atul Shah, founder of Diverse Ethics and author of *Celebrating Diversity*, and Irna Qureshi, anthropologist, writer and oral historian specialising in British Asian and Muslim heritage, whose views have informed this chapter. This chapter also draws on my own experience as a museum educator, writer and lecturer including as Head of Education at the British Museum and a growing (but still small) literature and accompanying case studies including those in the journal, *Material Religion*.

At the end of *Pilgrimage* (Coleman and Elsner 1995) there are three images of modern, secular places of pilgrimage: Lenin's tomb in Moscow, Elvis's grave at Graceland, and the British Museum in London. Since the Enlightenment, major museums, and especially art galleries, have looked and behaved as secular temples with their own high priests expecting worship and deference from their visitors (Duncan 1995). In many museum cultures this situation has changed under immense pressure from all quarters. In their role as forum and public 'neutral' space or 'town square' (Gurian 2005) many museums and galleries have now taken on some of the functions traditionally served by religious or civic leaders: asking moral questions about slavery, diversity, scientific and medical ethics, war and violence, the environment, gender and exploitation. As tools of state policy, in support of the national school curriculum or in response to public expectation, museums and galleries may now be expected to address diverse beliefs (and the results of fanaticism) as well as to exhibit and interpret the great art, literature and thought inspired by faiths.

Considering the central position that 'religion' has occupied in civilisations worldwide, it is strangely neglected in museums (O'Neill 1996; Paine 2000). According to the theologian, former nun and British Museum trustee Karen Armstrong (2007), this neglect is part of a wider and longer-term phenomenon. It can be explained as the result of: secularisation from the Enlightenment onwards; scientific rationalism undermining the literal truthfulness of events as set out in the Bible, for example; and of scholarship showing the extent to which sacred texts are not 'timeless' but were coloured by the conditions of their times, a potentially controversial theme in the British Library's *Sacred* exhibition catalogue to which Armstrong contributed the keynote essay. However, despite all this, as Armstrong (2007: 14) points out:

> Scripture has . . . made a comeback, and once again the Bible and the Qur'an are in the news. Terrorists quote the Qur'an to justify their atrocities . . . Jewish fundamentalists cite the Hebrew prophets to validate their settlements in the West Bank . . . In the United States members of the Christian right scour the book of Revelation to sanction their government's policies in Israel and the Middle East; they are convinced that the first chapter of Genesis is a factual account of the origins of life, and campaign for the school curriculum to include the teaching of what they call Creation Science.

This is a worldwide phenomenon. As Karen Chin reports from Singapore, 'In Asia, and even in cosmopolitan Singapore, religion still plays a major role in national affairs as well as in the everyday lives of many ordinary people'. Yet the Asian Civilisations Museum where Karen Chin is Head of Education is the first, and so far, the only one in the region, to present religions holistically and effectively in a wider cultural context and with a strong civic and educational purpose (Chin 2010: 193).

It has been suggested that the increasing engagement with forms of religion worldwide is due to a number of reasons including: 'dissatisfaction with a global, consumerist world culture; the search for protective frameworks to support different identities and world-views; and a return to tradition when those world-views are attacked, misunderstood and misrepresented' (Reeve, 2006: 6; cf. Ruthven 1989). On the other hand, the humanist philosopher A. C. Grayling points to what he sees as the dangerous unreason at the heart of religious faith and claims (in contrast to Karen Armstrong) that what the world is witnessing is not a lasting revival of religious sentiment but rather religion's death throes (Grayling 2007: 57).

Richard Dawkins (evolutionary biologist at Oxford University, prominent atheist and author of *The God Delusion*) has commented that before the 11 September 2001 attacks on the World Trade Center in New York:

> Many of us saw religion as harmless nonsense. Beliefs might lack all supporting evidence but, we thought, if people needed a crutch for consolation, where's the harm? September 11th changed all that. Revealed faith is not harmless nonsense, it can be lethally dangerous nonsense. Dangerous because it gives people unshakeable confidence in their own righteousness . . . dangerous because it teaches enmity to others labelled only by a difference of inherited tradition. And dangerous because we have all bought into a weird respect, which uniquely protects religion from normal criticism. Let's now stop being so damned respectful!
>
> *Dawkins 2001*

Critics of Dawkins, such as the philosopher John Gray (2007), argue that science has latterly become a religion substitute and that bigotry also exists among non-believers such as Dawkins. So, in the context of this larger picture, without any comforting consensus, who do museums listen to, how much respect should they show to unpalatable views and which expressions of which faiths (and none) do they represent? By whom are they advised and how much of the story gets edited out?

What is happening and what works best?

Mark O'Neill, Director of Policy, Research & Development, Culture and Sport Glasgow, is one of the pioneers of presenting religions in museums, at St Mungo Museum of Religious Life and Art in Glasgow (Figure 9.1) and at Kelvingrove Art Gallery and Museum (O'Neill 1996; Da Silva 2010). At an international conference, *From the Margins to the Core? Exploring the Shifting Roles and Increasing Significance of Diversity and Equality in Contemporary*

FIGURE 9.1   *The Gallery of Religious Art*, St Mungo Museum. Photograph by kind permission of Glasgow Museums.

Museum and Heritage Policy and Practice held at the V&A in March 2010, O'Neill proposed four key issues that beset any publicly funded curator of religious material:

1. Whether to present objects in a cultural or religious context and whether to include the views of believers in their interpretation.
2. Whether museums could promote mutual understanding and respect amongst people of all faiths and none in their presentation of religious themes.
3. Whether museums have a duty to present the destructive histories of religions as well as their positive contributions.
4. How museums might respond to fundamentalist lobby groups who are increasingly turning to human rights legislation to censor museum work and personnel.

He suggested that debates around these issues went to the core of the meaning of life in a pluralist society.

These questions, in particular the first three, will provide the framework to explore how museums should respond to issues of religion and belief in contemporary society.

Presenting, consulting and sharing interpretation

Clearly a major factor in museum reluctance to be involved in presenting and understanding religion is that this is potentially so controversial and divisive that people may be deeply offended (and would certainly be if Dawkins got his way). Curators and museum educators, like teachers, may feel ill-equipped to cope, be afraid of 'getting it wrong' or being seen as partisan, inept, prejudiced. Despite all this, the Challenging History Network of museum and heritage educators believes that we must 'acknowledge history is complicated and that we need to take risks in delivering it' and 'build our confidence in delivering contentious issues by creating process, supported by peer review, for sector staff to develop their expertise' (Challenging History Network 2010).

This is easier said than done as can be seen in the wider educational world. Teacher anxieties are well expressed in the report *Teaching Emotive and Controversial History* (T.E.A.C.H. 2007) where, for example, non-Muslim teachers in mainly Muslim areas of Britain express their concern about teaching topics such as the Crusades or even the Holocaust, to the extent of avoiding them. Various reports on religious education in the UK criticise its limitations in understanding faiths as experienced beliefs rather than a collection of externally driven facts. As Charlene Tan also stresses in the Asian educational context, 'knowing certain facts about a religion is not the same as appreciating the religion' (Tan 2008: 185).[1]

When it comes to museum anxieties we are beginning to understand more of the interplay of curatorial, educational and faith group concerns thanks particularly to work by Eithne Nightingale and Marilyn Greene at the V&A (Nightingale 2006, 2010; Nightingale and Greene 2010). They describe the work of the seven faith advisory groups that expressed views on everything from labels to programmes, new galleries and collecting. Atul Shah, a member of the Jain advisory group and whose subsequent views have informed this chapter, comments on the impact of curators' beliefs or non-beliefs on their practice:

> In recruiting curators, I suggest that a lack of faith in their personal life can be a disadvantage, and lead to inaccurate interpretation and presentation of objects. The nuances

[handwritten margin note: Same for all Objects]

of faith need to be respected, and where curators do not have the skills, they should consult with the living communities as to how they use and interpret the objects. Curators should be made as accountable to the living faith communities as to their peers and museum bosses. Their work should be assessed not on artistic merit, but on authenticity of presentation and interpretation.

Shah 2010

He also observes that, 'unlike the regular visit to temples, Jains rarely make regular visits to their own objects in these museums. They are felt as alien and not belonging to them, nor having a spiritual significance'. The Jain focus group as a whole was keen on both greater interactivity in the gallery and placing the object in its religious and cultural context. The curator, whilst acknowledging the importance of context, was keen to counterbalance this with the statement that, 'the central role of the V&A as an art museum must also be borne in mind'. In response, Nightingale and Greene (2010: 226) comment:

> The boundary between the V&A as a museum of art and design, a secular space rather than a spiritual space, is often a blurred, and sometimes disputed, issue. There seems to be a tipping point, often undefined, beyond which the museum will not go in incorporating the religious or indeed cultural dimensions of the collections.

This suggests the need for negotiation over issues of religion and belief in museums and galleries. As in so many areas of diversity policy and practice museum managers have to be highly conscious of their responsibility for the scope and sustainability of collections and the interpretation of them on behalf of diverse communities who hold diverse religious beliefs or indeed hold none. These communities, in turn, may or may not feel that their special connection with, and significance of these collections, is acknowledged by the museum or gallery or that they in any sense 'own' them. Accordingly the educator or curator may decide that something called 'neutrality' or 'objectivity' is a safer position to adopt. But 'academic objectivity' or institutional 'neutrality', as Atul Shah has pointed out, can all too easily be used to shut down more challenging, less comfortable ways of interacting with faith communities and religious art.

Some years ago a curator queried with me the need for a teachers' resource on Islam as a religion for a new gallery of Islamic art with the remark, 'we are not a mosque'. He considered it was not the job of the museum to interpret or ask others to help us interpret Islam. I would argue that, on the contrary, it is the job of the museum; that the curator was letting himself off the hook and inviting misinterpretation and confusion. More recent galleries such as the Jameel Gallery of the Islamic Middle East at the V&A (Plate 9.1), in displaying the objects as a series of safely distanced art forms, suggest similar reservations about presenting Islam as a living faith, today and in the past. This is in contrast to the touring exhibition *Palace and Mosque* and accompanying exhibition programmes based on the same collection (Stanley 2004). In 2006, for example, Irna Qureshi worked with older Muslim women in Leeds who, as part of the project *Pillars of Light Alive*, visited *Palace and Mosque* in Sheffield and *Speaking Art*, a calligraphy exhibition in Cartwright Hall art gallery in Bradford. The latter is notable for Nima Poovaya-Smith's work as curator and consultant in first collecting south Asian arts, both traditional and contemporary, and then integrating these collections with existing European arts in the collection. Nima has spoken and written inspiringly about this work and its impact (Merriman and Poovaya-Smith 1996).

What was thought appropriate interpretation and content for a temporary exhibit in Shef-field or Bradford was perhaps not felt to be appropriate for a permanent gallery in South Kensington. There appears to be an institutional rationale for this position. The V&A, like the British Museum in London, the Louvre in Paris or the Metropolitan Museum in New York, still uses a broadly neutral, aesthetic and distancing approach to the display of most of its religious art unlike its presentation of, for example, ceramics, architecture or British art and design. Strangely, for a museum with a strong contemporary mission and track record in inter-active and audience-focussed interpretation, the V&A doesn't include contemporary Islamic art, much faith context or interactivity for its Jameel Gallery. The absence of contemporary art or context in the actual gallery space is only partly compensated by the V&A's excellent website and by the Jameel Prize awarded to contemporary artists and designers inspired by Islamic traditions of craft and design (Figure 9.2), the basis for an exhibition which toured the Middle East in 2010, but which has not been incorporated into the permanent display on a long-term basis (Stanley 2004).

As museum educators know only too well, and as designers and curators surely should know by now, if the gallery or exhibit doesn't do the initial connecting and interpreting for visitors then they 'make their own meaning' and have to rely on previous knowledge, inven-tion, educational programming (if there is any), guidebooks, audio–guides and websites – or they just give up. In other words, the Jameel Gallery illustrates the familiar museum problem of keeping its concepts, structures, contexts and knowledge implicit and assuming visitors know what questions to ask and where to find the answers. If they don't know, then clearly they are the problem and not the museum. For example, the revelatory community voice for the Jameel Gallery is on the website but not visibly reflected or acknowledged in the display itself. The participants quoted on this website were asked to select which V&A objects struck them most, for whatever reason. The first group of objects, not surprisingly, all had a connec-tion with the Hajj and pilgrimage to Saudi Arabia (Greene 2007a).

The V&A website also includes comments by other faith communities on the personal and spiritual significance of museum objects. These were contributed through the faith advisory groups as part of the intercultural strand of a specially funded project, *Capacity Building and Cultural Ownership – Working with Culturally Diverse Communities* (Greene 2007b) and were carried out both after, and separately from, the development of the Jameel Gallery.

The website for the Norwich Castle Museum exhibition, *The Art of Faith* (Moore and Thøfner 2010) also includes the chance to see and hear members of local faiths and non-believers talk about their special objects. The British Museum's more generic online tour has comments across faiths, potentially a trickier option. This tour, created by young people over a week in the Museum, was part of a partnership with the charity Save the Children through the *Diversity and Dialogue* initiative to promote dialogue between people of different faiths (British Museum 2008).

A cross-collection, cross-cultural and contextual approach for other religions and relevant institutions is suggested by the successful collaboration between European and Middle Eastern museums and academics, both online and in book publishing, as part of 'Museum with No Frontiers' (Museum with No Frontiers 2004–11). Both the British Museum and V&A have contributed to this initiative and link to the programme through their respective websites.

Pilgrimage is a popular theme for looking at religious experience, and is accessible to modern audiences that may go to Santiago de Compostela, Canterbury, Iona, Assisi or other sacred hubs if only as secular tourists. It is a main thread in the education programmes of

FIGURE 9.2 Rachid Koraichi, *The Invisible Masters*, 2008. Jameel Prize winner 2009, V&A Museum. Courtesy of October Gallery, photo by Jonathan Greet.

the Singapore Asian Civilisations Museum (Chin 2010: 209–13) where one of the pilgrim testimonies was from a football pilgrim to Liverpool. The Ashmolean's admirable cross-faith pilgrimage exhibit was an important part of an interfaith project (Barnes and Branfoot 2006). Coleman and Elsner's wide-ranging pilgrimage book published by British Museum Press has already been cited above. The British Museum also has a major exhibit on the Hajj in preparation for 2012.

The issue of relics is another theme that can be explored from a multi-faith perspective. In summer 2011 the British Museum and the Walters Art Museum, Baltimore co-created *Treasures of Heaven: Saints, Relics and Devotion in Medieval Europe*. In spring 2011 ceramicist Grayson Perry made reliquaries working with students as part of a residency at the Foundling Museum in London. Although relics may appear initially to be of no contemporary relevance or interest except to the devout, thousands queue every day to view the holy body relics of Communism in Moscow and Beijing, and others visit the graves of Elvis, Marx or Princess Diana.

Mutual understanding and diverse identities

Mark O'Neill's second question was 'Whether museums could promote mutual understanding and respect amongst people of all faiths and none in their presentation of religious themes'. The museologist and cultural historian Tony Bennett talks of 'parity of representation for all groups and cultures' as one of the 'distinctive political demands' on the modern museum (Bennett 1995: 9). A museum director or educator might well respond to this by asking 'how far can we realistically meet the needs of so many faiths and versions of faiths ("and none" as St Mungo aims to)?'. Certain religions appear to be prioritised and integrated into museum narratives or agendas because of their art (mainstream and historic Buddhist, Christian, Hindu, Islamic, Jewish, and sometimes Jain) and, within that prioritisation, certain art forms are privileged – icons and altarpieces or Indian sculpture for example (Guha–Thakurta 2008). The scale and quality of that representation is dependent often on who is providing financial sponsorship for the acquisition or display of religious art. Some faiths may be seen as more ethnographic and less worthy of representation, regardless of how many adherents there are in the modern world or the local community (e.g. Sikhs, Rastas, evangelical black churches, Hare Krishna, etc.). Religions or beliefs largely without art or material culture are usually ignored altogether, such as Quakers or Humanists. Contemporary Druids or various new kinds of pagans, revealed as a significant minority by recent UK demographic surveys, are not taken seriously by museums although their ancient equivalents are.

A major problem in creating a thematic and more anthropological gallery of religions within a comprehensive museum, like the V&A or British Museum, would be such omissions. One reviewer of my *Visitor's Guide to World Religions* (Reeve 2006) pointed out that it didn't address his own faith, Sikhism, which, as the guide explains, is not featured in British Museum displays. The British Museum's organisation collections of Sikh material, unlike the V&A's, are minimal. However that doesn't prevent the British Museum collecting to fill the gap as many UK museums (Leicester, Ipswich, Bradford, Birmingham, Museum of London, etc.) have done in recent years in order to reflect the 'home' cultures of local populations. In fact in 2010 the British Museum exhibited an impressive ceremonial Sikh turban and its conservation alongside multi-voiced meanings in the experimental exhibition space just by the main entrance doors. The permanent displays remain unaffected, however, not least because there is no ethnographic gallery for beliefs outside the main world religions. One exception is the problematic *Living and Dying* gallery with its strong emphasis on health and well-being as dictated by the financial sponsorship. The main Asia gallery has virtually no material after 1900 despite the enormous amount of contemporary collecting in recent years. Who is deciding these display priorities and who still finds them acceptable?

The main faiths are, of course, not monolithic across time, space, generations, gender and class. Different sects and groups have different interpretations of faith. This was acknowledged successfully by the V&A online initiative where every effort was made to involve different branches of the main religions. It was also acknowledged by the multi-voiced treatment on the British Library's *Sacred* exhibition website where the three featured faiths were represented by different ages and perspectives and discussed by atheist philosopher, Julian Baggini (Reeve 2007).

There have been other successful multi-voiced exhibitions. Displays in the Museum of the Bible in Amsterdam featured a commentary and selection of significant objects by a range of young people from different faiths including a Rasta and a Hare Krishna follower (van der Meer 2010). In 2010 the exhibition *Marvellous Miracles* showed Bible stories through the eyes of artists with mental impairments. The Bible Museum is now under the same director as the remarkable Catholic church that is concealed in the attic of a canalside house, now being reinterpreted with discreet interactivity for the twenty-first century: *Museum Ons' Lieve Heer op Solder, Our Lord in the Attic* (Kiers 2008).

There is therefore growing evidence of multi-voicing and the varied registers of response to religious objects. Chin describes beautifully how students respond to the Singapore displays (Chin 2010: 201–6); Wingfield looks at encounters between adult visitors and the 'charismatic' Buddha in Birmingham Museum (Wingfield 2010) and sculptor Antony Gormley responds to the new Buddhist sculpture gallery at the V&A (Gormley 2009); helpfully linked from the V&A website.

The spiritual and personal significance of religious art to faith communities is clearly revealed by Irna Qureshi when she describes what happened when she took a group of Muslim women to see exhibitions of Islamic arts in Sheffield and Bradford:

> Their negotiation of the spaces they entered as well as their interpretation of the objects they saw was very revealing. They regarded the museum space as sacred, partly because they had no other term of reference for dealing with something 'Islamic' . . . In anticipation, some performed ablutions beforehand, as Muslims would before entering a mosque or a sacred space. This was their way of showing respect to the space and a way to prepare themselves for a spiritual connection. They wondered whether to remove shoes before entering, and kept their heads covered throughout, as they would do in a mosque.
>
> Although they regarded the space as sacred, the women were not familiar with the notion of religious objects being on display purely for aesthetic appreciation. Thus, they imposed their own meaning upon the artefacts and could only appreciate them as functional objects. Perhaps for this reason, the women preferred to focus on familiar objects whose function they understood – the Quran, astrolabes, pulpit, calligraphy – viewing them purely in terms of their religious significance and function, and not as works of art or as works of historical significance.
>
> *Qureshi 2010*

It is clear that a gallery of Islamic art needs to address different needs and expectations if it is to connect, not only with its core audiences, but also specifically with Muslims of different generations, levels of education and often with very limited experience of museum going. Few galleries or exhibitions even begin to do this. The challenge of the under-interpreted gallery is well illustrated by the Addis Islamic gallery at the British Museum. Before looking at a single object on the tour of the Islamic gallery the *Visitor's Guide to World Religions* asks the visitor to sit and read a double spread of context that isn't available in the gallery itself (Reeve 2006: 70–2). This gallery is still largely collections-led despite recent improvements. These include some visual connections with contemporary Islamic and Victorian art, with China, and science showing some aspects of inter-connectedness between cultures, and between the viewer, Islam and Islamic art.

A temporary exhibition in 2010–2011 at the British Museum, *Images and Sacred Texts: Buddhism across Asia*, is another classic example of this neutral, object-centred, implicit kind of display: curatorial in tone and purpose without any context in contemporary religious practice or any visible effort to engage the visitor except aesthetically. It asks no overt questions and invites no reactions. Its main purpose appears to show objects that are normally in store. Although it aims 'to show the shared heritage and the pan-Asian and trans-national nature of Buddhism' the actual work of relating the small sample in this exhibition to the much richer array of Buddhist art from across Asia in the galleries is left to the visitor and to the public programme. There is no learning resource or publication and no sustainable afterlife to this project. So what, might we ask, is the strategic point of mounting this display when there is so much one could do with religious art in a world class collection (British Museum 2010)?

Elsewhere there is more sense of engagement and of prompting outcomes and responses. At the Horniman Museum in south London, by contrast to the V&A and British Museum, religious art is widely defined and presented in different kinds of hybrid cultural contexts, such as in the *African Worlds* gallery and as the result of varied consultation (Da Silva 2010; Golding 2009). Karen Chin from Singapore's Asian Civilisations Museum describes good practice in an Asian context as part of a state strategy for civic education (Chin 2010). The book that accompanies the south Asian part of this museum (Krishnan 2007) is a model of how such a collection should be interpreted accessibly and reflects a strong public and educational as well as art historical purpose, combining art and faith, art history and ethnography, ancient and modern.

Also in *Material Religion* Indian educator Shobita Punja explains how she created a course for Hindu sixth formers in Delhi, introducing other faiths including Islam at a time of major political tension over faith and identity. Central to the development of this initiative was meeting with representatives of other faiths and accessing resources of both museums and places of worship (Punja 2010). Indian state museums or government bodies are generally very wary of presenting or exhibiting Islam.

During the aftermath of 11 September 2001 many more visitors came to the Islamic galleries of major US and UK museums; extra talks and tours were provided and some adjustments made to displays. However, long term, have these initiatives made any difference (cf. Cuno 2003: 49)? In 2011 the Metropolitan Museum in New York opened new galleries for the *Arts of the Arab Lands* and the Louvre, a new Islamic wing. Both are likely to follow the usual expensive art treasures approach which is also taken in the Middle East. For example, the new Museum of Islamic Art in Doha, Qatar also treats sacred artworks as expensive treasures in isolation. I. M. Pei's monumental ziggurat replaces an earlier more modest project by a Middle Eastern architect that grounded Islamic art and culture in the physical contexts and lives of Muslims. The challenge in all the contexts referenced is how to combine the art and faith aspects of objects and other media (not necessarily in the same space): the high art and art history with the low art and anthropology of religion. Norwich, Amsterdam, Singapore, Glasgow and the Horniman Museum have probably got as close as anyone. The old ethnography department of the British Museum, the Museum of Mankind, used to do this as a matter of routine. For example, a simulated altar in the exhibition *Vasna* (as part of the 1982 Festival of India) took on a life of its own as south Asians left offerings. But the Museum of Mankind approach and collections were subsumed long ago into the aesthetic and 'world' meta-narratives of the main British Museum.

Now many museum ethnographers have major reservations about contextual displays in recreated environments, although these did appear to have major interpretive and educational advantages. Guha-Thakurta (2008: 157) describes how the Newark New Jersey Museum (which has one of the world's greatest Tibetan collections), created a realistic Tibetan altar which was subsequently blessed by the Dalai Lama. Other Tibetan collections, such as for example at Itanagar in north-east India, have also been blessed by the Dalai Lama. In the UK, Burmese priests inaugurated and blessed the newly commissioned throne for the British Museum's Burmese Buddha in its main Asian gallery and a group of Chinese Buddhist monks blessed the Robert H. N. Ho Gallery of Buddhist Sculpture at the V&A (Plate 9.2a). Also at the V&A religious officials and representatives from diverse Christian and Jewish traditions participated in the opening of the Sacred Silver and Stained Glass Gallery, many of them having advised on different aspects of the content, interpretation and display (Plate 9.2b).

Providing sacred spaces in secular museums for active worshippers is a real challenge. The British Museum provides such a space for Ethiopian Christians to access some of their sacred objects. The Fowler Museum at the University of California, Los Angeles acknowledges that, whatever the faith on show in its current exhibition, other faith groups may wish to take advantage of such a 'sacred' space in which to meet (Nooter Roberts 2010: 92–5). On a training course in Bangkok I was told firmly by students that I had omitted a key audience in discussing audience profiles – monks and other Buddhists, who would want to do homage in front of Buddhist art. A different kind of faith activity in a museum is described by Guha-Thakurta (2008: 158–9): the creation in public in a museum of images for the Durga Puja festival by Bengali craftspeople, with subsequent ceremonies elsewhere. In the case of the British Museum in 2006, the images were eventually immersed in the Thames (Matti 2006). Tibetan sand mandalas are another instance of this kind of sacred 'performance/installation art' in museums and galleries.

Telling the whole story?

O'Neill's third issue was 'whether museums had a duty to present the destructive histories of religions as well as their positive contributions'.

As Sandell points out (2007: 1), St Mungo Museum shows commonalities between religions as well as differences and conflicts. It also doesn't claim to be objective. The British Library decided not to present destructive histories in planning the *Sacred* exhibition on the texts and objects of Judaism Christianity and Islam. This was partly to encourage a sense of ownership and ensure sponsorship from all three faiths. The emphasis was on 'what we share' (Reeve 2007a). On joining the team as catalogue editor at an advanced stage of the project, and as a historian, I had problems with this decision initially. Surely omitting the Crusades, Inquisition or pogroms, let alone contemporary events, would be seen as dishonest, distorting and self-censoring? As it turned out, the positive public and press reaction suggested that the British Library's decision was the right one and particularly in the context of a high profile national institution (Reeve 2007a).

The exhibition did tackle a number of potentially controversial issues – such as Shia representation of Muhammad and Jewish images of God, which were included after consultation with faith focus groups. It also treated faiths not as monoliths through time or as single entities through multi-voicing (varied ages, genders) on the substantial online resources (British Library 2007).

The exhibition also related objects to religious practice. Video stations illustrating rites of passage were placed alongside sacred texts and related exhibits, including Jemima Khan's wedding dress. Behind the success of this exhibition was a very complex process in which at least five interest groups could be defined: curators (all but one from the faith group whose objects they were curating); interpreters (designers, catalogue editor, publishers, learning department); high level faith representatives and sponsors; faith community focus groups convened by the British Library and British Library senior management. Publishing, interpretation and programming were all layered to appeal to a very broad range of audiences from academic to family and community.

While museums may deal with many faiths, art galleries, certainly in the UK, often display Christian art with minimal focus on its religious contexts. Yet this is now a big challenge given that many, perhaps most, gallery visitors will need help with Christian subject matter thus needing, but seldom getting, as much interpretation as Islamic or Buddhist art (cf. O'Neill 1996; Da Silva 2010: 179–85). I was conscious of being highly inconsistent in not explaining Christian iconography and ideas to the same degree as other faiths in the *Visitor's Guide to World Religions* (Reeve 2006), a book aimed at an international audience visiting the British Museum. Should not truly 'universal' secular museums and galleries explain the Virgin Mary in as much depth as Tara and Durga?

Contemporary art can be a potent ally in responding to and reconsidering older religious art. The National Gallery showed this with *Seeing Salvation* (MacGregor 2000; Howes 2007; Paine 2000). Other recent examples from across Europe are discussed by Bauduin (2010). Rowena Loverance (2007) draws on a range of contemporary Christian art in the British Museum collections, particularly graphic art not on display, and integrates these with historic displays. *Beyond Belief: Modern Art and the Religious Imagination* (Crumlin 1998) is the catalogue of a fascinating Australian exhibition on modern art and 'the religious imagination'.

But, in line with a familiar looseness of definition and thought in post-modern art, religion (or spirituality or the sacred) is now also invoked like the environment as an umbrella for work that may not at first seem closely related:

> It's rather stinky and kind of loud, but an exhibit [Carsten Hoeller's *Soma*] that allows visitors to bed down with 24 golden canaries and a dozen reindeer is one of the most popular ever at a Berlin museum. While the goal of the unusual installation is to acquaint the public with spiritual Hinduism, the gallery says the combination of reindeer and the approaching holidays has many visitors thinking just one thing: Christmas.
>
> *artdaily.org 2010*

A much tighter focus is in evidence in the exhibition *The Art of Faith: 3,500 Years of Art & Belief in Norfolk* which examines the long history of religious diversity in Norfolk. It brings together rare and beautiful religious objects from the Bronze Age to the present day (Moore and Thøfner 2010) As the press release explained:

> Within the exhibition, historical pieces are set beside contemporary works, revealing that what was important in the past is still relevant today. One of the most memorable pieces is John Goto's *Loss of Face, Iconoclasts Zealots and Vandals* (2002) – a series of photographs showing church rood screens attacked by iconoclasts during the Reformation. The show also features a specially commissioned film by Chris Newby. Working in collaboration with an interfaith group and as many local communities as possible, Chris Newby's film *Something Understood* focuses on the act of prayer.
>
> *Art of Faith 2010*

Conclusions

As we have seen, examples of good practice with religion in museums and galleries include: fruitful but boundaried collaboration with faith focus groups; more open-ended debate within museums and galleries about the nature of religious interpretation; sustained educational partnerships and sponsored programmes in various media; multi-voiced interpretation in displays, publications, websites and programmes; a responsiveness to public debates while mindful of the museum's public role; an engagement with contemporary culture and its responses to faith; ongoing audience research. An example of the latter is the current research project at the Centre for Religion and Contemporary Society, Birkbeck College, University of London entitled, *Seeing the Sacred in the Museum: Exploring the Significance of Religious and Secular Subjectivities for Visitor Engagement with Religious Objects* and developed in collaboration with the British Museum.

Critics of active museum involvement with current issues and potential controversy appear to believe that the overriding consideration is to play safe and maintain public trust, especially in the United States (Cuno 2003: 18–20). Art museums, in this view, should stay true to their aesthetic and art historical mission because that is all they are competent to do (Appleton 2004; cf. Weil 1988). They should not, it is maintained, be controversial or seen as partial as this will risk undermining relations with the wider community. One can see why this might be the case in the United States for example, where faith groups are very successful at closing down contemporary art exhibitions with religious material they don't like, or having offending items removed (Ruthven 1989; Dubin 1999; Cuno 2003: 13; Zongker 2010). This only serves to highlight the determination of museums in polarised faith communities such as Scotland and Northern Ireland that have tackled religions head on and met with opposition (Arthur 2000).

Richard West of the National Museum of the American Indian described it as a 'safe place for unsafe ideas' (Lewis 2007: 3). Ferguson, in her discussion of controversial topics in Australian and US museums observes that 'visitors perceive museums to be "safe" places – perhaps because they offer comfort or reassurance that society still values certain things, or that society's values haven't changed' (Ferguson 2006: 32). In optimistic vein Ferguson's checklist includes to 'Emphasize and defend the role of museums as a place to learn about controversial issues' (Ferguson 2006: 37). As David Anderson (Chapter 15, this volume) emphasizes:

> Museums have an obligation to recognize the legitimacy of many of the claims that faith groups make upon them, where these do not unreasonably interfere with the cultural rights of others . . . What museums cannot do (I would argue) is to cede open cultural space or the interpretation of collections to the control of faith adherents.

At the aspirational meta-level one might end with President Obama's speech in Cairo to a Muslim audience, *On a New Beginning*, on 4 June 2009. 'There must be a sustained effort to listen to each other. To learn from each other, to respect one another and to seek common ground.' These are the active aims of an organisation like the St Mungo Museum (O'Neill 1996: 198). In Singapore, in a newly-created museum, Karen Chin and her fellow museum educators aim 'to help visitors see religion with new eyes, not as exclusive sets of beliefs but an ecosystem of diverse ideas bound by rich civilisations that are connected by centuries of trade and cultural exchange' (Chin 2010: 193). From the V&A case studies, however, we see some of the tensions when the 'curatorial' voice meets the 'community' voice (Nightingale and Greene 2010: 235). Atul Shah (2010) advises that:

> Museums and curators need to be very humble about their interpretations, especially so if they do not have faith or if they come from a culture which is significantly different from the object they are interpreting. This is an inner quality which cannot be pre-scribed in a recruitment advertisement, but should be a living value for curators.

At whatever level, as Ian Blackwell (2009) observes in his advice on community consultation:

> the process will be intellectually challenging, with evolving definitions of 'engagement', 'community', 'authority' and 'knowledge'; there will be challenges and the excitement of negotiation and debate; [and as a result] the organization will find that its collections are appreciated more and their future is more secure.

A good example of this kind of community work, with a Muslim community education officer at Cartwright Hall art gallery in Bradford, is provided by Irna Qureshi (2010):

> What really impressed them [Muslim women from Leeds] was seeing what they per-ceived as the prominence and respect given by museums to Islamic objects. The com-munity group may not have been attuned to current affairs, but coming from Beeston (home of some of the London bombers) they understood that Islam had taken a very public battering. The museum visits gave them a sense of pride and raised their self esteem.

So we ask for and listen to a lot of advice, sometimes conflicting, often critical or inconclu-sive. We share the role of curator and interpreter so far as we can, but at the end of the day it is for us, as the museum professionals, to decide what we feel is right for the sustained life and reputation of the museum and its collections and in the interests of all its community stakeholders. The best practice described in this chapter acknowledges that a museum is a secular space for sharing views and experiences of the sacred; 'a secular guardian of religious artefacts' (Chin 2010: 213–15). We have to be sensitive to faith groups, but also thick-skinned if other pressure groups, religious and political bigots or the media kick up a fuss. We cannot do what everyone wants and need to be upfront about this and not raise false expectations. Above all we need to be braver and more consistent about evaluating whether our cherished projects actually make any difference. Our main task is to bring together religious objects and concepts with audiences both secular and religious. As Karen Chin rightly observes, 'Many people . . . find it difficult to understand religious concepts without visual aid' (Chin 2010: 213–15) which is why so many of these objects were created in the first place.

Note

1   For the challenges of religious education more broadly see also Lenga *et al.* (2000), Miller (2008) and Reeve (2010).

References

Appleton, J. (2004) 'The Object of Art Museums', *spiked*, Online. Available at: www.spiked-online.com/index.php?/site/article/2496 (accessed 8 September 2011).

Armstrong, K. (2007) 'The Idea of Sacred Text', in J. Reeve (ed.) *Sacred: Books of the Three Faiths: Judaism, Christianity, Islam,* London: British Library: 14–20.

Art of Faith (2010) *The Art of Faith: 3500 Years of Art & Belief in Norfolk.* Norwich. Online. Available at: www.artoffaith-learning.co.uk (accessed 2 September 2011).

artdaily.org (2010) *Bed Down with Reindeer at Carsten Hoeller's Berlin Show at Museum fuer Gegenwart.* Online. Available at: www.artdaily.org/index.asp?int_sec=2&int_new=43019 (accessed 2 September 2011).

Arthur, C. (2000) 'Exhibiting the Sacred', in C. Paine (ed.) *Godly Things: Museums, Objects and Religion,* London: Cassell: 1–27.

Barnes, R. and Branfoot, C. (eds) (2006) *Pilgrimage. The Sacred Journey,* Oxford: The Ashmolean Museum.

Bauduin, T. (2010) 'The True Artist Helps the World by Revealing Mystic Truths: Recent European Exhibitions on Art and Spirituality', *Material Religion* 6(2): 257–62.

Bennett, T. (1995) *The Birth of the Museum,* London: Routledge.

Blackwell, I. (2009) 'Community Engagement: Why are Community Voices still Unheard?', *Journal of Education in Museums* 30: 29–36.

British Library (2007) *Online Gallery: Sacred Contexts: Elements of the Abrahamic Faiths: Judaism, Christianity, Islam.* Online. Available at: www.bl.uk/onlinegallery/features/sacred/wheel.html (accessed 2 September 2011).

British Museum (2008) *Explore Online Tours/Faith Tour.* Online. Available at: www.britishmuseum.org/explore/online_tours/museum_and_exhibition/faith/faith_tour.aspx (accessed 8 September 2011).

British Museum (2010) *Images and Sacred Texts: Buddhism across Asia.* Online. Available at: www.britishmuseum.org/the_museum/news_and_press_releases/press_releases/2010/buddhism_across_asia.aspx (accessed 2 September 2011).

Challenging History Network (2010) Online. Available at: www.city.ac.uk/cpm/challenginghistory (accessed 2 September 2011).

Chin, K. (2010) 'Seeing Religion with New Eyes at the Asian Civilizations Museum', *Material Religion* 6(2): 192–216.

Coleman, S. and Elsner, J. (1995) *Pilgrimage,* London: British Museum Press.

Crumlin, R. (ed.) (1998) *Beyond Belief: Modern Art and the Religious Imagination,* Victoria: National Gallery of Victoria.

Cuno, J. (ed.) (2003) *Whose Muse? Art Museums and the Public Trust,* Princeton: Princeton University Press.

Da Silva, N. (2010) 'Religious Displays: An Observational Study with a Focus on the Horniman Museum', *Material Religion* 6(2): 166–91.

Dawkins, R. (2001) 'Has the World Changed?', *Guardian,* 10 November. Online. Available at: http://books.guardian.co.uk/writersreflections/story/0,1367,567546,00.html (accessed 21 October 2010).

Dubin, S. (1999) *Displays of Power: Controversy in the American Museum from the Enola Gay to Sensation,* New York: New York University Press.

Duncan, C. (1995) *Civilizing Rituals: Inside Public Art Museums,* London: Routledge.

Ferguson, L. (2006) 'Pushing Buttons: Controversial Topics in Museums', *Open Museum Journal.* Online. Available at: http://hosting.collectionsaustralia.net/omj/vol8/ferguson.html (accessed 21 October 2010).

Golding, V. (2009) *Learning at the Museum Frontiers: Identity, Race and Power,* Aldershot: Ashgate.

Gormley, A (2009) 'Fine Figures', *Financial Times,* 25 April.

Gray, J. (2007) *Black Mass: Apocalyptic Religion and the Death of Utopia,* London: Allen Lane.

Grayling, A. C. (2007) *Against all Gods: Six Polemics on Religion and an Essay on Kindness,* London: Oberon Books.

Greene, M. (2007a) *Community Views of Islamic Collections*. Online. Available at: http://media.vam.ac.uk/media/documents/islamic_community_views_objects_in_collection.pdf (accessed 12 October 2011).

Greene, M. (2007b) *Community Views on Buddhist, Hindu, Jain and Sikh Collections*. Online. Available at: http://media.vam.ac.uk/media/documents/buddhist_community_views_objects_in_collection.pdf; http://media.vam.ac.uk/media/documents/hindu_community_views_objects_in_collection.pdf; http://media.vam.ac.uk/media/documents/jain_community_views_objects_in_collection.pdf; http://media.vam.ac.uk/media/documents/sikh_community_views_objects_in_collection.pdf (accessed 12 October 2011).

Guha-Thakurta, T. (2008) 'Our Gods, Their Museums: The Contrary Careers of India's Art Objects', in D. Cherry and F. Cullen (eds) *Spectacle and Display*, Chichester: Blackwell/AAH: 154–83.

Gurian, E. H. (2005) 'Threshold Fear', in S. MacLeod (ed.) *Reshaping Museum Space: Architecture, Design, Exhibitions*, London: Routledge: 203–14.

Howes, G. (2007) *The Art of the Sacred*, London: I. B. Tauris.

Kiers, J. (2008) 'Delivering Learning in a Historic Building: A Dutch Perspective', *Journal of Education in Museums* 29: 20–4.

Krishnan, G. (2007) *The Divine Within: Art and Living Culture of India and South Asia*, Singapore: Asian Civilisations Museum.

Lenga, R.-A., Totterdell, M. and Ogden, V. (2000) 'Religious Education: Soul-searching in an Era of Super-complexity', in A. Kent (ed.) *School Subject Teaching*, London: Kogan Page: 179–212.

Lewis, G. (2007) 'Memory and Universality: A UNESCO Debate', *ICOM UK News*, Summer 2007, London: ICOM UK.

Loverance, R. (2007) *Christian Art*, London: British Museum Press.

MacGregor, N. (2000) *Seeing Salvation: Images of Christ in Art*, London: Yale/National Gallery.

Matti, N. (2006) *Durga: Creating an Image of The Goddess at the British Museum*. Culture 24. Online. Available at: www.culture24.org.uk/art/art40138 (accessed 2 September 2011).

Merriman, N. and Poovaya-Smith, N. (1996) 'Making Culturally Diverse Histories', in G. Kavanagh (ed.) *Making Histories in Museums*, Leicester: Leicester University Press: 176–87.

Miller, J. (2008) 'Learning in Sacred Space', *Journal of Education in Museums* 29: 37–44.

Moore, A. and Thøfner, M. (eds) (2010) *The Art of Faith: 3,500 Years of Art and Belief in Norfolk*, London: Philip Wilson.

Museum with No Frontiers (2004–11). *Discover Islamic Art in the Mediterranean*. Online. Available at: www.discoverislamicart.org/dia_pm_home.php (accessed 2 September 2011).

Nightingale, E. (2006) 'Dancing Around the Collections: Developing Individuals and Audiences', in C. Lang, J. Reeve and V. Woollard (eds) *The Responsive Museum*, Aldershot: Ashgate: 79–92.

Nightingale, E. (ed.) (2010) *Capacity Building and Cultural Ownership – Working with Culturally Diverse Communities*, London: V&A.

Nightingale, E. and Greene, M. (2010) 'Religion and Material Culture at the Victoria & Albert Museum of Art and Design: The Perspectives of Diverse Faith Communities', *Material Religion* 6(2): 218–35.

Nooter Roberts, M. (2010) 'Tactility and Transcendence: Epistemologies of Touch in African Arts and Spiritualities', in D. Morgan (ed.) *Religion and Material Culture: The Matter of Belief*, London: Routledge: 77–96.

O'Neill, M (1996) 'Making Histories of Religion', in G. Kavanagh (ed.) *Making Histories in Museums*, Leicester: Leicester University Press.

Paine, C. (ed.) (2000) *Godly Things: Museums, Objects and Religion*, London: Cassell.

Punja, S. (2010) 'Teaching Comparative Religions in India through Heritage', *Material Religion* 6 (2): 156–65.

Qureshi, I. (2010) 'Faith Exhibitions from a Muslim Audience Perspective'. Paper presented at *From the Margins to the Core? Exploring the Shifting Roles and Increasing Significance of Diversity and Equality in Contemporary Museum and Heritage Policy and Practice*, Victoria and Albert Museum, March.

Reeve, J. (2006) *Visitor's Guide to World Religions*, London: British Museum Press.

Reeve, J. (ed.) (2007) *Sacred: Books of the Three Faiths: Judaism, Christianity, Islam*, London: British Library.

Reeve, J. (2007a) 'Sacred – Discover What We Share: Exhibition at the British Library', *Material Religion* 4(2): 255–8.

Reeve, J. (2010) 'Editorial', *Material Religion*, special education issue, 6(2): 142–55.

Ruthven, M. (1989) *The Divine Supermarket: Travels in Search of the Soul of America*, London: Chatto.

Sandell, R. (2007) *Museums, Prejudice and the Reframing of Difference*, London: Routledge.

Shah, A. (2010) 'Faith in Museums'. Paper presented at *From the Margins to the Core? Exploring the Shifting Roles and Increasing Significance of Diversity and Equality in Contemporary Museum and Heritage Policy and Practice*, Victoria and Albert Museum, March.

Stanley, T. (2004) *Palace & Mosque: Islamic Art from the V&A*, London: V&A. Online. Available at: www.vam.ac.uk/collections/asia/islamic_gall/touring_exhib/index.html (accessed 8 September 2011).

Tan, C. (2008) 'Teaching of Religious Knowledge in a Plural Society: The Case for Singapore', *International Review of Education* 54: 175–91. Online. Available at: www.bl.uk/onlinegallery/features/sacred/homepage.html (accessed 8 September 2011).

T.E.A.C.H. (2007) 'Teaching Emotive and Controversial History', London: The Historical Association. Online. Available at: www.history.org.uk/resources/primary_guide_780_53.html (accessed 21 October 2010).

van der Meer, M. N. (2010) 'The Biblical Museum, Amsterdam', *Material Religion* 6(1): 132–5.

Weil, S. E. (1988) 'The Proper Business of the Museum: Ideas or Things?', in S. E. Weil (1990) *Rethinking the Museum*, Washington and London: Smithsonian Institution Press: 43 56.

Wingfield, C. (2010) 'Touching the Buddha: Encounters with a Charismatic Object', in S. H. Dudley (ed.) *Museum Materialities: Objects, Engagements, Interpretations*, London: Routledge: 53–70.

Zongker B. (2010) *Gallery Protests: Smithsonian's Removal of Video*, ArtDaily. Online. Available at: www.artdaily.org/index.asp?int_sec=2&int_new=43038 (accessed 2 September 2011).

10

A BOOK WITH ITS PAGES ALWAYS OPEN?

Oliver Winchester

The museum as mirror

Museums keep our cultural heritage safe. Their galleries and store rooms keep objects that have been selected as historically significant or socially representative secure, hauled up in elegant stasis and protected from physical decay. Once admitted into the museum, objects are kept alive on the vast life support of interpretation, narrative and meaning that the museum machine generates and sustains. Principally organised around a taxonomic categorisation of knowledge and its material remains, the museum project 'conjoin[s] multiple experiences of time and space . . . in order to preserve, order, educate and collate' (Mills 2008: 46). It is this drive to order that distinguishes a visit to a museum from a trip to a shopping mall. Visitors to museums expect to benefit from time spent there (willingly or under duress) and the stories suggested by the displays define the identity of a museum, in turn contributing to and reflecting our greater sense of individual and collective identity.

However this warm and fuzzy communitarian logic conceals the always present fact that museums function through exclusion in order to make sense of the material to hand, filtering ideas out from the chaos of things. A museum's potential to explain is always based on its ability to focus on a particular set of relations and meanings between objects. The contemplative silence of a museum gallery is that of a quiet suppression, where problematic, superfluous or redundant associations are dismissed in favour of a predetermined script, thus ensuring the delivery of a singular, coherent and audible, intellectual narrative. Accordingly, these narratives are always predicated upon exclusions. Unchecked such exclusions may slip into an authoritarian, exclusive or undeniably dismissive mould, intolerant of atypical ideas or unrepresentative stories.

Yet simultaneously, over a long trajectory, museums throng with change as the ideas, displays and objects that are considered important are modified over time. The growth, adjustment and significance of museums as self-regulating and relevant places of enlightened scholarship, where knowledge-as-thing is categorised, is thus wholly dependent upon the successful navigation between these twin currents of stability and progress, with the institution charting a steady course through the continual present as it becomes history. Meaningful collections interpretation consequently keeps step with society whilst judiciously remaining outside fashion or politics (Schubert 2000; Barron 1991).[1]

An inbuilt contradiction

Sexuality and its histories is a relatively new area for examination within the museums sector.[2] An area of research currently in its infancy, the telling of such histories and the methods for so doing are exciting, complex and difficult. A field littered with political, moral and personal challenges, any foray into this area throws up many questions and provides only partial answers. Perhaps the most complex issue at stake in any drive for inclusivity based on sexuality, stems from the inherent tension that lies at the centre of the gay liberation movement and its legacy – the desire to eradicate discrimination whilst enshrining difference (Levin 2010; Cruikshank 1992; D'Emilio 1983).

Indeed, when sexual identity is discussed with any kind of thoughtful sensitivity beyond that of a simplistic, restrictive trans-historical essentialism, the museum project hits a problem. Many recent exhibitions have sought to address the exclusion of same-sex desire from their collections and displays by presenting a series of 'discovered' identities and 'hidden' histories, telling self-consciously bright and optimistic narratives that are built upon a retrospective (and ethically questionable) outing of notable men and women of the past whose sexual desires could be described as non-normative (Atkins 1996; McIntyre 2007).[3]

Yet, as is well documented, the crystallisation of western homosexuality as an *identity* rather than a set of activities occurred only towards the end of the nineteenth century and the simultaneous medicalisation of desire led to the disregard for, and in many cases wilful persecution of, homosexuals (Kosofsky Sedgwick 1990; Terry 1999). How then can museums play 'catch up' without producing reductive and overly simplistic stories of gradual transition from repression to liberation over the course of history, a form of telling that fetishises a breaking free from the closet? Desire is chaotic and cannot be confined to neat binaries and tidy labels. How can radical queer, anti-assimilationist desire be translated into the museum without a tacit acknowledgement of the gaps, disruptions, geographical discrepancies and exceptions that such desires inflict upon the objective museum system? In other words, to what extent can the ways in which sexuality is approached by museums be seen as a sincere and preemptive expression of a shifting political base rather than a rear guard reflection of a changing social superstructure? Just how should museums position themselves in relation to this messier, confusing and far more chaotic queer reality?[4]

Getting the ball rolling: V&A Lesbian, Gay, Bi, Trans & Queer Network

In 2006 the V&A founded the Lesbian, Gay, Bi, Trans & Queer (LGBTQ) Network, a cross-museum group of interested individuals who sought to engage with issues of sexual identity as one of the newly emerging curatorial tools with which museum collections may be interrogated. The group's publicly stated intentions were broad and all-encompassing. These included the drive for an increased understanding of the issues faced by gay and lesbian staff members; the provision of a sexuality-themed public programme; an investigation of museum collections to pinpoint how issues of sexuality might best be productively put to use as an interpretative tool; and the forging of partnerships with academics, artists and designers for whom such questions posed particular interest. Activities straddled three core areas of museum business – ongoing personnel management; shorter term front-facing public programming; and longer term research into collections for the development of expertise.

In order to generate and sustain momentum from the outset, the network opted early on to generate a series of public events that would increase visitor footfall and broaden collections interpretation. Starting in 2007, the V&A offered a varied programme of talks each February as part of LGBT History Month, with discussions ranging from questions of lesbian spectatorship and desire in nineteenth-century fine art to the poetic allusions of young male beauty found on ceramics dating from eleventh-century Kashan (modern-day Iran). Programming soon expanded to include events such as the London Lesbian and Gay Film Festival (LLGFF), delivered with the express aim of offering V&A visitors a fresh, new, personal and vibrant framework with which to view the collection. Events were closely tied to objects and ideas that related to gallery displays and temporary exhibitions and were intended to attract new audiences and to broaden and enrich the experience of existing visitors. For example the 2009 LLGFF screenings were linked to the permanent fashion displays through a series of film screenings that focused on gay self-fashioning and identity through the lives and clothes of Leigh Bowery and Quentin Crisp.

Attracting over 3,000 visitors, Friday Late *Making a Scene*, one of a series of monthly late-night curated museum events, investigated desire and sexuality and represented a highlight within the network's programme. The programme was produced in collaboration with Pride Legacy Project, the event flyer mischievously stating that 'from clandestine liaisons to the joy of serendipity, the art of cruising to radical activism, Friday Late *Making a Scene* explores gender performance and identity politics'. Content included the presentation of *Queer Courtesan*, an installation by artist Qasim Riza Shaheen and a series of intimate one-to-one performances collectively titled *Cruising for Art*, curated by academic Brian Lobel, that provocatively explored the practices of cottaging and personal encounters in public space. In addition, visitors were invited to witness a reinterpretation of Oscar Wilde's 1883 lecture at the Royal College of Art by artist Chris Green and to join performer David Hoyle for a life class lesson which would irreverently deconstruct notions of traditional female beauty. Broad ranging, entertaining and yet thoughtful, Friday Late *Making a Scene* attempted to grapple with concepts that, for many visitors, were heavily invested with personal significance.

Only as good as the next curator?

Yet temporary events or talks are only as good as their next curator and, taking place over hours rather than weeks or years, can merely skim the surface of their subject. Events may be high profile, thoroughly curated and thought provoking, engaging their audiences in subject areas that may be familiar or alien, yet in general they cannot be said to have a legacy or weight comparable to permanent displays or major headline exhibitions. It is the third stated area of network activity – research and collections analysis – that lies at the core of the V&A's engagement with sexuality as a serious area of study.

Hence, in March 2009, the network convened a roundtable that sought to interrogate the possibilities of same-sex desire as a curatorial tool. Bringing together museum curators and invited academic respondents for a programme of papers that ranged from the sexual preference of Serge Diaghilev (a paper delivered in anticipation of a major forthcoming V&A exhibition) to a practical discussion of past LGBTQ inflected displays at different institutions, *Sexing the Collections* offered the opportunity for knowledge transfer, where curators and academics alike were asked to think beyond the boundaries of their respective specialisms (Winchester 2010).[5] *Sexing the Collections* is the kind of event that the network continues to favour, supporting, enabling and promoting scholarly investigation into what museums do, for whom and why. Furthermore, in order to avoid a condescending tenor or accidental endorsement of potentially offensive attitudes, such work must first deconstruct its own authorial position. Primary among the reasons for this drive for context is the ambiguous nature of objects themselves.

Complicated objects

Objects are the life blood of a museum and the word itself is a hallowed museum term. Yet objects by themselves, divorced from time and place, are often difficult to explain on their own terms. Objects displayed with only minimal interpretation can rarely speak for themselves and are easily reduced by visitors to mere remnants, lucky scraps of material culture that have survived the ravages of history and are all too easily fetishised as such. Likewise, contemporary and well-known objects, when displayed within the museum environment are often subject to a heavy weight of sentimental associations drawn from visitors' own experiences (think of *New Order* album artwork for example). These connotations or associations may interfere with or contradict the intentions set for that object within the display as planned by the curator. This is not to chastise audiences as lazy, but rather to highlight that objects can frequently suggest only narrowly defined meanings unless the audience can glean something more of their instrumentality, fathom their function and symbolic value or the ways in which they operated and circulated as markers of cultural capital.

Yet if such questions flow around all objects, these questions are complicated yet further in an LGBTQ inflected reading of objects. Gender and sexuality studies have consistently complicated notions of essential meaning (for example, what does this object mean? Where does this identity come from?) and suggestions of environmental connotation or conditioning (What does this context mean for this object? How did interaction and environment generate this identity?). Perhaps a figure in an object's history was LGBT or Q or the artist or designer could be considered gay or transgender? Likewise a collector or curator who crossed paths with an object may have been a lesbian or bisexual. Yet is an investigation into the biography and sexuality of an individual warranted or could such an endeavour be interpreted as superfluous at best and tokenistic political correctness at worst? What imprint, if any, can such histories leave on a physical object? Indeed is there such a thing as a queer sensibility and are contemporary cultural appropriations and queerings as valuable (or durable) as established and conventional values? (Duberman 1997; Katz and Ward 2010).[6]

Perhaps the initial impetus for a reappraisal of museum collections comes from a simpler, less theoretical (and long overdue) position. Whilst many members of LGBTQ communities within western urban centres now enjoy a vast array of supposed freedoms and the militancy of early gay liberation has given way to an altogether less easily defined picture, sexual identity remains a significant and useful construct. Straddling the extremes of separatism and assimilation, the simple recognition and presentation of LGBTQ histories alongside the identification of LGBTQ individuals and networks can suggest, however partially or awkwardly, that 'we' have always existed. Only from such a simple, anchored root point can the wider complexities and internal contradictions of desire, in all its forms, be adequately addressed.

Up front and clearly visible: content

Analysis of an object's content (what it appears to be saying on its surface) is perhaps the simplest form of fact that can frame an LGBTQ inflected reading of an object. Subject matter offers the curator an opportunity to explicitly and purposefully represent sexuality, especially when it lies at the core of the work. For example Gran Fury's poster *Kissing Doesn't Kill* (Plate 10.1) was created to effect political change for which visibility was all important. Invited by the American Foundation for AIDS Research to contribute to a group show called *Art Against AIDS On the Road*, the poster was originally designed to be seen as part of the landscape of the street, on bus shelters and on the side of buses. It is a vocal and emphatic object, a useful tool for exploring sexuality for a museum going public. Yet its move from the street to the gallery is not without issue (Crimp 1988, 1990; Felshin 1995; Griffin 2000; Triechler 1999; Watney 1986).

Co-opting the style of advertising *Kissing Doesn't Kill* depicts three interracial couples kissing, one heterosexual and two gay. A secondary text box reads 'Corporate Greed, Government Inaction, and Public Indifference make AIDS a Political Crisis'. Through the economic and highly effective use of a pre-existing visual language of commerce, this image communicates a variety of complex ideas, the most striking being the then publicly held misconception that AIDS could be transferred by social contact or kissing. In so doing the image re-affirms the validity of queer desire in the face of growing institutionally sanctioned homophobia and image and text challenge the root cause of the crisis, locating it outside the individual and calling attention to the larger social forces at work. The image challenges mainstream representations and, through the use of the familiar and mundane vocabulary of advertising, AIDS is brought into close proximity to the viewer without recourse to shock tactics. The success of the image depends on visual pleasure and the glossy seductiveness of the representation. In addition, the poster attempts to include a variety of ethnic groups and shows both men and women. Moreover, the intended mobility of this work, which was to be seen on the side of a bus, was not rooted in one community, subculture or geographical location. So successful was this image in fact that it was reproduced in both the mainstream and alternative press, reprinted several thousand times as a poster and was restaged as a music video broadcast on MTV.

Yet, even within the fine art commissioned context of this travelling show, Gran Fury's work provoked controversy. The American Foundation for AIDS Research (AMFAR), an organisation largely devoted to fundraising and therefore reliant on corporate donations, held exception to the secondary strap line. Faced with the stark choice of pulling out or accepting this editing of their work, Gran Fury agreed to remove the offending text, believing that the visuals were powerful enough to get their message across. Thus in San Francisco, Washington, DC and Chicago, *Kissing Doesn't Kill* was displayed in an incomplete fashion. The results were confusing for a large number of viewers, some of whom assumed the work was about the rights of gay men and lesbians to kiss in public. In Chicago this confusion led to City Alderman Robert Shaw suggesting that the graphic was 'directed at children for the purposes of recruitment'. Shortly before the posters went up in Chicago, the Illinois State Senate passed a bill outlawing the 'display of any poster showing or simulating physical contact or embrace within a homosexual or lesbian context where persons under 21 can view it'. The bill was later overturned thanks to local and national campaigning and the posters did go on display but nearly all were defaced by vandals, provoking national press coverage.

Kissing Doesn't Kill thus speaks of a significant and controversial moment in the history of gay sexuality. It insists upon the visibility of same-sex desire, both then (as object) and now (as image). Yet the preservation of this poster within the museum environment leads to an inevitable loss of the original urgency, denying the work its political significance and historical specificity in a manner that unintentionally reinforces the divisions and misconceptions that the poster originally sought to resist. *Kissing Doesn't Kill* loses its immediacy both as a historical document (much has changed) and as museum object (unable to speak for itself). It thus merely serves as a grim reminder of a moment of queer despair, reinforcing a simplistic binary of straight and gay, us and them, negative and positive, healthy and diseased, future and death – assumptions that are camouflaged under a patina of history. Objects, on whose surfaces same-sex desire is so clearly and undeniably written, are thus hostages to fortune in need of contextual explanation and sensitively considered juxtapositions. Such objects mean a great deal to those for whom they speak but say very little to those for whom their visual language and content is unfamiliar.

The back story: context

However, objects that speak explicitly of sexuality make up a very small percentage of the V&A collection (Plate 10.2). The personal histories of the men or women associated with objects offer a broader territory for exploration of queer themes through biography. One such figure is William Beckford, a voracious art collector of the eighteenth century (Figure 10.1).

FIGURE 10.1   William Beckford at the age of 21, engraved after a painting by Sir Joshua Reynolds, 1835. V&A Museum. Museum no. E.2046–1919.

The objects he amassed over his lifetime, which now find themselves spread throughout the V&A collections, include some of the most significant works held by the museum. The 'Mazarin Chest', one of the finest pieces of surviving Japanese export lacquer, originally dating from around 1640, was acquired by Beckford in 1800 (Plate 10.3). Furthermore, the Museum's British Galleries contain a dedicated vitrine to the man himself, a figure whose personal life was as rich and varied as his appetite for beauty (Malcolm 1996).

Born in 1760, aged nine, after the sudden death of his father, the young William inherited his family's immense fortune amassed in the sugar plantations of Jamaica. Called 'England's Wealthiest Son' by Lord Byron, Beckford was a one time pupil of the composer Mozart. Raised in the famous Fonthill Splendens mansion in Wiltshire, Beckford was educated at home by a series of teachers, the last of whom was the drawing instructor Alexander Cozens, with whom Beckford developed a close and sentimental bond, although the depth of this relationship can only be inferred. In the summer of 1777 Beckford travelled to Geneva, a favourite destination for English tourists, where he further developed his education. The highlight of this first trip abroad was undoubtedly Beckford's meeting with Voltaire, the famous French writer and philosopher, author of *Candide* (1759). However, letters home to his mother told of another exciting discovery, that of his passion for a young Genevan boy. Alarmed, Beckford's mother made the journey to Switzerland to collect her son.

On his return Beckford's mother sent her son on a tour of England, first to the West Country, and a trip to Powderham Castle in Devon, the family home of the Courtenays where Beckford formed a liking for the young William Courtenay, later Viscount Courtenay and 9th Earl of Devon. Courtenay was then aged eleven and reputed to have been particularly beautiful. Naming him 'Kitty' in his letters, Beckford wrote that 'of all human creatures male or female [Courtenay] is the only one that seems to have been cast in my mould' and that Courtenay was 'never so happy as when reclining by my side listening to my wild music or the strange stories which sprang up in my fancy for his amusement. Those were the most delightful hours of my existence' (Malcolm 1996: 17).

In June 1780 Beckford embarked on a Grand Tour. Whilst in Venice he formed a liking for the son of the aristocratic Cornaros family with whom he was staying, but nevertheless his letters continued to refer to his 'Kitty' and we are told that when Beckford heard directly from Courtenay, he would be thrown into ecstasy and would write back recklessly saying how he had kissed his letter a thousand times. On his return to England, Beckford moved to London, where he became involved with his cousin Louisa Beckford and the two of them plunged themselves enthusiastically into London's social scene, in time growing romantically and sexually involved, leading to an increasingly complex love triangle.

In 1872 Beckford began work on his novel *Vathek*, an extravagant exotic Arabic tale. Deeming the subject inappropriate, Beckford was sent on another Grand Tour by his mother and in his absence she arranged for her son to marry. On his return and following the marriage, however, Beckford began writing *The Episodes*. One of the more unconventional stories was that of Prince Alaso and Princess Firouzah, described by the historian Malcolm Jack as 'overtly pederastic and the denouement a thinly disguised attempt to avoid making its homosexual overtone overt' (Malcolm 1996: 17). Moreover in September 1784, on a visit to Powderham Castle in Devon, Beckford was accused of having been seen in a compromising situation with the now sixteen-year-old William Courtenay. The accusation was made by Lord Loughborough, whose family tutor was supposedly woken by a disturbance and witnessed an impropriety through the keyhole. Following its reporting in the press Beckford was forced to flee to Switzerland with his wife in July 1785.

Florid biographical description of this kind, contextualising the remnants of a life lived queerly, tells us much about the young Beckford's character, about who he was and what mattered to him. Yet this form of interpretation is dependent on secondary sources and requires a high degree of participation by visitors in order to project meaning onto mute objects. If the visitor is engaged, then a layered narrative can be built up around objects, breathing life into the seemingly inert detritus of another person's life. However modern sensitivities over any potential suggestion of paedophilia within Beckford's biography for example, which chimes with the unfortunate modern tendency to conflate homosexuality with pederasty, neatly highlight some of the potential complexities that an uncritical and pedestrian delivery of a single life story may involve.[7] Taken further, this form of interpretation, if performed uncritically, can imply that homosexuality is a trans-historical category outside designation, a suggestion that is both curatorially uncomplicated and wildly inaccurate. Yet biographical description is the most widely employed form of LGBTQ interpretation within museums.

Moving beyond biography

If one merely reads a life through its material remnants, then the objects become mere illustrations to a closed story and lead to an intellectual cul-de-sac. Broadening out beyond biography to include habits, patterns of living, social interactions between individuals or their collecting habits may help breach this impasse of analysis. In the case of Beckford we find his interest in collecting moved well beyond fine and decorative arts. The Bodleian Library holds Beckford's papers and distributed through these are the contents of scrap books he kept throughout his life which show a keen interest in molly (pre-modern homosexual) subculture, where he noted the arrest, prosecution and public disgracing of many homosexual men, including William Courtenay.[8] For example Beckford cut out a report concerning one of his neighbours in Wiltshire, Mr Seymour. In 1828 he and his servant Mr Macklin were discovered having sexual relations in the master's dressing room. The ensuing trial was attended by great numbers of the Wiltshire gentry and Mr Seymour claimed that the servants were conspiring against him. He protested that 'he had been leaning over Macklin, with one hand upon his shoulder, looking at a book of accounts' rather than indulging in any inappropriate behaviour.

Beckford's collecting and accumulation of such documents moves beyond the desire to surround oneself with decorous, fine objects and engages with the very meaning of collecting as an impulse. To quote Michael Camille 'the history of collecting is not the account of how groups of already-finished inert things are organized by individuals or institutions, so much as a process by which these objects are being constantly produced, reconfigured and redefined' (Camille and Rifkin 2001: 1). Such a shift in emphasis from one man's collection to one man's impulse to collect suggests a space for reading the activity of collecting as pathology and provides avenues through which the activity of acquisition may itself be read as a significantly queer activity. After all, collecting engages with themes of accumulation and categorisation that gesture towards broader notions of inheritance, reproduction and life legacy. Indeed gender and sexuality tend to be understood as 'things we see in images' but equally may be seen as 'inherent in the very structure of relations through which images have been inherited, bought, sold exchanged and enjoyed' (ibid.: 1–2). Consequently, collecting is not a homosexual drive to possess but, as Camille continues, 'it's not just that the unmentionable nature of same sex desire has often meant that the subject had to communicate the secret in a coded language, but the fact that this language was a system of objects' (ibid.: 2). What cannot be said, therefore, may be spoken of through things. Yet the coded language of objects does not remain static and objects accrete a succession of varying, and at times contradictory, meanings over their existence. Objects such as the V&A's plaster copy of Michelangelo's *David* gesture towards a third way for LGBTQ inflected analyses of museum displays, one that puts the museum visitor firmly at the centre of the encounter.

Meaning is in the eye of the beholder?

The V&A's plaster copy of *David* (Figure 10.2) was presented to Queen Victoria in 1856 by the Grand Duke Ferdinand III of Tuscany as a peace offering after he had vetoed the export of a painting by Ghirlandaio which the National Gallery had sought to acquire. The Queen received no advance notification of the gift and the cast was immediately redirected to the Foreign Office and then on to South Kensington. The cast, a full eighteen feet in height, was installed in February 1857 in the newly completed 'Brompton Boilers' (nicknamed on account of their appearance), the first permanent buildings on the South Kensington site. Displayed next to this cast of *David* is a plaster fig leaf which was hung on *David* on the occasion of visits by royal ladies. It was first used in the time for Queen Mary. According to anecdotal information, on her first encounter with the cast, Queen Victoria was so shocked by *David*'s nudity that a correctly proportioned fig leaf was created and stored in readiness for any visit members of the royal family might make. On these occasions the leaf was hung from two strategically placed implanted hooks.

As has been well documented elsewhere, in 1532, aged fifty-seven, Michelangelo fell in love with the adolescent Tommaso Cavalieri. A 2006 exhibition at the British Museum was one of the first to discuss the artist's work in relation to his homosexuality. Some reviewers of the exhibition thought that Michelangelo's sexuality was reflected in his interest in the male form. Indeed Michelangelo's contemporary, Ascanio Condivi, noted in his biography of the giant of Renaissance art that Michelangelo held the naked male form in particular admiration, although Condivi went on to stress the chaste nature of this interest. Sculpted from a single piece of perfectly white marble, the original statue (now housed in the Accademia in Florence, Italy) depicts a physically mature *David* holding a slingshot in one hand, his thoughts focused as he prepares to fight Goliath.

Whilst *David* was intended as a symbol of Florentine republican spirit (allegorically the giant represents Tyranny), its colossal, uncompromising nudity and its solid muscular form have become an icon of male sexual attractiveness, intimately linked with male same-sex desire (Rocke 1996; Saslow 1986). In 2001, the V&A's own marketing campaign used an image of *David*, with the strap line 'I'm Free' in a camp reference to the BBC situation comedy *Are You Being Served?* with its central effeminate character Mr Humphries, played by John Inman. This advert thereby mischievously played with the associated stereotypes that weigh down both the statue and catchphrase, each coded as a marker of queerness. Raymond-Jean Frontain has written on the importance of *David* in twentieth-century gay culture, noting that in the book *Fully Exposed: The Male Nude in Photography* (Cooper 1995) the author prints John S. Barrington's *Jack Cooper Posing as 'David'* (c. 1950), thereby 'presenting the photographer's physical ideal in the pose of Michelangelo's statue' (Cooper 1995: 106). In Lea Andrews's photographic self-portrait as *David* (1987), the statue's groin is superimposed over the model

FIGURE 10.2 Plaster cast of original statue of *David*, by Michelangelo, Florence, Italy, 1501–4. V&A Museum. Museum no. REPRO. 1857–161.

in a challenge to the cultural idealisation of erotic reality (Cooper 1995: 106). Both use Michelangelo's sculpture to comment upon contemporary social fashioning of masculinity. Frontain goes on to suggest that, whether transformed into a set of refrigerator magnets that allow the statue's naked figure 'to be dressed in such iconic gay guises as a California surfer boy, a leather-clad biker, or a jock' or taken up to advertise everything from health insurance to amyl nitrate, Michelangelo's *David* has become one of Western culture's most visible sexual fetishes.[9] Indeed, as Frontain points out, when director Franco Zeffirelli commissioned from Tom of Finland a contemporary reinterpretation of *David*, the artist produced, in the assessment of biographer F. Valentine Hooven:

> a figure with a broader chest, more prominent nipples, and a genital endowment 'at least quadruple the size of the one Michelangelo gave him. And . . . instead of wearing a frown of determination, Tom's *David* slyly peeks at the viewer as if to say, "I know what you're looking at!"'
>
> *Ibid.*

Even in the process of parodying Michelangelo's *David*, Tom of Finland reaffirms the Renaissance statue as an erotic, particularly homoerotic ideal (ibid.).[10]

David, through its accumulation of meaning and layers of association, offers a sophisticated entry point for discussion of concepts including beauty, the body and gender. A work whose very fame is itself an issue of significance, the issues at stake in the re-appropriation and reuse of *David* lead outside the strictly sexual, beyond the limits of a biologically determined essentialist view of gay or straight, open or closed, visible or invisible and move towards a queerer, overall messier and, in the end, perhaps more exciting space beyond inclusion/ exclusion. Indeed the question that confronts the visitor when confronted by the familiar and heavily loaded figure of *David* relates less to the sculpture itself than to the context in which it is viewed. The question is not so much 'what does that object mean' or 'was the artist who made this homosexual' as 'what *might* this object mean and what does it mean to *me* when I see it *here*?'.

David hints at another form of spectatorship that engages head on with the ways in which meaning is made through relationships and experiences. It makes clear that the museum, far from being a static sanctuary, is in fact filled with a conceptual chatter that we as visitors generate ourselves. It makes clear the contingency of meaning and brings to the fore the arbitrary nature of what we deem important and what we do not. As Robert Mills has noted, in these kinds of circumstances queerness is less a state-of-object than a position-as-subject, a

> relational concept that comes into view against the backdrop of the normal, the legitimate, the dominant, and the coherent – and it would be precisely the challenge that queer poses to the normative structures of the museum that constitutes its subversive potential.
>
> *Mills 2008: 48*

The museum visitor is thoroughly implicated in the creation of narratives and meaning through the use of jarring, confusing or 'provocative juxtapositions' in a model of active experiential participation. The meaning of objects and the narratives they suggest are thus shown to be an always unfinished process where meanings are necessarily provisional, dependent upon the freedom of the visitor to bestow significance upon a chaos of things and the subversive potential of desire. Emphasis is upon the

> provisional and partial, the ways in which meaning is made and felt by the visitor . . . a multiplicity rather than a single authoritative museum narrative, and the ways in which meaning becomes a process rather than a product, one in which the visitor is wholly implicated.

Mills 2008: 48

A book with its pages always open

The potential for a broad, inclusive and dizzyingly contingent conception of the museum as a place of relativism and relationships rather than as a pantheon of facts or the institutional gatekeeper of the artistic canon, holds within itself the potential to destabilise the museum as a meaning-making machine itself; it acts as a solvent to the layered and designated links, significances and ideologies that the museum project gives visible form to. It is, in other words, dangerous territory, a field that throws up many questions and provides only partial answers. Perhaps it is the partial, contingent and truly personal nature of sexuality, as manifested through material culture, that lies at the core of a form of engagement that can be all too easily simplified to the realm of inclusion and representation alone.

Henry Cole, founder of the South Kensington Museum, now the V&A, is described as having said that he wished the museum to be 'like a book with its pages always open and not shut' (Burton 1999). The stories suggested (and those that are not) define the identity of a museum. Whose values and histories such pages represent depend on how each museum is managed, how its collection is presented and which narratives seem important at the time. The key is to ensure that exclusions are considered rather than arbitrary, and meaningful in their absence, rather than pointed in their denial.

Notes

1 See especially chapter six of *The Curator's Egg* (Schubert 2000) which discusses the ill-fated Guggenheim Soho.
2 See www.vam.ac.uk/content/articles/l/lgbtq-histories-at-the-v-and-a for an introduction to the V&A LGBTQ Network.
3 For an introduction to the primary curatorial issues surrounding sexuality see Atkins (1996) and McIntyre (2007). An example of such an exhibition is the National Portrait Gallery's recent exhibition *Gay Icons* (2009).
4 The ideas discussed in this chapter were first outlined in brief form in the online exhibition catalogue essay 'Of Chaotic Desire and the Subversive Potential of Things', published to coincide with the show *Queering the Museum* at Birmingham Museum and Art Gallery in 2009. See www.bmag.org.uk/uploads/fck/file/Queeringbrochure-web.pdf.
5 See Winchester (2010).
6 A recent exhibition that investigated same-sex desire through portraiture was *Hide/Seek: Difference and Desire in American Portraiture* (2010), a show that provoked an international controversy reminiscent of the late 1980s US Culture Wars following the summary removal of *A Fire In My Belly* (1986–7), a video by the late, politically inclined New York artist David Wojnarowicz who died of HIV/AIDS related complications in 1992.
7 Two recent cases where paedophilia and sexuality (both straight and queer) have been closely intertwined spring to mind here. Both cases resulted in the removal of works from display following police intervention. An image of Brooke Shields aged ten by Richard Prince, heavily made up

and scantily clad, was removed from the Tate Modern leg of the touring exhibition *Poplife: Art in a Material World* (2009). Likewise a self-portrait aged fifteen taken of the photographer and inhabitant of the transgressive New York demimonde of the 1980s, Mark Morrisroe's *Sweet 16, Little Me as a Child Prostitute* (1984) was discretely removed from the 2007 Barbican Art Gallery exhibition *Panic Attack: Art in the Punk Years* following internal discussions, despite the work's status as a *self*-portrait.
8 For a discussion of Beckford's scrapbooks see Norton (1999).
9 See also Gunn (2003).
10 Ibid.

References

Atkins, R. (1996) 'Goodbye Lesbian/ Gay History, Hello *Queer Sensibility*', *Art Journal*, 55(4): 80–6.

Barron, S. (ed.) (1991) *Degenerate Art: The Fate of the Avant-Garde in Nazi Germany*, Los Angeles: Los Angeles County Museum of Art.

Burton, A. (1999) *Vision & Accident: The Story of the Victoria & Albert Museum*, London: V&A.

Camille, M. and Rifkin, A. (eds) (2001) *Other Objects of Desire: Collectors and Collecting Queerly*, London: Blackwell.

Cooper, E. (1995) *Fully Exposed: The Male Nude in Photography*, London: Unwin Hyman.

Crimp, D. (ed.) (1988) *AIDS. Cultural Analysis, Cultural Activism*, Cambridge, MA: MIT Press.

Crimp, D. (1990) *AIDS Demographics*, Seattle: Bay Press.

Cruikshank, D. (1992) *The Gay and Lesbian Liberation Movements*, London: Routledge.

D'Emilio, J. (1983) *Sexual Politics, Sexual Communities: The Making of a Homosexual Minority in the United States, 1940–1970*, Chicago: The University of Chicago Press.

Duberman, M. (ed.) (1997) *Queer Representation. Reading Lives, Reading Cultures*, New York: New York University Press.

Felshin, N. (ed.) (1995) *But is it Art? The Spirit of Art as Activism*, Seattle: Bay Press.

Griffin, G. (2000) *Visibility Blue/s. Representation of HIV and AIDS*, Manchester: Manchester University Press.

Gunn, D. (2003) *Covering David: Michelangelo's David from the Piazza della Signoria to My Refrigerator Door.* Online. Available at: www.gunnzone.org (accessed 9 September 2011).

Katz, J. and Ward, D. C. (2010) *Hide/Seek: Difference and Desire in American Portraiture*, Washington, DC: National Portrait Gallery & Smithsonian Books.

Kosofsky Sedgwick, E. (1990) *Epistemology of the Closet*, New York: Harvester Wheatsheaf.

Levin, A. (ed.) (2010) *Gender, Sexuality and Museums*, London: Routledge.

McIntyre, D. (2007) 'What to Collect? Museums and Lesbian, Gay, Bisexual and Transgender Collecting', *International Journal of Art and Design Education*, 26(1): 48–53.

Malcolm, J. (1996) *William Beckford: An English Fidalgo*, New York: AMS Press.

Mills, R. (2008) 'Theorizing the Queer Museum', in J. Fraser and J. E. Heimlich (eds) *Queer is Here, Museums & Social Issues. A Journal of Reflective Discourse*, 3(1): 45–57.

Norton, R. (1999) *William Beckford's Gay Scrapbooks*. Online. Available at: www.rictornorton.co.uk/beckfor2.htm (accessed 9 September 2011).

Rocke, M. (1996) *Forbidden Friendships. Homosexuality and Male Culture in Renaissance Florence*, Oxford: Oxford University Press.

Saslow, J. M. (1986) *Ganymede in the Renaissance: Homosexuality in Art and Society*, New Haven: Yale University Press.

Schubert, K. (2000) *The Curator's Egg: The Evolution of the Museum Concept from the French Revolution to the Present*, Santa Monica: One Off Press.

Terry, J. (1999) *An American Obsession. Science, Medicine, and Homosexuality in Modern Society*, Chicago: University of Chicago Press.

Triechler, P. (1999) *How to Have Theory in an Epidemic: Cultural Chronicles of AIDS*, Durham, NC: Duke University Press Books.

V&A (2007) *LGBTQ Histories at the V&A*. Online. Available at: www.vam.ac.uk/content/articles/l/lgbtq-histories-at-the-v-and-a (accessed 9 September 2011).

V&A *William Beckford*. Online. Available at: www.vam.ac.uk/people/w/william-beckford (accessed 11 September 2011).

Watney, S. (1986) *Policing Desire, Pornography, AIDS, and the Media*, London: Comedia.

Winchester, O. (2010) 'Diaghilev's Boys', in J. Pritchard (ed.) *Diaghilev and the Golden Age of the Ballet Russes*, London: V&A.

11

UNPACKING GENDER

Creating complex models for gender inclusivity
in museums

Amy K. Levin

In 2010, a major piece of legislation – the Equality Act – was passed in the UK reaffirming the obligations of public sector bodies – including museums and galleries – to contribute to the advancement of equality. For such a bill to pass, changes in both social demographics and in public institutions themselves had to be underway already and, indeed, museums and galleries have been increasingly mindful of issues of equality and inclusion in recent decades. In the light of these developments, this chapter seeks to trace the extent to which museums and galleries have progressed in their accommodation of gender diversity, not only by increasing the representation of women in displays and exhibitions, but also by transcending traditional gender binaries and challenging limited (and limiting) notions of human sexuality and gender expression.

The word *museum*, with its embedded reference to the Greek muses, implies that the institution has been gendered since its inception. Despite the word's suggestion that the museum might house the nine goddesses, the museum was originally very much man's home, and often his castle or palace. The Western museum grew out of the Renaissance cabinet of curiosities[1] into the private picture gallery on a nobleman's estate (think Darcy's ancestral portraits in Jane Austen's *Pride and Prejudice*). In the nineteenth century, large museums began to manifest themselves in one of two ways: as incarnations of the power of the state, such as the Louvre, the repository of treasures Napoleon looted from the rest of Europe (Duncan 1995), or as proof of industrial barons' wealth and their passport into higher echelons of society. For the populace, establishments such as Peale's Museum in the early American republic served as places of entertainment rather than edification (Brigham 1995) until they were supplanted later in the century by institutions with the goal of acculturating the masses.[2]

Females have long been represented in Western museums as objects of the male gaze, whether they were *odalisques* in gilt-framed oil paintings or nudes in a variety of sculptural forms. But living females were not always welcome in museums, either as staff or visitors. In the 1853 novel *Villette*, Charlotte Brontë records the ambiguous social position of her heroine as she scandalises her mentor (soon to be suitor) by looking at a painting in a gallery that depicts a scantily clad and curvaceous Cleopatra. In the nineteenth century, women were excluded from the professional museum workforce because they were unable to obtain the scholarly credentials to become curators; moreover, they were forbidden to join the male societies that sponsored academies and galleries. In the twentieth century, these restrictions began to yield as museums emphasised their roles as educational institutions, welcoming mothers and female teachers with their charges. During the Second World War, women entered the workforce not only as museum educators, but in some cases as curators replacing men gone to war.[3] Nevertheless, as we approach the present, feminist organisations such as the Guerrilla Girls continue to decry certain representations of females in museums.[4] Professional associations note the under-representation of women in the upper echelons of museum personnel, although, among the ranks of visitors, women generally constitute an overall majority (taking into account gendered patterns of visitation, with men preferring military and scientific museums, and women selecting artistic venues and historic homes).

Feminist and queer theories

Feminist theory provides a framework for discussing current and historical conditions that have led to the under- and misrepresentation of females in museums. Grounded in the notion that sex and gender are two distinct forms of categorisation, feminist theory argues that gender is a social construction, based on cultural and historical traditions. In the United States and Europe, both sex and gender have regularly been presented as binaries, with men and the masculine having a hierarchical advantage over women and the female. Other aspects of society have similarly been divided in binary fashion into such dualisms as mind/matter, public/private, science/creativity and subject/object. This gender schema has relegated women and their contributions to a secondary role in museums, and in Western works of art women have traditionally been objectified, rendered passive recipients of a male gaze. In contrast, feminist theorists have demonstrated that Western gender 'norms' are based on white middle class society, and that gender expression is variable across class, race and ethnic lines, as well as time. Relying on generalised gender schemas distorts history, as when a female African-American slave is presented as unfeminine because of the necessity for her to work.

The history of Western museums with regard to the LGBT population is more difficult to trace, largely due to the hidden lives forced upon so many individuals in this group. Nevertheless, it seems reasonable to assert that there have been gay, lesbian, bisexual and transgender artists longer than museums have existed in their current form, and that gay men and lesbians, together with bisexuals and transgender individuals, have worked for these institutions for a long time as well. They have worked in museums and galleries regardless of whether they have been made welcome (by institutional policies, practices and workplace cultures) and regardless of whether their artworks or histories were on display there. In the past forty years, as many Western societies have become more accepting of homosexuality, individuals who identify as LGBT (as well as the artworks they have created and the collections they have owned) have become more openly associated with museums.

The year 2003 saw the repeal of Section 28 of the Local Government Act of 1988 in England – an infamous piece of legislation which stated that a local authority 'shall not intentionally promote homosexuality … [or] promote the teaching in any maintained school of the acceptability of homosexuality as a pretended family relationship'. This repeal permitted institutions to present material relevant to LGBT lives without breaking the law.[5] Legislative changes did not, however, ensure the removal of other constraints. In 2004, Michael Petry curated an exhibition at the New Art Gallery Walsall – *Hidden Histories* – exploring male same-sex lovers in the visual arts. He experienced considerable interference from local authorities who 'insisted on having final approval of each artwork that was to be included and the label caption that accompanied it' (Sandell and Frost 2010: 160). More recently in the United States, the Smithsonian's National Portrait Gallery sparked an international debate over censorship following the decision to remove a video by David Wojnarowicz from an exhibition which explored portrayals of same-sex love, *Hide/Seek: Difference and Desire in American Portraiture*, in response to complaints by the Catholic League. While institutions such as the Walker Art Center in Minneapolis, Minnesota, have quickly comprehended the possibilities for marketing themselves as a social venue for gay and lesbian visitors, most institutions' family memberships are restricted to 'Mr' and 'Mrs' with their offspring. Moreover, natural history museums persevere in presenting ancient hominids and related species in distinctly heteronormative groupings and individuals who identify as gay or lesbian continue to have difficulty finding their experiences represented in historic sites.[6]

Other difficulties persist as well. While depictions of heterosexual relations are ubiquitous in museum settings, objects and materials related to homosexual relations frequently continue to be perceived as pornographic or otherwise inappropriate, and LGBT themed displays are often confined to sites children are unlikely to visit. Moreover, many museums tend to focus on a narrow range on the spectrum of LGBT experiences. The NAMES project AIDS quilt, for example, has been criticised for its emphasis on white middle class males.[7] The Leather Museum & Archives in Chicago offers a fresh alternative. This institution, devoted to collecting, preserving and displaying objects pertaining to leather and fetish communities around the world, including erotic art, publications and memorabilia related to alternative sexual practices, presents the history and achievements of a subgroup within the LGBT population, so that public perceptions of the experiences of these individuals gain complexity. Nevertheless, the controversy over *Hide/Seek: Difference and Desire in American Portraiture* suggests that sectors of the public are prepared for only sanitised images relating to homosexuality, particularly if their religions oppose same-sex relations.

Queer theory has provided a means for opening up museum discourse to include the lives of sexual minorities. 'Queering' the museum is not as simple as adding objects related to – or examples of art by – individuals who identify as gay, lesbian or bisexual. We must also be aware of persistently (and perniciously) presenting these populations as monolithic – as white, middle class, or adopting a shared set of sexual practices. Arguably, queer theory transcends dualisms, and particularly the gay–straight binary: 'the obverse of heterosexual need not be homosexual, and … the most visible resistance to gender norms can be a universal androgyny, where male and female meet somewhere in the middle' (Katz 2010: 27). Dynamism and energy may be found in recognising 'otherness' in the realms of gender and sexual identity. Thus, when we speak of 'queering' the museum, we are *estranging* ourselves from common modes of thought. The previously mentioned Leather Museum & Archives surprises many visitors with its collection of objects related to women – visitors tend to believe that this gay subculture achieves its expression primarily among males (Ridinger 2010). 'Queering' the museum leads us to question every aspect of the institution, especially the extent to which the traditional museum is infused not only with masculinity, but also, more generally, with a simplistic view of sex and gender as coming in only two forms. Such an approach requires us to seek out and include the stories of transgendered and intersex individuals as well and to problematise or reject common cultural plots that would have us believe that the path to recognising gender diversity is as simple as a narrative of progress leading from 'repression to liberation' (Mills 2008: 43).

There is a danger of replacing one set of exclusions for another when certain groups within (or images of) gay and lesbian communities dominate. Queer theory, with its emphasis on challenging heteronormativity and traditional gender roles, can help us avoid this danger. We must ask what unexamined gender assumptions continue to be unpacked every time we mount an exhibition or greet a visitor in our galleries. More specifically, as women have become increasingly visible in museums, how have we rendered our thinking about gender more complex, to encompass not only the experiences of individuals who identify as gay, lesbian, bisexual or transgender, but also those who are marginalised within these communities? In an attempt to answer these questions, I discuss the interactions of gender, race, ethnicity and class in temporary exhibitions at three different institutions in London during 2010; the Saatchi Gallery, the Wellcome Collection and the Whitechapel Art Gallery. Curators have an advantage when creating temporary exhibitions because they are not restricted to what is in institutions' permanent collections and have some flexibility in obtaining works on loan. Therefore, temporary displays like those under discussion are most likely to represent current thinking on an issue. Moreover, in this case, the displays all involved other themes related to diversity, such as race, class, nationalism and/or colonialism, rendering their treatment of gender even more complex. Thus this study yields rich insights into the role of gender in contemporary museums, as well as to the ways in which museums as public sites continue to be enmeshed in the expression of powerful and often competing social and political ideologies.

The Wellcome Collection

While I am primarily concerned with a temporary exhibition at the Wellcome Collection titled *Identity: 8 Rooms, 9 Lives*, a brief discussion of the permanent collection is necessary to contextualise the mission of the institution and the space in which the *Identity* display appeared. Two permanent exhibitions are located on the upper floors of the building: *Medicine Now* and *Medicine Man*. *Medicine Now* is subdivided into five sections: dealing with malaria, obesity, genomes, the body, and experiencing medical science. In each section, the museum presents current knowledge on the topic as well as contemporary art works that speak to or reflect thinking about the subject. A visually stunning example of one of these art works is a molecule of the HIV virus rendered in blown glass by Luke Jerram (Figure 11.1). The sculpture evokes conflicting emotions for those who have never seen a representation of the molecule, let alone one so beautiful, and it forces viewers to think about the virus from unusual perspectives. The piece 'queers' the museum not because it is represents a disease that has been stereotypically associated with gay males, but because it estranges us from commonplace ways of considering this sexually transmitted disease. The section on genomes includes droppings and fleece from Dolly, the cloned sheep. These mundane objects associated with life on farms take on new meaning: at once ordinary and extraordinary, they make cloning banal and familiar.

Medicine Man, the second permanent exhibition, is dedicated to the collections of pharmaceutical magnate Henry Wellcome. Instead of presenting a hagiography, the exhibit creators have focused on objects that might arouse curiosity, humour or historical interest. Juxtapositions jar visitors out of conventional modes of thinking, as when a Chinese torture chair is placed close to a birthing seat and a dentist's chair. Other objects include a leper clapper, a scrap of Jeremy Bentham's skin, a guillotine blade, a case of forceps, and seemingly random

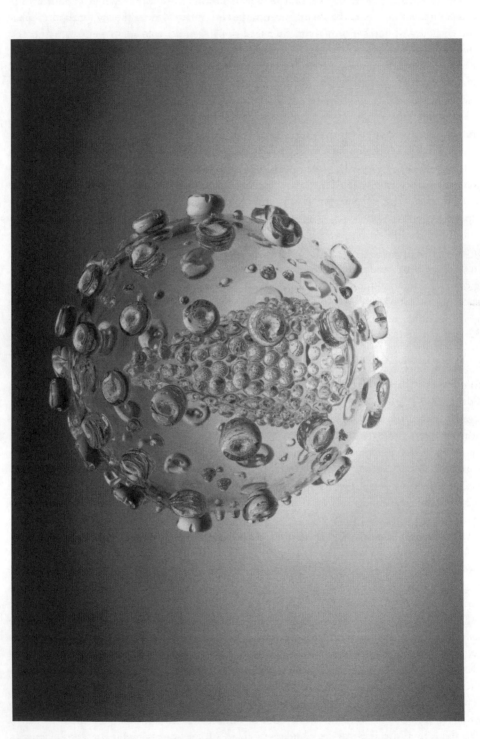

FIGURE 11.1 Luke Jerram, Glass sculpture of HIV virus, 2004. Courtesy of Luke Jerram/Wellcome Images.

examples of erotica. These fragments and objects create a post-modern montage. Relics of famous men become fetishes in the exhibitionary space, while items from the far reaches of the British Empire and beyond reify the privilege of white male industrialists to wander the world to indulge their curiosity. Nothing, it appears, is excluded from the totalising and acquisitive gaze of the collector. The exhibition's title, *Medicine Man*, gestures at gender, given the way the expression is used in various contexts to allude to men who are spiritual leaders, healers, dangerous 'quacks' and, in some cultures, transgender. Appropriately, within the exhibition, all of these aspects of 'medicine' come into play – the spiritual, the healing, the dangerous, and the sexual.

If *Medicine Man* presents the international pharmaceutical magnate as polymath, the temporary exhibition *Identity: 8 Rooms, 9 Lives* created environments for visitors to consider various aspects of identity, leading to theorising about what makes us ourselves. In each of the eight rooms, an aspect of identity was 'introduced by a figurehead [and in one case, twin figureheads] – a person whose ideas about, or experience of, identity issues opens up important areas of debate' (Wellcome Collection 2010: 1). In the same way that the *Medicine Now* exhibit is divided into sections that do not follow parallel categories (the spaces are not all focused on diseases, for example), so the *Identity* exhibit presented diverse categories of individuals, including those who were important for their work *on* identity, such as Alec Jeffrey, 'pioneer of DNA profiling', and those who were significant *in* their identities, such as Charlotte and Emily Hinch, identical twins born three years apart as a result of *in vitro* fertilisation. Significantly, the scientists and students of identity were all male: Samuel Pepys, diarist par excellence; Franz Josef Gall, instigator of phrenology; Alec Jeffrey; and Francis Galton, Darwin's first cousin, a proponent of eugenics. The Hinch twins were joined by Fiona Shaw, an actress who inhabits a range of identities, primarily those of strong and sometimes frightening females – Electra, Medea, Aunt Petunia in the Harry Potter films, and the daunting Miss Jean Brodie. The other two rooms concentrated on individuals who refused strict binary gender categorisation – April Ashley and Claude Cahun.

When I visited the exhibition, the room dedicated to the Hinch twins, and more so, the spaces allocated to Ashley and Cahun, were the most crowded. They took on the quality of sideshows, spectators clustered several deep in front of images and press clippings, while passing by more detailed text. April Ashley, born George Jamieson, began her professional life unhappily as a sailor in the Navy, occupying a typically masculine role, but later made a career as a female impersonator under the name of Toni April. In 1960, Ashley underwent one of the first full sex change operations, taking her current name. Her sex change was exposed by the British tabloid newspaper, *The People*, after which it was difficult for her to escape the limelight. Widely photographed and featured as a model in *Vogue* and other publications, Ashley has been recognised as a singular beauty. Nevertheless, at many points in her life she met bullying and prejudice. The room in the *Identity* exhibit evoked complex issues. On the one hand, the institution's open and honest presentation of what happens when an individual's bodily sex does not match his or her gender identity was surprising and thought-provoking. On the other hand, the swimsuit shots seemed designed as much to titillate and eroticise Ashley's transformation as to normalise it.

The room devoted to Claude Cahun raised many of the same issues. Cahun, born Lucie Schwob, (Figure 11.2) was a photographer interned on Jersey during the Second World War, where she joined the Resistance. Cahun was included in the exhibition for her defiance of gender norms. Not only did she (here, gendered pronouns are inadequate) take the ambiguous

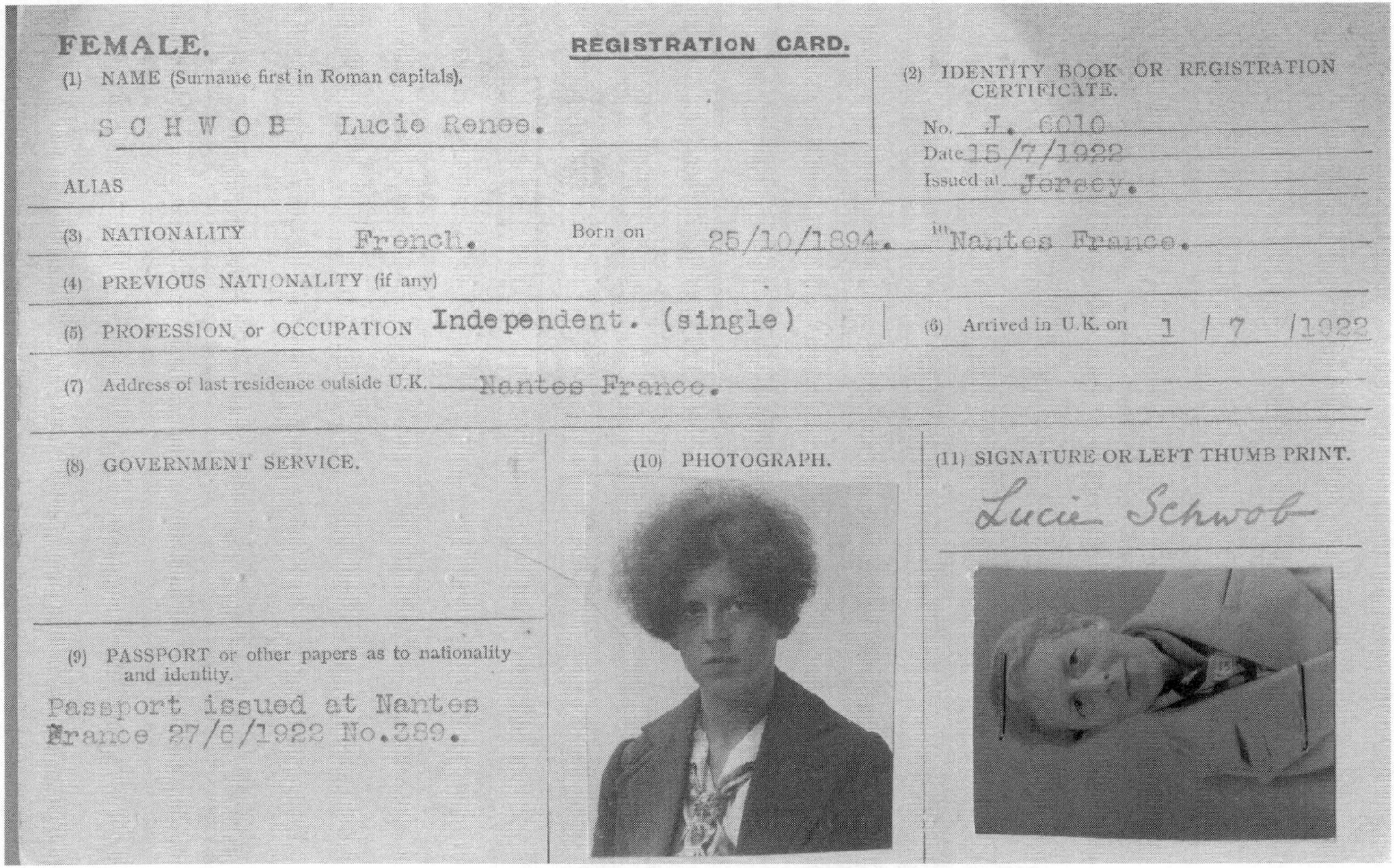
FEMALE. REGISTRATION CARD.

(1) NAME (Surname first in Roman capitals).
S C H W O B Lucie Renee.

ALIAS

(2) IDENTITY BOOK OR REGISTRATION CERTIFICATE.
No. J. 6010
Date 15/7/1922
Issued at Jersey.

(3) NATIONALITY French. Born on 25/10/1894. in Nantes France.

(4) PREVIOUS NATIONALITY (if any)

(5) PROFESSION or OCCUPATION Independent. (single)

(6) Arrived in U.K. on 1 / 7 /1922

(7) Address of last residence outside U.K. Nantes France.

(8) GOVERNMENT SERVICE.

(9) PASSPORT or other papers as to nationality and identity.
Passport issued at Nantes France 27/6/1922 No.389.

(10) PHOTOGRAPH.

(11) SIGNATURE OR LEFT THUMB PRINT.
Lucie Schwob

FIGURE 11.2 Claude Cahun Resident Alien Card. Courtesy of the Jersey Heritage Collections.

name, Claude, but she claimed that she was of 'neuter' gender, wearing clothes that were androgynous. Her partner, Suzanne Malherbe, also took an ambiguous name, Marcel Moore. Their photographic montages explored the seemingly arbitrary nature of gender boundaries that are so carefully policed by society. Whereas the room dedicated to Ashley focused primarily on her gender identity, the space occupied by Cahun's memorabilia demonstrated how her works expressed her ideas about gender. This made her appear less freakish, though her identity drew considerable attention.

The disjunction between the presentation of male scientists and writers who studied identity and the presentation of females and individuals of ambiguous gender whose identities were rendered as spectacles for a voyeuristic audience was somewhat disturbing. This aspect of the display served to reinforce traditional formulations of strict gender binaries, in contrast to the *Medicine Now* exhibition, which 'queers' the museum by instigating theorising about health, the body and gender in unconventional ways. At the same time, the valuable work achieved by the exhibition in making visible diverse gender expressions – primarily in the rooms devoted to Cahun and Ashley – illustrates a difficult dilemma in curatorial practice. The public is so unused to exhibitions featuring individuals who challenge gender norms that it is almost inevitable that these displays will draw crowds. Too often, the alternative appears to be maintaining silence and invisibility around the experiences of gender minorities, when in fact the challenge is to present their experiences with dignity and in a manner that invites respect.[8]

The Saatchi Gallery

The Empire Strikes Back: Indian Art Today, an exhibition at London's Saatchi Gallery in the spring of 2010, was free and open to the public. It attracted a fashionable, cosmopolitan crowd, indicating the ways in which certain kinds of post-colonial art have become accepted by the world of high culture. The exhibition was displayed along with another temporary exhibition; an installation on the top floor of the gallery by Emily Prince titled *American Servicemen and Women Who Have Died in Iraq and Afghanistan (But Not Including the Wounded, Nor the Iraqis Nor the Afghans)*. Prince's work incorporated more than 5,100 drawings of the dead based on photographs she found on a memorial website. Prince adds drawings regularly; her sketches are on identical small cards with pencilled inscriptions of the names of the dead, their ages and the dates of their death. The cards covered three walls of the room. This installation, reached after seeing the main exhibit, offered a reminder of the proximity of India to conflict as well as of the continuing presence of individuals of European descent in Asia. As mentioned with some irony in its title, the installation's focus on Americans mirrored the manner in which Westerners tend to view themselves as central in global conflicts.

Even if visitors missed Prince's installation, it was impossible for them to consider *The Empire Strikes Back* in isolation from global capitalism and post-colonialism, in part because its title referred to Paul Gilroy's co-edited volume on racism in 1970s Britain (Centre for Contemporary Cultural Studies 1982). In addition, the first piece to be encountered in the exhibition was Jitish Kallat's wall-sized transcription of Ghandi's 1930 speech on the salt marsh tax, which laid down his notions on civil disobedience and nonviolence. In Kallat's *Public Notice 2*, the speech was 'written' in 4,500 bone-shaped letters, commemorating the dead on the road to freedom and independence. Viewers were dominated by the enormous text, which stood several heads high and crossed multiple panels.

The exhibition continued to confront viewers with images of racism and oppression, and gender discrimination was also challenged. Huma Mulji's constructions used taxidermy specimens of animals to comment on the status of women. In *Her Suburban Dream*, a water buffalo had a pipe around her neck, which was elongated by a concrete collar. As a result of its weight, the cow could not stand; she was in a subservient position with her head and front legs down and back legs partly elevated. The pipe that carried water to the 'suburban dream' seemingly confined the females who lived there and strangled traditional lifestyles. Atul Dodiya's *Woman from Kabul* offered an image of an emaciated woman, virtually a skeleton except for the black burqa on her head. Rashind Rana's *Veil Series, I, II, & III* criticised the hypocrisy which clothes females in head to floor burqas, even as pornography is widely commercialised. In Rana's works, images of women in burqas were revealed to be composed of tiny pornographic photos of women. Chitra Ganesh used her own body in the photographs *Twisted* and *Hidden* to express the way females are distorted and mutilated by violence and the oppression of traditional roles.

Ganesh and other female artists in the exhibit were not solely occupied with presenting victims of gender oppression. They used conventional forms and icons in subversive ways to create works that empowered women. Excerpts from Ganesh's comic book–like series, *Tales of Amnesia*, commented humorously on the role of females in traditional Indian society and global popular culture, as well as on their function as Western icons. In *Secrets*, for example, the image includes references to powerful Hindu goddesses Durga and Kali – a sword, a lotus, a three-headed figure with multiple arms (significantly, this goddess is mother to the god Ganesh, whose name the artist bears).

Pushpamala N. and Clare Arni were represented in the exhibition through selections from their *Ethnographic Series, Native Women of South India: Manners & Customs*, which re-appropriated the genre of ethnographic photography through pictures of Pushpamala in stylised poses. The images drew attention to the controlling yet artificial nature of the ethnographic gaze. These artists challenged gender traditions by inserting images of themselves in their works, their bodies resisting traditional objectification, reconstructing the spectator's gaze.

Other works gestured at Indian traditions only: Bharti Kher's untitled 2008 work at first appeared to be pop art, but on closer inspection was revealed to be a collage of *bindi* of multiple sizes and colours. According to the exhibition guide, 'the artist is signalling a need for social change and challenging the role of the women entrenched in tradition, whilst also commenting on the commoditisation [*sic*] of the bindi as a fashion accessory' (Saatchi Gallery 2010: n.p.). The layered *bindi* took on the appearance of targets, suggesting the vulnerability of women.

T. Venkanna's *Dream in a Dream* focused on male sexuality. A version of Henri Rousseau's painting *The Dream*, it depicted the artist instead of a female nude reclining on a couch in the jungle, suggesting that male sexuality may be exoticised and objectified, too. The black figure in the background of Rousseau's painting was replaced by a brown nude female. On the right side of the image was a comic-strip version of a jungle resembling a Disney cartoon, with the nude woman back in place – a comment on the ways certain artistic images have become so common as to be cartoons of themselves, cultural commodities without depth. A blood red inscription noted, 'My dream never comes true but I am not a pessimist'. Despite these rich examples, the exhibition for the most part limited itself to (re)presenting a fairly narrow range of gender identities, which perhaps suggested a lack of acceptance for other possibilities within contemporary, post-colonial Indian culture as well as the global art market.

The Whitechapel Art Gallery

Where Three Dreams Cross: 150 Years of Photography from India, Pakistan and Bangladesh was shown in the Whitechapel Art Gallery in East London in early 2010. Distant from the elegant Kings Road art galleries in the neighbourhood of the Saatchi, the Whitechapel Art Gallery, founded in the nineteenth century by middle-class social reformers with the mission of acculturating London's working men (and later women),[9] is situated in a working-class neighbourhood that houses many Asian immigrants. The gallery was always intended to address the needs of its community; in this sense, the photographic exhibition was well placed, though it appeared odd that of all the exhibitions at the gallery that year, this was the only one with an admission fee. Perhaps for this reason, *Where Three Dreams Cross* was less crowded than the other exhibitions.

Many of the photographs in the exhibition tended to be less self-consciously artistic or concerned with Western culture than the works at the Saatchi. This is not to say that the display existed or could exist in isolation from the West; indeed, its title alluded to *Ash Wednesday* by T.S. Eliot (1962: 66):

> This is the time of tension between dying and birth
> The place of solitude where three dreams cross
> Between blue rocks.

Eliot's lines situated the exhibition in a liminal space and time and at a crossroads – a place both marginal and central – in much the same way as the subcontinent and its cultures can be considered with respect to today's global economy originating in the West. But the title was also ambiguous. Did the reference to three dreams allude to the artificial national borders drawn in the creation of Pakistan, Bangladesh and India? Were the dreams the collective imaginary or individual imaginations leading to the photographs? Did they allude to the spaces of possibility inherent in every culture?

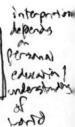

[handwritten margin note: interpretation depends on personal education/understanding of world]

The images in the exhibition addressed these questions and more. Like the identity display at the Wellcome Collection, *Where Three Dreams Cross* was organised by themes that were not necessarily parallel or easily categorised; in this case, the portrait, the family, the body politic, the performance, and the street. Reviewers for the *Observer* and *Time Out* noted that the topics overlapped, rendering the division of the exhibition into thematic sections 'confusing' (O'Hagan 2010) and 'garbled' (Caplan 2010) respectively. Indeed, the boundaries separating the sections at times appeared as artificial as those that created the three nations featured in the exhibition.

Moreover, Nina Caplan stated in *Time Out* that 'the interesting predilection in both Pakistan and India for senior female politicians, despite harsh restrictions on women elsewhere, remains unexamined' (ibid.). In fact, Raghu Rai's 'Indira Gandhi being escorted by Security Guards, Delhi' did examine this issue: his image emphasised Gandhi's vulnerability and reliance on males by showing her surrounded (and virtually suffocated by) guards and spectators. Gandhi was virtually invisible behind her sari, which was pulled over her head.

The exhibition presented diverse gender expressions, offering a possibility for a 'third dream' beyond the binaries of male and female identities. Early in the exhibition, hand-painted studio portraits displayed the wealthy and powerful, posed rigidly in photographs that emphasised Western norms of masculinity and femininity, as well as individuals in traditional Indian garb. Within this section, Nony Singh's image, 'My sister, Guddi, posing as Scarlett O'Hara from Gone with the Wind', subverted the Western icon, for Guddi was posed (and poised) in a sari. Scarlett O'Hara is famously shown against the great expanse of the Tara estate; in contrast, Guddi is in a corner bounded by a brick wall, leaning against a wood fence. The photographer replaced the icon of Western beauty with her own vision.

Images later in the exhibition increasingly challenged gender roles. *Matinee Show, Sreerampore (Best Friend)*, by Saibal Das, appeared to depict a tiger being managed by its stick-wielding tamer. Closer examination revealed that the tamer was surrounded by two other tigers. The photograph was cropped in such a way that the tamer's head was cut off, further disempowering him. A female lay still under the first tiger, composed and smiling.

Pushpamala N., whose works were also featured in the Saatchi exhibition, was represented with photos from the *Navarasa Suite*, part of her *Bombay Photo Studio* series. These dramatic gelatine silver prints 'combine the conventions of classic Bollywood studio portraiture and types with allusions to characterisations of the nine *rasas* – essential human emotions found in traditional Sanskrit literature and drama'.[10] Like *Matinee Show*, these images suggested the power of female performance.

Variant gender expressions were visible as well. Kriti Arora's[11] *Caught in Disarray* (2006) depicted a woman in a burqa examining guns in a case. The photograph gestured at popular images of women in front of shop windows, but the title suggested that the female was breaking out of her traditional role by looking at the forbidden. Her transgression was akin to being 'caught' improperly dressed.

The exhibition also included photographs of members of 'third gender' or transgender male-to-female communities in photographs of Karachi 'Lady Boys' by Asim Hafeez. *Karachi Lady Boys* illustrated the ways in which individuals in these subgroups gather to perform and celebrate their sexuality through glamorous clothes, make-up and shoes. *Bobby* was based on an exhibition and book named *Kaaya: Beyond Gender*. This photograph referred to cross-dressing and transgender in Indian society, both of which are severely marginalised. The self-consciousness of the photographs' male-to-female subjects echoed the stylised self-performances evident in the images of Bollywood.

Although these individuals are often targets of hatred, in this small section of the exhibition, 'three dreams' did cross, as the images captured a space of possibility that was neither traditionally male nor female. The curators responded to Robert Mills' 'concern' regarding 'the marginalisation of transgender as an interpretative lens', so that 'the T in "LGBT" is often a fake T' (Mills 2006: 256). It was unclear, however, whether this space could exist because the exhibition was less visited or because the representations belonged to cultures that have often been eroticised by Westerners. Beyond the confines of the gallery, the subjects of the photographs continue to be treated as outsiders.

Conclusion

Through such examples, the three exhibitions constitute a conversation about visibility and change in the presentation of sex and gender in museums, crossing cultural and national boundaries. All three exhibitions broke down gender binaries and included images of males and females in nontraditional roles. The Wellcome Collection presented individuals of ambiguous gender and persons whose lives were affected by technologies such as artificial insemination or sex reassignment surgery, but struggled to negotiate the significant challenge of presenting its subjects without sensationalising their lives. The Saatchi and Whitechapel exhibitions focused on the Indian subcontinent; inevitably perhaps, the displays were significant in the ways they treated the intersections of British gender mores with local gender traditions, both before and after colonisation. The Saatchi Gallery also incorporated the most explicit works on homosexuality, while the Whitechapel Art Gallery introduced images of male-to-female transgender individuals within limited spaces of visibility.

Although all three exhibitions were promising in many ways, they ultimately left the unsettling conclusion that the task of 'queering' the museum is far from accomplished. We continue to have before us the mission of rendering our institutions ever more inclusive, even as we continue to encounter resistance from regional and transnational forces that bind together local gender schema with the so-called 'norms' brought by colonising Europeans.

Notes

1 For more on the origins of museums see MacGregor and Impey (1985).
2 See, for example, Koven (1994).
3 On the history of women as museum workers see Taylor (1994); and on women museum workers in the Second World War, see Schlievert and Steuber (2008).
4 See www.guerrillagirls.com.
5 See Sandell and Frost (2010) for further discussion of the impact of legislation on museum practice.
6 See Vanegas (2002) for further discussion of the challenges of representing lesbian and gay histories in museums.
7 Christopher Bell was writing on this topic from the perspective of an African-American, HIV-infected male at the time of his death in December 2009. See Bell (2010).
8 See also Chapter 14, this volume, for discussion of transgender representation.
9 For the gallery's early history, see Koven who demonstrates how gallery exhibitions functioned as 'instruments of social control' (1994: 39), although the 'working-class East Londoners challenged the ideological underpinnings of the exhibition' (ibid.: 44).
10 See comments on these works when they were exhibited in *Public Places, Private Spaces*, at the Newark Museum (New Jersey), www.newarkmuseum.org/podcast/india/NewarkMuseumIndia.xml (accessed 12 December 2010).
11 Kriti Arora's works were also featured in the Saatchi Gallery show; however, her pieces at the Saatchi Gallery focused primarily on working-class men and are less relevant to this discussion.

References

Bell, C. (2010) 'Is Disability Studies Actually White Disability Studies?', in L. Davis (ed.) *The Disability Studies Reader*, third edition, London and New York: Routledge: 275–82.

Brigham, D. (1995) *Public Culture in the New Republic: Peale's Museum and Its Audience*, Washington, DC: Smithsonian Institution Press.

Caplan, N. (2010) 'Where Three Dreams Cross: 150 Years of Photography from India, Pakistan, and Bangladesh', *Time Out*, 28 January. Online: Available at: www.timeout.com/london/art/event/170110/where-three-dreams-cross-150-years-of-photography-from-india-pakistan-and-bangladesh (accessed 22 July 2011).

Centre for Contemporary Cultural Studies (1982) *The Empire Strikes Back: Race and Racism in 70s Britain*, London: Routledge.

Duncan, C. (1995) *Civilizing Rituals: Inside Public Art Museums*, London: Routledge.

Eliot, T.S. (1962) 'Ash Wednesday', in *The Waste Land and Other Poems*, New York: Harcourt Brace: 57–66.

Katz, J.D. (2010) 'Hide/Seek: Difference and Desire in American Portraiture', in J.D. Katz and D.C. Ward (eds) *Hide/Seek: Difference and Desire in American Portraiture*, Washington, DC: Smithsonian Books: 10–61.

Koven, S. (1994) 'The Whitechapel Picture Exhibitions and the Politics of Seeing', in D. Sherman and I. Rogoff (eds) *Museum Culture: Histories, Discourses, Spectacles*, Minneapolis: University of Minnesota Press: 22–48.

MacGregor, A. and Impey, O. (1985) *The Origins of Museums: The Cabinet of Curiosities in Sixteenth- and Seventeenth-Century Europe*, Oxford: Oxford University Press.

Mills, R. (2006) 'Queer is Here? Lesbian, Gay, Bisexual and Transgender Histories and Public Culture', *History Workshop Journal*, 62(1): 253–63.

Mills, R. (2008) 'Theorizing the Queer Museum', *Museums & Social Issues* 3 (1): 41–52.

O'Hagan, S. (2010) 'Where Three Dreams Cross: 150 Years of Photography from India, Pakistan and Bangladesh', *The Observer Review*, 24 January: 17.

Ridinger, R. (2010) 'Sister Fire: Representing the Legacies of Leatherwomen', in A.K. Levin (ed.) *Gender, Sexuality, and Museums: A Routledge Reader*, London and New York: Routledge: 172–81.

Saatchi Gallery (2010) *The Empire Strikes Back: Indian Art Today. Picture by Picture Guide*, London: The Saatchi Gallery.

Sandell, R. and Frost, S. (2010) 'A Persistent Prejudice', in F. Cameron and L. Kelly (eds) *Hot Topics, Public Culture, Museums*, Newcastle upon Tyne: Cambridge Scholars Publishing: 150–75.

Schlievert, C. and Steuber, J. (2008) 'Collecting Asian Art, Defining Gender Roles', *Journal of the History of Collections* 20 (2): 291–303.

Taylor, K. (1994) 'Pioneering Efforts of Early Museum Women', in J. Glaser and A. Zenetou (eds) *Gender Perspectives: Essays on Women in Museums*, Washington, DC: Smithsonian Institution Press: 11–27.

Vanegas, A. (2002) 'Representing Lesbians and Gay Men in British Social History Museums', in R. Sandell (ed.) *Museums, Society, Inequality*, London and New York: Routledge: 98–109.

Wellcome Collection (2010) *8 Rooms/9 Lives* [booklet], London: Wellcome Collection.

PLATE 1.1 John Everett Millais, *The Blind Girl* (1856). With permission of Birmingham Museums & Art Gallery. In 2008 the painting was part of an audio trail throughout the Museum's fine art galleries which highlighted artworks with a link to disability and invited disabled artists to interpret the works and explore their resonance with contemporary lived experience of disability.

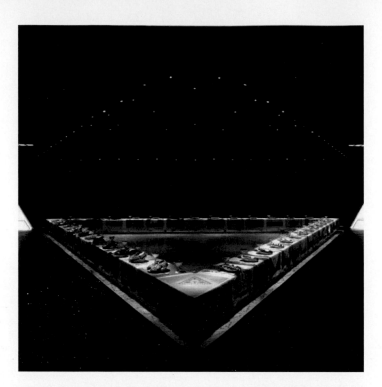

PLATE 1.2a Judy Chicago, *The Dinner Party* (1974–1979). Mixed media: ceramic, porcelain, textile. Brooklyn Museum, Gift of The Elizabeth A. Sackler Foundation, 2002.10. © Judy Chicago, Photo © Donald Woodman.

PLATE 1.2b Judy Chicago, *Sojourner Truth* place setting from *The Dinner Party* (1974–1979). Mixed media: ceramic, porcelain, textile. Brooklyn Museum, Gift of The Elizabeth A. Sackler Foundation, 2002.10. © Judy Chicago, Photo © Donald Woodman.

PLATE 1.3 James Tissot (French, 1836–1902), *Jesus Ministered to by Angels [Jésus assisté par les anges]*, 1886–1894. Opaque watercolor over graphite on gray wove paper, Image: 6 11/16 x 9 3/4 in. (17 x 24.8 cm). Brooklyn Museum, Purchased by public subscription, 00.159.54.

PLATE 1.4 The Singh Twins, *EnTwinED* (2009), is a commissioned response by the Singh Twins (Amrit and Rabindra Singh) to the Museum of London's paintings by Henry Nelson O'Neil, *Eastward Ho!* and *Home Again*, acquired in 2004. These pictures are displayed in the Museum's Galleries of Modern London. O'Neil's canvases, painted in 1857 and 1858, show British soldiers embarking for the First Indian War of Independence and then disembarking after completing their tour of duty. The Singh Twins have used this idea of disembarkation to develop an image which touches upon the experience of the Indian diaspora throughout the British Isles. With permission of the Museum of London.

PLATE 1.5 Marshall D. Rumbaugh, *Rosa Parks*, Painted limewood, 1983. With base: 99.1 × 96.5 × 30.5cm (39 × 38 × 12"). Without base: 95 × 88.9 × 18.4cm (37 × 35 × 7 ¼"). Base: 96.5 × 30.5cm (38 × 12"). National Portrait Gallery, Smithsonian Institution. NPG.83.163

PLATE 3.1a The Golden Throne made by Hafez Muhammad Multani, Lahore, about 1820–1830. Sheets of gold worked in repousse, chased and engraved, over a wooden core. Height approximately 93cm. Museum no. 2518(IS). With permission of the Victoria and Albert Museum, London.

PLATE 3.1b Jain manuscript, *The Mortal Realms of the Universe*. Painting on cotton. Deshnok, Rajasthan, dated 1844. V&A 6565(IS). © Victoria and Albert Museum, London.

PLATE 6.1 Fred Wilson, *The Museum: Mixed Metaphors* (detail), 1993. Seattle Art Museum, Seattle, WA. Courtesy, Seattle Art Museum.

PLATE 6.2 Fred Wilson, *SO MUCH TROUBLE IN THE WORLD – Believe it or Not!* (detail), 2005 Hood Museum of Art, Dartmouth College, Hanover, NH. Courtesy, Hood Museum of Art, Dartmouth College, Hanover, NH 03755 USA.

PLATE 6.3 Caspar Mayer, American, 1871–1931. *Bust of Ota Benga*, A Bachichi man, as displayed by Fred Wilson in the installation *SO MUCH TROUBLE IN THE WORLD – Believe it or Not!*, 2005. 1904. Plaster cast made from a life mask, Hood Museum of Art, Dartmouth College, Hanover, NH. Courtesy, Hood Museum of Art, Dartmouth College.

PLATE 8.1 Sonia Boyce, *Mr close-friend-of-the-family pays a visit whilst everyone else is out*, 1985. Arts Council Collection, Southbank Centre, London. With kind permission of Sonia Boyce.

PLATE 9.1 Islamic Middle East: The Jameel Gallery, V&A Museum.

PLATE 9.2a Blessing of the space by Chinese Buddhists at the opening of the Robert H.N. Ho Buddhist Sculpture Galleries, 28 April 2009, V&A Museum.

PLATE 9.2b The opening of the Sacred Silver & Stained Glass Galleries, 22 November 2005, V&A Museum. Members of different branches of Christianity and Jewish communities advised on the development and interpretation of the galleries. With permission of the Victoria and Albert Museum, London.

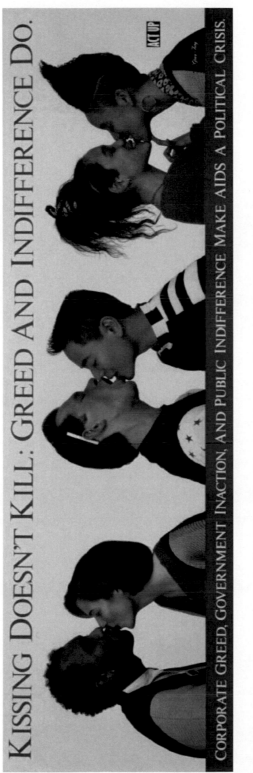

PLATE 10.1 *Kissing Doesn't Kill. Greed and Indifference Do.* Poster by Gran Fury (designer), ACT UP (publisher). Museum no. E.472-1993. Given by Shaun Cole. Reproduced courtesy of Gran Fury/Avram Finkelstein.

PLATE 10.2 'Lesbians are coming out . . .' Screenprint by See Red Women's Workshop. V&A Museum. Museum number: E.786-2004. Gift of the American Friends of the V&A; Gift to the American Friends by Leslie, Judith and Gabri Schreyer and Alice Schreyer Batko.

PLATE 10.3 The Mazarin Chest, Japan, about 1640. V&A Museum. Museum no. 412–1882. With permission of the Victoria and Albert Museum, London.

PLATE 14.1 David Hockney, *We Two Boys Together Clinging*, 1961. Oil on Board. 48 x 60". © David Hockney. Collection: Arts Council, Southbank Centre, London. Photo Credit: Prudence Cuming Associates.

PLATE 14.2 Sadie Lee, *Holly Woodlawn Dressing II*. Oil on canvas 2007. With kind permission of Sadie Lee.

PLATE 14.3 Grayson Perry, *Transvestite Looking in Mirror*, 2009. Glazed ceramic. 71 × 43.5 × 5 cms, 28 × 17 1/8 × 2 inches. (GP 295). Courtesy the Artist and Victoria Miro Gallery, London. Copyright Grayson Perry.

PLATE 14.4 Kristiane Taylor, *Self-Med Woman*, 2009. Courtesy of the artist.

PLATE 16.1 Aboriginal Tent Embassy outside Parliament House, Canberra, 1972. Image supplied by National Archives of Australia. NAA: A7973, INT1205/1.

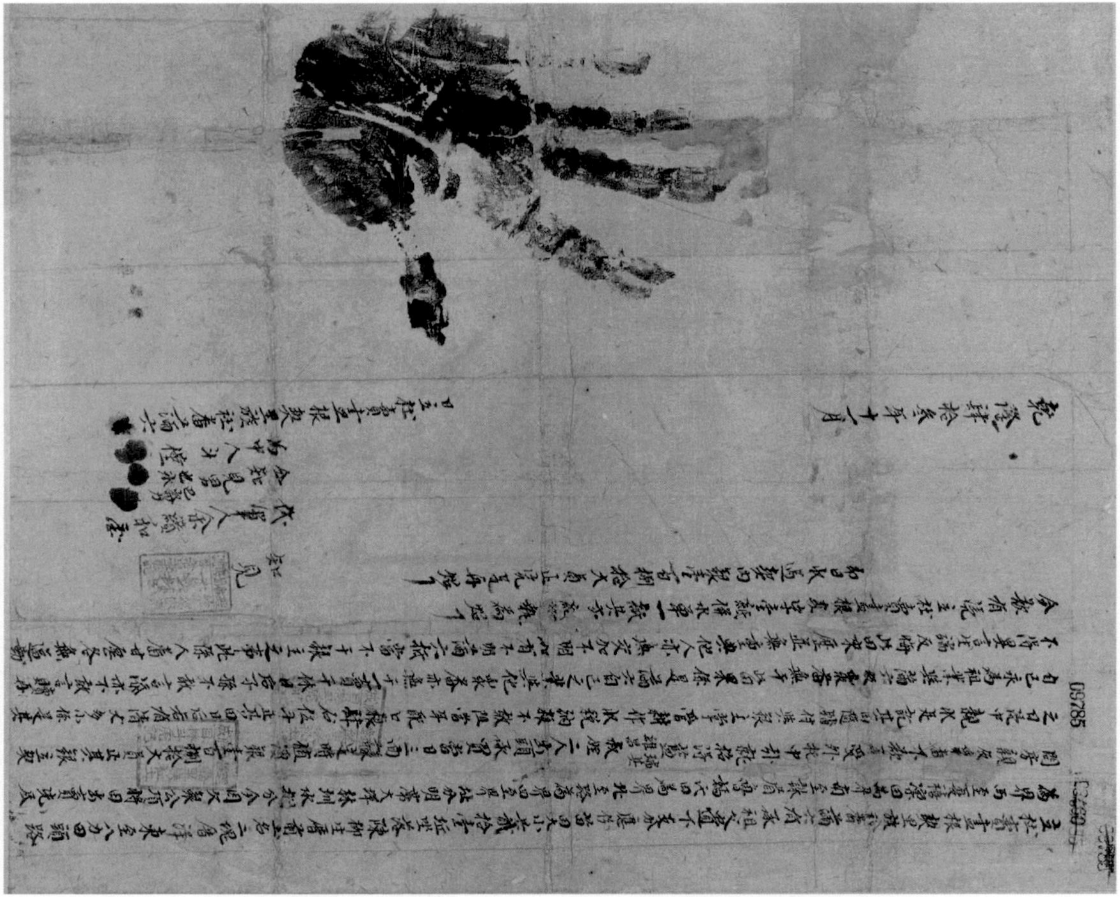

PLATE 17.1 Deed of lease of indigenous lands issued by Han Chinese officers of the Qing government, late eighteenth century. Photo courtesy of the National Taiwan Museum.

PLATE 18.1a Interviewing local residents. Photo courtesy of Susan Kamel.

PLATE 18.1b School group during an interview. Photo courtesy of Christine Gerbich.

PLATE 21.1 Chris Ofili, *Afro Lunar Lovers*, 2003. With permission of the Victoria and Albert Museum, London.

PLATE 21.2 *The West Indian Front Room: Memories and Impressions of Black British Homes.* Geffrye Museum, London. Photographer: John Nelligan.

12

MUSEUMS AND AUTISM

Creating an inclusive community for learning

Susan Davis Baldino

Museums and their academic partner, museum studies, comprise an interdisciplinary group of professionals and scholars who not only study, care for and exhibit our cultural and natural heritage, but offer progressive learning solutions and proactively work toward making positive differences for diverse populations. This chapter discusses how museums can use social learning theory and practice to provide an inclusive and effective program for learners on the autism spectrum. The model I describe here is a 'museum learning community' and the focus of my research is a group I established in 2006, known by its members as the 'Museum Learners Club' or MLC.

The development of the Museum Learners Club coincides with three crucial trends: pressing mandates for museums to be more relevant to society; the increasing prevalence of autism; and the growing need for accessible and inclusive education. While the museum learning community I examine cannot ameliorate the condition of autism, it embraces diversity, accommodates differences and offers a viable context for inclusion that is a worthwhile alternative or enhancement to typical school education. Museums can use it as a vehicle for learning that affirms the abilities of autistic learners and others like them who may frequently be labeled as outcasts, be misunderstood or underserved.

From traditional teaching to communal learning

Today's rapidly changing world demands new educational forms and processes (Gardner 2006a: 9–11). Standard educational institutions persistently rely on didactic methods that remove learning from everyday cultural, social and economic life. Teaching is often practiced through a model of linear transmission that posits teachers as experts and students as passive receivers. In this scenario, only the teacher's side of the information exchange is active. Psychologist Jerome Bruner describes it as an impoverished pedagogical tradition whereby 'a single, presumably omniscient teacher explicitly tells or shows presumably unknowing learners something they presumably know nothing about' (1996: 20). Bruner calls for a reformation of this omniscient teaching model, because 'only a very small part of educating takes place on such a one-way street—and it is probably one of the least successful parts' (ibid.: 21).

He asks us to consider whether the human mind is a computational device that processes finite information or a mind that is informed by our experiences and makes meaning within cultural and social contexts. If we understand humans as reflective of the societies and culture in which they live, they cannot be passive receivers. Therefore, we should be skeptical of educational institutions that extract knowledge from our cultures and present it in a linear, decontextualized manner.

Bruner endorses a cultural-psychological approach to education that reconceives the classroom as a community of mutual learners. This community is a cultural context where all students work together, helping one another learn according to their individual abilities. There is no teacher in the traditional sense, but rather a guide or coach who enables and encourages the learning process by providing supportive scaffolding and sharing authority. The pedagogy of mutuality is carried on by dialogue, discussion and interaction. If we create school cultures that operate as mutual communities of learners we will better prepare our students to create and negotiate meaning and assume workable identities in more complex cultures outside school (Bruner 1996: 68).

Other scholars, including social anthropologist Jean Lave, learning theorist Etienne Wenger and learning scientists Brown, Collins and Duguid work in the same vein as Bruner. They view the combination of communal setting and co-participation as fertile ground for learning. They understand that cognition is situated in the context and culture in which it occurs and have investigated the processes of apprenticeships where the phenomenon of situated learning is readily apparent.

Lave and Wenger's study of apprenticeships identified 'legitimate peripheral participation', or LPP, as the elemental learning process (1991). LPP occurs when the learner joins the actual practice of an expert, absorbing and being absorbed in the culture of that practice. The learner does not acquire a discrete body of facts, but rather the skill to eventually become a full member of the practice. In the initial stages of LPP, the newcomer's tasks are short and simple and responsibility is minimal. As the newcomer moves toward full participation there is an increased sense of belonging and motivation for learning. With full participation comes expertise and knowledge of the practice. Learning is thus conceived as a process of becoming a full participant in a sociocultural practice. Their investigation of this process prompted Lave and Wenger to devise a social learning framework they term a 'community of practice'.

Brown and his colleagues developed a similar community model they call the 'cognitive apprenticeship' (1989). The cognitive apprenticeship is collaborative learning that stresses the enculturated, context-dependent, situated nature of learning. The term *apprenticeship* anchors the notion that participatory activity is requisite for learning. Like historical apprenticeships, it begins with coaching and modeling in situ and continues with a scaffolding process that supports learners during tasks and includes a gradual withdrawal of support until learners can manage on their own. The modifier *cognitive* emphasizes that the apprenticeship techniques go beyond physical skills to include cognitive skills. To illustrate situated learning in a cognitive apprenticeship, Brown and his co-authors point to the ease with which we learn the meaning of words through dialogue, conversation, storytelling and other types of everyday discourse. This contextual learning is far more effective than reading definitions in dictionaries. Reading a dictionary, like the didactic teaching of abstract concepts, does not consider how knowledge and meaning is built through continual situated use across our cultural communities.

Education, as conceived by social learning theorists, is rarely found in our schools that rely on prescriptive teaching and standardized testing, but it can thrive in museums. Museums offer an alternative environment for learning where learners can interact in a more natural community atmosphere, outside the more artificial classroom environment to which they are accustomed. It is a place where they can relate to objects and experiences directly, not via intermediary texts and contrived procedures.

Museum learning theorists and social learning theory

Social learning theory has become increasingly influential for museum studies. The potential for community learning was introduced to the field by prominent developmental psychologists and cognitive scientists at the 1994 conference, 'Public Institutions for Personal Learning: Understanding the Long-Term Impact of Museums' (Falk and Dierking 1995). In a conference 'background paper', Matusov and Rogoff contributed a Vygotskian inspired participatory approach they call a 'community of learners' and view the museum as a bridge between such communities and their practices (1995). In another background paper on interactive learning environments, Roschelle considered the work of Dewey, Vygotsky, Lave and Wenger, and Brown, Duguid and Collins to conclude that only part of knowledge exists when we acquire explicit information; the rest comes from community engagement (1995). As Roschelle states, 'Growing ability *to participate* in a community-based culture has precedence over the ability *to know*' (1995: 47).

In their own right, museum theorists have made invaluable contributions to our understanding of learning. They recognize that museums are not restricted to didactic practices; rather they are freer to encompass a variety of learning processes. George Hein advances the constructivist learning theory, a view of learning as building upon existing knowledge through learner-centered methods (1998). Since he first began writing about museums and constructivism, other museologists have further developed constructivist learning theory and practice. Much of it is based on the social constructivism of Vygotsky who keenly understood that higher mental functions are 'socially formed and culturally transmitted' (1978: 126). Through her study of cultural communications and interpretive communities, Eilean Hooper-Greenhill develops the idea that meaning is achieved by mutual processes of sharing and participating in social and cultural frameworks (1994, 2000). John Falk and Lynn Dierking, like Matusov and Rogoff, see the museum as the intersection of community learning experiences (2000). Gaea Leinhardt and Karen Knutson study learning in the museum as 'conversational elaboration', a decidedly sociocultural view (2004). All of these theorists see the museum as an ideal locus for learning. All deem learning as inherently social, and recognize its communal aspect and the positive prospects for learning in communities.

Museums as common ground for human diversity

Alongside increasing recognition of the social character of learning in museums can be found growing interest in the significance and value of more inclusive approaches to museum practice evidenced, for example, in recent studies by Sandell (2002 and 2007) and Janes (Janes and Conaty 2005; Janes 2007). As museums break from an elitist and discriminatory past, they are exercising their exceptional capacity to reach out to existing and potential users who have suffered segregation and marginalization. Among these marginalized users are people with exceptional physical, intellectual and emotional differences; people who experience disability and constitute a large but often overlooked minority (World Health Organization 2011).

People with autism spectrum disorders make up a significant segment of the disabled population, one that is growing at an alarming rate. The Centers for Disease Control in the United States (CDC) cite the incidence of autism as an average of one in 110,[1] and regard autism as an urgent public health concern. The Autistic Society in the United Kingdom measures the prevalence of autism as one in 100,[2] and views it as a lifelong disabling condition that can be devastating without appropriate supports. Autism has been referred to as a global crisis.[3] The United Nations has designated April 2 as Autism Awareness Day.

Developing inclusive programs for learners on the autism spectrum focuses on a significant population that has not always experienced full and open access to education and everyday social activities. The Museum Learners Club invites autistic learners to join others as equals in motivating environments. It fits into a worldwide movement toward inclusive education that utilizes learner-centered pedagogies and supports differences (World Health Organization 2011). Inclusion benefits autistic students by eradicating inequities. Perhaps more importantly, it benefits *all* students, autistic and non-autistic, by expanding individuals' experiences of difference in ways that diminish prejudice.

Autism and learning

Autistic learners present a complex set of physical, intellectual, developmental and behavioral manifestations that spans a wide-ranging continuum. Autism is therefore known as a spectrum disorder. The autism spectrum includes such diagnoses as autistic disorder, Asperger's Syndrome and Pervasive Developmental Disorder.[4] Each person who displays autistic characteristics does so in a uniquely individual way; however, every person with an autism diagnosis endures debilitating neurologically based information processing difficulties that can result in mild to severe learning differences and behaviors.

Minshew and Williams explain that regions in the autistic brain are not integrated, do not work in synchrony or harmony and thus may hinder complex abilities and functions (2008). Someone whose neural networks are not integrated may experience challenges in receiving and responding to information from another person. For example, as one person communicates with another, the typical brain simultaneously processes facial expressions, gestures and postures along with linguistic and contextual information. This wholly integrated process does not occur in the autistic brain (Gutstein 2009: 9). Inadequate neural integration is not only revealed in acts of communication but also in perception and motor coordination that can cause physical unease or irritation.

Students on the autism spectrum can confront barriers in a traditional classroom. They may find it difficult to relate to teachers and classmates. They may not be able to follow or elaborate on what they are taught. They may be both distractible and distracting and physically and emotionally uncomfortable. Even those autistic learners who are easily able to master curricular subjects and are considered 'high functioning' can remain socially and emotionally isolated.

Table 12.1 encapsulates cognitive, communicative and physical challenges for learners on the autism spectrum. The chart is based on Greenspan and Wieder's work that sorts learning challenges of autism into foundational areas of relating, communicating and thinking (2006) and includes an additional area that addresses physical comfort. The chart matches learning fundamentals to behaviors and symptoms of autism, many of which I encountered during my fieldwork with the Museum Learners Club.

TABLE 12.1 Classroom learning challenges in school-aged and older learners on the autism spectrum

Fundamentals necessary for learning in the classroom	Indications of Autism Spectrum Disorder	Associated Symptoms
COGNITIVE ABILITY		
Creative and logical use of ideas: Ability to express needs, intentions, desires, feelings in meaningful conversation and connect ideas logically	'Under-connected thinking' and an inability to use ideas in meaningful ways; using ideas without logical connections; inconsistent perception	Illogical and inappropriate use of ideas, echolalia, repeating scripted language
Abstract and reflective thinking: Ability to use high level thinking skills; make inferences	Concrete thinking that is rigid and lacks subtlety; restricted interests	Exaggerated reactions or avoidance of social situations
SOCIAL COMMUNICATION		
Attention, engagement, emotional interactions: Ability to pleasurably relate to another person and initiate interactions	Fleeting, intermittent or no engagement or interaction; difficulty regulating arousal; speech delays	Aimless, random or self-stimulatory behaviors; self-absorption or withdrawal, inattention
Continuous purposeful social communication: Ability to negotiate, play, and read emotional intentions of others	Limited or no interaction; little initiative taken toward relating	Impulsive or repetitive behaviors (perseveration); aggressive behavior, vulnerability
PHYSICAL COMFORT		
Strength to endure classroom activity: Ability to sit quietly, follow directions and conform to class expectations	Low muscle tone; delayed fine and gross motor functioning; lack of sensory integration	Repetitive motions; shaking and flapping; avoidance of noise and touching, need for frequent breaks

Faced with inabilities to socially integrate and make meaning in typical ways, autistic learners seem to live and learn in a manner detached from their typical peers. Their world is often dominated by anomalous perception and literal information that remains disjointed and not synthesized into meaningful analyses. It can include painful sensitivities and inappropriate communication styles. Without meaningful analysis, autistic learners often prefer repetition to novelty and predictability to new situations. With overwhelming sensory input, they may recede from the tasks at hand. Without the ability to relate in familiar ways, they may be dismissed, rejected and bullied.

The autistic population needs education solutions. The number of autistic students who receive educational services is steadily rising. These students are often isolated with special education teachers in therapeutic settings with the hope that they will 'catch up' with their peers. In the United States as many as 40 percent of students on the autism spectrum are outside the classroom for more than 60 percent of the school day (US Department of Education 2009). Underlying this statistic is a singular paradigm for learning that does not take into consideration multiple learning styles and leaves students with special needs feeling excluded and actually deterred from realizing their potential.

Most research on autism deals with areas other than education. Primary goals are determining incidence, identifying risk factors and cause, examining brain anatomy, developing pharmacological treatment, and gauging economic cost. Too little work is applied to quality of life issues for those who are growing up on the spectrum. There is also an overwhelming dependence on interventions based on theories of behaviorism that attempt to alter autistic behaviors with instructional control and induce socially acceptable and school-appropriate conduct.[5] Behaviorism teaches 'right' and 'wrong', while ignoring subtle, reflective, more advanced ways of thinking. More acceptable behaviors may be realized; however, there is growing concern that behavioral approaches aim to correct symptoms rather than address fundamental differences and generate a brittle type of knowledge that is difficult to generalize. More research is needed on learning and concomitant social skills that will generate a happier and more productive existence for autistic students.

Autism and social learning strategies

There is emerging research on social learning for those who have autism spectrum disorders. Diverging from behaviorist methods, these newer approaches utilize social interaction to increase cognitive ability. They emphasize communicative, relational and problem solving skills more than the aptitude to produce correct responses. Among them is the SCERTS educational model that places learning firmly in social contexts and daily routines and measures learning by degrees of participation and communication (Prizant *et al.* 2006).

The SCERTS acronym signals its priorities: social communication (SC), emotional regulation (ER) and transactional supports (TS). The social communication domain addresses the need to relate to others in order to learn. The emotional regulation domain refers to support that help learners maintain social engagement. The domain of transactional supports specifies the guiding strategies used across all learning situations at home, in school and in the community. SCERTS takes into account a broader definition of learning that includes not only academic skills but communicative, emotional and motor skills. It considers learners as active participants in their own learning and views inclusion with non-autistic peers as advantageous to all. SCERTS has been implemented in educational settings where its principles are employed with a 'semi-structure' to promote consistent social interaction when needed yet retain flexibility and learner initiation where appropriate.

The SCERTS approach was designed to be adaptive to different environments and flexible enough to incorporate into compatible learning designs. Because of its similarities to progressive museum learning, it could be integrated with social learning programs in museums such as the Museum Learners Club.

Museum learning community research and the MLC

My study of socially mediated learning led me to create an inclusive learning community for autistic learners. The design is indebted to pathfinders of museum studies who promote the museum as an important setting for learning and instill the value of theory-based research for museum practice. Their revelations about constructivist and sociocultural learning remain my keystone; however, my learning framework is primarily linked with theorists from the fields of knowledge management and organizational learning science. Derived from notion of the community of practice, I designed it as a 'museum learning community'. I organized and tested it with young learners who renamed it the 'Museum Learners Club' and referred to it as the 'MLC'.

Underpinning the framework of the MLC is an essential understanding of the multi-dimensional nature of knowledge and the process of learning. Knowledge does not solely consist of independent facts and explicit information. It also involves culturally embedded personal backgrounds and an indescribable tacit component. Although individuals can ingest explicit information by singular effort, more balanced and meaningful learning results from participation – the activity that exposes cultural affinity and unleashes the tacit component of knowledge.

Organizational scientists in today's 'knowledge age' count knowledge as the most valuable asset of the firm. They conduct profound studies of knowledge and learning to expand the learning capacities of their employees. Their research on organizational knowledge creation – the theory that examines how people learn within the organization – reveals the relative importance of explicit and tacit knowledge. Explicit knowledge includes easily expressible data, facts and information that enterprises can access and use in a straightforward manner. Tacit knowledge, however, is embedded in individual minds and bodies and remains stubbornly resistant to articulation. As scientist and knowledge philosopher Michael Polanyi wrote, 'tacit knowing is more fundamental than explicit knowing: we can know more than we can tell and we can tell nothing without relying on our awareness of things we may not be able to tell' (Polanyi 1964: ix). Much of today's organizational research is based on Polanyi's ideas about the tacit dimension. Although both explicit and tacit knowledge are integral to an organization's success, it is the harnessing of tacit knowledge that results in true innovation and increased competitive advantage.

Polanyi believed that tacit knowledge can only be released when we are connected socially and culturally, as he explains in his seminal work on personal knowledge:

> Tacit assent and intellectual passions, the shaping of an idiom and of a cultural heritage, affiliation to a likeminded community: such are the impulses which shape our vision of the nature of things on which we rely for our mastery of things. No intelligence, however critical or original, can operate outside such a fiduciary framework.
>
> *Ibid.: 266*

To capture and mobilize tacit knowledge, business organizations cultivate social groups distinct from their structural hierarchies. These groups allow employees to participate in a more natural context and generate new ideas from the existing personal and tacit knowledge of group members. I looked at several such groups to build the MLC, and drew particularly on the concept of microcommunities of knowledge, developed by von Krogh *et al.* (2000), and the idea of communities of practice, developed by Wenger (1998).

In both communal constructs, innovations result from active participation. The microcommunity comprises five to seven participants who share tacit knowledge through observation, narration, imitation, experimentation and joint execution to develop a concept. An enabling system includes 'knowledge activists' who initiate dialogue and assure continual participation through which conversions of knowledge take place: from tacit to explicit and explicit to tacit. Wenger's community of practice also involves the communal negotiation of explicit and tacit knowledge and has been proven effective in numerous case studies. With four interdependent components, it combines a *practice* with a coherent *community* where mutual engagement and reification generates *meaning* and enables a transformation of *identity*.

The foundational aspects of organizational learning communities can be applied in a variety of settings including museums and schools. Wenger, for example, has used his organizational form of the community of practice to develop a specific design for education. His educational conception depends on managing the forces of four dualities: participation and reification; teaching and learning; the local and the global; identification and negotiability. The design favors participation over reification; privileges learning over teaching; encourages local engagement to widen its boundaries; and promotes identity development. It is accompanied by successive 'modes of belonging' or steps in the transformation of learners' identities because, as Wenger puts it, 'Education, in its deepest sense and at whatever age it takes place, concerns the opening of identities—exploring new ways of being that lie beyond our current state' (1998: 263). The three steps in identity transformation are engagement (community building), imagination (reflection and exploration) and alignment (connecting learning to broader enterprises outside school) (ibid.: 263–7).

I adapted Wenger's framework to produce a blueprint for the MLC as seen in Figure 12.1. It reflects most of Wenger's ideas and those of others who have designed such learning communities. The quadrants of 'context' and 'adaptive guidance' provide the frame for the museum learning practice that occurs in a small inclusive group without teaching as we typically conceive of it. The areas of 'participation' and 'identification' denote knowledge enablers within the frame that encourage interactivity and a sense of belonging. The modes of engagement, imagination and alignment indicate successive stages of identity transformation that begin when a community coalesces, grows with members' exploration of themselves and others and moves beyond the immediate community as members are exposed to other communities and practices. The conception represents a new form and process for learning, as called for by Gardner and Bruner, and is similar in character to the SCERTS approach to learning with its emphasis on participatory contexts, guidance and individual identities within a flexible structure.

The interactive participatory MLC, guided by a facilitator and attentive to individual identities, provides a learning environment situated in everyday activities, away from the constraints of a classroom and traditional teaching system. It trades traditional pedagogy for a pedagogy of mutuality. It relies on participation in which meaningful activity supersedes reified materials such as textbooks, rubrics and standardized tests. It is a place where learning

CONTEXT	PARTICIPATION
Community of Practice: Inclusive group learning in museums Shared purposes and a balance of local and expanded engagement	Make meaning through sharing and participation not reification Incorporate reification that arises naturally within the context
IDENTIFICATION	ADAPTIVE GUIDANCE
Empower meaningful identities Encourage membership Provide opportunities for each participant to lead	Stress the emergent over the designed: less teaching, more learning Community coordinator assumes facilitative, guiding role

Engagement	→	Imagination	→	Alignment
Coming together		Reflecting and Exploring		Crossing boundaries

FIGURE 12.1 Learning architecture and modes of belonging for the Museum Learners Club.

can be contoured by each individual yet scaffolding is available where needed. Here, learning is measured by degrees of participation and transformation of identities as participants are first encouraged to become full and active members (engagement); allowed to reflect and explore their identities and those of others (imagination); and to move beyond school walls into the community.

Museum Learners Club in practice

The MLC operates as a microcommunity of practice with six learners: three on the autism spectrum and three who are neurologically typical. I experimented with the model in a museum-school collaboration in which the MLC augmented class curriculum by visiting museums. In my initial test group, the three students with autistic characteristics had difficulties learning in the classroom.[6] Their cognitive abilities, social and communication skills, and physical manifestations of disability varied. They experienced common autistic sensory issues such as aversions to loud noise, commotion and touching and responded with perseveration, repeated movements and self-stimulatory behavior. They exhibited various physical discomforts, withdrew rather than related to others and were rigid in their conceptions and desires. The school considered them disabled, issued them government mandated Individual Education Plans and segregated them from other students for special education sessions several times during the week. Three neurologically typical students joined the MLC. I rounded out the group, not as an authoritative teacher, but as a guiding 'knowledge activist'.

To coordinate the MLC, I laid out an elaborate yet flexible scheme for learning in museums. Our plan roughly followed the social studies curriculum of the school term, but made allowances for collective and individual exploration and reflection. The MLC left campus to visit museums for an entire school day once a week and conceived and built a project that was presented to the class at the end of the term. Our goals mirrored those of the students left in the classroom who were conducting social studies research in class by using texts, lectures and online resources for a term-end presentation, but our learning processes were completely different.

As participant observer during the MLC process, I clearly witnessed growing participation and identification. Each club member contributed to joint activity with increasing frequency. Each assumed leadership roles and/or new responsibilities at various times. Attitudes toward involvement changed, especially for those on the autism spectrum who became more involved with other participants and worked together in spontaneous partnerships and group undertakings. Learners on the autism spectrum were also able to negotiate identities within the MLC that were prohibitive in the classroom. They were given the time and support necessary to shape and communicate their thoughts. For them, the MLC was a transformative experience. They could assume positions equivalent to those of their peers and did so with regularity.

The Museum Learners Club also enabled participants' identities to reach a point where they imagined themselves in the world around them. Not only learners in a school, they had become learners in museums and in the surrounding community. They connected to a broader enterprise that was inhabited by varied institutions, primary resources, historic collections, experiences with professionals and learning activity apart from standardized rubrics. Their understanding became deeper and wider than the curriculum.

The positive results of the MLC experiment were remarkable. The students not only learned subject area content but increased social and communication skills. Each student gained a sense of belonging. Formerly ostracized students became full participants. Passive learners became active learners as reticence gave way to full participation. Followers became leaders. There was unprecedented interaction between autistic learners and non-autistic learners, acceptance of differences and enhanced tolerance. There was an increase in confidence and friend-making. The joy of being together in a purposeful practice in museums was palpable (Baldino 2010).

Implications for the future

People with autistic spectrum disorders are part of our collective history and integral to our society. As such they should be part of our collective meaning-making and should not be intentionally or incidentally excluded or dissuaded from learning. The Museum Learners Club is a framework for diversity and a place where these people can be heard and respected as equal partners. Museums can use the Museum Learners Club to engage and affirm the abilities of autistic learners and others like them who have dealt with discrimination.

In addition to the merits of social inclusion, the successful working out of the MLC proved to me that humans with varying abilities can work together to solve problems, and correct misunderstandings. I agree with Howard Gardner who writes:

> If we can mobilize the spectrum of human abilities, not only will people feel better about themselves and more competent; it is even possible that they will also feel more engaged and better able to join the rest of the world community in working for the broader good. Perhaps if we can mobilize the full range of human intelligences and ally them to an ethical sense, we can help increase the likelihood of our survival on this planet, and perhaps even contribute to our thriving.
>
> *2006b: 24*

Notes

1 For further information see Centers for Disease Control and Prevention (2011).
2 For further information see National Autistic Society (2011).
3 For example, see the May 2011 hearing on global perspectives on autism conducted by C. Smith, chair of the US House of Representatives Foreign Affairs' Subcommittee on Africa, Global Health and Human Rights, www.c-span.org/Events/Hearing-Examines-Global-Perspectives-on-Autism/10737421894/ (accessed 30 September 2011).
4 Definitions and a guide to diagnosis for autism in the United States are delineated in the *Diagnostic and Statistical Manual of Mental Disorders*, published by the American Psychiatric Association (www.psych.org). Other countries follow similar guidelines but may include a somewhat different list of disorders on the autism spectrum.
5 I do not want to imply that all behaviorist strategies are inappropriate. They may be useful in some cases – for example, where extreme behaviors such as aggression and tantrums persist. For the majority of educational settings, however, social or socio-developmental approaches produce knowledge that is better suited for an integrated life.
6 The students who exhibited autistic characteristics were 'learning-ready' and spent much of their school day in the classroom with typical students. They could generalize skills to independent settings and were selected for the study because I wanted my work to be remedial not compensatory.

References

Baldino, S. D. (2010) 'Museum Learners Club: Social Environments for Inclusive Learning', unpublished thesis, University of Leicester.

Brown, J. S., Collins, A. and Duguid, P. (1989) 'Situated Cognition and the Culture of Learning', *Educational Researcher*, 18(1): 32–42.

Bruner, J. (1996) *The Culture of Education*, Cambridge, MA and London: Harvard University Press.

Centers for Disease Control and Prevention (2011) *Autism Spectrum Disorders (ASDs)*. Online. Available at: www.cdc.gov/ncbddd/autism/index.html (accessed 5 September 2011).

Falk, J. H. and Dierking, L. D. (1995) *Public Institutions for Personal Learning: Establishing a Research Agenda*, Washington, DC: American Association of Museums.

Falk, J. H. and Dierking, L. D. (2000) *Learning from Museums: Visitor Experiences and the Making of Meaning*, Walnut Creek: AltaMira Press.

Gardner, H. (2006a) *Five Minds for the Future*, Boston: Harvard Business School Press.

Gardner, H. (2006b) *Multiple Intelligences: New Horizons*, New York: Basic Books.

Greenspan, S. I. and Wieder, S. (2006) *Engaging Autism: Using the Floortime Approach to Help Children Relate, Communicate, and Think*, Cambridge, MA: Da Capo Press.

Gutstein, S. E. (2009) *The RDI Book: Forging New Pathways for Autism, Asperger's and PDD with the Relationship Development Intervention Program*, Houston: Connections Center Publishing.

Hein, G. E. (1998) *Learning in the Museum*, London: Routledge.

Hooper-Greenhill, E. (ed.) (1994) *The Educational Role of the Museum*, London and New York: Routledge.

Hooper-Greenhill, E. (2000) *Museums and the Interpretation of Visual Culture*, London and New York: Routledge.

Janes, R. R. (2007) 'Museums, Social Responsibility and the Future We Desire', in S. J. Knell, S. MacLeod and S. Watson (eds) *Museum Revolutions: How Museums Change and are Changed*, London and New York: Routledge: 134–46.

Janes, R. R. and Conaty, G. T. (eds) (2005) *Looking Reality in the Eye: Museums and Social Responsibility*, Calgary: University of Calgary Press.

Lave, J. and Wenger, E. (1991) *Situated Learning: Legitimate Peripheral Participation*, Cambridge: Cambridge University Press.

Leinhardt, G. and Knutson, K. (2004) *Listening in on Museum Conversations*, Walnut Creek: AltaMira Press.

Matusov, E. and Rogoff, B. (1995) 'Evidence of Development from People's Participation in Communities of Learners', in J. H. Falk and L. D. Dierking (eds) *Public Institutions for Personal Learning*, Washington, DC: American Association of Museums: 97–104.

Minshew, N. J. and Williams, D. J. (2008) 'Brain–Behavior Connections in Autism', in K. D. Buron and P. Wolfberg (eds) *Learners on the Autism Spectrum: Preparing Highly Qualified Educators*, Shawnee Mission: Autism Asperger Publishing Co: 25–43.

National Autistic Society (2011) *Autism and Aspergers Syndrome: Some Facts and Statistics*. Online. Available at: www.autism.org.uk/about-autism/some-facts-and-statistics.aspx (accessed 5 September 2011).

Polanyi, M. ([1958] 1964) *Personal Knowledge: Towards a Post-Critical Philosophy*, New York: Harper & Row.

Prizant, B. M., Wetherby, A. M., Rubin, E., Laurent, A. C. and Rydell, P. J. (2006) *The SCERTS Model: A Comprehensive Educational Approach for Children with Autism Spectrum Disorders*, Vols. I and 2, Baltimore, London and Sydney: Paul H. Brookes Publishing.

Roschelle, J. (1995) 'Learning in Interactive Environments: Prior Knowledge and New Experience', in J. H. Falk and L. D. Dierking (eds) *Public Institutions for Personal Learning: Establishing a Research Agenda*, Washington, DC: American Association of Museums, 37–51.

Sandell, R. (2002) *Museums, Society, Inequality*, London and New York: Routledge.

Sandell, R. (2007) *Museums, Prejudice and the Reframing of Difference*, London and New York: Routledge.

United States Department of Education (2009) *28th Annual Report to Congress on the Implementation of the Individuals with Disabilities Education Act, 2006.* Online. Available at: www.ed.gov/about/reports/annual/osep/2006/parts-b-c/28th-vol-1.pdf (accessed 22 January 2009).

Von Krogh, G., Ichijo, K. and Nonaka, I. (2000) *Enabling Knowledge Creation: How to Unlock the Mystery of Tacit Knowledge and Release the Power,* New York: Oxford University Press.

Vygotsky, L. S. ([1962] 1978) *Mind in Society,* Cambridge, MA: Harvard University Press.

Wenger, E. (1998) *Communities of Practice: Learning, Meaning, and Identity,* Cambridge and New York: Cambridge University Press.

World Health Organization (2011) *World Report on Disability 2011,* Geneva: The World Health Organization.

13

MUSEUMS AS INTERCULTURAL SPACES

Simona Bodo

Many museums were founded in order to represent and validate national, local or group identities and have been understood to function as spaces which have tended to work against contemporary social and political concerns for cultural diversity and inclusion. Increasingly, however, museums are being perceived as places which might nurture respect for cultural differences and foster dialogue between groups (Bodo *et al.* 2009; Sandell 2007). This chapter draws on recent European research to examine this trend in museological thinking and practice and, in particular, looks at contemporary, experimental initiatives from Italy to consider the role that museums might play in promoting equality and mutual understanding between communities in multicultural societies.

Heritage, museums and intercultural dialogue: a problematic relationship

The very notion of 'heritage' can be problematic when we begin to consider these issues. For many it can seem to refer to something that is attained 'once and for all' by birthright, rather than developed by an individual throughout their lifetime (Matarasso 2006); a perception that has informed the views of many policy-makers and museum professionals but also underpinned broader public understandings of heritage. As Matarasso has highlighted, it is commonly assumed that:

> one can become a cultured person; one can learn to understand and appreciate art, music, or ballet . . . one can accumulate cultural capital . . . But one cannot acquire a heritage: it is given, fixed at birth. Heritage claims an essential, and ineradicable, difference between someone born in a village, or a country, or a faith, and someone who has chosen to make their life within that social and cultural framework; and that distinction, paradoxically, disadvantages the person who has freely chosen an identity, making a conscious commitment to a place, a group or a set of values. In this world, a migrant can only ever be an honorary member, an affiliate whose status, whether welcomed or merely tolerated, is always at risk of revocation.

2006: 53–4

For Matarasso, however, heritage should not be 'mistaken for the neutral remains of the past, as most heritage bodies imply . . . Rather, it is how people interpret evidence of the past for present use; and one of those uses is to define themselves' (ibid.: 53). Building on this understanding of the constructed nature of heritage, it is possible to determine two main interpretive paradigms (Besozzi 2007) with radically different implications for museums. The 'essentialist paradigm' sees heritage as the 'neutral remains of the past': static, consolidated, 'of outstanding universal value'[1] and, as such, something to be 'transmitted' through a linear communication process from the curator (as the only reliable source of authority and expertise) to the cognitively passive visitor. The 'dialogical paradigm', on the other hand, understands heritage as a set of cultural objects – both material and immaterial – that should not only be preserved and transmitted, but also renegotiated, reconstructed in their meanings and made available for all to share in a common space of social interaction.[2]

In the real world, both paradigms represent legitimate concerns and interests and, in fact, need not be understood to be entirely in conflict with each other. Whilst in the former, decisions are made on what is worth preserving and transmitting to future generations, in the latter, this heritage is constantly questioned and rediscovered by individuals who breathe new life into it. As museum mediator Rita Catarama observes, 'heritage is not something separate from life' (Pecci 2009a: 129).

Tensions emerge, however, since the essentialist paradigm has dominated most institutional policy and practice thereby constraining dialogical notions of heritage, compromising the accessibility of museums and excluding those who do not possess an 'adequate' level of cultural literacy, let alone a sense of belonging.

In light of this tension between a more traditional, self-referential, and a more inclusive, participatory way of conceiving heritage, how are museums responding to a political agenda which is increasingly urging them to play a role in the promotion of intercultural dialogue? I began to address this question in 2007, through my involvement in a study on European Union member states' approaches to intercultural dialogue in different policy domains (culture, education, youth and sport), carried out by the European Institute for Comparative Cultural Research (ERICarts Institute) on behalf of the European Commission Directorate General for Education and Culture (Bodo 2008). My brief within this project was to investigate the different understandings of intercultural dialogue and the resulting policy approaches to its promotion in museums across Europe.[3] In this chapter I provide an indicative selection of the approaches found in the study and focus on whether and how museums have been successful in encouraging interaction between different cultural groups.

Understandings of intercultural dialogue

One of the prevailing understandings of a museum's responsibility to promote intercultural dialogue has been to encourage increased knowledge and greater recognition and appreciation of 'other' cultures. Although this approach may take very different forms (for example, by showcasing difference as an educational strategy to inform audiences about cultures which have traditionally been misrepresented or made invisible in museum spaces; or by exposing and challenging past and present stereotypes concerning certain cultural traditions), what often distinguishes these initiatives is not so much a will to encourage attendance and participation on the part of migrant communities, as to promote a 'knowledge-oriented multiculturalism' directed principally at an autochthonous public. Here, the 'other' is conceived as an object of knowledge – rather than an individual with whom we engage in a relationship – and is constructed from the point of view of a dominant culture; one 'unmarked by ethnicity in relation to which the differences of other cultures are to be registered, assessed and tolerated' (Bennett 2006: 24).

At the opposite end of the spectrum, the promotion of intercultural dialogue has often been associated with the integration of 'new citizens' within mainstream culture, by helping migrant communities to become familiar with a country's history, values and traditions. In the best of cases, these initiatives are rooted in communities' needs and expectations, rather than driven by curatorial and institutional interests, or transitory political and social agendas (Bodo 2009b). For example, some museums are actively supporting groups of recent arrivals and helping them settle into the new country by assisting them with language learning. Others are encouraging an inclusive mediation of the local heritage by experimenting with a participatory approach to the interpretation of collections. However, some initiatives, typically including guided tours to museums and heritage sites targeted at specific groups, have turned out to be rather more problematic due not only to a lack of consistent outreach policies and limited direct involvement of participants but, in some cases, to a patronising attitude,[4] intended 'to make it easier for those who are not yet believers to learn to appreciate what they are missing' (Matarasso 2004: 493).

A further option which is being increasingly explored by museums across Europe is 'culturally specific programming', for example the development of exhibitions and events drawing on collections that might hold particular significance for an immigrant community. Alongside these initiatives, intended to redress the under- or misrepresentation of specific minority groups, there has been a growing interest in collections or programmes that reflect the cultural heterogeneity of a region or city's population and those which explore topics (such as the history of immigration, colonialism and slavery) that enable diverse cultures to be represented.[5] Some communities are actively involved by museums in the interpretation of collections or assisted with preserving and presenting their own cultural heritage (whether it be material or immaterial), while other communities are attempting to establish their own museums or community archives.

The ERICarts survey found that these approaches, as different as they may be, often have some key features in common (Bodo 2008). First, they tend to utilise a static, essentialist notion of heritage, which is primarily seen as a 'received patrimony' to safeguard and transmit. Second, they generally target communities exclusively in relation to their own cultures and collections, while cross-cultural interaction across all audiences is generally avoided. Third, by keeping 'majority' and 'minority' cultures and communities apart – and by generally treating the latter as 'unified, traditional, unchanging and thereby exotic' (Bloomfield and Bianchini 2004: 98) – they sometimes operate to reinforce rather than to challenge stereotypes. Fourth, they are inclined to embrace the rhetoric of 'diversity as a richness', rather than acknowledging and confronting tensions and frictions between communities. Lastly, these approaches are generally based on an understanding of 'intercultural dialogue' as a *goal* to be attained rather than as a *process*, ingrained in a museum's practice, through which it might promote 'multiple visions and interpretations' (Veini and Kistemaker 2003: 20). In other words, the concept of multiple and shifting identities – which is so central to intercultural dialogue as it permits a move beyond the prevailing rationale of cultural representation (including diverse communities in museum narratives) – may well be widely accepted in theory but, in reality, is very seldom placed at the heart of a museum's work.

By highlighting these common features, however, I am not suggesting that these approaches are to be discredited or abandoned. Indeed they all have an important role to play – not least, in supporting diverse communities and helping individuals and groups to maintain a vital link with their cultural traditions – and provide the basis for the promotion of museums as inter-cultural spaces (Bodo 2009a). Rather, what I wish to contend is the need to work towards what Young refers to as 'a more integrative model of diversity, rather than the current model with its tendency to reify difference and put people into discrete categories without interaction or overlap' (Young 2005).

we want separation

This approach will demand an honest, open and comprehensive rethinking on the part of museums around what it really means to carry out intercultural work. Does such work involve enhancing the cultural literacy of immigrant communities through familiarity with a country's history, art and culture, or 'compensating' for the misrepresentation of minorities in cultural narratives, as many museums and heritage institutions have understood it? Or, might inter-cultural work be conceived more productively as a bi-directional, dialogical process which is transformative of all parties (majority as well as minority representatives; those from host as well as immigrant backgrounds) and in which all are equal participants?

Museums as 'intercultural spaces': exploring new paradigms

Based on an overview of the most recent developments in Italian museums' thinking and working practices,[6] I wish to argue here that alongside the more established policy responses to the growing diversity of museum audiences – and ideally as their culmination – there is a pressing need for strategies and programmes aimed at creating 'third spaces', where individuals are permitted to cross the boundaries of belonging (Bodo 2008) and are offered genuine opportunities for self-representation.

To explore the ways in which Italian museums are responding to this need for 'third spaces' I wish to highlight three significant strands of experimental practice. First, some museums are taking on the training of immigrant cultural mediators[7] with a view to exploring a more dia-logical, multi-vocal interpretation of collections. Second, some institutions are actively engag-ing mixed groups in the development of new, shared narratives around collections through storytelling, theatre techniques and other mediation methodologies, starting from the premise that project participants can provide a significant contribution to the knowledge, understand-ing and interpretation of museum objects. Third, some museums are facilitating interaction with contemporary artists in order to develop new perspectives on the notions of heritage or identity, and to experiment with unconventional communication and relational methodolo-gies, mediated through contemporary art languages.[8]

The potential of the first area of experimentation – cultural mediators as 'new interpreters' of the museum's heritage – is evident in a project called *Tongue to Tongue: A Collaborative Exhi-bition*, jointly promoted by the Museum of Anthropology and Ethnography of the University of Turin and the Centre for African Studies (Pecci and Mangiapane 2010; Pecci 2009b; Bodo *et al.* 2009).

Tongue to Tongue was based on a participatory approach to the interpretation and display of collections, involving mediators,[9] the museum's staff and an architect/exhibition planner (playing the threefold role of exhibition designer, facilitator and 'translator' of the mediators' knowledge and expertise) in the planning and mounting of a multi-vocal exhibition. The voice or 'tongue' of the museum – institutional, scientific, didactic – engaged in dialogue with the mediators' voices – autobiographical, evocative, emotional – hence the title of the exhibition. At the heart of the project was a training course primarily conceived as a process of cultural empowerment, providing 'first and second generation migrants and cultural mediators with genuine opportunities for self-representation and cultural re-appropriation of tangible and intangible heritages' (Pecci 2009b).

During the course – which developed participants' skills in a range of areas from the use of storytelling as a heritage mediation tool to youth engagement – each mediator freely selected from the museum's ethnographic collections one or more objects, not necessarily directly related to their own cultural backgrounds, but nevertheless 'holding a particular significance for them, as they revealed sometimes unexpected links with their personal history, past and present, or with their knowledge systems and memories' (Bodo *et al.* 2009: 36). The selection of objects from the collection was followed by the planning of 'narrative routes' for visitors, developed in close cooperation with the museum's staff. Finally, the objects were displayed in showcases alongside the 'subjective heritage' of mediators (souvenirs, pictures, books, clothes and so on), thereby creating an impressive range of autobiographical installations. Through this project: 'Museum objects . . . revealed their capacity to evade the classifications and narratives into which they had been institutionally inscribed and to be re-presented into a new, more connective display' (Pecci and Mangia-pane 2010: 149).

The visit to the exhibition, mainly addressed to local students attending the last two years of secondary school, but also to the general public of the Museum and to under-represented audiences (in particular, young people and immigrant communities), consisted of dialogical 'narrative routes' resulting from the interaction and exchange of knowledge and perspectives between a museum educator and a mediator.

> The [museum educator] gave an account of the 'journeys', both geographical and museological, of the displayed object; through storytelling, the [mediator] helped the educator and the audience put the objects in context, by highlighting their history, their functions and interpretations, and sometimes their ideological use. The autobiographical approach also allowed mediators to incorporate their individual (and migratory) stories in the displayed objects and exhibition spaces.
>
> *Pecci 2009b*

[handwritten margin note: multiple peeps at play interpreting]

A key achievement of *Tongue to Tongue* is the reciprocity it encouraged between the museum and mediators, by bringing into dialogue their different perspectives, experiences and knowledge bases, and incorporating them not only in interpretation (the development of the 'narrative routes'), but also in display (the planning and mounting of a multi-vocal exhibition). Overall, the project demonstrates that:

> the potential role of museums as agents of social change lies in their contribution to the recognition as well as to the reflective deconstruction of the cultural identity of individuals and groups. But in order for this to be achieved, the museum's areas of work must be conceived as *processes*, rather than as tightly defined 'mechanical' functions such as conservation, exhibition and education.
>
> *Pecci 2009a: 15*

The second strand of experimental practice I would like to explore – the engagement of mixed groups in the development of new, shared narratives around collections – found an ideal testing ground in the Guatelli Museum. The history of this most peculiar museum is closely connected with the personal story of its creator, Ettore Guatelli, a primary school teacher born in 1921. Interested in objects as evidence of the history of mankind, Guatelli was particularly fascinated by the narratives they embody and unfold. The collection reflects daily life through the poetry of objects (utensils from rural culture and everyday objects such as boxes, toys, shoes and pottery), evocatively displayed on the museum walls. In trying to initiate intercultural dynamics and participation patterns in the local community's life, the project *Plural Stories* (Turci 2009; Bodo *et al.* 2009) drew inspiration from the museum founder's vision, in that it aimed at collecting histories and experiences of participants in some way connected with the collections. As Mario Turci, director of the Guatelli Museum, observes, 'women became part of a "provisional community" interested in developing new interpretations of the relationship between personal biographies and the biographies of objects' (Turci 2009: 65).

Project participants (ten native and migrant women, aged between 18 and 60) were identified outside formal learning contexts through contacts with local associations and with the support of two neighbouring local authorities. One of the key aims of *Plural Stories* was to help participants 'recognise, interpret and conceptualise tangible and intangible elements acquiring a heritage value with respect to both their original culture and the culture of the place where they have settled' (Bodo *et al.* 2009: 52).

The initial intention to invite participants to describe objects in written form was subsequently revised due to significant differences in literacy levels amongst the women. The project team opted instead for a theatre workshop (run by FestinaLente Teatro, one of the museum's partners in this project), where women were free to express themselves through verbal and non-verbal language (Figure 13.1). In fact, the use of theatre techniques helped overcome linguistic barriers and enabled a strong interaction between project participants. This was achieved through the shared recovery of 'gestural memories' drawing inspiration from the museum's spaces and objects (for example, the gesture of washing clothes, of lighting a fire and so on), as well as through storytelling and the exchange of narratives triggered by the participants' own objects (a sort of 'personal museum'), and connected with their respective life experiences and contexts of origin. Through *Plural Stories*, 'The past embodied in objects was conceived and explored as a "foreign country", which helped define a "third space" where participants could share the development of new knowledge systems, skills and experiences' (Bodo *et al.* 2009: 53).

The project ended with an itinerant theatre performance held across the museum's spaces, in which women gave life to their stories through spoken and body language. The title of the performance, *Plural Stories: From Hand to Hand*, reflects the belief that heritage, conceived in its dialogical dimension, is constantly re-created and enriched by being passed on from one individual to the other, from one generation to another.

A third strand of practice with which Italian museums are increasingly engaging is the interaction with artists with a view to visualising intercultural dynamics through contemporary art languages.

The *City Telling* project, launched by the Sandretto Re Rebaudengo Foundation in Turin (Bodo *et al.* 2009; Pereira *et al.* 2010), offers an interesting example of how this can be achieved. The underlying goal of the project was to increase the opportunities for cultural participation of young immigrants (students of a local centre for adult education and training), as well as to build a common ground of cultural, linguistic and aesthetic interaction, by helping participants to

FIGURE 13.1 Rehearsal of the final theatre performance in the exhibition spaces of the Guatelli Museum.

'develop a critical understanding of the reality surrounding them; increase their ability to analyse and communicate their own experience of the world; acquire the necessary skills to carry out personal inquiry and re-discover the urban territory where they live' (Bodo *et al.* 2009: 34).

City Telling started with the setting up of a team composed by the education staff of the Foundation, teachers from the Drovetti Centre for Adult Education and Training, artist-director Gianluca De Serio and photographer Anna Largaiolli, who exchanged views and expertise with respect to the methodological approach as well as to their respective knowledge of the territory to explore during the project. For six months, the group of young students were actively involved in discovering their local urban space. The project began by enabling the students to share their geo-cultural origins through storytelling and the use of objects, photographs, postcards and web technologies. In the following phase of the project, De Serio and Largaiolli guided the students in two parallel itineraries respectively devoted to video and photographic storytelling, a methodology with which the education staff of the Foundation was very familiar. The two working groups developed a personal route across urban space, by identifying significant spots in the city (schools, museums, libraries, private homes, gardens, places of worship, urban installations, services and meeting spaces) and collecting their manifold impressions in a journal made of photographs, observations and audiovisual creations. A key strength of the project was the chance for participants to work at leisure in the Foundation's exhibition spaces, where the artworks provided opportunities for reflection, writing and the production of audiovisual materials.[10]

One of the photographic series produced by *City Telling* project participants drew inspiration from an artwork in the Sandretto Re Rebaudengo Foundation's permanent collections – *A-Z Living Unit*, by Californian artist Andrea Zittel – which is concerned with travelling through different cultural contexts and discovering what is essential for living. Dina and Belen, the two young participants who produced their own photography inspired by this piece, spent a lot of time in the room where *A-Z Living Unit* was exhibited, as they knew the idea of 'being here and somewhere else at the same time' was central to their own story. The series opens with the parallel awakening of Dina and Belen in two different parts of the city; both feel an initial sense of being *at home*, before their dreaming gives way to reality. Walking around Turin, across different kinds of spaces (changing spaces, empty spaces, spaces full of memory, spaces of desire), Dina and Belen talk about their past, present and future, how they see and don't see themselves, the trace they want to leave in the city.

Conclusions

Whilst these three projects involved different groups, heritage institutions and working practices, they can nevertheless be understood to have grown out of a shared assumption: that the rethinking of heritage from a participatory, dialogical, intercultural perspective is an important pursuit, one which holds the potential to impact all citizens. Museums as intercultural spaces can function to not only promote the cultural rights of migrant communities but also to nurture in *all* individuals ('natives' and 'migrants'), those attitudes, behaviours and skills (including cognitive mobility; the ability to question one's own points of view and to challenge stereotypes; the awareness of one's own multiple identities) which are indispensable in a world of increasing contact and interaction between culturally different groups.

The exploratory and experimental projects discussed in this chapter show a willingness on the part of some museum professionals to go beyond policies targeting individuals and groups according to their racial origin and ethnicity; initiatives which are often based on the over-simplistic assumption that a 'community' will be interested exclusively in objects and issues that are specifically and directly related to its cultural background. As Pecci and Mangiapane (2010: 147) argue, 'Migrants are not representatives of the cultures they come from, but interpreters or witnesses who, instead of wearing the uniform of culture, creatively escape from its essentialist definition of a bounded and confined unity'. In other words, these projects work on identity as 'the start rather than the end of the conversation' (Khan 2010), and work with a notion of the museum as a space for generating new (inclusive and liberatory) meanings (Pecci and Mangiapane 2010; Sandell 2007). Moreover, they highlight methodological issues which are key to the development of 'third spaces'. In such spaces, the use of a thematic approach to the presentation of collections is not simply an alternative way of transmitting content or specialist knowledge but rather it is aimed at helping participants develop a critical understanding of the reality surrounding them and increasing their ability to analyse and communicate their own experience of the world. Similarly, autobiographical storytelling is explored, not simply as a one-off chance for self-expression but instead as an opportunity to facilitate an ongoing reflection on the role of the museum and to lay down foundations for continued dialogue and cooperation. Finally, such spaces emphasise the evocative and emotional power of objects, not only to strengthen group allegiances but also to disengage objects and audiences from the prevailing rationale of cultural representation (Bodo 2009b).

Museums' increasing concern to function as spaces for intercultural dialogue represents a significant international trend in museological thinking and practice. Underpinning such efforts is the recognition that this work can promote more diverse and less stereotypical images of communities by providing participants with the opportunity for self-representation; it can create shared spaces where meaningful, interactive communication takes place and all participants are recognised as being equal. At the same time, the experiences of museums working in this field highlight how hard it still is, even for the most forward-looking institutions, to break the dichotomy between curatorship as a core function (carried out by museum experts) and education, outreach and community engagement as an activity which takes place in the margins, where project ownership and the active involvement of participants are more easily tolerated, precisely because they do not seem to threaten the authority and expertise of curators and scientific staff.

Further challenges for the museum sector, therefore, lie in ensuring that the outcomes of programmes and activities aimed at promoting cross-cultural interaction between different audiences are more clearly visible and easily retrievable, whether in the museum's collections documentation system or permanent displays; and, perhaps most importantly, in a rethinking of all the fundamental functions of a museum (from collections management and conservation to exhibition strategies) through an intercultural perspective, so that this is built into its institutional fabric. As the museum anthropologist Christina Kreps observes, 'achieving interculturality is a step by step process that may help, with every project and every action, to not only transform our societies, but also our museums and the nature of public culture' (2009: 4).

Notes

1 See article 1 of the UNESCO World Heritage Convention (1972: 2).
2 See article 2 of the UNESCO *Convention for the Safeguarding of the Intangible Cultural Heritage* (2003: 2), which acknowledges heritage as being 'constantly recreated by communities and groups in response to their environment, their interaction with nature and their history'.

3 A growing body of research around good practice in intercultural dialogue in museums across Europe and beyond is available, arising from a number of surveys and action-research projects: see for example Bodo et al. (2009); Gibbs et al. (2007); CLMG – Campaign for Learning through Museums and Galleries (2006).

4 In Italy, this attitude is best exemplified by initiatives aimed at 'explaining Italian art to non-EU citizens'.

5 Sandell (2004) offers a useful categorisation of museum initiatives such as these and their underpinning motivations and potential social effects and consequences.

6 In 2007, Milan-based Fondazione Ismu (Initiatives and Studies on Multiethnicity) launched *Patrimonio e Intercultura* (http://fondazione.ismu.org/patrimonioeintercultura, English version available), an online resource exclusively devoted to heritage education in an intercultural perspective, which regularly monitors projects carried out in Italian museums. For an overview of the Italian museum sector in terms of cultural diversity and intercultural policies see also Bodo and Mascheroni (2009).

7 As the term 'mediator' is interpreted differently across the museum sector in Europe, it is worth clarifying that, in the Italian context, the expression 'cultural/linguistic mediator' is mainly used to describe professionals with an immigrant background acting as 'bridges' with their respective communities in sectors such as formal education and the healthcare system. Only recently has this profession started to be developed in a museum/heritage context.

8 The three case studies presented in this section of the chapter were all carried out in the framework of the European project, *MAP for ID – Museums as Places for Intercultural Dialogue* (www.mapforid.it; see also Bodo et al. 2009), funded by the European Commission as part of the Grundtvig Lifelong Learning Programme.

9 Trained mediators' countries of origin ranged from Chad, Congo and Senegal to Italy, Morocco and Romania.

10 The short films and photographic series produced through this project can be viewed in the 'Videos' section of the website *Patrimonio e Intercultura*.

References

Bennett, T. (2006) 'Cultura e differenza: teorie e pratiche politiche', in S. Bodo and M. R. Cifarelli (eds) *Quando la Cultura Fa la Differenza. Patrimonio, Arti e Media nella Società Multiculturale*, Roma: Meltemi: 21–37.

Besozzi, E. (2007) 'Culture in gioco e patrimoni culturali', in S. Bodo, S. Cantù and S. Mascheroni (eds) *Progettare Insieme per un Patrimonio Interculturale*, Quaderni Ismu 1/2007, Milan: Fondazione Ismu: 19–28.

Bloomfield, J. and Bianchini, F. (2004) *Planning for the Intercultural City*, Stroud: Comedia.

Bodo, S. (2008) 'From "heritage education with intercultural goals" to "intercultural heritage education": conceptual framework and policy approaches in museums across Europe', in ERICarts Institute (ed.) *Sharing Diversity. National Approaches to Intercultural Dialogue in Europe*, final report of a study carried out on behalf of the European Commission – Directorate General for Education and Culture. Online. Available at: www.interculturaldialogue.eu (accessed 25 August 2011).

Bodo, S. (2009a), 'The challenge of creating "third spaces": guidelines for MAP for ID pilot projects', in S. Bodo, K. Gibbs and M. Sani (eds) *Museums as Places for Intercultural Dialogue: Selected Practices from Europe*, Dublin: MAP for ID Group: 22–4.

Bodo, S. (2009b) 'Introduction to pilot projects', in S. Bodo, K. Gibbs and M. Sani (eds) *Museums as Places for Intercultural Dialogue: Selected Practices from Europe*, Dublin: MAP for ID Group: 26–30.

Bodo, S. and Mascheroni, S. (2009) 'Il patrimonio culturale, nuova frontiera per l'integrazione', in Fondazione Ismu, *Quattordicesimo Rapporto sulle Migrazioni 2008*, Milan: FrancoAngeli: 253–61.

Bodo, S., Gibbs, K. and Sani, M. (eds) (2009) *Museums as Places for Intercultural Dialogue: Selected Practices from Europe*, Dublin: MAP for ID Group.

Campaign for Learning through Museums and Galleries (2006) *Culture Shock: Tolerance, Respect, Understanding . . . and Museums*, London: Home Office.

Fondazione Ismu (Initiatives and Studies on Multiethnicity) (2007) *Patrimonio e Intercultura*. Online. Available at: http://fondazione.ismu.org/patrimonioeintercultura (accessed 25 August 2011).

Gibbs, K., Sani, M. and Thompson, J. (eds) (2007) *Lifelong Learning in Museums. A European Handbook*, Ferrara: Edisai.

Khan, N. (2010) *The Artist as Translator*, paper delivered at the seminar 'Super Diversity – Who Participates Now? Discussion on the Phenomenon of "Super Diversity" in the Visual Arts', Institute of International Visual Arts, London, 2 February.

Kreps, C. (2009) 'Foreword', in S. Bodo, K. Gibbs and M. Sani (eds) *Museums as Places for Intercultural Dialogue: Selected Practices from Europe*, Dublin: MAP for ID Group: 4–5.

Matarasso, F. (2004) '*L'Etat, c'est nous*: arte, sussidi e stato nei regimi democratici', *Economia della Cultura*, Journal of the Italian Association for Cultural Economics (themed issue edited by S. Bodo and C. Da Milano on Culture and Social Inclusion), 4: 491–8.

Matarasso, F. (2006) 'La storia sfigurata: la creazione del patrimonio culturale nell'Europa contemporanea', in S. Bodo and M. R. Cifarelli (eds) *Quando la Cultura Fa la Differenza. Patrimonio, Arti e Media nella Società Multiculturale*, Rome: Meltemi: 50–62.

Pecci, A. M. (ed.) (2009a) *Patrimoni in Migrazione. Accessibilità, Partecipazione, Mediazione nei Musei*, Milan: FrancoAngeli.

Pecci, A. M. (2009b) 'Tongue to Tongue', in 'Projects', *Patrimonio e Intercultura*. Online. Available at: http://fondazione.ismu.org/patrimonioeintercultura/index.php (accessed 24 August 2011).

Pecci, A. M. and Mangiapane, G. (2010) 'Expographic storytelling: the Museum of Anthropology and Ethnography of the University of Turin as a field of dialogic representation', *The International Journal of the Inclusive Museum*, 3 (1): 141–53.

Pereira, M., Salvi, A., Sani, M. and Villa, L. (2010) *MAP for ID. Esperienze, Sviluppi e Riflessioni*, Bologna: Istituto per i Beni Artistici Culturali e Naturali della Regione Emilia-Romagna.

Sandell, R. (2004) 'Strategie espositive nei musei e promozione dell'uguaglianza', *Economia della Cultura*, Journal of the Italian Association for Cultural Economics (themed issue edited by S. Bodo and C. Da Milano on Culture and Social Inclusion), 4: 539–46.

Sandell, R. (2007) *Museums, Prejudice and the Reframing of Difference*, London and New York: Routledge.

Turci, M. (2009) 'Dell'impossibilità che il dialogo possa essere interculturale', in *Antropologia Museale*, Journal of the Italian Society for Demoethnoanthropologic Heritage and Museography (themed issue edited by V. Lattanzi on Heritage, Museums and Collaborative Practices), 20/21: 64–5.

UNESCO (1972) *Convention Concerning the Protection of the World Cultural and Natural Heritage: Adopted by the General Conference at its Seventeenth Session, Paris, 16 November 1972*, Paris: United Nations Educational, Scientific and Cultural Organization.

UNESCO (2003) *Convention for the Safeguarding of the Intangible Cultural Heritage*, Paris: United Nations Educational, Scientific and Cultural Organization.

Veini, E. and Kistemaker, R. (2003) 'Dancing with diversity', *Muse*, XXI (4), Canada Museums Association: 20–3.

Young, L. (2005) *Our Lives, Our Histories, Our Collections*, paper commissioned by the Museum of London. Online. Available at: www.museumoflondon.org.uk/Collections-Research/Research/Your-Research/RWWC/Essays/Essay2 (accessed 25 August 2011).

PART III
Museums and the good society

14

MUSEUMS AND THE HUMAN RIGHTS FRAME

Richard Sandell

The idea of human rights – as a set of values, norms and beliefs, as a moral framework and an ideal standard through which social equality and fairness might be achieved – is one that enjoys considerable support worldwide, capable of generating an extraordinary level of consensus amongst diverse social groups, institutions and governments, and across national and cultural boundaries (Donnelly 2003). Despite this widespread, global appeal, attempts to apply rights at the local level, to redraw the boundaries that distinguish those who enjoy rights from those who are denied them, rarely proceed uncontested. Indeed, such attempts frequently reveal conflicting moral positions and mobilise opposing parties to deny or seek to undermine rights claims, resulting in fiercely fought and highly visible battles. This chapter explores how and why museums, typically risk-averse institutions that prefer to avoid controversy, are increasingly taking up human rights as an interpretive frame through which to address, and engage visitors in debating, diverse contemporary social concerns.

Despite a remarkable proliferation in the number and type of museum and gallery projects internationally that have, over the last decade, taken up the language and idea of human rights to frame their approach to wide ranging subjects, very little research has yet been carried out to empirically investigate this phenomenon and its implications for museums, audiences and those agencies and social groups actively engaged in human rights struggles. Whilst a growing body of literature over the past twenty years has significantly developed our understanding of museums as sites in which political struggles over issues of identity, belonging and citizenship are played out (Karp and Lavine 1991; Hooper-Greenhill 2000) and recent studies have begun to consider the implications of museums' engagement with controversial and morally charged topics (Macdonald 2008; Sandell and Dodd 2010; Cameron and Kelly 2010), little is known about the social and political effects and consequences of museums' increasing engagement with human rights. How are museum staff negotiating the ethical dilemmas bound up in their human rights work? How are visitors responding to the moral standpoints they encounter? And how are museums viewed and utilised by those actively involved in contemporary struggles to secure human rights?

This chapter develops an interdisciplinary analysis that combines theoretical perspectives from social anthropology, social movement studies, and museum and cultural studies to address this under-researched area. Responding to calls within social anthropology for in-depth empirical investigation of rights processes within specific settings, I take a single case study to examine how a rights project is constructed through negotiation between *local* agendas and interests on the one hand and, on the other, a *global* rights discourse that transcends local and national boundaries (Cowan *et al.* 2001). Furthermore, I explore the ways in which this particular articulation of rights is perceived, taken up, appropriated and resisted by diverse constituencies.

The approach and methods proposed and described below are designed to generate 'thick descriptions' of the setting under investigation; ones which are rich, nuanced and drawn from multiple perspectives. Social anthropologist, Richard A. Wilson, argues that such methods are helpful for countering the legalistic and mechanistic approaches which have predominated in human rights studies, for capturing the complexity of rights talk and processes and 'the richness of subjectivities immersed in complex fields of social relations which legalistic accounts of human rights often omit' (1997: 170).

The Gallery of Modern Art in Glasgow (GoMA) offers a rich and highly pertinent site for this investigation. From 9 April to 1 November 2009, GoMA presented the fourth in a biennial series of programmes that used contemporary art as a platform for public and community engagement around diverse social justice-related themes. Building on the success of earlier programmes – that examined the rights of asylum-seekers and refugees, violence against women, and religious sectarianism – the fourth programme, entitled *sh[OUT]*, focused on lesbian, gay, bisexual, transgender and intersex rights. During this time the Gallery attracted more than 320,000 visitors but, at the same time, generated a political and media storm unprecedented in the institution's history.

This chapter examines the ways in which a particular regime of rights came to be inscribed through *sh[OUT]* and traces the social effects and consequences of this project from a number of different perspectives. First, I consider how particular notions of gender and sexual diversity came to be produced and explore the ways in which ideas about the rights of lesbian, gay, bisexual, transgender – and, ultimately, intersex – communities were constructed by Gallery staff through negotiation with intersecting local, national and transnational agendas. I then consider key moments in the media controversy sparked by particular aspects of the *sh[OUT]* programme before focusing in greater depth on audiences and, through quantitative and qualitative analyses of visitor responses, examine how individuals perceived, negotiated and made use of the moral standpoints and ethical narratives they encountered in the gallery. My purpose here is to consider how – if at all – public understandings of rights-related issues are informed or reconfigured by visitors' engagement with museum and gallery projects. Lastly, I explore the potential role and agency of museums in addressing rights issues from the perspective of those communities engaged in the struggle for equal rights. Drawing on focus groups and interviews with transgender activists and artists, I explore how members of this minority group – at a critical moment in their long-standing struggle for rights – viewed the Gallery of Modern Art as a vehicle for advancing their cause. Taken together, these diverse perspectives aim to shed light on a broader set of questions museums in many parts of the world increasingly face. How might practitioners begin to negotiate the multiple moral positions they encounter and select which, of various competing visions of the good society, will be privileged in their interpretations? How do museums interpret and respond to situations in which the rights of one group are perceived to impinge on those of another? Ultimately, I argue that controversy – generated by activities and stated moral positions that frequently challenge normative conceptions of fairness and equality – might usefully be seen as an inevitable, indeed necessary, part of the human rights work that museums do. Anticipating and managing this controversy in productive ways is likely to become increasingly important for museums that purposefully seek to shape a more equitable and fair moral order.

The human rights project

Over the past few decades, human rights thought and practices have been taken up in wide ranging global contexts and appropriated by myriad causes, social movements, institutions and governments. Human rights, it is increasingly recognised, has become 'one of the most globalised political values of our times' (Wilson 1997: 1).

The growing influence of rights discourse can be seen in international museum rhetoric, policy and practice, particularly over the last two decades and in the emergence of a growing number of museums whose primary purposes and rationales are concerned with the promotion of equal rights and the promulgation of humanitarian values (Duffy 2001; Sandell 2007).[1] Whilst these museums address diverse topics and historic events it is nevertheless possible to discern commonalities amongst them, both in terms of the language they each deploy to frame their interpretive approach and, more fundamentally, in a shared belief that the capacity for museums to function as 'sites of persuasion' (Morphy 2006) can be harnessed to build public and political support for equity, fairness and justice. These specialised institutions have emerged against a backdrop of increasingly ubiquitous concern, in museums of all kinds, to represent cultural differences in more respectful ways (Bennett 2006; Sandell 2007). In recent years, museums have become more confident in proclaiming their value as agents of progressive social change and, in particular, articulating their capacity to function as fora in which the rights, interests and viewpoints of diverse communities can be represented and debated. Indeed, exhibitions and displays purposefully designed to engage audiences in debates around rights-related issues (especially pertaining to women, indigenous and minority ethnic communities but also those linked to faith groups, disabled people and sexual minorities) have appeared in museums in many parts of the world.

Universalism and relativism

The ubiquity of human rights – and the capacity they hold to engender relatively consensual support across cultures – owes much to what Donnelly terms their 'moral universality' (2003); the notion that a common set of universal rights are naturally held by all human beings regardless of the circumstances in which they live and the institutional structures (legal, political and social) which may govern their daily lived experience. Whilst claims regarding the moral universality of rights have been enormously influential they have also given rise to fierce debate amongst human rights researchers, especially within social anthropology where considerable support for a cultural relativist position has been deployed to critique the universal human rights project. For much of the second half of the twentieth century, anthropological thought and practice favoured a relativist standpoint which valued respect for cultural differences and rejected the very notion of universal norms of justice. Indeed, supporters of anthropological relativism argued that the universal human rights project could more accurately be read as an attempt by the West to claim – as natural and morally superior – a highly particular set of values and to impose them onto other cultures (Rapport and Overing 2000; Wilson and Mitchell 2003).

Over the last two decades however, in the face of growing concerns for notions of global justice and high profile instances of rights violations in many parts of the world, there has been increasing support for the view that a relativist standpoint is untenable and that anthropologists can no longer avoid making moral and ethical judgements on the cultural and social practices they encounter and seek to understand (ibid.). It is only in the last decade that progress has been made to move beyond the impasse created by the idea that universalism and relativism are inherently irreconcilable and instead to view the tension between them 'as part of the continuous process of negotiating ever-changing and interrelated global and local norms' (Cowan *et al.* 2001: 6).

Evolving rights regimes

What the long-standing debate between universalists and relativists serves to highlight is the situated, highly contingent and dynamic character of human rights discourse. Whilst the idea of rights as held universally by all human beings across space and time represents an ideal to which many would subscribe, any concrete attempt to inscribe rights is necessarily historically, culturally and geographically situated, shaped by an interplay between local normative conceptions of fairness and a global rights discourse that, despite the rhetoric of universalism and immutability is, in fact, shifting and dynamic. Although, for many, human rights stands for emancipation, inclusion and fairness, specific rights regimes (and the policies, laws, institutional structures and resource priorities they inform) invariably involve ongoing forms of exclusion and oppression. As Donnelly (2003: 228) illustrates:

> women and nonwhites were until well into [the twentieth] century widely seen as irreparably deficient in their rational or moral capacities and thus incapable of exercising the full range of human rights. These racial and gender distinctions, however, were in principle subject to moral and empirical counterarguments. Over the past several decades dominant political ideas and practices in Western and non-Western societies alike have been transformed by national and international movements to end slavery and, later, colonialism; to grant women and racial minorities the vote; and to end discrimination based on race, ethnicity, and gender. A similar tale can be told in the case of Jews, non-conformist Christian sects, atheists, and other religious minorities.
>
> In each case, a logic of full and equal humanity has overcome claims of group inferiority, bringing (at least formally) equal membership in society through explicitly guaranteed protections against discrimination.

Whilst it would be inaccurate to assume from Donnelly's account that all regimes proceed smoothly along an ever more progressive and inclusive linear trajectory, his analysis is nevertheless helpful for highlighting the fluidity and permeability of the constantly contested boundaries that distinguish between those who can claim the rights that accompany full and equal membership of societies, and those from whom rights are withheld. His analysis turns the spotlight on the social and political struggles that – at any given moment – are seeking to extend or reconfigure the boundaries inscribed by (formal) regimes to confer rights upon previously disenfranchised groups. At the same time, however, as Donnelly highlights, a focus on the *formal* instruments and processes through which rights are conferred (such as national and international law) potentially overlooks the everyday experience of social groups for whom formal recognition constitutes only a part of the struggle for equal rights. Whilst rights regimes at a supra-national level and in many states have evolved to encompass, for example, women, indigenous groups and minority ethnic and religious groups, such formal recognition does not, of course, preclude discrimination and a denial of opportunities to exercise the full range of rights at the level of lived experience. In other words, whilst discrimination on the grounds of race, for example, might be outlawed by equality laws and other formal mechanisms, such instruments do not necessarily eliminate racism.

Museums and human rights

Given this understanding of the human rights landscape as continually shifting in relation to political struggles, new social movements and changing norms of justice, what role might museums play – both in terms of the reconfiguring of boundaries through which formal rights are inscribed and the nurturing of more cosmopolitan social norms that shape the lived experiences of marginalised groups? To what extent can museums negotiate the difficult territory between globally framed (often more inclusive and cosmopolitan) normative understandings of justice and locally inscribed (frequently more exclusive and conservative) rights regimes? To examine these issues, I turn now to Glasgow, Scotland and the Gallery of Modern Art to consider the ways in which both local moral norms and conventions and globalised conceptions of human rights inspired and constrained the construction of rights.[2]

A new direction for GoMA

Around 2001, Glasgow's Gallery of Modern Art began to develop a programme of biennial exhibitions, public events, and education and community outreach activities which sought to deploy contemporary and modern art to directly and explicitly engage visitors in debates pertaining to different human rights issues.[3] The 'social justice programme' emerged out of what Mark O'Neill, then Head of Museums and Galleries, describes as a 'combination of opportunism and principle' (Sandell, Dodd and Jones 2010: 14). Glasgow City Council (of which GoMA was then part)[4] had recently agreed to take around 10,000 asylum-seekers as part of the UK government's dispersal programme to relieve pressure on the south-east of England (Bruce and Hollows 2007: 8), a controversial decision which led to criticism of the way in which new arrivals were integrated into areas of already high deprivation. Growing political concern over social unrest and negative perceptions of asylum-seekers in both local media and amongst Glasgow's communities reached a peak following the high profile murder of a young Turkish refugee, Firsat Yildiz, in the Sighthill area of Glasgow. The City Council subsequently asked its various departments, including Culture and Leisure Services of which Glasgow Museums was part, to consider how they might both develop services targeted at new arrivals to the city and address negative public attitudes towards these groups (ibid.). At around the same time, Glasgow Museums was approached by Amnesty International about the possibility of an exhibition linked to their activities and discussions began around the possibilities of partnership. These events fitted well with the ethos and practice of Glasgow Museums that had, for many years, pioneered museum developments that sought to extend access to new audiences and to address social issues but posed particular problems for the Gallery. For many years, GoMA had had a difficult relationship with the thriving Glasgow art scene and had come to be viewed, by both local artists and the art world more broadly, as populist and lacking credibility as a venue for showing quality work. So, despite a framework of institutional commitment and prior experience within Glasgow Museums as a whole, the idea of an exhibition that explicitly addressed political and social concerns represented an entirely new direction for GoMA's practice and one of which staff were initially very wary. As Victoria Hollows, Museum Manager, explained:

> We had been suffering in the early years at GoMA in terms of its reputation and credibility as an art gallery. To be absolutely honest, when we were first asked to do something about asylum seekers and refugees we thought 'do we have to?' We were just starting to get support in the arts community and we thought it would be perceived completely wrong. We didn't want this to be the final nail in the coffin. I think it's fair to say that the staff had a very strong belief that we can have good quality art and embrace current contemporary practice *and* we can still have strong audience support. So this was our moment to prove that can happen. It was a huge gamble in some respects.

The project nevertheless gained momentum and a philosophy of practice emerged which centred on the use of art as a platform for engaging audiences in debate and dialogue around a series of human rights related topics – a philosophy maintained through all four biennial programmes. The first programme to be launched in 2003 entitled *Sanctuary: Contemporary Art and Human Rights* sought to raise awareness of the plight of asylum-seekers and refugees worldwide and to redress negative media portrayals and local public perceptions. It featured work by 34 artists from 15 different countries including established names such as Bill Viola, Louise Bourgeois, Leon Golub and Hans Haacke (Bruce and Hollows 2007). Since *Sanctuary*, three further programmes have been delivered, each with the same strapline, 'Contemporary art and human rights'. The second programme, *Rule of Thumb* (2005), explored the issue of violence against women with a range of activities based around a solo exhibition of work by American artist Barbara Kruger. The third programme, *Blind Faith* (2007), explored the sensitive issue of sectarianism, again through a range of outreach and education projects and a public events programme built around a high profile exhibition, this time of specially commissioned work by Glasgow-based artist, Roderick Buchanan. The fourth programme – *sh[OUT]* – opened in 2009 and explored rights issues pertaining to lesbian, gay, bisexual, transgender and intersex communities. In common with the previous three programmes, *sh[OUT]* was presented in partnership with Amnesty International and developed through collaboration with an advisory group comprised of representatives of a range of community based agencies in Scotland.[5]

At the heart of the programme was an exhibition featuring work by 18 artists including Patricia Cronin,[6] Robert Mapplethorpe (Figures 14.1 and 14.2) David Hockney, Nan Goldin, Sadie Lee and Grayson Perry (Plates 14.1, 14.2 and 14.3) and, in a small adjoining gallery, visitors could find out more about the struggle for LGBT rights and examples of rights violations from around the world through a documentary exhibition developed by Amnesty International. In a further space, a resource area (with books, leaflets, oral history material and so on) featured a wall on which visitors were invited to share their responses to the programme through comments cards. Accompanying the main exhibition was a series of smaller, changing exhibitions including work produced by participants in LGBT community groups (developed with support from professional artists and gallery staff). A series of striking posters, featuring quotations related to the programme's central concerns and selected by the advisory group, were used to promote the programme across the city (Figure 14.3).

FIGURE 14.1 Patricia Cronin, *Memorial to a Marriage*, 2002. Bronze, 17 × 26.5 × 52 inches. Collection of Glasgow City Council. With kind permission of the artist and Glasgow Museums.

FIGURE 14.2   Robert Mapplethorpe, *Brian Ridley and Lyle Heeter*, 1979. ©Robert Mapplethorpe Foundation. Used by permission.

Who's in and who's out: inscribing LGBT(I) rights

As planning for the fourth programme got underway, the seemingly straightforward aim to fairly represent, within the main exhibition, lesbian, gay, bisexual and transgender identities (in accordance with the familiar acronym, LGBT) proved increasingly problematic. The lead curator for *sh[OUT]*, Sean McGlashan, was able to identify, with relative ease, a range of high quality work which spoke to lesbian and gay experiences but other aspects of sexuality and gender identity proved more challenging to address – although for very different reasons. Representing bisexual experience, for example, was constrained by the paucity of artworks that could be found on this theme.[7] In contrast, a wealth of arts practice was identified that, in some way or another, spoke to issues of gender diversity (and, interestingly, around a third of the works that were included in the final selection were either by transgender/intersex artists or otherwise referenced some aspect of gender diversity). Understanding and negotiating the

FIGURE 14.3 Exhibition poster for *sh[OUT]: Contemporary Art and Human Rights, Lesbian, gay, bisexual, transgender and intersex art and culture*, 2009, Gallery of Modern Art, Glasgow.

political implications bound up in representing transgender identities and experience, how-ever, proved to be a complex curatorial challenge. Here, James Morton, Project Coordinator at the Scottish Transgender Alliance and a member of the advisory board for *sh[OUT]*, offers reflections on early discussions in the planning process that highlight how a developing under-standing of the transgender rights movement (and the overlapping – sometimes conflicting – local and national agendas involved) influenced the gallery's position on trans issues.

> When I first heard about *sh[OUT]* it was sounding like it was going to be very much focused on sexuality – but once we realised that, yes, they were taking this seriously and they wanted to be trans-inclusive then I started going along to the meetings . . .
>
> Down in England there are a lot more tensions around whether the T gets included in LGBT so you see more organisations that are just LGB. So, for example, Stonewall, based in London just deals with sexual orientation but Stonewall Scotland, it does do LGBT, it does do gender identity as well. In Scotland there's been a lot of effort within national LGBT organisations to make sure trans doesn't get over looked but it hasn't always gone to plan and even where it has been integrated it's still an area which is much less well understood and the population is much smaller so it can be hard – even if you're trying to be representative – to achieve transvisibility within an event.
>
> I was stressing [through the advisory board] that, in Scotland, we try and show there are not just transsexual people but people who see themselves as in-between genders, there's intersex as well, there's cross dressing . . . ideally you should be trying to find bits that tie into that range – so, keep going, try to find more. Don't just go 'we've got one [artist], that will do'.

As Sean in particular (and Gallery staff more broadly), learned more about the realities of transgender experience and the politics of trans identity, increasing effort was made to shape an exhibition that could accommodate this complexity. In particular, a nascent understanding of the intersex rights movement coupled with the discovery of work by artist Ins Kromminga, led to the addition of the term 'intersex' to the more familiar L, G, B and T that featured in the programme's subtitle. (This prominent inclusion of work related to gender identity and diversity subsequently proved pleasantly surprising and significant for transgender visitors and community participants whose experiences of projects purporting to represent the range of LGBT experience were more typically characterised by disappointment.[8])

Nevertheless, it is fair to say that the Gallery's openness to representing diverse aspects of trans identity and experience raised its own set of challenges for GoMA staff, increas-ingly concerned to develop a more inclusive approach to the programme. As James Morton explained:

> I think I kind of acted as a reassurance because they were worried at one point . . . There are so many different aspects of trans . . . and so it was like . . . 'Grayson Perry, Del LaGrace Volcano . . . who do we need to have in? Do we have to have *one*? Do we have to have *more*? Will they both be prepared to be in together? Are trans or other communities going to react really badly to particular representations of trans?' . . . I was like, 'yes, there are differences of opinion but you can't only represent one side. If you're trying to represent diverse aspects of sexual orientation you need to be trying to represent diverse aspects of gender identity too'. So yes, there will be people who don't

see Grayson Perry as exactly how they identify as trans . . . and might object to the fetish aspect of the cross dressing element but that's still a part of the community diversity and to just hide it away and go 'that's going to be contentious' wouldn't be appropriate.

Gallery staff were faced with a number of possibilities concerning which aspects of sexuality and gender identity to include in *sh[OUT]*. For curator Sean McGlashan and other colleagues, engagement with transgender politics, it seemed, led to a transformed understanding of the lived experience of transgender people which, in turn, translated into a desire to pass on some of this new insight to visitors. Resisting alignment with more narrowly framed rights regimes, staff eventually chose to develop a project which reflected support for a cosmopolitan, progressive and more inclusive articulation of LGBTI rights – a decision which, I will argue, is significant for our understanding of the role and agency of museums in engendering support for human rights. I return to this issue of choice shortly but first turn attention to further dilemmas Gallery staff faced in shaping a programme designed to lend support to LGBTI rights.

'Sex, sex, sex. Morning, noon and night': negotiating the politics of difference (and sameness)

Alongside challenges concerning which groups and identities were included (or given priority) within the exhibition were equally thorny dilemmas concerning how LGBTI lives should be portrayed and presented to the visiting public. From the outset, there was considerable consensus amongst advisory group members that the show should be celebratory in tone and avoid notions of victimhood and, indeed, this was reflected in the curatorial decision to select works 'mainly concerned with pride, confidence and respect of differences' (McGlashan 2009: 9). However, differing opinions quickly surfaced amongst advisory group members concerning the extent to which the exhibition might give emphasis to the distinctiveness of LGBTI lives or, alternatively, support readings which highlighted a common humanity with non LGBTI visitors through an emphasis on universal themes such as love, desire, family and so on.

This tension between, on the one hand, a political demand for respect for difference and, on the other, an assertion of sameness and shared humanity was most evident in debates concerning the exhibition's treatment of sexual practices and preferences. As ideas for artworks began to emerge and were presented to the advisory group by Gallery staff, anxieties around the inclusion of works depicting or related to sexual practices were raised by some members. Debate was particularly animated around the two Robert Mapplethorpe images – *Brian Ridley and Lyle Heeter* (1979), and *Jim and Tom, Sausalito* (1977), the latter being part of Mapplethorpe's infamous *X Portfolio* featuring images of sadomasochistic sex acts. Opinion on the appropriateness of these works for *sh[OUT]* ranged considerably, reflecting the internal complexity behind the familiar acronym, LGBT. Some voiced a concern that the Mapplethorpe images would likely alienate some members of the public and undermine the project's attempts to elicit mainstream support for LGBTI equality by encouraging visitors to read off the exhibition a natural association between 'deviant' sexual practices and homosexuality. Others believed the inclusion of the images that, twenty years earlier, had prompted a notorious censorship lawsuit over their display in the United States, was an exceptionally powerful way of communicating shifts in social mores and, moreover, a reflection of Glasgow City Council's willingness to take a stand on LGBTI rights. For example, Hugh Donaghy, Glasgow Team Leader for LGBT Youth Scotland, commented: 'When the Council said "yeah, you can have the Mapplethorpes" . . . that's when I saw the Council was 100% behind it – that was a real turning point for me'.

The final selection of works that eventually opened to the public portrayed diverse aspects of LGBTI lives. Both proposed Mapplethorpe images were selected, alongside other works which, to varying degrees and in different ways, were felt to be more challenging for audiences (and which can be understood to reflect support for a more radical LGBTI identity politics). However, these works – which prompted one visitor to comment, 'Sex, sex, sex, morning noon and night. Why can they only put their message over by being sexually explicit?' – were accompanied by many others which emphasised a common humanity, irrespective of sexual orientation and gender identity. How then were these carefully crafted articulations of LGBTI rights received by news media and gallery visitors?

'Hardcore gay porn'/'a celebration of tender portraiture'

Whilst gallery staff anticipated a degree of press interest (and, indeed, some negative reporting) based on their experiences with the previous social justice programmes, the scale of the media storm prompted by *sh[OUT]* took everyone by surprise. The first controversy, which erupted just a few days before the exhibition opened, centred on the inclusion of artworks with sexual content. The *Daily Mail* (2 April 2009) reproduced Mapplethorpe's *Brian Ridley and Lyle Heeter* (1979) with the headline 'Hardcore gay porn in public art gallery (and the organisers want children to go along and see it)'. The article deployed modes of attack with which many art galleries have long been familiar, including the ridiculing of modern art and an account of the costs of the project to the taxpayer (a criticism given additional potency by increasing awareness at the time of looming public sector cuts as a result of the economic recession). Around the same time, *sh[OUT]* also attracted a number of very positive reviews, including some which referenced the sensationalist reporting typical of the UK's tabloid newspapers, especially in their treatment of stories concerning both sexuality and modern and contemporary art. Moira Jeffery, writing in *The Scotsman*, commented:

> What could have so easily been an explicitly political show about gay rights is instead a celebration of tender portraiture . . . When I visited the Gallery of Modern Art in Glasgow this week, I was told there had been a number of serious complaints about the exhibition shout. But visitors lured by recent Daily Mail headlines screaming about hardcore gay porn will have been seriously disappointed by the lack of it.

The second main wave of media attention came some months into the programme and focused on one of the series of small, changing exhibitions, featuring work by different community groups which ran alongside the main exhibition. Whilst most of these smaller shows had avoided negative media attention (including *Our Vivid Stories* – an exhibition of work by members of LGBT Youth Scotland and *Rendering Gender* – work by members of the Scottish Transgender Alliance's TRANSforming Arts group), *Made in God's Image*, supported by artist Anthony Schrag, which opened in June 2009 and featured work by LGBT people of faith, sparked a controversy which ran for many weeks, gaining momentum and ultimately attracting the attention of national and international news journalists. At the centre of the controversy was a work by Jane Clarke, a minister at Glasgow's Metropolitan Community Church which involved an open Bible and an invitation to visitors who felt they had been excluded to write themselves back in; a work based on her own religious practice of writing notes and comments in the margin of her own Bible. Mark O'Neill (2011: 234) provides an account of the controversy that ensued:

> The tabloids, notably the *Daily Mail*, represented the exhibition as a deliberate attack on Christianity, claiming that we had 'invited' people to 'deface' the bible. They solicited and received condemnatory comments from the Church of Scotland and from the Archdiocese of Glasgow. The Gallery of Modern Art was picketed by evangelical groups, and disturbances led to the police being called on two occasions. Eventually, we received over a thousand letters and emails, many of which were copied to City Councillors and to Culture and Sport Glasgow's board members.

Over a period of more than two months, the controversy continued to gather momentum with new angles emerging in the press each week. On 28 July, the *Daily Mail* claimed that even Pope Benedict had personally condemned the exhibition and accused the Gallery of mounting a 'stunt' that 'would not have been contemplated with a copy of the Koran' (Grant 2009).

Capturing the complexities of public engagement and response

Even taking into account the sensationalist tone of much of the coverage, the scale and tenor of media reporting seemed to suggest that the moral standpoint embodied in *sh[OUT]* constituted a significant affront to prevailing moral codes and conventions. However, whilst media coverage was suggestive of widespread and deeply felt public outrage, a closer examination of visitors' engagement with the exhibition reveals a much more complex, contradictory, picture of the ways in which diverse audiences perceived and responded to the issues they encountered on their visit to the Gallery. Indeed, the interviews we conducted with visitors and our analysis of more than 1,300 comments cards revealed both the capacity for the programme to prompt debate amongst visitors and, importantly, considerable agency on the part of the Gallery in shaping the ways in which visitors perceived and talked about the issues presented.

In common with previous social justice programmes at GoMA, *sh[OUT]* featured a 'response room' in which visitors were encouraged to reflect on the ideas they encountered and to share their views and opinions with others in the form of comments cards that quickly populated the wall space available for their display. Books, leaflets and catalogues linked to LGBTI art and culture and details of both human rights organisations and a variety of LGBTI support groups were available for browsing, alongside audio points through which visitors could listen to oral histories of LGBT people. A comments book, entitled *Your Stories*, provided an opportunity for visitors to add accounts of their own experiences.

Not surprisingly, responses were enormously variable in content, tone and style. Some visitors chose to comment (both positively and negatively) on individual artworks; the Gallery's approach to display and interpretation; and the appropriateness of art exhibitions as the basis for tackling political and social issues. Others shared their opinions on diverse aspects of LGBTI rights, sometimes agreeing with, or taking to task, other visitors for the personal viewpoints they expressed. Taken as a whole, the written responses appear to suggest both considerable public interest in the topic (reflected in the prevalence of particularly extensive written comments) and a keen interest in debating the issues raised by the exhibitions (reflected in the significant numbers of responses that directly referred to other visitors' comments). Although fieldwork at GoMA did not include a large scale study of visitor demographics, analysis of comments cards (through which many declared some information about their own background) suggested that *sh[OUT]* had engaged a diverse body of visitors. These included regular gallery goers and first time visitors; local residents and tourists; those who visited specifically to see *sh[OUT]* and those who stumbled across the exhibition as part of a general visit to the Gallery or to the public library that occupies the same building; a range of age groups; and people whose life experiences and identities cut across categories of sexual orientation and gender diversity. Previous studies at GoMA have similarly found a visitor profile that suggests a broader appeal than that generally associated with galleries of contemporary and modern art (Bruce and Hollows 2007).

A preliminary analysis of response cards identified considerable support for *sh[OUT]* amongst visitors with a significant majority (more than two thirds) expressing positive views on the programme; the exhibition content or interpretative approach; the Gallery's stated aims; or the perceived message of equal rights for all. In order to probe more deeply the ways in which visitors engaged with the particular ethical narratives around LGBTI rights embodied in *sh[OUT]*, the research team drew upon and, crucially, adapted[9] analytical categories used in studies of media-audience reception to make sense of the enormously variable responses made by visitors, either verbally through interviews or in written form through comments cards left in the response room. Reponses could readily be identified in four main categories.

First, *confirmatory* responses (which constituted the vast majority) were comprised of those declaring their support for LGBTI rights or for the Gallery's perceived ethical standpoint. Many in this category explicitly drew upon a discourse of rights and equality to express their views: 'What does it matter if someone is gay, straight, a different race or religion? If it doesn't affect you in any way or hurt anyone then let them live their lives in peace and with equal rights.'

Other confirmatory responses expressed their support by invoking universal ideals of a shared humanity. One visitor to the Gallery in June wrote, 'Women, men, black, white, gay straight one thing in common – all human!!!' whilst another in August commented, 'Human rights are for us all. We're all human & all have the right to love'.

The second category – *oppositional* responses – encompassed those through which visitors expressed objection, either to the notion of LGBTI human rights in general or, more particularly, to GoMA's support for the issue. Also included in this category were those comments which were explicitly homophobic or transphobic: 'Absolutely disgusting! Homosexuals deserve abuse and should not promote it. Shame on GAYS. Shame on GOMA'; 'There is more to love than this rubbish. And so much more to Art. A real waste of taxpayer's money so that perversion can be spread'.

The third category of audience response included those which evidenced a *negotiated* position on the issue of LGBTI rights presented through *sh[OUT]*. These responses were particularly revealing of the capacity for human rights to elicit broad support at an abstract level and, at the same time, to prompt resistance towards attempts to confer those rights on specific groups deemed by some to be morally undeserving. Typically, a negotiated response might be one which states that human rights are a 'good thing' but that such rights should not be available to, for example, people who are gay or lesbian. As one visitor wrote: 'Love is a human right but all the behaviours out of love are not necessarily right.'

A fourth category of response brought together comments that were less straightforward in either expressing their support for, or rejection of, the ideas they encountered but instead took the opportunity to engage in debate or raise questions about the numerous complex themes and issues raised by the exhibition. Here, for example, visitors combined an expression of support for human rights with a questioning of the value of focusing on minority experiences whilst others declared their acceptance of sexual and gender diversity but complained about the inclusion of works that depicted or alluded to sexual practices.

Threaded through all these categories of response (and of particular interest for our under-standing of the agency of the Gallery) were numerous comments suggestive of the capacity for engagement with *sh[OUT]* to inform the ways in which visitors thought about and discussed LGBTI rights. Shifts in position – sometimes subtle and cautious, others more explicit and transformative – suggested the Gallery and its deployment of the human rights frame had, in different ways, shaped visitor understandings of an issue which many found challenging. One visitor, for example, wrote:

> Eye opening and, for me, with little exposure/interaction with LGBT people, somewhat surreal; however, great to see people are becoming more accepting of different sexuali-ties, because, in the end, being human is about acceptance or at least it should be.

During the controversy related to the Bible exhibit, another young visitor commented:

> I don't know what I think about this exhibition yet . . . it takes me a while to process things . . . I think it's really important that the Church is inclusive and engages with all people. I'm a Christian 20 years old and my best friend is gay and recently became a Christian. Most of all I believe God loves everyone and wants us to do the same.

This fine-grained analysis of individual responses arising out of the encounter between visi-tor and exhibition begins to build a picture of the role that museums and galleries might play in engendering public support for more progressive conceptions of human rights, but, at the same time, raises further questions. Crucially, how might these localised, highly personal-ised encounters be understood in relation to the broader aims and ambitions of new social movements that seek to reconfigure both formally constituted rights regimes (through which legally recognised rights are conferred) and localised moral codes and conventions that shape the lived experience of disenfranchised minorities? To consider these questions, it is helpful to look again at the events in Glasgow but this time from the perspective and experience of a minority group for whom the focus of the Gallery's social justice programme in 2009 proved to be especially timely.

Rights in the making

In April 2010 – one year after the opening of *sh[OUT]* – a landmark piece of legislation gained Royal assent in the UK, representing 'the biggest reform of British equality legislation since its inception in the 1960s' (Bell 2011). For the transgender community – The Equal-ity Act 2010 – (although imperfect[10]) represents an important milestone in the struggle for equal rights. Although there is considerable debate about the Act – its effectiveness, incon-sistencies and flaws (ibid.) – its symbolic significance for the transgender community cannot be underestimated since, for the first time, it places the rights of individuals who intend to undergo, are undergoing, or have undergone gender reassignment on the same platform as other more familiar equality strands (race, religion/belief, age, sexual orientation and so on).[11]

Of course, it would be misleading to suggest that GoMA's prominent inclusion of transgender issues had a direct effect on the passing of this significant piece of legislation. Nevertheless, for both the Scottish Transgender Alliance (STA) and members of the transgender community, participation in *sh[OUT]* was perceived to afford unique opportunities through which public support for trans equality could be mobilised. For James Morton, project coordinator at the STA, a lack of prior experience of working with arts and cultural organisations led to initial scepticism about the value of such collaboration. However, as the project gained momentum, the benefits of a partnership, particularly in terms of the potential to shape public opinion, began to emerge. As Morton asserted:

> In terms of trying to raise public awareness of issues and raising a positive public representation of transgender people, GoMA could reach such a larger audience than we could ever hope to reach on our own. I think the social justice programme, by having as much space as it's got, particularly dedicated to intersex and transgender, it means that a whole range of people that have never really thought about that, it starts to make it more familiar and therefore in due course it becomes slightly less scary, less alien . . . because it's like, 'I vaguely remember seeing something about that when I was going around the Gallery . . . and it was being considered significant enough to be within a public service space'.

A concern for changing the ways in which transgender people are represented and perceived by members of the public similarly underpinned motivations for involvement with *sh[OUT]* expressed by three of the participants in the arts project that culminated in the exhibition *Rendering Gender* that ran alongside the main exhibition from 25 June to 22 August 2009. Amy, Kristi and Finn each expressed a desire to use their exhibition as a vehicle for communicating ideas about trans experience to a wider public; although the tone, purpose and content of the message they wanted to convey varied. Amy's tone was explicitly political. She viewed the work she produced for display in *Rendering Gender* as 'an artistic extension of political activism': 'I see it as a mischief making. I am a gender commando. I identify as female but cannot escape my past. Part of me wants to grow a goatee to bend people's heads.'

Finn and Kristi were similarly intent on changing public perceptions although their motivations for involvement were expressed in more personal terms. Finn wanted to tackle transphobia by educating the public, specifically by conveying a message that 'trans people are not freaks'. He did not see himself as fighting a cause ('we are not all in combat with the rest of the world') but rather wanted to inform visitors to the exhibition about the realities of trans experience:

> Being trans is not about changing your genitalia, it is about your whole sense of identity. It is about having lived vicariously . . . not having an identity . . . about life opening up and getting a sense of identity . . . I wanted to show that.

Kristi wanted to create new representations of trans people that offered alternatives to the toxic images that currently circulate in mass media settings, images that promote ridicule and misunderstanding rather than empathy. Getting involved with GoMA was 'a once in a life-time opportunity to educate and inform people who would not normally come into contact with transgender people'. Kristi set about creating a series of works for *Rendering Gender* that were poignant, challenging and often very witty and drew very directly on her own personal experiences. In the following comments, Kristi reflects on one print in particular, entitled *Self-Med Woman* (Plate 14.4):

> This was one of my favourites and by a consensus vote, became the image for the flyer for the exhibition. I feel it asserts my right to self determination in a way that presents both humour and self-confidence and that is important to me. I don't want to be pitied or seen as some timid creature hiding under a wig, wearing tasteless clothes and ill-fitting shoes. I made myself by my sheer determination to survive in spite of everything, I made myself in a world that largely does not accept or understand me.
>
> The two circles actually represent the two medications I have been taking to facilitate my transition and the title also refers to the practice of self-medicating within the trans-sexual community. When presented with the hoops you have to jump through to prove you are transsexual it is sometimes easier to buy your drugs online . . . self-medicating was a powerful psychological and political act for me. I alone determine my future and who I am. I am a self med woman.

Of course it is impossible to gauge the extent to which *Rendering Gender*, and the *sh[OUT]* programme, more broadly succeeded in subverting or supplanting the negative stereotypes in the media and the public perceptions of trans people highlighted by Kristi, Amy and Finn. Nevertheless, amongst those explicitly transphobic visitor comments and statements which rejected the notion of transgender rights were some which suggested a growing openness to new ways of seeing and understanding gender diversity and others which implied or explicitly declared support for transgender equality:

> Didn't realise it was such a difficult/confusing situation. Good luck to all who go through it. Much respect for those who have.

> Very interesting and thought provoking. Recognition and acceptance of homosexuality (and bisexuality) has come a long way in the past 50 years and with hope will continue to progress. The rights of intersexuals still have a long way to go.

What might this exploration of rights processes in a particular setting – viewed from the diverse vantage points and moral positions held by different actors caught up in the negotiation of LGBTI rights – tell us about the roles, responsibilities and agency of museums more broadly?

Museums and moral activism

Although human rights work in museums is experimental, potentially high risk and relatively under-explored (compared to more established and long-standing areas of practice), the findings from this research evidence the potential for museums and galleries to play a unique – albeit undeniably challenging – role in relation to human rights. As a growing number of institutions worldwide claim, museums provide a space in which complex and contested rights issues can be explored and publicly debated, although it would be reductive and inaccurate to suggest that their role is simply one of enabling or facilitating debate, or to view museums as offering an objective, neutral forum in which diverse opinions can be voiced.

Museums mediate between and are influenced by diverse moral positions but they are also *active* in shaping them. Navigating the multiple moral perspectives bound up in intersecting local and global rights discourse, museum staff encounter numerous choices. The decisions and choices they make have social and political effects and consequences that, whilst sometimes diffuse and difficult to trace, nevertheless impact individuals' lives and influence more broadly the relations between mainstream and marginalised constituencies.

In making these (often complex and ethically challenging) decisions, curators, educators, interpreters and museum managers cannot, of course, ignore local agendas and the interests of their funders, governing bodies and audiences that might potentially encourage a more conservative (relativist) position on rights issues. After all, museums need to nurture ongoing political and public support for their work. At the same time, however, if human rights are understood as an evolving project, a contested territory in which struggles for greater equity and fairness are always in play, there is little value in museums taking up a position that simply reflects and reinforces the moral consensus. Rather, I argue that museum practitioners engaging in this work should, as far as is possible within the contexts that they operate, look towards more cosmopolitan (universalist) understandings of human rights in their framing of the rights issues they present.

Alignment with more progressive conceptions of rights that challenge locally framed moral codes and conventions will, of course, invite controversy of which museums are generally (and understandably) wary. Indeed, exhibitions that explore potentially sensitive topics and which manage to avoid major media controversies or which attract few or no complaints are frequently viewed internally as successful. However, the analysis of media and audience responses to GoMA's human rights project suggests that institutions seeking to engender support for more progressive social norms might need to reconsider their approach to controversy. Taking up a position which seeks to reconfigure or call into question, normative ideas about justice and fairness will *inevitably* generate conflict and provoke some groups to express their counter opinions. Controversy, although frequently painful, potentially damaging and difficult for institutions to manage, might then need to be viewed as a necessary, valuable part of the human rights work that museums can accomplish.

Museums that highlight injustices and point to ways in which they might be overcome – even when such a position confronts prevailing social norms – can be understood as sites of moral activism (Sandell and Dodd 2010) that do not simply reflect and reinforce the consensus but actively seek to build public and political support for more progressive human rights values. Whilst such work is enormously challenging, it is through such attempts to redefine (or at least to generate informed debate around) prevailing ideas about justice and fairness that human rights work in museums can have greatest impact.

Notes

1 These include the National Civil Rights Museum, Lower East Side Tenement Museum, the National Underground Railroad Freedom Center and the Japanese American National Museum in the United States; the District Six Museum and Constitution Hill in South Africa; the St Mungo Museum of Religious Life and Art in Scotland and the Anne Frank House in Holland. The Canadian Museum for Human Rights – currently under construction – aims to be 'a centre of learning where Canadians and people from around the world can engage in discussion and commit to taking action

against hate and oppression' (Canadian Museum for Human Rights 2011). In 2010, the Federation of International Human Rights Museums was established by National Museums Liverpool creating a global network of museums engaged in rights-related issues. See Chapter 5, this volume.

2 The Research Centre for Museums and Galleries, University of Leicester, was commissioned to carry out an evaluation of *sh[OUT]* by Culture and Sport Glasgow, utilising a mixed methods research design to assess the impact of GoMA's social justice programmes on visitors and community groups. This chapter draws on data gathered through that project and additional fieldwork (in particular, interviews and focus groups with transgender activists and artists) I undertook as part of a longer term research project exploring museums and human rights. I am grateful to colleagues in RCMG, especially Jocelyn Dodd and Ceri Jones with whom I worked on the project and whose insights have enriched this work; and to the Australian National University's Humanities Research Center for their invaluable support through the award of a fellowship which I took up in 2008.

3 As Mark O'Neill explained, the project was originally conceived as a biennial programme with the first three themes agreed early on.

4 Glasgow Museums was later reorganised to become part of Culture and Sport Glasgow, a body that delivers services on behalf of the City Council.

5 For *sh[OUT]*, these included OurStory Scotland (a charity that collects, archives and presents life stories of LGBT people in Scotland), the Scottish Transgender Alliance (the only publicly funded equality body in Europe that is dedicated specifically to advancing equality for transgender people) and LGBT Youth Scotland (a national organisation working to improve the health and wellbeing of LGBT young people).

6 *Memorial to a Marriage*, a large bronze sculpture (based on the marble version permanently installed in Woodlawn Cemetery, New York) was frequently referred to by visitors to *sh[OUT]* who found the combination of personal and political themes in Patricia Cronin's work highly affecting. As Cronin states in the exhibition catalogue; 'Deborah (my partner, the artist Deborah Kass) and I have all the legal documents one can have to try to simulate the legal protections of marriage, but they are wills, health care proxies and power-of attorney documents. They are so depressing because they are all about if one of us gets incapacitated or dies. I wanted something official that celebrated our life together and if all I will be officially allowed is death, I decided to make the most elegant and dignified statement I could about the end of our life together. In 2002 I created *Memorial to a Marriage,* an over life-size three ton Carrara marble mortuary sculpture, which is a double portrait of Deborah and me. It is permanently installed on our actual burial plot in the Woodlawn Cemetery, in New York . . . The statue addresses issues of lesbian invisibility, gay marriage, love and loss, power and status. In this sculpture I chose a nationalist form – nineteenth-century American neo-classical sculpture – to address what I consider a federal failure. In death I make official my "marriage" which is still not legal while we are alive'. The political timeliness of Cronin's work and the contested nature of the rights issues which *sh[OUT]* sought to highlight were subsequently underscored when same-sex marriage was eventually legalised in the state of New York on 24 July 2011.

7 At an early meeting of the advisory board Sean voiced his concerns around the challenge of identifying works specifically commenting on bisexuality and, indeed, the introduction to the exhibition catalogue subsequently acknowledged the limited presence of works on this theme. Later on, the issue reappeared through our analysis of visitor responses, where some visitors expressed considerable disappointment at the perceived absence of works reflecting their own (bisexual) identity and life experience (Sandell, Dodd and Jones 2010).

8 Although the attempt to represent trans identities in a particularly comprehensive and inclusive manner (including work which explored intersexuality, transvestism, drag cultures and other forms of gender transgression alongside transsexuality) was largely welcomed, especially by those politically active in the field of trans rights, James Morton later reported some criticism from a minority of trans visitors reflecting internal disagreements within the trans community over what constitutes 'the right way to be trans'.

9 Many influential audience studies widely cited in the literature – for example, David Morley's (1980) classic study of viewers' responses to the *Nationwide* television programme and Janice Radway's (1984) research into romance readers – have sought to understand and explain media/text–audience/reader relationships in the context of the distribution of power and have variously argued for the primacy of text or audience in the construction of meaning. Research over the past two decades has increasingly challenged this approach to understanding the complex ways in which audiences engage with, and participate within, the contemporary mediascape (Abercrombie and Longhurst 1998).

For the purposes of this study, audiences are understood not as recipients of (or resistors to) fixed and non-negotiable messages but rather as participants in the co-production of meaning. Similarly, museum exhibitions are not viewed simply as *texts* (to be accepted, rejected or negotiated) but rather as *resources* available for use and appropriation by audiences active in the processes of making meaning. For further discussion of this conception of media and audience in the museum context, see Sandell (2007).

10 The Equality Act, though welcomed by many LGBT campaigners, adopts a limiting understanding of gender diversity that focuses on individuals undergoing or intending to undergo gender reassignment, overlooking alternative forms of gender diversity.

11 Crucially, it extends the concept of what is called the 'public sector equality duty' which requires all publicly funded bodies (including of course most museums) to have due regard to the need to: eliminate unlawful discrimination, harassment and victimisation; advance equality of opportunity between different groups; and foster good relations between different groups (Home Office 2011).

References

Abercrombie, N. and Longhurst, B. (1998) *Audiences: A Sociological Theory of Performance and Imagination*, London, Thousand Oaks and New Delhi: Sage.

Bell, M. (2011) 'British Developments in Non-Discrimination Law: The Equality Act', in R. Schulze (ed.) *Non-Discrimination in European Private Law*, Tübingen: Mohr Siebeck Verlag: 209–31.

Bennett, T. (2006) 'Civic Seeing: Museums and the Organisation of Vision', in S. Macdonald (ed.) *A Companion to Museum Studies*, Massachusetts and Oxford: Blackwell Publishing: 263–81.

Bruce, K. and Hollows, V. (2007) *Towards an Engaged Gallery*, Glasgow: Culture and Sport Glasgow (Museums).

Cameron, F. and Kelly, L. (eds) (2010) *Hot Topics, Public Culture, Museums*, Newcastle upon Tyne: Cambridge Scholars.

Canadian Museum for Human Rights (2011) *Mission Statement*. Online. Available at: www. humanrightsmuseum.ca (accessed 20 September 2011).

Cowan, J.K., Dembour, M. and Wilson, R.A. (eds) (2001) *Culture and Rights: Anthropological Perspectives*, Cambridge: Cambridge University Press.

Donnelly, J. (2003) *Universal Human Rights in Theory and Practice*, 2nd edn, Ithaca and London: Cornell University Press.

Duffy, T.M. (2001) 'Museums of "Human Suffering" and the Struggle for Human Rights', *Museum International*, 53(1): 10–16.

Grant, G. (2009) 'It Wouldn't Happen to the Koran: Pope Attacks Glasgow Art Gallery's Invitation to Vandalise a Bible', *Daily Mail*, 28 July.

Home Office (2011) *Equality Act 2010*. Online. Available at: www.homeoffice.gov.uk/equalities (accessed 20 September 2011).

Hooper-Greenhill, E. (2000) *Museums and the Interpretation of Visual Culture*, London and New York: Routledge.

Karp, I. and Lavine, S.D. (eds) (1991) *Exhibiting Cultures: The Poetics and Politics of Museum Display*, Washington, DC and London: Smithsonian Institution Press.

Macdonald, S. (2008) *Difficult Heritage: Negotiating the Nazi Past in Nuremberg and Beyond*, London and New York: Routledge.

McGlashan, S. (2009) 'Introduction', in Culture and Sport Glasgow, *sh[OUT]: Contemporary Art and Human Rights. Lesbian, Gay, Bisexual, Transgender and Intersex Art and Culture*, Glasgow: Glasgow Museums Publishing: 9–10.

Morley, D. (1980) *The Nationwide Audience*, London: BFI.

Morphy, H. (2006) 'Sites of Persuasion: Yingapungapu at the National Museum of Australia', in I. Karp, C.A. Kratz, L. Szwaja and T. Ybarra-Frausto (eds) *Museum Frictions: Public Cultures/Global Transformations*, Durham, NC and London: Duke University Press: 469–99.

O'Neill, M. (2011) 'Religion and Cultural policy: Two Museum Case Studies', *International Journal of Cultural Policy*, 17(2): 225–43.

Radway, J. (1984) *Reading the Romance: Women, Patriarchy and Popular Literature*, Chapel Hill, NC: University of North Carolina Press.

Rapport, N. and Overing, J. (2000) *Social and Cultural Anthropology*, London: Routledge.

Sandell, R. (2007) *Museums, Prejudice and the Reframing of Difference*, London and New York: Routledge.

Sandell, R. and Dodd, J. (2010) 'Activist Practice', in R. Sandell, J. Dodd and R. Garland–Thomson (eds) *Re-Presenting Disability: Activism and Agency in the Museum*, London and New York: Routledge: 3–22.

Sandell, R., Dodd, J. and Jones, C. (2010) *An Evaluation of sh[OUT] – the Social Justice Programme of the Gallery of Modern Art, Glasgow 2009–2010*, Leicester: Research Centre for Museums and Galleries.

Wilson, R. (1997) *Human Rights, Culture and Context: Anthropological Perspectives*, London: Pluto.

Wilson, R. and Mitchell, A. (eds) (2003) *Human Rights in Global Perspective: Anthropological Studies of Rights, Claims and Entitlement*, London: Routledge.

15

CREATIVITY, LEARNING AND CULTURAL RIGHTS

David Anderson

International law and human rights theory are unequivocal in including cultural rights as an essential component in the indivisible and irreducible body of human rights. Yet serious discussion of the concept of cultural rights in plural, democratic societies is still relatively rare. Many states are signatories to the legally binding International Covenant on Economic, Social and Cultural Rights (1966) but most have ignored its requirement that they take steps to achieve the full realisation of the cultural rights of their citizens. Surprisingly, cultural institutions have also shown little interest in addressing the issue, being fearful, perhaps, that they would have to divert resources from other (and perhaps in their view, higher) priorities. The public at large is almost entirely unaware that, as citizens, they have cultural rights for which their governments are required by law to provide.

One of the reasons why progress in providing for cultural rights has been so slow may be that there is no agreed list or classification of cultural rights. Often, media debate in this area is limited to consideration of the rights of high profile artists to free cultural expression, such as Ai Weiwei in China,[1] eclipsing discussion around the broader cultural rights of all citizens. This chapter explores other, potentially more productive analyses. I draw on human rights theory and debates within politics, international relations and creativity research to propose a more comprehensive and ethically informed way of thinking about cultural rights, one that highlights the responsibility of museums to reduce inequalities of social participation. I conclude by focusing on the issue of faith and cultural rights, examining the obligations of museums, to both faith groups and others, and arguing for museums as a critical resource for the realisation of rights and the fostering of critical thinking and debate in a democracy.

Culture and creativity in an international context

There are two reasons why museums should consider cultural rights from an international perspective: the first is the impact of globalisation on their work and the second is the emergence of creativity as a focus for debate about the role of cultural institutions across the world. Both developments are forcing museums to look again at the relationship between culture and broader values.

The publication in 2002 of Richard Florida's book, *The Rise of the Creative Class*, attracted attention from city and national governments worldwide because it appeared to provide a template with which to measure the creative potential of a local economy in relation to its competitors. Central to the success of any city or state, Florida claimed, is the presence of a thriving Creative Class. Florida acknowledged that not everyone can join the new elite Creative Class and that, in the United States which was the focus of his study, there is a large pool of creativity among other groups in society. The issue of equity, however, is not a major concern of the book, occupying only a few pages in the last chapter; in effect, for Florida, this is someone else's problem.

Members of the Creative Class, because they are well compensated and work long and unpredictable hours, he argues, 'require a growing pool of low-end service workers to take care of them and do their chores' (2002: 71). The degradation of nearly half of the American workforce is then, for Florida, a 'necessity'. So, too, presumably, is the even greater poverty of hundreds of millions of service and manufacturing workers in developing countries, whose labour also supports the relative wealth of the Creative Class in the United States and the rest of the western world. Do these workers not have the right to expect more creative lives also?

The work of Howard E. Gruber, who died in 2005, provides an alternative, ethically informed perspective on creativity and rights. Mark A. Runco, in a Festschrift for Gruber published in 2003, recalled a walk he took with the distinguished psychologist through Central Park in New York a decade earlier. Halfway through this walk, Gruber asked the question, 'Where are we going to hang all the paintings?'. The question, as Runco understood it, stuck with him afterwards; Gruber was puzzling over how all the creativity he believed was waiting to be uncovered and expressed in the wider population (and not just in the visual arts) could be presented (Runco 2003). Gruber's exceptional contribution was to identify the moral and ethical dimensions of creativity and his work helps us to understand how creative practices intersect with issues of human rights and social justice.

We should not assume that creativity is necessarily put to a positive purpose. Robert McLaren, writing in the *Creativity Research Journal* in 1993, says, 'If we are to be honest in our quest for understanding of creativity, we cannot evade acknowledging that, like all human endeavors, it too has its dark, and even, to use Plato's word, its daemonic side' (1993: 137). Museum practice and public participation in cultural and creative activity has, then, moral and ethical implications, as the debate surrounding a recent exhibition in the United States helps to illustrate. In 2005, the Bowers Museum in Santa Ana, California, and other venues in the United States for the show *Tibet: Treasures from the Roof of the World*, attracted criticism for their plans to show the exhibition which had been curated by Tibet's Bureau of Cultural Relics and staff of Lhasa's three central cultural institutions, in collaboration with staff of the Bowers. Critics accused the Bowers Museum, Houston Museum of Natural Science and the Rubin Museum of Art, New York, of complicity in the occupation of Tibet and the destruction of Tibet's cultural heritage. Lhandon Tethong, executive director of Students for a Free Tibet, said, 'We are not telling people not to go and see the exhibition. But it is damaging if the average person sees it with no mention of the problems. See it, but know what you are seeing'. At the same time, the Dalai Lama welcomed the exhibition for revealing the magnitude of Tibet's artistic traditions. 'Despite the wholesale destruction that has taken place in recent decades', he wrote in a letter to the Bowers Museum, 'some works of art have survived. I hope that such efforts will contribute to saving Tibetan culture from disappearing forever' (Morrow Flanagan 2005: 5a).

The case for cultural rights

This is, then, as good a time as any to review the relationship between culture and human rights. The starting point is the 1948 United Nations Universal Declaration of Human Rights (UDHR), Article 27 (i), which states: 'Everyone has the right freely to participate in the cultural life of the community, to enjoy the arts, and to share in scientific advancement and its benefits' (United Nations 1948). In 1948 'art' was primarily understood to be high art, and 'culture' the local and indigenous. Yet, with allowance for changing concepts of culture, art and participation, the declaration retains its value as a living document (Hewison and Holden 2004). Soon after the UDHR was adopted, the influence of the Cold War and ideological differences about the limits of state power and the balancing of individual and social interests, resulted in the splitting of the Declaration. At the urging of the United States, two legally binding documents were created instead of one – the International Covenant on Economic, Social and Cultural Rights (ICESCR 1966), and the International Covenant on Civil and Political Rights (ICCPR 1996) (Otto 2002). Article 15 of the ICESCR identifies the right to take part in cultural life, to enjoy the benefits of scientific progress, and to benefit from intellectual property interest of authorship of scientific, literary or artistic productions.

Also at the urging of the United States, all economic, social and cultural rights, no matter how vital their fulfilment, were declared less genuine rights with less binding duties, a position later described by Henry Shue, a leading US theorist of human rights, as intellectually bankrupt.

Every state that is a signatory to the ICESCR is obliged to implement the rights in the Covenant by giving them domestic effect, taking steps:

> individually and through international assistance and co-operation, especially economic and technical, to the maximum of its available resources, with a view to achieving progressively the full realisation of the rights . . . by all appropriate means, including particularly the adoption of legislative measures.
>
> *United Nations 1966*

Whilst accepting that cultural rights cannot immediately be guaranteed in full, the Covenant requires states to be active and to achieve implementation as quickly as possible. Yet it is evident that, in the United Kingdom and elsewhere, this has not happened.

Unfortunately, unlike some other major treaties, the ICESCR did not provide for a monitoring committee, an omission which reflected the secondary status of economic, social and cultural rights during the Cold War. Although a Committee on Economic, Social and Cultural Rights was later established in 1985 to encourage states to comply with their obligations, there has nevertheless been slow progress in achieving cultural rights over the last twenty-five years.[2]

Defining cultural rights

On 3 April 2011, there was an international outcry when the Chinese artist and activist Ai Weiwei was arrested on charges of alleged 'economic crime'. Tate Modern, which was then displaying Ai Weiwei's *Sunflower Seeds* exhibition, placed a large sign on the exterior of the building demanding his release. Ai Weiwei was eventually released on 22 June 2011.

It is impossible to separate such protests against the arrest of high profile artists from their contexts. Current perceptions of cultural rights are, in part, a product of the Cold War. While the primary focus of western media attention has shifted from the USSR to China, the fundamental assumption that the issues of cultural rights are essentially those of individual cultural expression have remained unchanged. This assumption, and its political origins, should not pass unchallenged.

There is, however, no agreed list or classification of cultural rights with which to critique this reductive perspective. The Nobel prize-winning economist Robert William Fogel has suggested that:

> The *modernist* egalitarian agenda was based on material redistribution. The critical aspect of a *post modern* egalitarian agenda is not the distribution of money income, or food, or shelter, or consumer durables. Although there are still glaring inadequacies in the distribution of material commodities that must be addressed, the most intractable maldistributions in rich countries such as the United States are in the realm of spiritual and immaterial assets.
>
> *2000: 2*

Those assets, I would argue, include civic spaces that provide the opportunity for reflection and spirituality (as broadly defined) such as libraries, art galleries, museums and parks (Leadbeater 2002), and also the public educational resources that help and enable people to express themselves creatively.

As Rodolfo Stavenhagen points out, 'a cursory look at the way the concept of "culture" has been dealt with in some international documents and legal instruments shows a variety of usages' (1998: 5–7). Stavenhagen identifies three broad concepts of culture embodied within international legal or inter-governmental frameworks. The first is *culture as capital* – the accumulated material heritage of mankind. According to this position, the right to culture might mean the equal right to access by individuals to the accumulated cultural capital. A goal of government might then be 'more culture' (as capital) and better access to this culture by more categories of people – a quantitative measure that often pays little regard to qualitative dimensions. For example, do more television channels really represent further enhancement of cultural rights, or greater imposition of a dominant culture (western or other)?

A second concept identified by Stavenhagen is *culture as creativity* – the process of artistic and scientific creation. Within this perspective, the right to culture in practice often means (although it need not) the right of certain individuals to freely create their own cultural oeuvres, and the right of all persons to enjoy these in cultural venues such as museums, concerts, theatres and libraries. Cultural policies are therefore focussed on support for these individual cultural (often artistic) creators, whose right to free cultural expression is celebrated as a cherished symbol of human rights. This leads to a distinction between 'high' and 'low' culture, with official policies frequently directed towards the development of elite (high) forms of culture.

Stavenhagen's third concept is *culture as a total way of life* – an anthropological view. In this, culture is the sum total of the material and spiritual activities and products of a given social group, that identifies it from other groups. At one level this is an inclusive concept, yet at another it opens the door to culture wars by groups that use real or perceived cultural differences for political (often oppressive or discriminatory) ends. While the UN Declaration focuses on individual human rights, the concept of culture as a total way of life is often collective (Stavenhagen 1998).

By definition, cultural rights (as articulated by the United Nations Declaration) are universal and non-negotiable. Yet in practice the concept of cultural rights is most often perceived to apply to indigenous peoples whose way of life is under threat, or artists and intellectuals in societies controlled by authoritarian governments (Stavenhagen's third and second concepts).

None of these three classifications of cultural rights is entirely satisfactory. All, potentially, ascribe an essentially passive role to citizens in plural democratic societies such as the United Kingdom or United States. Yet many people want not just to consume their share of cultural assets, but to contribute something to the wider good of society, something that is valued by others – in other words, they want to be able to *give*. Having the opportunity to give may be one of our most significant sources of fulfilment and self-actualisation, and a stimulus to creativity. This could be particularly important for older people. The evaluators of an Irish Museum of Modern Art project led by older adults found that:

> the members of the group, because they have got so much from their own involvement with the Museum, feel that they ought to give something back, and this is the motivation for their involvement as key workers. This concept of giving back has the merit of being built on a sense of equality and reciprocity.
>
> *Fleming and Gallagher 1999: 37*

Cultural rights as commons

One difficulty with cultural rights is that (depending upon how they are defined) some or all are experienced within, by the individual or community concerned; they cannot be distributed directly by the state in the way that is possible for basic commodities like food and shelter. Nevertheless, the achievement (by individuals and communities) of cultural rights is a responsibility of the state. In so far as they are immaterial, cultural rights depend primarily upon the attitudes and behaviour as well as the actions of intermediaries (such as local communities, institutions like museums, and individuals) more than the state itself. Cultural rights depend, then, upon the cultural environment – the public sphere, which the state or community to some degree creates or manages – as much as upon direct interventions by the state in the lives of the individual.

One of the central issues facing all providers for human rights is the 'Tragedy of the Commons' (Hardin 1968). The 'Commons' referred to here once included the common lands that until the early modern period in England were shared by the inhabitants of most villages; if everyone were to attempt to take as large a share of the grass on the commons for their own animals as they could, the land would rapidly be denuded and the system would fail. In practice, because of the operation of the wisdom of the group, this rarely happened – ways were found to commensurate the incommensurables, balancing individual and communal interests.

But the issue of management of finite resources – including museum resources – is universal. Governments are used to controlling usage and setting priorities for some things, where there is a publicly accepted need for regulation to ensure controlled distribution (such as spaces for cars in cities), but not for others which are degraded less immediately and visibly (such as the air which cars pollute). The problem is in part a moral question, and depends on an assessment of the impact of the action concerned: how much harm will result if abuse of the commons is allowed to happen? Unrestricted fishing, for example, would be a more significant problem today than it was a hundred years ago.

Public cultural resources – such as the services of museums and galleries – represent commons of this kind. If each person living in this country attempted to use museums and galleries to the maximum of their theoretical personal capacity, these facilities in their present form would, in many respects, become degraded and intolerable for everyone. Such a situation is prevented at the moment by the barriers of many different kinds placed by museums in the way of usage (as well as by other factors which are outside the control of museums) (Sandell and Dodd 1998). The question then is whether these barriers are the right ones or even acceptable at all in a society which has legally committed itself, by signing the International Covenant on Economic, Social and Cultural Rights, to actively create the conditions for its citizens to enjoy those rights?

[handwritten margin note: Public cultural space cannot be barred]

Are cultural rights important?

One argument against provision for cultural rights is that they are not, at the end of the day, important – certainly not as important as provision for basic sustenance, or liberty of the person, for example. There are at least two objections to this argument. One is that every international definition of human rights states that they are fundamentally interdependent and indivisible. Even in 1966, when separating human rights into two instruments, the United Nations General Assembly reaffirmed in the preambles to both Covenants that the conditions must be created for the enjoyment of *all* rights; civil, political, economic, social and cultural. Second, there are plenty of examples of where humans living under conditions of extreme deprivation, danger or duress have clung to their right to cultural expression, even at the risk of their lives. It would not be appropriate for those who may take their own cultural rights for granted to belittle their value for others who are not in so fortunate a position.

In 1977, when she was only sixteen, soldiers in Buenos Aires came to E.D. Benchoam's home, killed her seventeen-year-old brother, and took her as a political prisoner. During more than four years in prison she used many psychological strategies for survival, and creative activity was primary among them. As Benchoam later said:

> art became a necessity for me in my functioning as a human being because it provided me with a calm environment, that of the inner self. Both of these enterprises – commitment and the arts – have shaped my life and given meaning to my existence.

Her artistic activities were so important to her (and other prisoners') preservation of self that they continued to create, despite the fact that such creative actions were regarded as a form of resistance and prohibited (Benchoam 1993).

There is, of course, a huge gap between Benchoam's concept of cultural rights, and its usage in other contexts. As Eithne McLaughlin (2002: 3) has warned:

> In recent years, the language of rights has proliferated and people now use it to describe a very broad range of potential and actual rights as well as end states, that is, states of being . . . The problem with prolific use of the language of rights . . . is that this may have the unintended effect of reducing rather than increasing the public legitimacy of 'core' or basic social and economic rights. Judicious, even parsimonious use of rights language and claims may be strategic, in terms of developing public opinion.

The casual use of rights language to which McLaughlin refers risks downgrading cultural rights to the status of lifestyle accessories.

Henry Shue, in his classic study, *Basic Rights: Subsistence, Affluence and U.S. Foreign Policy*, describes the discussion of rights as being about the 'moral minimum' – the least that every person can demand and the least that every person, every government and every corporation must be made to do (1996: xi). A moral right, he says, provides:

> (1) the rational basis for a justified demand (2) that the actual enjoyment of a substance be (3) socially guaranteed against standard threats . . . Those who deny rights do so at their own peril . . . It is only because rights may lead to demands and not something weaker that having rights is tied as closely as it is to human dignity.
>
> *Ibid.: 13–14*

Rights, by Shue's definition, are very different from entitlements, which may vary according to the decisions of an authority or local custom and practice. Shue says he does not suggest the absurd standard that a right has been fulfilled only if it is impossible for anyone to be deprived of it, or only if no one is ever deprived of it. The standard can only be some reasonable level of guarantee against a standard threat. He adds that it is impossible to deduce precisely what sort of institutions are needed to ensure this reasonable guarantee, as these will vary with circumstances, but what *is* universal is a duty to make and keep effective arrangements.

Social participation and cultural institutions

At this level of abstraction, it may be difficult for cultural institutions to relate rights theory to their own practice. Shue's discussion of social participation, on the other hand, addresses issues that relate very directly to the work of cultural institutions. With regard to the liberty of participation, he makes three points. First, to be meaningful, participation must be effective and include influence over fundamental choices and strategies, implementation and operation of social institutions and policies, as they affect oneself. Second, participation must affect the outcomes; it is not sufficient, he explains, for people to 'be heard but not listened to' (ibid.: 71). Third, participation should not be construed in a narrowly political sense as, for example, the right to vote; it also relates to having the power to influence public and private organisations (like museums and galleries). The fact that not everyone wants to exercise the right to participation does not make it any less a right. Shue adds that the supplying of information is barely, if at all, a form of basic participation.

He addresses the objections that may be raised to fulfilment of rights to security, subsistence, social participation and physical movement. One of these is that it would place inordinate burdens on everyone except the poorest (that is, it would hurt *me*); another is that it cannot be anyone's responsibility to fulfil the rights of strangers on the other side of the globe, in place of the responsibility one may have to the deprived within one's own country (that is, it would hurt the *local poor*).

He concludes that there is no evidence, with regard to the duty to aid the poor in one's own country, that anything even approaching the sacrifice of all preferences (those things which are neither basic rights or non-basic rights in his definition) would be required in order to aid all who are deprived of basic rights, and that 'social institutions should be used to preserve rather than to eliminate extreme and degrading and unfair inequalities is beyond rational justification' (ibid.: 130). He also concludes that the duty to eliminate inequality is universal across individual institutions; we all, regardless of nationality, share in the universal duty to enable people in other countries, as well as our own, to achieve their basic rights.

To sum up the implications of Shue's analysis, this might be that museums, as significant social institutions, have a duty to be active in fulfilling (within the limits of their available resources) the basic cultural rights of their populations, and these obligations also extend in principle (and this is crucial in the context of museums' international activities) to people in other countries. Many major museums have international strategies that ignore this principle, and assume that the ethical obligations placed upon them within their own countries do not apply when they operate abroad. Shue's analysis shows this to be unethical and indefensible.

[handwritten margin note: borders don't exist for human rights]

One significant responsibility of museums, then, is to fulfil people's rights to effective social participation. Of course, individual museums are not states, and they need to set priorities in deciding how best to fulfil these duties. But the option of retaining the status quo, rather than making every effort to reduce inequalities of participation, is not an acceptable option from a rights perspective.

Onora O'Neill suggests cultural rights can derive more effectively from an ethical theory that takes *obligations* rather than *rights* as its foundation. This is necessary, she says, in order to protect us from the damaging consequences of, for example, pornography and the trivialisation of culture. One of the obligations in a democracy is to maintain a social environment that creates space for plural public communication without the destruction of languages, vulgarisation of cultural traditions, coercion or deception by governments, or manipulation by the communications industry. This, in turn, leads to the concept of corporate or organisational citizenship, which places an obligation upon all organisations – but not least public institutions like museums – a responsibility to foster genuine and critical public debate, rather than a cynical policy of communication manipulation (O'Neill 1990 cited in Turner 2001).

Implications for museums

Because social and educational theorists have given relatively little attention to the issue of cultural rights and obligations in general, and the role of cultural institutions like museums and galleries in particular, it is hardly surprising that the ways in which museums might contribute to development of cultural rights have scarcely been discussed.

Through education and participation in cultural activities, children and adults can learn not just how to understand design, or to make a bowl, painting or film. By practising these activities in a public space, they can also learn that it is their right to participate in cultural activities. A model of learning, and of museums, which fails to encourage wider participation by the public in cultural activities, is antithetical to the development of a strong and healthy democracy as well as contrary to the Universal Declaration of Human Rights.

Museum-based cultural learning in England has been marginal in museum policy, and, for very different reasons marginal in state education policy for over a century. In museums, this neglect has reflected the strenuous efforts many institutions have made to avoid their social responsibilities. For many (not all) education officials in government, museums and other cultural bodies lie beyond the known world of formal education and, what's more, are institutions which themselves often do not want educational responsibilities. These traditional views of the role of museums in learning fail to acknowledge the vast body of research that now exists on the value of informal and self-directed learning through culture

(Hooper-Greenhill 2007). Cultural rights can only be achieved if museums and other institutions give priority to public learning.

Are museums to be regarded as 'corporate citizens'? If so, many have been poor citizens. Many have been thoroughly modernist, believing themselves free from any wider integrating framework of social responsibility, picking and choosing those obligations they might fulfil, yet demanding the funding and other resources they wanted on the grounds of the intrinsic value of art, and their intrinsic 'right' as organisations to exist. Some might even be said to manifest characteristics of institutional psychological disorders including an indifference to what visitors are feeling and thinking, an obsession with collecting and categorising, and anxiety in the face of change.

What rights in western democracies do our citizens have in relation to our museums, based on international law? I propose that all have the rights to: (1) recognition of their own cultural identity; (2) engagement with other cultures; (3) participation in cultural activities; (4) opportunities for creativity; and (5) freedom of expression and critical judgment. How may these rights be addressed in practice?

What this will require of museums in practice would vary in different countries and different kinds of museum. But some elements would be found in every institution: (1) a commitment in principle to redressing inequalities in cultural engagement; (2) acceptance that the population as a whole is as wise, clever and culturally experienced as museum professionals; (3) effective action to support more public learning and creativity; (4) participation and personalisation for priority groups in gallery development, collections work and public programmes; (5) extension and distribution of services beyond the institution into social communities; (6) sustained investment in learning research and evaluation to support all of this; and (7) a refocusing of our thinking away from what we want to offer, towards what is needed for individual and community well-being.

Museums face many difficult challenges in making practical provision for cultural rights. Just one example, related to issues around faith, will be explored briefly here.

Faith and cultural rights

Faith adherents claim for themselves personal and exclusive insights and experiences that are not accessible to people who do not share their beliefs, and are not amenable to rational enquiry. In some instances, faith identity also depends on ethnicity, excluding all who do not share their ethnic background, whatever their beliefs. Some faith groups claim divine sanction for cruel, oppressive or unequal treatment of (for example) women in their own communities, or people of other faiths or cultures.

Museums have an obligation to recognise the legitimacy of many of the claims that faith groups make upon them, where these do not unreasonably interfere with the cultural rights of others – for example, for restitution of objects not legally acquired, or where the circumstances of acquisition were ethically dubious. Museums also have an obligation to display objects with sensitivity to the implications of public exhibition (Chapter 9, this volume). Acknowledgement of cultural rights can also bring benefits for other museum staff and users. Faith adherents can correct curatorial ignorance, and share their expertise on the cultural context of their faith with other members of the public.

Museums should not deny that faith is an important dimension of human culture, and this should be fully reflected in the interpretation of faith-related artefacts. If someone is contemplating objects quietly in a gallery, museum staff have no right to ask whether the individual concerned is engaged in religious observance or is deep in secular thought.

What museums cannot do (I would argue) is to cede open cultural space or the interpretation of collections to the control of faith adherents. Such space is a vital resource for the achievement of cultural rights in a democracy, and all people should feel welcome there. If an object is legitimately held by a museum, and is displayed with sensitivity, then it has become part of an especially valuable kind of public space, the integrity of which we should defend, for everyone's benefit. Demands for control by faith groups (along with commercial pressures and abuse of their professional power by museum staff themselves) can be one of the greatest threats to the integrity of gallery space as a forum for cultural rights. Nor should museums permit faith adherents to engage in intrusive acts of public worship in gallery space. Museums are, in essence, secular institutions with a responsibility to foster critical thinking and debate. It is not the job of museums to protect faith from such engagement and enquiry.

At the heart of the issue is a question – to whom are publicly funded museums, and museum professionals, accountable? In a democracy, this should be the elected government, acting on behalf of the people as a whole, not just any group with a particular set of beliefs. This is why restitution issues, for example, should be negotiated within a framework established between governments.

If museums are to be places for expression of the cultural rights of all humanity, then humane secular philosophies must take precedence over faith. But is the secular museum the home of all faiths or of none? Is the secular truly in opposition to all faiths, or only those that are exclusive, intolerant and oppressive? In societies where particular faith groups are oppressed, do museums have a responsibility to make special provision for such groups, in ways that would not be appropriate in a more tolerant social environment?

Conclusion

Museums now urgently need a strong organising principle that is intellectually and morally credible, and offers them a purpose in society that is rooted in their unique identity as institutions of material and non-material culture. For all its complexity, a role as centres for cultural rights and cultural democracy could provide just such an organising principle. Human rights has become, arguably, the biggest issue facing us at an international level, and museums could make a modest but important contribution to their spread.

If museums are to do so, it is important that they value the rights of citizens of their own country to social participation through provision for learning and creativity. This goes beyond campaigns for the rights of high profile artists to freedom of expression, and is arguably a more effective, democratic and socially inclusive way to address the responsibilities of museums to promote human rights. Crucially, this same fundamental legal and ethical responsibility applies to the international activities of museums, and, in particular, their engagement with citizens of other countries. Cultural rights, like other human rights, know no boundaries.

Notes

1   See, for example Searle (2011).
2   For more information on the monitoring role of the Committee on Economic, Social and Cultural Rights see Office of the United Nations High Commissioner for Human Rights (2007).

References

Benchoam, E.D. (1993) 'Art, Refuge and Protest: Autobiography of a Young Political Prisoner in Argentina', *Creativity Research Journal*, 6 (1–2): 111–28.

Fleming, T. and Gallagher, A. (1999) *Even Her Nudes were Lovely: Toward Connected Self-Reliance at the Irish Museum of Modern Art. A Research Report On The Museum's Programme For Older Adults*, Dublin: Irish Museum of Modern Art Kilmainham.

Florida, R. (2002) *The Rise Of The Creative Class: And How It's Transforming Work, Leisure, Community And Everyday Life*, New York: Basic Books.

Fogel, R.W. (2000) *The Fourth Great Awakening and the Future of Egalitarianism*, Chicago: University of Chicago Press.

Hardin, G. (1968) 'The Tragedy of the Commons', *Science*, 162: 1243–8.

Hewison, R. and Holden, J. (2004) *The Right to Art: Making Aspirations Reality*, London: DEMOS.

Hooper-Greenhill, E. (2007) *Museum Education: Purpose, Pedagogy, Performance*, London and New York: Routledge.

Leadbeater, C. (2002) *Up the Down Escalator: Why the Global Pessimists are Wrong*, London: Penguin Books.

McLaren, R. (1993) 'The Dark Side of Creativity', *Creativity Research Journal*, 6: 137–44.

McLaughlin, E. (2002) *The Challenges of a Social and Economic Rights Approach to the Development of Social Policy in Ireland*. Online. Available at: www.ispa.ie/documents/120902emclaughlin.doc (accessed 21 August 2011).

Morrow Flanagan, S. (2005) 'Treasures in Cultural Crossfire', *Financial Times*, 4 April: 5a.

Office of the United Nations High Commissioner for Human Rights (2007) *Committee on Economic, Social and Cultural Rights*. Online. Available at: www2.ohchr.org/english/bodies/cescr (accessed 21 August 2011).

Otto, D. (2002) 'Economic, Social and Cultural Rights', *Human Rights Law Resources*. Online. Available at: www.austlii.edu.au/au/other/HRLRes/2002/3 (accessed 21 August 2011).

Runco, M.A. (2003) 'Where Will We Hang all the Paintings? An Introduction to the Festschrift for Howard E. Gardner', *Creativity Research Journal*, 15(1): 1–2.

Sandell, R. and Dodd, J. (1998) *Building Bridges: Guidance on Developing Museum Audiences*, London: Museums and Galleries Commission.

Searle, A. (2011) 'Where is Ai Weiwei?', *Guardian*, G2: 19.

Shue, H. (1996) *Basic Rights: Subsistence, Affluence, and US Foreign Policy* (second edition), Princeton: Princeton University Press.

Stavenhagen, R. (1998) 'Cultural Rights: A Social Science Perspective', in H. Niec (ed.) *Cultural Rights and Wrongs*, Paris: UNESCO: 1–20.

Turner, B.S. (2001) 'Outline of a General Theory of Cultural Citizenship', in N. Stephenson (ed.) *Culture and Citizenship*, London: Sage Publications: 12–15.

United Nations (1948) *Universal Declaration of Human Rights*, in M.R. Ishay (ed.) (1997) *The Human Rights Reader: Major Political Essays, Speeches and Documents from the Bible to the Present*, New York and London: Routledge: 407–12.

United Nations (1966) *International Covenant on Economic, Social and Cultural Rights*, in M.R. Ishay (ed.) (1997) *The Human Rights Reader: Major Political Essays, Speeches and Documents from the Bible to the Present*, New York and London: Routledge: 433–40.

16

EXCEEDING THE LIMITS OF REPRESENTATION?

Petitioning for constitutional change at the Museum of Australian Democracy

Kylie Message

Opened in May 2009, the Museum of Australian Democracy (MoAD) is a museum of social and political history located in the nationally listed heritage building, Old Parliament House (OPH), in Canberra, the capital city of Australia. The Museum of Australian Democracy was conceptualised as a 'constitution' museum that would represent the creation and establishment of the Australian state (MoAD n.d.). The decision to change nomenclature from 'constitution' museum to 'museum of democracy' reflects the adoption of an expanded remit by which the museum sought to be inclusive of a more widely and less formally defined Australian experience of citizenship and to contextualise Australian democracy against historical and contemporary global trends. The name change has not distracted from the museum's main focus, however, and it remains strongly committed to exploring the rights and obligations that are associated with the legal–political citizenship contract between the individual and the state that provides the basis for Australian citizenship, as awarded by the state, where the state is aligned directly with the nation. The museum's focus on citizenship, the Australian Constitution, and constitutional transactions means that its approach to interpretation (in regard to both the house and its individual exhibitions) emphasises 'constituted' power, as that which extends – rather than challenges – typical affiliations between the museum and governmentality to engender a particular moral code and kind of behaviour within its visitors (Bennett 2006). The museum's overarching obligation to educate Australians about their constitution and the nation's parliamentary system and history risks further delimiting understandings about citizenship to a restrictive typology whereby individuals can only be categorised as citizens or non-citizens. A significant challenge for the museum is thus how to reconcile the fact that the Australian Constitution is identified by progressive law scholars as being without the capacity to account for, address, or define the contemporary experience of citizenship (Australian Citizenship Council 2000; Rubenstein 2000).

The museum's focus on the rights, responsibilities and obligations outlined in the Australian Constitution also risks undermining the transformations which have occurred in the fields of museology and (some quarters of) constitutional and public law discourse over the last thirty years which have argued for formal recognition of a wider diversity of citizenship experiences. Critical or 'new' museology and 'critical legal studies' (constitutional and public law in this context) exist as areas of professional practice/application as well as academic scholarship. They sit quite comfortably together under an interdisciplinary academic rubric aligned with the 'legal humanities'. Despite differences in motivations and approaches to progressing discrete agendas, these fields share the contention that law and society interact with and affect one another in critical pragmatic, as well as theoretical, ways. This means, for example, that while the new museology presents museums as having the ability to act upon the social (this is a position reinforced by policy frameworks, especially in the UK throughout the 1990s and early 2000s), critical legal studies argues for the importance of factoring debates occurring within society into the legislative decision-making process. In addition to exploring the similarities apparent between the ideological premises and intentions associated with these fields of study, dialogue between them may create another pathway through which we can explore the increasingly ubiquitous idea that museums might progress a social justice agenda. This line of thinking typically positions museums as agents that either respond to, or are open to being acted upon, by constituent groups, for the greater public good (Peers and Brown 2003; Kreps 2003). Such thinking attempts to make the case that culture can have a positive effect on society and that culture (and museums) can influence the political juridical structures which regulate society. The new museologist's argument may provide evidence to support the contention by constitutional and public law scholars who have contributed to the establishment of a 'critical legal studies' by arguing that all the functions of law are deeply imbued in the social nexus which it impacts upon, and which also provides the law with fluidity and changeability (Anderson 2009; Rubenstein 2000; Tsosie 2003).

The theoretical work presented in this chapter is largely experimental, and the legal humanities framework has not been previously applied to the museum studies sector in this way. Although limitations and possibilities both arise from this innovation, my objective is to provide a platform from which to explore the clash between 'constituent' power (exemplified by the Aboriginal Tent Embassy and the Yirrkala Bark Petitions) and 'constituted', or governmental, power (exemplified by MoAD as a constitution museum) to assess whether culture may be seen to act on legal process as well as outcomes, consistent with what many legal scholars are now arguing. I focus primarily on events at Australia's 'old' Parliament House (prior to the transformation of the heritage-listed site into MoAD in 2009) that invoked legal, political and cultural measures in order to activate change. These events are each related to the landmark 1971 Gove Land Rights Case (*Milirrpum v Nabalco Pty Ltd*, 1971), which was a legal challenge that drew and impacted on culture and national institutions, as well as understandings of citizenship in contemporary Australia.

Old Parliament House

The attempt to identify whether a causal relationship may exist in some instances between museums and social justice requires a consideration of the engagement between 'bottom up' approaches toward grassroots activism and the formal instruments of constituted power. Since opening in 1927, Old Parliament House (within which MoAD is now located) and its external areas have been witness and host to many interactions and debates, and the museum now seeks to show how 'much that is now the essence of democratic practice worldwide has strong roots in Australia – the secret ballot, votes for women, salaried parliamentarians, and the principle of constitutional change by majority vote' (Comm. of Aust. 2008: 1). In recognition of this role, the site's heritage management plan identifies it as significant for having provided a physical focus for events that reflect Australian democratic values, and political and social rights. It argues that through its physical design, the building embodies the federal government's separation of the legislature (the Commonwealth or Federal Parliament, which has the power to pass, amend and appeal laws) from the judiciary (the High Court and affiliated system of courts that interprets and applies the law in the name of the state) and executive functions (from which administration of the state bureaucracy occurs). The heritage management plan also recognises that it is important to acknowledge the events of critical national significance that occurred beyond the parliamentary halls and chambers, principally those dramatic events which occurred at the austere main entrance of the building and the front grassed area, which hosted numerous gatherings and demonstrations over time, and became recognised as a key site for Aboriginal protest with the establishment in 1972 of the Aboriginal Tent Embassy, opposite the building's main entrance.

Contestation about what was to be done with this 'Provisional Parliament' when it was no longer in use started from the building's earliest days (MoAD n.d.). An early proposal suggested transforming the building into a museum of constitutional history, while others preferred the idea of establishing a parliamentary museum and an Australian political history interpretation centre. In a 1983 submission to the Joint Standing Committee on the New Parliament House, the architects of New Parliament House suggested that if re-purposed as a museum, the 'old' Parliament House would continue to stand in close relationship with the new building; visitors would find in the core of the Parliamentary Triangle the beginning and the history of the parliamentary process, and would then proceed to the working parliament on the hill. In the report on the use of Provisional Parliament House, the Joint Standing Committee on the New Parliament House stated that 'the most appropriate future use would be a museum related to the Australian Constitution, Federation and the Commonwealth Parliament' (in MoAD n.d.; see also Joint Standing Committee on National Capital and External Territories 2004). In 1988 an ideas forum was held to provide advice on the future of the building. Contributors included academics and high profile representatives from the historical and cultural community. They provided specific themes for future exhibitions, proposing that the museum should 'display political history in its broad rather than its narrow context', 'be "inspirational" to make Australians reflect on their identity and how the nation became what it is today' and 'encourage visitor interaction with the display material' (MoAD n.d.). The building was closed in 1988, at which time its operations were transferred to the 'new' Australian Parliament that opened on Capital Hill to coincide with the nation's Bicentenary. Debate intensified about what to do with the (old) 'Provisional Parliament' building, which had, by this stage, come to be associated by many Australians with significant formal and informal (vernacular) events that had contributed to shape legal and political conceptions of citizenship and continued to symbolise to many the broader sense of the civic value of membership in the Australian community (Figure 16.1).

The building remained a popular target for demonstrations and protests even after its closure. Prime amongst these was the occupation of the building that occurred in 1992, when it was briefly taken over by residents and supporters of the Aboriginal Tent Embassy. Associated with protests that were held to commemorate the twenty-year anniversary of the establishment of the Tent Embassy, the demonstrators protested against the lack of progress that had been made in the intervening period, exemplified, they believed, by the Labor government's abandonment of the idea of committing to a treaty with Aboriginal people in favour of a ten-year reconciliation process (which sought to redress the unjust colonial past from 'within' the existing constitutional order). At a press conference held within the building, in King's Hall, during the occupation, spokesperson Billie Craigie said that the Embassy had relocated from

FIGURE 16.1 After the Gove Land Rights Case in 1971, public attention to the legal problems of Indigenous people increased and so did campaigns for change to the law. Here, Aboriginal people and supporters demonstrate at Parliament House on 5 March 1974. Image supplied by National Archives of Australia. NAA: A6135, K5/3/74/10.

Old Parliament House's margins to the building's interior. The Embassy would stay, he said, 'indefinitely until we can work out our own Aboriginal government and maybe fill up the rest of the building with elected members from our own, Indigenous, sovereign nation' (cited in *The Advertiser*, 28 January 1992). The hundred or so demonstrators ultimately retreated to the Tent Embassy two days later, and the building was reopened with the formal name of 'Old Parliament House' not long afterwards.

The building served as a venue for exhibitions from various cultural institutions throughout the next stage of its life, including the important 1993 National Museum of Australia (NMA) exhibition, *Landmarks: People, Land and Political Change*. From 1994 to 2005 the National Portrait Gallery was housed as a separate entity in one section of the building, while the rest of it became a house museum that interpreted Australia's political and parliamentary history. Following the 2005 move of the National Portrait Gallery into a purpose-built building, research conducted by Old Parliament House revived interest in former ideas about developing the site as a museum that would put Australian parliamentary democracy into its historical and global contexts.

The 1963 Yirrkala Bark Petitions

The 'Petitions of the Aboriginal people of Yirrkala 14 August and 28 August 1963' (Figure 16.2) are an important example of actions taken by Indigenous peoples and communities to secure their rights within the Australian constitutional and legal system. Sent from Yirrkala, Northern Territory, to the House of Representatives in 1963, the petition was presented in both Yolngu and English and was signed by seventeen leaders. It was typed on paper and glued to a sheet of stringy-bark on which a border of traditional symbolic motifs had been painted. Protesting the Commonwealth Government's sale of part of the Arnhem Land reserve to a bauxite mining company and the absence of consultation with traditional owners prior to the sale, the petitions were put on display in Parliament House in 1977 (Figure 16.3), and then moved to the new Parliament House in 1988 (Comm. of Aust. 1963: 1795–7). While a number of petitions have since been presented to Australian prime ministers and the Commonwealth parliament by Aboriginal claimants (1968, 1988, 1998 and 1998), the Yirrkala Petitions are the only ones that have been formally accepted by the Australian Federal Government. While the Minister for Territories, Paul Hasluck, had lobbied to have the petitions rejected, a seven-member bipartisan select committee recommended the payment of compensation, the protection of sacred sites, and the creation of a permanent parliamentary standing committee to scrutinise developments at Yirrkala (Comm. of Aust. [House of Reps] 1963). Most importantly, the committee acknowledged the people's moral right to their lands (Howie-Willis 1994).

Despite the findings of the select committee, the petitions did not achieve the constitutional change sought at the time. They are nonetheless considered significant for leading to the later recognition of Indigenous rights in Commonwealth law, and for making a specific contribution to the 1967 amendment of the Australian Constitution (S.51, S.127), the 1976 statutory acknowledgment of Aboriginal land rights by the Commonwealth, and in *Mabo v Queensland (No. 2)* (1992), in which the High Court of Australia recognised native title and in so doing overturned the claims of *terra nullius* that had been used to defend British colonisation. Indicating their status as founding documents, the petitions continue to be exhibited (not at the museum but) in the political space of (new) Parliament House, alongside the

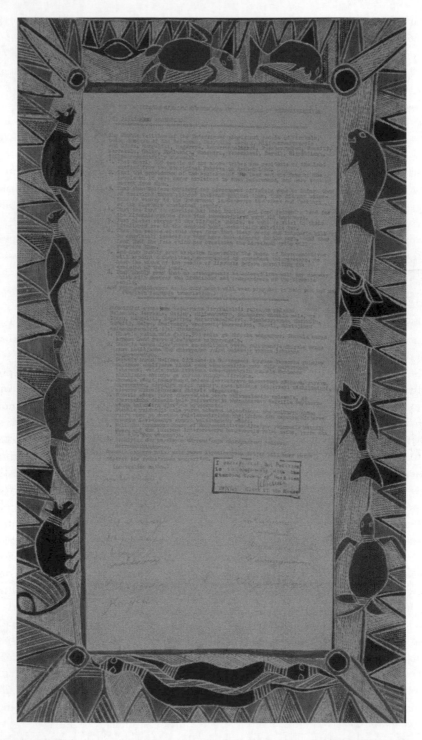

FIGURE 16.2 Yirrkala artists, Yirritja moiety, Yirrkala Bark Petition 28.8.1963, 46.9 × 21 cm natural ochres on bark, ink on paper, House of Representatives, Canberra (Accession number 02/0020.002). Image courtesy of Parliament House Art Collection, Canberra.

FIGURE 16.3 Yolngu leaders Galarrwuy Yunupingu (left) and Silas Roberts at Parliament House in 1977 with Jeremy Long and the Minister for Aboriginal Affairs, Ian Viner (right), looking at the two bark petitions presented to the House of Representatives in 1963. These petitions are displayed in the glass case with a 1968 petition and message stick, also presented by the people of Yirrkala in the Northern Territory. Image supplied by National Archives of Australia. NAA: A8739, A11/3/77/4.

Australian Constitution and a copy of the Magna Carta. The success of the Yirrkala Bark Petitions in drawing attention to the social and cultural impact of legal decision-making was also significant for increasing public attention to the legal problems of Indigenous people in the lead-up to the 1967 Referendum. Technically a vote on the *Constitution Alteration (Aboriginal People) 1967*, the amendment was overwhelmingly endorsed, and became law on 10 August 1967.

The Aboriginal Tent Embassy

A chronological and thematic continuum connects the earliest precedent for political protest by Aboriginal rights activists at Parliament House – when Jimmy Clements disrupted the opening ceremony of the building in 1927 (Aust. Govt. n.d. [Heritage Register]) – with the submission of the Yirrkala Bark Petitions in 1963, and the subsequent establishment of the Tent Embassy in 1972 (Plate 16.1). While each of these protests marked different eras for the building and for Australian society (the Yirrkala Bark Petitions are, for example, often attributed as being the 'start of the land rights movement', Aust. Govt. n.d. [Heritage Register]), the latter protests were associated directly with the same landmark legal case that Prime Minister McMahon had put forward in his 1972 Australia Day speech as providing evidence for his support of mining in the Northern Territory and his rejection of the Yolngu people's claims to occupy their land free from interference to their sovereign rights. The case, *Milirrpum v Nabalco Pty Ltd* (1971) 17 FLR 141 (known as the Gove Land Rights Case), was the first litigation on native title in Australia. It was notorious not just because Justice Blackburn ruled against the claimants on nearly every possible issue of law and fact, but because he rejected the doctrine of Aboriginal title in favour of *terra nullius*.

The first step in this sequence of events occurred when the Yolngu people petitioned the Australian House of Representatives with the Bark Petition in 1963. Preparing the bark petitions helped the Yirrkala groups gain the confidence to mount their historic 1970 action before the Northern Territory Supreme Court against the Nabalco mining company and the Commonwealth. Their goal was to establish in law their rightful claim to the homelands over which they assert sovereign rights. Justice Blackburn's ruling against the claimants combined with Prime Minister McMahon's Australia Day speech to fuel anger amongst Aboriginal-rights activists. Contrary to expectations, raised in part by the findings of the select committee discussed in the previous section (Comm. of Aust. [House of Reps] 1963), McMahon's speech offered Aboriginal people of the Northern Territory general purpose leases rather than the land rights for which they and others had lobbied. He also allowed companies to continue mining Aboriginal land without applying for the consent of the residents of the land – relying, in so doing, on Justice Blackburn's highly contested Northern Territory Supreme Court ruling that the doctrine of *terra nullius* continued to exist (McMahon 1972; *The Australian* 1972). Building on plans that had already been brewing for a national demonstration, a small group of activists responded to the speech by travelling from Sydney on Australia Day and erecting the initial 'Tent Embassy' on the lawns of Parliament House, Canberra.

By virtue of being formally accepted by the Commonwealth Government and displayed at Parliament House, the bicultural Yirrkala Bark Petitions have come to be associated with institutional legitimacy. Existing forcefully on both the physical margins of Old Parliament House and psychological edges of the national political imaginary, the Aboriginal Tent Embassy is, in comparison, a rogue assertion of Aboriginal sovereignty. Following its establishment (the erection initially of a beach umbrella and sign) in 1972, the Embassy was removed by police and re-established several times until February 1975, when it closed. The following year parliament passed the first Commonwealth law on land rights. A second tent embassy, opened on the same site in January 1992 while the High Court was deciding the Mabo Case, still stands in front of the first Parliament House. Now associated with an encampment of tents, the Embassy is accompanied by large letters spelling 'sovereignty' that face outwards toward the parliamentary axis. The Tent Embassy was controversially granted national heritage significance in 1995, when it was added to the Australian Register of the National Estate (following the earlier listing of the OPH building and verge, upon which it is located). The Australian Heritage Council recognised its role as a place for demonstrations and reform movements that is 'unique because it is the only Aboriginal site in Australia that is recognized nationally as a site representing political struggle for all Aboriginal and Torres Strait Islander people' (Aust. Govt. n.d., n.p. [Heritage Register]). According to the listing, the Aboriginal Embassy Site has, from the moment of its inception in 1972, been 'the focus for Aboriginal and Torres Strait Islander people's political struggle for land rights, sovereignty, autonomy, equality and self-government. The Aboriginal Embassy Site is also important as a place that has focused international attention on these political activities' (Aust. Govt. n.d., n.p. [Heritage Register]).

Despite being a heritage-listed site within a heritage-listed site, the Tent Embassy is not easily contained by the Parliament House Vista heritage area, which is both central to Walter Burley Griffin's designed landscape of Canberra, and a key element of the parliamentary axis that connects Australia's major national parliamentary, legal, cultural and administrative institutions. The establishment, maintenance and reconstruction over time of the Aboriginal Tent Embassy can be considered acts of constituent power that have acted upon the space of Australian parliament both figuratively and pragmatically. The focus of agency and action is exemplified by a statement made by Indigenous activist, Kevin Gilbert, in a speech delivered at the Aboriginal Tent Embassy to mark a day of protest and mourning for the twenty-fifth anniversary of the 1967 referendum (2000: 99). Gilbert's words – 'We can't be done to anymore' – assert the authority of constituent over constituted power that is embodied by the Aboriginal Tent Embassy which visually disrupts the grassed lawns of Old Parliament House's verge and provides a constant reminder that it is a contested space that speaks to greater issues of colonial dispossession and the founding of the Australian nation. The antagonism at the heart of the constitutional contract between Indigenous people and the Australian state was writ large in the activists' decision to call the protest site an 'Embassy', as an institution that typically speaks with authority when representing one sovereign group to another government. Embassies are also usually established architectural complexes that provide a symbolic, legislative and political 'home' for citizens living in the foreign country. The Aboriginal Tent Embassy stands in contrast to these images. Its tents and makeshift structures demonstrate both the dispossession and lack of representation of Indigenous people in their own land. Considered by some to be an 'eyesore' (Dow 2000), the Embassy's tents create an unsettling visual presence which reminds governments and people of a continuing Indigenous underclass with more health problems, less education and a much shorter life span than other Australians.

Like the Yirrkala Bark Petitions, the significance of the Tent Embassy is both political and cultural. Attempts in recent years to diminish the ongoing political impact of the Tent Embassy have included proposals to replace the living protest site with a memorial to the Aboriginal-rights reform movement, as if to suggest the struggles over civil rights and land rights have been resolved. One such suggestion was put forward in 2005 by Territories Minister, Jim Lloyd, who proposed replacing the Embassy with a permanent exhibition (where camping would be banned) (Truscott 2005). Here politics risks being reduced to a cultural artefact, where the material residue of the Tent Embassy and its residents are recast as the 'stuff' of traditional anthropology museums which were historically associated with the colonial enterprise. Similar plans (proposed in 1991) to establish an area designated as 'Reconciliation Place' met with resistance from Tent Embassy activists and others who continued to demand a treaty between the Australian nation and Aboriginal nations rather than reconciliation (Lawson 2001).

Proposals for replacement memorials and museums have typically been couched in language that claims to offer something 'that all Australians would be proud of'. This language overlooks the point that the Tent Embassy was not designed to accommodate the interests of the general Australian polity. It implies that Aboriginal-rights activists are being 'un-Australian' in continuing to claim both self-government rights and the systematic political acknowledgement of difference. This language is problematic for assuming homogeneity and consensus amongst 'Australians', and has no capacity to recognise the diversity within the general population, let alone the different levels of support and criticism asserted by Aboriginal people in relation to the Tent Embassy activists' claims for separate nationhood and a government-to-government treaty. A member of the general public effectively summed up the argument against replacing politics with culture (should it be possible) and generalities by arguing against the 2005 proposal by Minister Lloyd in the following terms:

> Mr Lloyd wants to end the campaign and replace the embassy with a permanent museum. That is, he wants to sanitise the embassy project to make it acceptable to non-Aboriginals. The embassy should remain as a disturbing controversial and totally unassimilated political symbol.
>
> *Letter to the editor, Canberra Times, 1 September 2005,*
> *in Truscott 2005: n.p.*

The Museum of Australian Democracy at Old Parliament House

Although all exhibitions at MoAD are committed to telling the story of Australian democracy, *Living Democracy: The Power of the People* is most relevant for discussion here because of its aim to explore the potential for culture and grassroots activism to effect political and legal change. An interpretive panel within the exhibition announces that:

> the boundaries between formal/informal and legal/informal participation have changed throughout Australian history as people have fought to be included, to have their voices heard and to create a better quality of life. We invite you to explore and reflect on how your participation can shape democracy.

The exhibition's aims, plus its location in the very building which was the focus of Aboriginal political protest means that it is the ideal vehicle to host a conversation about the history of Aboriginal reform movements and constitutional exclusion within the parliamentary triangle, and even to do so collaboratively with the current-day residents of the Tent Embassy, who are still camped on the museum's 'front lawn'. However, while the exhibition includes an image of the Bark Petition and a large photograph of the Tent Embassy in the early 1970s, and accompanies each with brief statements, it does not reflect upon or engage with these issues. The image of the Tent Embassy is accompanied by a short wall text which simply states that the Aboriginal Tent Embassy is currently located on the OPH verge but there is no interpretation of the site, or indication of any relationship between MoAD and the site or its residents – despite the fact that the Tent Embassy exemplifies the processes of 'living democracy' that are featured in the exhibition, and despite the fact that, rather than being an artefact, it remains both the longest lasting, and still ongoing, demonstration to occur at OPH.

The Yirrkala Bark Petitions and the Aboriginal Tent Embassy are just two, separate encounters in a wider political reform movement that, although motivated by different specific and diverse participant groups, combine to raise a number of important challenges for MoAD. The main tensions revolve around the fact that MoAD is effectively a constitution museum that occupies the site at which these protests took place. On the one hand, the development of MoAD was shaped and informed by the principles of the new museology, which means that it is concerned to promote the concepts of access and inclusivity and to encourage and enable participation in its operations by constituent groups. It is guided by the principle that – within a democracy – ultimate authority rests with 'the people', the constituent power that the state represents and to whom it is accountable. On the other hand, however, its location at OPH and status as a constitution museum means that its constituent groups are as outlined in the Australian Constitution and hence reflect or repeat the limitations of that document. These inadequacies are outlined by legal scholars who argue (typically according to critical legal studies), that the Constitution is a limited legal document that requires significant reform if it is to recognise and adequately account for the recognition of diverse social and cultural forms of identification and belonging that are embodied in the diverse lived experiences of Australian citizenship. Furthermore, the Australian state, like many other settler societies, has effectively excluded Indigenous people from the constituent power that authorised their constitutions (Muldoon and Schaap in press: 3), even in the period following the 1967 Referendum. At an event held at the Aboriginal Tent Embassy (27 May 1992) to protest and mourn the twenty-fifth anniversary of this earlier landmark, for example, Tent Embassy activist Kevin Gilbert made this point when he asserted 'And we can never become, and we will never become, Australian citizens. For we are Aboriginal People. We are Sovereign Aboriginal People' (2000: 99).

The Yirrkala Bark Petitions and the Aboriginal Tent Embassy each provoke a study of justice. Although ostensibly motivated by the desire to achieve legislative change (formal recognition of civil rights and land claims), each protest employed a strategy that refocused the study of law away from court-based legal regimes and towards the 'contexts of, and contestations between, the formal (conventionally known as legal) and informal (conventionally known as social) sites of socio-legal practices' (Cramer 2005: xii). Rather than simply arguing that the historical and current social, economic and political disadvantage of Aboriginal people needs to be more adequately taken into consideration by law- and policy-making bodies, activists involved in each of these instances effectively used culture as a tool to act upon and call into question the current legal-political policies of the Australian nation and parliament, at Parliament House, as the pre-eminent political site in Australia. Although activists in both cases sought to make the point that their culture is excluded by the parliament and Australian nationhood, in using culture as both the form and content of the communication, Yirrkala petitioners and Tent Embassy activists also asserted a challenge to the constituted order of the Australian polity from its excluded 'outside'. This means that rather than lobbying simply for political reform that would lead to improved recognition of Aboriginal people according to a doctrine of equal or special rights, the protest enacted a challenge to the very legitimacy of the nation, and its founding documents, including the Constitution. These encounters question the presumptions which exist at the heart of constituted power, that is, the idea of political unity (a shared identity) among 'the people' from which it claims both its credibility and authority. Or, as Muldoon and Schaap (in press: 2) suggest in relation to the Tent Embassy:

> The Tent Embassy demonstrates Aboriginal Sovereignty by acting as if it is a form of constituted power. As such, the Tent Embassy is a manifestation of constituent power, which makes available the possibility of a fundamental break with the colonial past, which has so far eluded the constituted power of the Australian state.

MoAD also provides a nexus for debate over the different opinions and understandings about reconciliation. This is because museums in post-settler societies are often praised for their potential to provide inspirational models of reconciliation through their inclusive practices and ways of bringing demographically marginalised groups into the museum where they are encouraged to become active producers of meaning (Kelly and Gordon 2002). Despite the increasing attention by museums to grassroots activities (community curated exhibitions) and outreach programmes, however, reconciliation as a political concept in Australia has been criticised as a process that exists 'within' the existing constitutional order and so does not offer up real opportunities for structural change. 'The reconciliation process can achieve nothing', said Kevin Gilbert in 1993 (2), 'because it does not at the end of the day promise justice. It does not promise a treaty'. So the alliance between museums and reconciliation risks repositioning museums as instruments that promote government policy initiatives. This can, of course, compromise the interest or trust that marginalised constituents might have in the site. Reflected in every element of the OPH site as well as the debates over the establishment of 'Reconciliation Place' in the 1990s and in the proposals for other exhibit-based replacements for the Tent Embassy at various points in the last twenty years, the tensions over reconciliation might indicate that MoAD can do little more than reproduce the limitations of the existing legal-political governmental system, and in such a way that means the museum can only operate in the guise of what Bennett (2006) calls an exhibitionary apparatus.

However, a more optimistic counter-reading of MoAD is also possible. Such a reading might recognise the museum's agency and its intention to do something more progressive than the governmentalist interpretation can allow. It might seek to identify the ways that MoAD has actively borrowed strategies from the protests discussed in this chapter, and then consider how these strategies and the representations which follow have been informed by the discourses of new museology and critical legal studies which both have a bearing on the representational approach developed by MoAD's developers and curators. This interpretation might also attempt to present culture (the museum itself) not as a riposte or antagonist to political-legal structures, but as an internal (that is, governmental) institution that is well-positioned to draw from its experience of working with constituents (offering constituents a platform from which to express their own opinions) to provide informed advice and evidence supporting the claims by legal scholars for the necessary reformation of some founding documents, presumptions and biases. It is easy to accuse MoAD of conspiring with attempts to assimilate Indigenous culture into the mainstream polity on the grounds that any content it represents is brought into what persists (because of the restrictions that accompany the site's official heritage listing) in being a highly bureaucratic and regulated ex-government space (giving further credence to the 'exhibitionary apparatus' concept). However, the counter-argument may become more compelling if we continue to identify and assert the importance of the Yirrkala Bark Petitions and the Tent Embassy as acts in which people who exist as 'outside-insiders' challenge the authority of the government not just for the purpose of reform, but with the aim of achieving sovereignty and recognition of their rights to constitute an independent government that is separate to (and would thus disrupt) the constituted order of the Australian polity. This can ultimately be achieved in MoAD only if the museum engages with a diversity of people involved in the events and narratives that accompanied or contested Australia's founding moments and documents – including current or former residents of the Tent Embassy, which continues to sit just a few hundred metres from the front door of OPH.

The National Museum of Australia

Although the new museology seeks to be increasingly 'constituent-focused' – that is democratic and inclusive – new museums that receive their support primarily from government are often bound by the infrastructural limitations to justice that may result from these political ties. A key question arising from this paradox is whether the museum – and here I am specifically thinking about MoAD – can, through its allegiance to the new museology, offer a space of constituent, rather than constituted, power to progress its interests in social justice, regardless of the seeming unlikelihood of this proposition. I will offer a tentative response to this question by briefly contextualising the 'encounters' presented in this chapter against a number of exhibitions developed by or for the NMA, which was legislated for in 1980 and opened in 2001 as a social history museum. Also located in Canberra, the NMA aims to represent 'Indigenous histories and cultures, histories of European settlement and the interaction of Australians with the environment'. According to its vision statement, the museum aims to 'celebrate the stories of ordinary and extraordinary Australians and provide a dynamic forum for discussion and reflection'. The museum's mission statement is important for providing something of a rationale for exhibitions developed by or for the NMA that demonstrate ways in which culture aims to act upon political structures, systems and assumptions. One early example of the NMA's consideration of social justice issues was the exhibition (held in 1993, at OPH) called *Landmarks: People, Land and Political Change*, which examined land ownership through the lens of Australia's political history, and focused on three recent 'landmarks' – the end of the White Australia Policy in 1973, the Franklin Dam dispute of 1983 and the Mabo High Court decision in 1992 – 'that have challenged traditional assumptions about these issues' (NMA 1993). The museum's interest in representing social justice, political reform, and the civil and land rights movements of Indigenous Australians also led to a range of more recent exhibitions including *'67 Referendum: Spin, Myths and Meanings* (March 2007 to March 2008), which marked the fortieth anniversary of the 1967 Referendum; *70% Urban* (March 2007 to March 2008), which drew on the Museum's collection to explore Indigenous culture in the city; and *From Little Things Big Things Grow* (September 2009 to March 2010), which traced the story of Indigenous and non-Indigenous activists who fought for Indigenous civil rights.

Beyond providing a glimpse into the 'playing field' or background context within which MoAD operates, the NMA is notable for having produced particular exhibitions which have been able to perform beyond the representational (or cultural) sphere by bringing into view the direct clash that can result from different understandings held about political issues and the cultural frame of the museum. The main example of this occurred in relation to the plans to establish a *yingapungapu* sand sculpture and performance as part of the NMA's opening ceremony in 2001. This exhibition – a collaboration between the Yolngu people from Yirrkala, north-eastern Arnhem Land (from where the Bark Petitions originated) and anthropologist Howard Morphy – demonstrated the museum's potential to provide a significant space for political advocacy (if not recognition or protest) to the extent that the exhibition may be considered a clear assertion of constituent power. Like the act of submitting the Yirrkala Bark Petitions and the act of establishing and maintaining the Aboriginal Tent Embassy, the creation of the *yingapungapu* sculpture was connected with an intention to create a public place that would 're-order' the traditional museum as a space of constituted power by re-configuring what could be seen, done and named within it. These aims – and the associated political statement inherent within the actions – are suggested by Morphy's claim that Yolngu leaders saw an exhibition in Canberra as a way to demonstrate to a national audience their native title rights over the coastal waters of Blue Mud Bay (Morphy 2006: 482). Indeed, the potential the Yolngu saw for the museum to play a role in their struggle for land rights was reiterated by their subsequent (unrealised) request for the hearing into their claim to be held at the NMA rather than at the High Court of Australia (Morphy, pers. correspondence, 2008).

Conclusion

The NMA example gives some sense of how political and social reform movements might be represented in the cultural sphere of the museum, and in such a way that can exceed the limitations of representation and may even contribute to the social justice project at the heart of the protests, demonstrations and actions that they invoke. It also demonstrates a challenge to the authority of the traditional notion of citizenship as a legal instrument represented exclusively by the legal apparatus (the High Court of Australia). This relationship indicates that the 'national' museum was valued by Yolngu precisely for its ties to government, and that this connection was understood to demonstrate governmental legitimation of the representation being made – at least symbolically. The cultural politics that motivated the decision to include the *yingapungapu* sculpture and performance in the NMA shows that the museum was identified as a site of productive (albeit contested) understandings of national identity and history by players who had traditionally been excluded by Commonwealth Government policies. Furthermore, in continuing to promote the legitimacy of cultural forms and practices of citizenship, the museum might increasingly become what Morphy (2006) calls a 'site of persuasion' to counteract its traditional role as an exhibitionary complex or surface of government (Bennett 2006).

MoAD is different in many ways to the NMA, and is younger, but while it may be seen as having a narrower mandate, in the sense that it is bound to expand knowledge about the constitution, it also has a responsibility to represent the reaction of its constituents to centrally significant or contested events and actions occurring at the site, as well as the founding documents associated with democracy. Indeed, it would seem to me that MoAD is perfectly located to explore, perhaps in the form of an exhibition, the interplay of law, culture and society. One possible narrative might work to connect the encounters I have addressed in this chapter – that is the OPH, the Yirrkala Bark Petitions, the development of the Aboriginal rights movement and establishment of the Aboriginal Tent Embassy – with the Gove Land Rights Case which provided a nexus for and point of motivation for each. Further, the OPH site has been crucial to each of these events and encounters, not just as a neutral space, but as a national forum in which the very essence of constituent versus constituted power has been played out. Such an exhibition would make a significant contribution to the way Australians understand the limits of the Australian Constitution, and it would expand knowledge about protest and reform movements in Australia. Lastly, it would encourage greater understanding of the active role and impact that culture exerts on legal process as well as outcomes, and vice versa.

[handwritten margin note: emphasize importance of culture]

References

Anderson, J. E. (2009) *Law, Knowledge, Culture: The Production of Indigenous Knowledge in Intellectual Property Law*, Cheltenham, UK and Massachusetts: Edward Elgar Publishing.

The Australian (1972) 'A price on our guilt', Australia Day editorial, 26 January.

Australian Citizenship Council (2000) *Australian Citizenship for a New Century: A Report by the Australian Citizenship Council*, Canberra: Australian Citizenship Council.

Australian Government, Department of Sustainability, Environment, Water, Population and Communities (n.d.) *Aboriginal Embassy Site, King George Tce, Parkes, ACT, Australia* (Australian Heritage Database Place Details), Commonwealth of Australia, Online. Available at: www.environment.gov.au (accessed 14 December 2010).

Bennett, T. (2006) 'Exhibition, difference, and the logic of culture', in I. Karp, C. A. Kratz, L. Szwaja and T. Ybarra-Frausto (eds) *Museum Frictions: Public Cultures/Global Transformations*, Durham, NC and London: Duke University Press: 46–69.

Commonwealth of Australia (1963) Parliamentary Debates (Hansard), House of Representatives, 23 May, Canberra: Commonwealth of Australia. Online. Available at: www.indigenousrights.net.au/files/f104.pdf (accessed 14 December 2010).

Commonwealth of Australia [House of Representatives] (1963) *Report of the Select Committee on Grievances of Yirrkala Aborigines, Arnhem Land Reserve 1963*, Canberra: Australian Government Printing Service. Online. Available at: www.aph.gov.au/House/committee/reports/1963/1963_PP311.pdf (accessed 14 December 2010).

Commonwealth of Australia (2008) *Old Parliament House and Curtilage Management Plan 2008–2013*. Canberra: Commonwealth of Australia.

Cramer, R. A. (2005) *Cash, Color, and Colonialism: The Politics of Tribal Acknowledgement*, Norman: University of Oklahoma Press.

Dow, C. (2000) 'Aboriginal Tent Embassy: Icon or Eyesore?', Social Policy Group, Parliament of Australia (Chronology 3 1999–2000), 4 April. Online. Available at: www.aph.gov.au/LIBRARY/Pubs/chron/1999-2000/2000chr03.htm (accessed 14 December 2010).

Gilbert, K. (1993). *Aboriginal Sovereignty: Justice, the Law and the Land*, Canberra: Burrambinga Books.

Gilbert, K. (2000 [1992]) 'For we are Aboriginal People. We are Sovereign Aboriginal People'. Speech delivered by Kevin Gilbert at the Aboriginal Tent Embassy, 27 May 1992, to mark a day of protest and mourning for the twenty-fifth anniversary of the 1967 referendum, in S. Kleinert, M. Neale and R. Bancroft (eds) *The Oxford Companion to Aboriginal Art and Culture*, Oxford and New York: Oxford University Press: 98–9.

Howie-Willis, I. (1994) 'The Yirrkala Bark Petitions', in D. Horton (gen. ed.) *The Encyclopaedia of Aboriginal Australia: Aboriginal and Torres Strait Islander History, Society and Culture*, Canberra: Aboriginal Studies Press for the Australian Institute of Aboriginal and Torres Strait Islander Studies: 100–1.

Joint Standing Committee on National Capital and External Territories (2004) *A National Capital, a Place to Live: Inquiry into the Role of the National Capital Authority* (July), Committee activities (inquiries and reports), Joint Standing Committee on National Capital and External Territories, Commonwealth of Australia. Online. Available at: www.aph.gov.au/house/committee/ncet/nca/report/fullreport.pdf (accessed 14 December 2010).

Kelly, L. and Gordon, P. (2002) 'Developing a community of practice: museums and reconciliation in Australia', in R. Sandell (ed.) *Museums, Society, Inequality*, London and New York: Routledge: 153–74.

Kreps, C. F. (2003) *Liberating Cultures: Cross-Cultural Perspectives on Museums*, London and New York: Routledge.

Lawson, K. (2001) '"Sorry" design unveiling: Reconciliation Place could replace tent embassy', *Canberra Times*, 16 June: 7.

McMahon, W. (1972) 'Australian Aborigines Commonwealth Policy and Achievements Statement by the Prime Minister – The Rt Hon. William McMahon, C.H., M.P.', 26 January (Pamphlet), Canberra: Commonwealth Government Printing Office. Online. Available at: www.indigenousrights. net.au/files/f61.pdf (accessed 4 December 2010).

Morphy, H. (2006) 'Sites of persuasion: *Yingapungapu* at the National Museum of Australia', in I. Karp, C. A. Kratz, L. Szwaja and T. Ybarra-Frausto (eds) *Museum Frictions: Public Cultures/Global Transformations*, Durham, NC and London: Duke University Press: 469–99.

Muldoon, P. and Schaap, A. (in press) 'Aboriginal sovereignty and the politics of reconciliation: the constituent power of the Aboriginal Tent Embassy in Australia', *Environment and Planning D: Society and Space*.

Museum of Australian Democracy (n.d.) *Twenty Years in the Making – the Museum of Australian Democracy*, Canberra: Museum of Australian Democracy. Online. Available at: http://moadoph.gov.au/blog/ article/twenty-years-in-the-making-the-museum-of-australian-democracy (accessed 14 December 2010).

National Museum of Australia (1993) *Landmarks: People, Land and Political Change*, Canberra: National Museum of Australia.

Peers, L. and Brown, A. K. (eds) (2003) *Museums and Source Communities*, New York: Routledge.

Rubenstein, K. (2000) 'Citizenship and the centenary – inclusion and exclusion in 20th century Australia', *Melbourne University Law Review* 24(3): 576–608.

Truscott, M. C. (2005) 'Reconciling two settings: responding to threats to social and scenic heritage values', in International Council on Monuments and Sites (ICOM), Proceedings of the Scientific Symposium, *Monuments and Sites in their Setting – Conserving Cultural Heritage in Changing Townscapes and Landscapes*, ch. 37. Online. Available at: www.international.icomos.org/xian2005/papers/2-37.pdf (accessed 14 December 2010).

Tsosie, R. (2003) 'Tribalism, constitutionalism, and cultural pluralism: where do Indigenous peoples fit within civil society?', *Journal of Constitutional Law* 5(2): 357–404.

17

TOWARDS SOCIAL INCLUSION IN TAIWAN

Museums, equality and indigenous groups

Marzia Varutti

In contemporary Taiwan, museum exhibitions and initiatives increasingly engage with a broad spectrum of social issues – including human rights, gender equality, immigration, and the healing of collective traumas – and there is a growing concern amongst practitioners with the representation of social and cultural diversity, particularly in relation to indigenous groups. Drawing on recent fieldwork, this chapter explores the changing, increasingly significant role that Taiwanese museums are playing in the pursuit of social justice and equality.

The chapter focuses, in particular, on the representation of indigenous groups and ethnic minorities since the country's transition to democracy, marked by the lifting of martial law in 1987, and reflects on the 'emergence' of indigenous peoples and other Taiwanese ethnic groups as they have moved from a position of social invisibility to gradually becoming subjects of museum representations as well as actors in the process of shaping museum narratives.[1] The analysis is inscribed in the political and historical changes affecting Taiwan and, most notably, the recent reformulation of Taiwanese national identity to more fully include indigenous and ethnic groups. Recent and ongoing museum initiatives devoted to (or involving the participation of) indigenous groups provide a platform for the discussion of the potential opportunities and challenges for museums seeking to nurture a more equitable and inclusive society in Taiwan.

Museums, equality and social issues in Taiwan

As social institutions with political mandates and public funds, museums in many parts of the world are increasingly being required to tackle social issues, often demanding the relinquishing of institutional claims to 'objectivity' and 'impartiality' in order to take up a position on contemporary debates. It is often from this stance of commitment and partiality that museums are able to make the most significant contributions to public debates and to have an impact on collective perceptions and assumptions (Sandell 2007). Thus, the engagement of museums with social issues is gradually extending to new areas previously considered marginal to institutional core priorities and interests. These include, for instance, the protection and implementation of human rights (Langfield *et al.* 2010), the reduction of discrimination and prejudice against specific groups (Sandell 2002, 2007; Skartveit and Goodnow 2010) and more controversial topics such as LGTBQ rights (Levin 2010; Chapter 14, this volume) and the representation of disability (Sandell *et al.* 2010).

But what does it imply for a museum to embrace social responsibility and pursue social equality, and to what extent might such goals demand an institutional commitment beyond the somewhat generalized aim to become more inclusive? Pursuing social equality often demands *active* recognition and *explicit* legitimation of multiple forms of difference. As Richard Sandell explains; 'through the thoughtful representation of difference and diversity . . . all museums, regardless of the nature of their collections, the resources available to them, their mission and the context within which they operate, can contribute towards greater social equity' (2002: 4). In most instances, fulfilling these social roles demands that museums rethink and modify their institutional remits, priorities and resources. These kinds of structural changes require a supportive political context, a strong and motivated institutional leadership and, not least, a shared concern among a museum's staff. Not surprisingly then, relatively few institutions are able and willing to embark upon such transformations in purpose and priority.

In the light of these considerations, it seems all the more significant that an increasing number of museums in Taiwan have become sites for engagement with often challenging contemporary issues of social and political concern. For example, in reaction to the earthquake that seized central Taiwan on 21 September 1999, a whole new museum, the *921 Earthquake Museum of Taiwan*, was created by the government in 2001 in Wufeng, Taichung county. The museum is a compelling (and rather unusual) instance of a cultural institution fully devoted to the processes of acknowledgement, recollection, elaboration and healing related to a collective trauma (Chen 2009). Similarly, the National Taiwan Museum has devoted increasing attention to the social as well as environmental threats posed by the natural disasters that have afflicted Taiwan over the last few years and developed innovative approaches to interpretation that include information on disaster prevention and mitigation.[2]

Of course, social equality also has an historical dimension. A concern for justice in the present day demands that the historical record be presented (sometimes re-presented) in a balanced, accurate way that accommodates multiple points of view, including those of the victims of past atrocities. From this perspective, it is significant that in Taiwan, following the democratic movement of the early 1990s when the authoritarian regime of the Kuomintang (KMT) started to lose its grip and the Democratic Progressive Party (DPP) came to the political forefront, a number of new museums and heritage sites have been dedicated to human rights, the promotion of peace and the commemoration of historical incidents.

In 1995, for instance, a museum devoted to the infamous 2–28 Incident – a violent suppression of anti-government activity by the KMT army that occurred on 28 February 1947[3] – was inaugurated in Taipei (Chen 2003), and another national museum devoted to this subject is in preparation (*Taipei Times* 2009). In a similar vein, the Green Island Human Rights Memorial Park was inaugurated in 2002 to remember the victims of the 'white terror', the period of political persecutions perpetrated by the KMT between 1947 and the abolition of martial law in 1987. Also, the Taiwan Human Rights Memorial, which opened in 2007 on the site of a former prison, commemorates former political prisoners persecuted by the KMT during the 'white terror' period (Tsao 2006). From 2012, the Jing Mei Human Rights Memorial and Cultural Park and the Green Island Human Rights will be administered by a national-level museum group under the Ministry of Culture, specifically devoted to human rights (*Taiwan Today* 2010a).

In addition to these high profile, government-initiated developments in the re-presentation of national history, there are also examples of museum engagement with grassroots rights movements, for example relating to disability (Chen 2010b).

Taken together, these initiatives bear witness to the engagement of museums with social issues in a wide range of contexts; it is however in the domain of ethnic equality that Taiwanese museums have deployed most of their efforts. In this regard, of particular relevance is the representation in museum displays of indigenous and ethnic groups with specific reference to the (re)definition of Taiwanese national identity, as well as the negotiation of the inclusion of new immigrant communities in contemporary Taiwanese society.

Taiwanese nation-building, ethnicity and museums

Museums have become important sites for the re-definition of Taiwanese national and cultural identities (Chen 2010a). The contemporary situation is the result of more than two decades of major political and ideological changes in Taiwan – indeed, as anthropologist Scott Simon notes, 'ethnic tension is the background for all political behaviour in Austronesian communities' (2010: 727).

The lifting of martial law in 1987 led to a growing political awareness of the need to include previously marginalized groups. The late 1980s were also a period of civic mobilization which saw the coalescence of citizens' associations around new social movements seeking equal rights for groups including women, Hakka, Aborigines and political victims, and the emergence of protest groups such as those opposing nuclear power (Hsiao 1990: 167ss).

From 1989, the political rhetoric of the Democratic Progressive Party (DPP) started to emphasize the concept of 'Taiwan's four ethnic groups' comprising Min-nan people (70 per cent of the Taiwan population, immigrants from Fujian Province of China); Hakka people (15 per cent of the population, immigrants from Guangdong Province of China); Mainlanders (13 per cent, immigrants from various provinces of China after 1945); and indigenous groups (2–3 per cent of the population, comprising 14 officially recognized groups) (Allio 1998: 54). This ethnic partition had long been implicitly shaping ethnic relations in Taiwan and had become particularly acute after 1945, with the arrival of millions of Chinese supporters of the KMT fleeing Communist China. During the decades of the KMT government, Mainlanders had benefited from preferential treatment (such as preferential access to government positions, housing facilities and so on) which contributed to deepen ethnic divisions, especially between Mainlanders and the rest of the population (Chen 2010a; Wachman 1994: 91–2).

The contested issue of the political status of Taiwan polarized the debate between the supporters of Taiwanese independence and those in favour of the reunification with the People's Republic of China. But more than the political status of Taiwan, it was the issue of Taiwanese *cultural* identity that was at the centre of political and intellectual debates in the early 1990s. Gradually, the notion of a 'new Taiwanese' cultural identity started to gain substance and definition. This notion encompasses the cultures of ethnic and indigenous groups and stresses the present experience of living together, translated in political jargon through the concepts of Taiwan's 'shared community' or 'life-community' (*Taiwan shengming gongtongti*) (Chen 2010: 21; Rudolph 2001). This approach generated a long-term governmental programme called the *Community Construction Movement* (*shequ zongti yingzao*) launched in 1995 to revitalize local communities. The programme brought impetus to the development of a 'Taiwanese consciousness' through the strengthening of ties with local history and community (Chang

acknowledge people already there

2004: 4) and led to a rapid growth of local museums in the early part of the 1990s (Chen 2002, 2007, 2010a). In this new political climate, cultural institutions such as museums were also charged with the task of making visible the multicultural and local character of Taiwanese culture (Wang 2004: 805). So, for example, a number of museums were created to illustrate Hakka culture in Taiwan (including the Taipei County Hakka Museum, the Pingtung County Hakka Museum, the Meinung Hakka Culture Museum and the Historical Hakka Museum in Kaohsiung).

In a line of relative continuity, governmental cultural policy in the new millennium has been geared towards the territorialization and localization of Taiwanese culture and the development of creative and cultural industries (such as design, tourism, an independent film scene and so on) (Chang 2004). Whilst keeping up with these priority areas, over the last decade cultural institutions have started to develop a sharper focus on socially relevant issues, and questions of ethnicity and national identity – with special reference to the representation of indigenous groups – have become increasingly important.

Since the early 2000s, the political and ideological framework in Taiwan has been characterized by a more marked emphasis on multicultural nationalism, implying the full recognition that Taiwan is a multi-ethnic and multicultural society and bringing with it acknowledgement of the state obligation to protect minority rights and guarantee ethnic and cultural identities (Schubert 1999: 59). Moreover, the re-evaluation of Taiwan's non-Chinese ethnic features has been a key factor in the re-definition of the island as culturally autonomous from mainland China (Rudolph 2001). National narratives of Taiwanese identity have therefore been reformulated in multicultural terms to account for the plurality of ethnic groups inhabiting the island (Brown 2004: 21).

This political turn has exerted a significant influence on museums. For instance, since 2002 the Taiwanese Council of Cultural Affairs has been developing a programme called the 'Local Cultural Museum Development Scheme'. The programme set parameters for the re-evaluation and re-use of historical buildings and sites, aiming to develop Taiwan's 'multi-cultural features, including the recording, collection, collation, research, promotion and hosting of activities involving different ethnic groups, localities and international backgrounds' (Chen 2008: 128). In the changed ideological context, the preservation of the culture of different ethnic and indigenous groups has become one of the most important tasks of museums. The valorization and promotion of respect for Taiwan's ethnic cultural diversity have thus become institutionalized and inscribed in the remits of public museums.

The refashioning of Taiwanese cultural identity in multicultural terms, together with the re-writing of Taiwanese history to include the history of indigenous peoples and ethnic minorities, are major, long-term projects undertaken by national museums in Taiwan. In particular, as will be discussed later on, the new National Museum of Taiwan History (NMTH) located in the southern city of Tainan, is proposing a new reading of Taiwanese national history to account for the island's past of inter-ethnic interactions and cultural hybridity. Similarly, a number of special exhibitions, such as *The Legacy of the Pingpu Group* held at the National Taiwan Museum in spring 2010, examined the historical relations between Chinese settlers and indigenous groups. The exhibition included historical documentation evidencing the unequal relations between Han Chinese settlers and indigenous populations (Plate 17.1).

Other initiatives have focused on more recent immigrant communities (for example from the Philippines, Vietnam and other south-east Asian countries) with the purpose of including these previously marginalized ethnic groups in an updated notion of Taiwan's national identity. The touring exhibition, *Voyage 15840*, organized in 2007 by the Taiwan International Worker's Association was devoted to the country's migrant workers (Taiwan International Workers Association 2007). The figure in the exhibition title – 15840 – is the minimum wage for workers in Taiwan, and it often corresponds to the salary of migrant workers. The exhibition, which opened in May 2007 at the FuXun Park in downtown Taipei, was later displayed in a number of sites including community colleges. The display included photos taken by 19 migrant workers in Taiwan; it aimed to cast light upon their working and living conditions, to make migrant communities visible, and ultimately to dispel negative stereotypes surrounding them.

Whilst Taiwan's immigrant communities are only starting to gain visibility in museums, other communities such as indigenous peoples have long been the subject of practices of collection, display and interpretation in museums.

Displaying indigenous cultures as Taiwanese

In Taiwan there are currently 14 officially recognized indigenous groups. The material culture of indigenous groups features prominently in a significant number of major Taiwanese museums, including the Taiwan National Museum, the Museum of Ethnology of the Academia Sinica, the National Museum of Natural Science, the National Museum of Prehistory and the Shung Ye Formosan Aborigines Museum. The ways in which museums have collected, displayed and interpreted indigenous cultures in Taiwan have been deeply entangled with colonial and post-colonial policies. During the Japanese occupation (1895–1945), Japanese ethnologists, linguists and archaeologists conducted in-depth studies on indigenous cultures with the purpose of providing scientific evidence of their 'primitive' character. The construction of indigenous groups as 'savage' and inferior to the Japanese civilization was crucial to legitimize Japanese colonial rule which, conversely, was framed as the purveyor of modernization (Kikuchi 2007). Museums played a key role in the validation and dissemination of such ideology. Writing about the collection and exhibition of indigenous material culture during the Japanese era, anthropologist Chia-yu Hu explains; 'the collected objects as a whole became a symbol that signified the subordinated position of indigenous people' (2007: 203). This situation started to change with the lifting of martial law in 1987 when the gradual process of revitalization of indigenous cultures started to gain momentum.

The creation in 1996 of the Council for Indigenous Peoples (CIP) – a Ministry-level body within the Taiwanese government solely devoted to indigenous affairs – represented a milestone in the promotion and implementation of indigenous human rights. Today, increasingly, the projects of the CIP are carried out in collaboration or in parallel with a large number of indigenous NGOs and local indigenous associations, contributing to the recognition and protection of indigenous rights (Hsieh 2006; Ku 2005). These developments have contributed to an increased awareness among indigenous communities of the importance of museums as showcases of indigenous cultures (Chen 2008). For instance, the Ketagalan Culture Center – a ten-floor building devoted to the display and promotion of indigenous cultures – was created in 2002 on the impulse of the Council of Indigenous Peoples and the Taipei City Government. Similarly, the Shung Ye Museum of Formosan Aborigines, a major private museum entirely devoted to traditional and contemporary indigenous arts and crafts, opened in Taipei in 1994. With their innovative, art-focused and aesthetically pleasing museological approaches to the representation of indigenous cultures, this new generation of museums set a stark contrast with the more conservative, didactic exhibitionary style of historical institutions such as the Museum of Ethnology of the Academia Sinica.

More recently, the representation of indigenous groups in museums has been enmeshed in nationalistic projects aiming to reformulate Taiwanese national history and identity as independent from mainland China. This is one of the main tenets of the National Museum of Taiwan History (NMTH) in Tainan. Professor Lu Li Cheng, current director of the Museum, points out that, 'Taiwan history is a multicultural interactive history . . . the aim [*of the museum*] is to describe Taiwanese history from different points of view, from different historical sources'. Consistent with this aim, the NMTH permanent exhibition – entitled *Our Land, Our People. The Story of Taiwan* – includes sections on 'the early inhabitants', 'the encounter of different cultures' and 'pluralistic development in regional societies' which look at the interactions of different cultures (the Dutch, the Spanish, the Japanese, the Han Chinese) with indigenous groups and explores their impact on the making of a Taiwanese identity. In the same vein, the NMTH's special exhibition *Encountering Different Cultures: Opportunities and Choices*, aimed to show that:

variety of identity [handwritten margin note]

> Taiwanese people are not one single group, but a combination of different people from different places, including immigrants coming to Taiwan and becoming Taiwanese. For a long time indigenous groups have been seen from the point of view of other cultures. In this exhibition we see that indigenous groups are the subject not the object. The 'other' culture, including the Han culture here, is the Other – this is another way to see Taiwan's history.
>
> *Lu 2010*

The words of Director Lu strongly resonate with the official position of the NMTH, which defines itself as 'a history museum that belongs to all the people of Taiwan',[4] with the following, socially purposeful mission:

> to construct the shared historical memories of Taiwanese . . . we endeavor to construct this museum for all Taiwanese that are living on this island . . . in an attempt to display a pluralistic cultural vista of Taiwan's history . . . to explore a range of wider ethnicity and cultural vision, as well as to enhance the mutual understanding and respect of Taiwan's citizens.
>
> *National Museum of Taiwan History 2009: 10*

Heightened concerns with attaining more democratic, equitable and respectful museum representations of indigenous cultures are not only reflected in the changing narratives about such cultures and their relation to the rest of the population, but also in the processes through which such narratives are being constructed. A number of recent initiatives between museums and indigenous groups point to an increased awareness of the need to develop more inclusive and collaborative practices. In 2009, for example, the National Taiwan Museum together with the Museum of Natural History of the University of Colorado developed the joint project *iShare: Connecting Museums and Communities East and West*. The project aims to set up an online platform enabling the Paiwan indigenous group to 'gain remote access to museum collections, document intangible aspects of their culture and disseminate information about their heritage to a broader public, including indigenous groups abroad' (*Taiwan Today* 2010b).

The Taiwanese government has also taken an active role in fostering collaboration between mainstream and indigenous museums. In 2006, government authorities, through the Council of Indigenous Peoples, launched an umbrella programme called *Big Museum Leads Small Museum*, promoting a series of collaborative projects between major museums holding indigenous collections and local indigenous museums (Lee 2010). The National Taiwan Museum (NTM) has been particularly active in this programme, sponsoring a number of collaborative initiatives. For example, since 2009 the curatorial team of the anthropological section of the NTM has been working in tandem with representatives of the Amis indigenous group to set up exhibitions in the Amis local museum located in Chi-Mei indigenous village, in the mountains on the east coast of Taiwan. The first exhibition, set up in 2009, offered Amis communities in Chi-Mei the opportunity to re-establish a connection with historical artefacts collected in the village by Japanese ethnographers in the early twentieth century and which subsequently had never left the storage of the NTM (Lim 2009; Li 2010). A similar project with representatives of the Atayal indigenous group aiming to set up an exhibition at the Datong Museum in Yilan county in the east of Taiwan is under way and a future similar project with the Paiwan indigenous groups in the Laiyi village in southern Taiwan is planned (Li 2010).

Outside the framework of collaborative projects managed by governmental bodies and major museums, members of indigenous groups are also gradually gaining visibility and legitimacy as curators. The participation of indigenous women in the organization of exhibitions of contemporary art such as *Mind and Spirit: Taiwanese Women's Arts in Taiwan*, held at the Fine Arts Museum of Taipei in 1998, and *Journey of the Spirits*, held at the Kaohsiung Fine Arts Museum in 2000–2001 is an illustration of such renewed opportunities (Ming 2008: 29).

These kinds of collaborative endeavour are of crucial importance as they set the ground for new relationships, new practices and new ways to understand what a museum is and what its contribution can be to the making of a more equal and inclusive society. As Michael Brown, writing about collaborative museum practices, notes; 'curators and cultural critics who think of themselves as progressives see these shifts as inherently democratizing: by putting oral tradition and community sentiment on the same footing as professional expertise, indigenous peoples achieve something like cultural equality' (2009: 151).

The broader social impact of this kind of initiative is amplified by the museum's capacity to reach wider audiences. To this end, museums in Taiwan have invested in ambitious digitization projects aimed at enhancing and democratizing audiences' access to collections and information. For instance, the National Taiwan Museum has developed digital learning projects and various archival projects such as 'Pazeh An-Li Village' on Pingpu indigenous groups of Central Taiwan and several other archival projects on official documents, maps and historical portraits in the Museum's collections are being planned (Hung 2009: 57). Similarly, the Museum of the Institute of Ethnology of the Academia Sinica has set up an online archive of its anthropological collections about indigenous groups ('The Digital Archives of Formosan Aborigines'). In the same vein, touring exhibitions have become a popular and well established practice for major museums wishing to collaborate with smaller museums and cultural institutions at local level and, at the same time, a means to reach broader audiences. So, for example, each year the National Taiwan Museum selects the most successful among its temporary exhibitions, whose contents are reassembled in formats suitable for touring exhibitions. The exhibition *The Shells Stories*, exploring the trade in shells among indigenous peoples, was met with great interest and was held in seven different local museums and cultural centres between 2007 and 2008.

Challenges and future directions

An increasing number of museums in Taiwan are devoting attention to socially relevant top-ics. Whilst it can be difficult to determine the impact of such museum initiatives on visitors' perceptions, this trend is nevertheless noteworthy since it signals an increased awareness at institutional level of the social responsibilities of museums and their potential to act as agents for social change.

Cameron and Kelly (2010: 1), writing about the challenges associated with the tackling of controversy, comment:

> While some museums have successfully and meaningfully engaged hot topics, in reality few are willing to do so because they are seen as high risk due to a fear of political and social repercussions, such as funding withdrawal or the alienation of audiences.

It might then be argued that museums in Taiwan are becoming increasingly courageous and progressive in their practices. In recent years, a growing number of institutions have sought not simply to act as sites for the validation of government approved positions, as might have been the case only a decade ago, but have increasingly attempted to take up the role of facilitator in proc-esses of socio-cultural transformation. Pressing contemporary social and political concerns such as the place of indigenous groups in contemporary Taiwan or the marginalization of migrant workers, are being addressed in museums as a way to democratically increase public awareness of (and sensitivity towards) such issues and to construct consensus around issues of difference, belonging and national identity. The many recent initiatives tackling equality issues, notably in the representation of ethnic and indigenous identities, suggest that museums in Taiwan are key agents in the transition towards a more equal and inclusive society. Yet, these same initiatives also raise a number of questions around museums' priorities and practices.

First, in most of the examples referenced in this chapter, museums tackle inequality issues in the context of special or temporary exhibitions; seldom are such concerns integrated in the permanent galleries. This implicit dichotomy between the opportunities afforded by the short-term, dynamic nature of temporary exhibitions, and the conservative approaches deployed in the permanent galleries, suggests that engagement with socially relevant issues is still being negotiated within museums.

Moreover, internationally the promotion of equality in museums has been linked to such phenomena as the rise of human rights and social movements; demographic changes leading to increasingly plural, multicultural societies; and an increased accountability of museums, especially where they are financed primarily through public sources (Sandell 2007: 6). Whilst Taiwanese museums are not immune to these dynamics, it would be inaccurate to attribute their growing concern with contemporary social issues solely to such phenomena as this would downplay the critical role that political considerations and Taiwan's historically, culturally and socially-specific trajectories have played in shaping museum thinking and practice. This is particularly marked in relation to the re-definition of Taiwanese identity, which requires construction through complex processes of negotiation and consensus-building. Taiwanese museums are fully engaged in these processes.

Indigenous peoples in Taiwan are today the target of a form of positive discrimination; their cultural difference is extolled rather than suppressed. In the museums of Taiwan, the cultural difference of indigenous groups is not diminished and contained, as it would be in the context of assimilationist discourses. Rather such differences are increasingly celebrated, historicized and actualized, and presented as a manifestation of Taiwan's cultural autonomy from China in the framework of nationalistic discourses. At the same time, whilst indigenous cultures are preferentially presented through historical or ethnographic perspectives, some of the most pressing issues affecting indigenous communities – such as high levels of unemployment, AIDS, prostitution and poverty – are absent from museum narratives. Moreover, displays are still largely conceived and set up by non-indigenous curators, whilst members of indigenous groups are, at best, *invited* to collaborate with museum staff in a consultative mode. Whilst this should not imply that all displays of indigenous cultures in Taiwan are manipulative, the largely unilateral authorship of such displays (by non-indigenous curators) suggests the persistence of unequal power relations between the subjects that organize the displays and the objects of representation.

These considerations denote a discrepancy between the growing concern of museums in Taiwan with social issues and the way ethnic and indigenous groups continue to be represented in museum displays. In other words, there appears to be a lack of consistency between the general progressive character of museum practices engaging with social and ethnic issues in Taiwanese society, and the modes of museum representation of indigenous groups. This reveals the highly political stakes inherent in ethnic representations in contemporary Taiwan. Whilst indigenous groups are not absent from, discriminated against or marginalised within museum representations – indeed they are increasingly visible and integrated in the national ethnoscape – their actual participation in the decision-making process remains limited.

If unilaterally conceived, museum representations aiming to 'be equal' may be at risk of reproducing and reinforcing forms of inequality. One way out of this situation might be the development of strategies that integrate multiple external perspectives (of indigenous and ethnic groups in this instance) with an internal, purposefully cultivated and shared awareness of social justice which informs ideas, working methods, institutional priorities and goals at every level of decision-making. In this way, it might be possible to construct a common platform of shared values within museums and across society – a platform that might help museums, in Taiwan and beyond, to achieve more equitable representations that support the construction of a genuinely inclusive and just society.

Notes

1 Fieldwork research in Taiwan was generously financed by a British Academy Small Grant.
2 Over the last few years Taiwan has been affected by a number of natural disasters including earthquakes (the most destructive was in September 1999), typhoons, floods and landslides.
3 For a discussion of the long-term implications of the 2–28 Incident for ethnic relationships in Taiwan and the development of a Taiwanese cultural identity see Chen 2010a (especially chapter 6).
4 For further information, see the website of the National Museum of Taiwan History: www.nmth.gov.tw.

References

Allio, F. (1998) 'La Construction d'un Espace Politique Austronésien', *Perspectives chinoises*, 47(1): 54–62.
Brown, M.F. (2009) 'Exhibiting Indigenous Heritage in the Age of Cultural Property', in J. Cuno (ed.) *Whose Culture? The Promise of Museums and the Debate over Antiquities*, Princeton, NJ and Woodstock, Oxfordshire: Princeton University Press: 145–64.
Brown, M.J. (2004) *Is Taiwan Chinese? The Impact of Culture, Power, and Migration on Changing Identities*, Berkeley: University of California Press.

Cameron, F. and Kelly, L. (eds) (2010) *Hot Topics, Public Culture, Museums*, Cambridge: Cambridge Scholars Publisher.

Chang, B. (2004) 'From Taiwanisation to De-sinification: Culture Construction in Taiwan Since the 1990s', *China Perspectives*, 56. Online. Available at: http://chinaperspectives.revues.org/document438.html (accessed 9 December 2010).

Chen, C.-L. (2002) 'The Museum in Transition: Community Involvement in North East Taiwan', *Museological Review*, 8: 37–50.

Chen, C.-L. (2003) 'Interpreting History: Adults' Learning in the Taipei 228 Memorial Museum', *Museological Review*, 9: 16–29.

Chen, C.-L. (2007) 'Museums and the Shaping of Cultural Identities: Visitors' Recollections in Local Museums in Taiwan', in S.J. Knell, S. MacLeod and S. Watson (eds) *Museum Revolutions: How Museums Change and are Changed*, London and New York: Routledge: 173–88.

Chen, C.-L. (2009) 'Trauma, Knowledge & Memories: On the Exhibition and Interpretation of the 921 Earthquake Education Park' (in Chinese), *Taiwan Wen Hsien*, 60(4): 439–69.

Chen, C.-L. (2010a) *Museums and Cultural Identities: Learning and Recollection in Local Museums in Taiwan*, Saarbrucken: VDM Publishing House.

Chen, C.-L. (2010b) 'Disability, Human Rights and the Public Gaze: The Losheng Story Museum', in R. Sandell, J. Dodd and R. Garland-Thomson (eds) *Re-Presenting Disability: Activism and Agency in the Museum*, London and New York: Routledge: 244–56.

Chen, K. (2008) 'Museums in Taiwan and the Development of Cultural Awareness', *Museum International* (UNESCO), No. 237–238, 60(1–2): 123–31.

Hsiao, H.M. (1990) 'Emerging Social Movements and the Rise of a Demanding Civil Society in Taiwan', *The Australian Journal of Chinese Affairs*, 24: 163–80.

Hsieh, J. (2006) *Collective Rights of Indigenous Peoples: Identity-Based Movement of Plain Indigenous in Taiwan*, London and New York: Routledge.

Hu, C. (2007) 'Taiwanese Aboriginal Art and Artifacts: Entangled Images of Colonization and Modernization', in Y. Kikuchi (ed.) *Refracted Modernity: Visual Culture and Identity in Colonial Taiwan*, Honolulu: University of Hawaii Press: 193–216.

Hung, S. (ed.) (2009) *National Taiwan Museum*, Taipei: National Taiwan Museum Publisher.

Kikuchi, Y. (2007) 'Introduction', in Y. Kikuchi (ed.) *Refracted Modernity: Visual Culture and Identity in Colonial Taiwan*, Honolulu: University of Hawaii Press: 1–20.

Ku, K. (2005) 'Rights to Recognition: Minority/Indigenous Politics in the Emerging Taiwanese Nationalism', *Social Analysis*, 49(2): 99–121.

Langfield, M., Logan, W. and Nic Craith, M. (eds) (2010) *Cultural Diversity, Heritage and Human Rights: Intersections in Theory and Practice*, London and New York: Routledge.

Lee, S. (2010) Director, Beitou Folk Art Museum, and project manager of the governmental programme 'Big Museum Leads Small Museum'. Interview with the author, 22 June.

Levin, A.K. (ed.) (2010) *Gender, Sexuality and Museums: A Routledge Reader*, London and New York: Routledge.

Li, T. (2010) Curator, anthropological section of the National Taiwan Museum. Interview with the author, 30 April.

Lim, S. (2009) 'A Hundred Years of Waiting: Chi-Mei Heritage goes back to Chi-Mei'. Exhibition notes (in Chinese), *National Museum of Prehistory Newsletter*, 167. Online. Available at: http://beta.nmp.gov.tw/enews/no167/page_01.html (accessed 31 March 2010).

Lu, L. (2010) Director, National Museum of Taiwan History. Interview with the author, 28 June.

Ming, T. (2008) *Visualising Culture and Gender: Postcolonial Feminist Analyses of Taiwanese Women's Exhibitions, 1996–2003*. Unpublished PhD Thesis, Loughborough University.

National Museum of Taiwan History (undated) *Encountering Different Cultures: Opportunities and Choices*, exhibition brochure.

National Museum of Taiwan History (2009) *A Brief Introduction to the National Museum of Taiwan History*, Taiwan: National Museum of Taiwan History.

Rudolph, M. (2001) 'The Emergence of the Concept of "Ethnic Group" in Taiwan and the Role of Taiwan's Austronesians in the Construction of Taiwanese Identity'. Online. Available at: www. taiwanfirstnations.org/mem.html (accessed 8 December 2010).

Sandell, R. (2002) 'Museums and the Combating of Social Inequality: Roles, Responsibilities, Resistance', in R. Sandell (ed.) *Museums, Society, Inequality*, London and New York: Routledge: 3–21.

Sandell, R. (2007) *Museum, Prejudice and the Reframing of Difference*, London and New York: Routledge.

Sandell, R., Dodd, J. and Garland-Thomson, R. (2010) *Re-Presenting Disability: Activism and Agency in the Museum*, London and New York: Routledge.

Schubert, G. (1999) 'The Discourse on National Identity in Contemporary Taiwan', *China Perspectives*, 25: 44–59.

Simon, S. (2010) 'Negotiating Power: Elections and the Constitution of Indigenous Taiwan', *American Ethnologist*, 37(4): 726–40.

Skartvcit, H. and Goodnow, K.J. (2010) *Changes in Museum Practice: New Media, Refugees and Participation*, New York: Berghahn Books.

Taipei Times (2009) '228 Foundation to Open Memorial Museum in 2011', 3 November. Online: Available at: www.taipeitimes.com/News/taiwan/archives/2009/11/03/2003457535 (accessed 25 July 2011).

Taiwan Today (2010a) 'CCA Unveils Human Rights Museum Plan', *Taiwan Today*, 23 July.

Taiwan Today (2010b) 'Museum Project puts Paiwan Culture Online', *Taiwan Today*, 15 December.

Taiwan International Workers Association (2007) 'Voyage 15840. Migrants as Photographers', *Inter-Asia Cultural Studies*, 8(3): 438–48.

Tsao, R. (2006) 'Museums for Peace: Identity of Taiwan's Peace Museums and Human Rights Parks'. Paper presented at the INTERCOM/ICOM conference *New Roles and Missions for Museums*, Taipei, 2–4 November 2006. Online. Available at: www.intercom.museum/documents/2–6Tsao.pdf (accessed 18 December 2010).

Wachman, A.M. (1994) *Taiwan: National Identity and Democratization (Taiwan in the Modern World)*, London: An East Gate Book.

Wang, H. (2004) 'National Culture and Its Discontents: The Politics of Heritage and Language in Taiwan, 1949–2003', *Comparative Studies in Society and History*, 46(4): 786–815.

18

SOCIAL JUSTICE AND COMMUNITY PARTICIPATION IN NON-WESTERN CONTEXTS

The Marib Museum Project in Yemen

Susan Kamel and Christine Gerbich

Prologue: the origins of the Yemen salmon project

Fitzharris & Price
Land Agents & Consultants
St James's Street
London

Dr Alfred Jones
National Centre for Fisheries Excellence
Department for Environment, Food and Rural Affairs
Smith Square
London

15 May
Dear Dr Jones,
We have been referred to you by Peter Sullivan at the Foreign and Commonwealth Office (Directorate for Middle East and North Africa) – We act on behalf of a client with access to very substantial funds who has indicated his wish to sponsor a project to introduce salmon, and the sport of salmon fishing, into the Yemen.

We recognize the challenging nature of such a project, but we have been assured that the expertise exists within your organization to research and project-manage such work.

Torday 2007: 1–2

This chapter explores three intersecting questions which, despite the increasingly globalised character of debates surrounding the social agency and responsibilities of museums, have received relatively little attention (Kreps 2008; Chapter 17, this volume). How do museums in non-Western societies address social justice and inclusion? Can a participatory (Simon 2010) and inclusive (Dodd and Sandell 2001; Sandell 2002) museum project be successful in 'hierarchically organized societies and conflict situations where tribal networks and power are more important than impositions of a central government' (Jones 2005: 301)? In such settings, which forms of exclusion might be challenged (and which issues might remain sidelined)?[1]

Recent events in Yemen demonstrate both the call for democratisation by the Yemeni people and the strong oppression of human rights from the president Ali Abdullah Saleh.[2]

Within this context, to conceptualise a museum in Yemen as a social actor might seem reminiscent of Paul Torday's satirical British comedy of absurd development projects, *Salmon Fishing in the Yemen*, described by one reviewer as a novel about impossibility but also belief in the impossible (Mackintosh-Smith 2007). Indeed, one might ask if an inclusive museum is really what the Yemeni people need at the moment. We are aware of the enormous challenges facing the region and hope we can prevent the planning of a regional museum in Marib from becoming another neo-colonial enterprise if we, as members of the museum team, work in close cooperation with our Yemeni colleagues and the various publics of Yemen. We also aim to critically reflect upon our own position in the project at all times.

Along the Incense Road

Some 2,800 years ago, Marib, the capital of the Sabaean Kingdom, was a prosperous town. Saba was an influential territorial state which ably utilised its geographical location to control the trade along the Incense Road (Hitgen 2005). This blossoming of ancient times stands in stark contrast to the region's current situation (Figure 18.1). Today, Marib has a relatively poor infrastructure and a high rate of unemployment. It also suffers the consequences of the regularly recurring conflicts between the government and the ruling tribes.[3] It is one of the poorest regions in a country whose economical and social situation has been shaped by immense political eruptions in the recent past. Today, Yemen is defined as a presidential republic. Yemen is also a member state of the Organization of the Islam Conference which adopted the Cairo Declaration of Human Rights in 1990. Generally seen as an Islamic response to the Universal Declaration on Human Rights adopted by the United Nations in 1948, the Cairo Declaration affirms Islamic Shari'ah as its sole source.[4] Both Declarations differ for example in respect to the status of men and women and the freedom of religion.

A strategy paper of the European Union for the period 2007–2013 defines the political and social situation of the country as follows:

> Yemen is one of the poorest countries in the world and belongs to the Least Developed Countries. High population growth, slow economic development, declining oil resources, depleting water resources, poor standard of public health and education, widespread poverty, poor governance and internal insecurity remain the key challenges for the country. At present, Yemen is unlikely to meet most of the Millennium Development Goals by 2015. The government has shown commitment to democratization, to economic liberalization and to political and economic reforms. However, this has not yet resulted in concrete progress. In the absence of reforms, the social and political situation is likely to deteriorate.
>
> *European Community 2007*

Nowadays, the situation is declining further as a result of military conflicts. In the field of education, the lack of basic skills and low standards in formal education are striking (UNESCO 2008).

FIGURE 18.1 Tank in front of the ruins of the Sabaean town of Sirwah close to Marib. DAI, Orient–Department. Photo by Iris Gerlach. Copyright: German Archaeological Institute, Oriental Department.

The origins of the Marib Museum Project

To improve the country's economic situation, the government under President Ali Abdullah Saleh (in office since 1990[5]) promoted tourism to ancient sites as this is an important source of income for the country. The country's historical sites are administered by the General Authority for Antiquities and Museums (GOAM). This institution is also responsible for over twenty museums throughout the country.[6]

As a result of this, the government of Yemen, namely GOAM, has started exerting its influence to preserve the historical sites and monuments by providing funding for excavation, preservation and protection and by promoting and funding cooperation with foreign experts (Bawazir 1994). The government has also set up a monitoring unit to observe border entries, sea ports and airports in collaboration with security forces and the army, as a response to the severe looting and smuggling of ancient objects.

To preserve the rich cultural heritage in the region of Marib, the Yemeni Social Fund for Development (SFD) commissioned Iris Gerlach, head of the Sana'a Branch of the German Archaeological Institute (DAI), to plan and build a regional museum in Marib.[7] The DAI is in charge of developing the scientific and museological concept, setting up the museum building and designing the exhibitions. The institution has not only been chosen for its scientific expertise in regard to the findings in Marib, but also for its knowledge of the local socio-political conditions and its promotion of capacity-building through workshops and training programmes. With the planned regional museum (Figure 18.2), the Yemeni government aims to promote tourism in this region and, in addition, to change the country's museum landscape, bringing it closer in line with international standards – both conceptually and in terms of administration.

While the DAI is responsible for the practical realisation of the museum, the overall responsibility for the project lies with the Yemeni Social Fund for Development (SFD). This institution was established as an autonomous state organisation under the Council of Ministers in 1997 and is financed by the International Monetary Fund and the World Bank.

The implementation of structural adjustment programs (SAP) initiated by the International Monetary Fund (IMF) and the World Bank have induced in the adjusting countries negative social effects which have been subject to harsh criticism. In order to socially mitigate SAPs, the World Bank has been promoting the creation of social safety nets. Social development funds (SFDs) were established as parts of these safety nets to alleviate the impact on poor and vulnerable groups of the reduction in income and employment caused by the economic reforms (Weidnitzer 1998).

The SFD aims at decentralisation and community development (Weidnitzer 1998: 4) in order to reduce poverty and strengthen participation in society as a whole. It defines certain Special Needs Groups (SNGs) which include: disabled people; children at risk, such as orphans and street children; women at risk, including women in prisons; socially marginalised groups like the *Akhdam*;[8] those in psychiatric hospitals; isolated elderly people and returnees living in shanty dwellings (Coleridge 2004: 4).

As a project under the auspices of the SFD, the Marib Museum has been conceptualised as a development project with two aims in mind: first, to boost the attractiveness of the province of Marib for both national and foreign tourists; and second, to improve employment opportunities by creating jobs in the museum, at the historical sites and in the tourist supply industry (for example, by increasing the demand for accommodation and restaurants). Moreover, it

FIGURE 18.2 About 80 per cent of the objects to be shown in the new museum are from German excavations. Grave Stelae from the Awam cemetery, including representations of the heads of the deceased. DAI, Orient-Department. Photo: Johannes Kramer. Copyright: German Archaeological Institute, Oriental Department.

is expected that the Marib Museum will have positive effects on social conditions: it will help reduce poverty in the area; support local economic initiatives, including initiatives for women; strengthen the self-esteem of the population and, it is hoped, have a positive impact on safety and security in the region.

Towards a new museology in Yemen

When we began to work on a museological concept for the Marib Museum, we were trained in Western museology, critical postcolonial theory, empirical research and Islamic studies. We also had experience of working in other Arab countries[9] – notably Egypt – which, to some extent, was helpful. In Yemen, however, we were absolute beginners.

The museological concept acknowledged the demands of the new museological movement and was welcomed by the SFD and its commitment to improving social conditions in Yemen. New museology is an umbrella term for different approaches to museum thinking and practice that reflect a paradigm shift towards an understanding of museums as social actors (Macdonald 2006; Meijer-van Mensch 2009). New museologies emerged out of the representational critique of socially marginalised groups. They have in common a critical interrogation of the very foundations of traditional museology and museum practices. New museologies or community museologies (Karp *et al.* 1992; Watson 2007) affect all areas of work in museums: collecting, preserving, researching and mediating. They challenge the canonical positioning of collections, and also expand the collections to include intangible cultural heritage. Preservationists and conservationists are invited to consider questions regarding what (and for whom) something should be preserved. Research is directed away from questions *about* 'the others' and towards research *with* 'the others' – including those often described as 'source communities' (Peers and Brown 2007). Also, the concept of the public as a unitary mass is replaced by an acknowledgement of diversity within society (Hooper-Greenhill 2006: 362). The hitherto static sphere of the museum is stretched beyond its physical boundaries, contextually as well as spatially: the area of the museum is expanded by large outdoor installations and the groups represented in museums are entitled to present their cultural heritage by means of varied publicity and workshops. The results of these developments are materialised in a variety of forms including ecomuseums, where the aim is to correlate human beings with their environment; community museums; tribal museums; and cultural centres.

The opportunities and challenges presented by the application of new museology in non-Western settings is 'appropriate museology' – a 'bottom-up, community-based approach that combines local knowledge and resources with those of professional museum work to better meet the needs and interests of a particular museum and its community' (Kreps 2008: 23); an approach developed in theory and practice by Christina Kreps for Indonesia. In her analysis of the role of museums in social development in non-Western societies, Kreps pointed out: 'Today, it has become widely accepted in development circles that, in order for development efforts to be sustainable in the long run, they must take local people's values, traditions, knowledge, and resources into account' (Kreps 2008: 27).

These concerns also impact the planning process for the future museum in Marib. The museum aims to be physically, socially and intellectually accessible to as many visitors as possible (Hein 1998, 2006). In the way it is conceptualised, it recognises that knowledge is constructed by visitors on the basis of their prior knowledge and experiences (Hooper-Greenhill 2006: 367). Research into the cultural heritage of Yemen will therefore take place, wherever possible, in cooperation with local experts. Also of great importance is the social responsibility of the museum *during* the planning process and, as a result, an inclusive approach has been adopted. Not only will research be conducted about potential visitors, their learning styles, their knowledge and their perceptions of the exhibition's contents (Wilk and Humphrey 2004; Yousuf 2006; O'Neill 2009), but different social groups will be included in the planning of the exhibition from the very beginning.

If we consider the theoretical advances achieved by the new museology, the choice of an inclusive museum concept – one based on community participation and social justice – seems entirely logical. However, if we look at the development of museology in the Arab world, it becomes obvious that such an approach constitutes a tremendous challenge to established perceptions of museum purposes and functions.

Ilm al-mutahif al-gadida[10] – new museological approaches in the Arab world?

The discussions about the changing role of museums that have taken place in the Western world – especially in Great Britain, Canada and the United States – have led not only to different understandings about institutional responsibilities, purposes and priorities, but also to structural changes in, for example, the proportion of staff employed in the areas of museum education, outreach and interpretation. To our knowledge, no analogue development can be observed in the Arab world.

We started our project with a survey of museums in the Arab world. For this, we examined museums in countries which are often homogenised as 'Arabic' (Popp 2004). Of course, museums in Egypt, Yemen, Saudi Arabia and the United Arab Emirates differ greatly in respect to their socio-political contexts: we can safely say that museums in a centralistic state like Egypt play a different role than museums in the Republic of Yemen, in the Wahhabiyyan monarchy of Saudi Arabia or in the booming megapolis of Dubai. Despite this variation, it is nevertheless crucial for our work in Yemen to reflect on the role and history of museums in Arab countries as they do share some important features; a common language, the influence of Islam and a history of imperialism and colonialism amongst others. As Gülrü Necipoglu (forthcoming) and others (Reid 2002) have pointed out, museums were introduced into Arab countries by colonisers and their local allies. Museums as representatives of the dominant culture played a leading role in the construction of orientalism through an essentialising presentation of the 'other' culture (Kamel 2004, 2009; Gerbich 2010; Kamel 2010).

Museums in Yemen – as in Egypt – were imperial showcases. Donald M. Reid's analysis of the situation in Egypt also seems to be true for Yemen: 'Archaeology and Imperialism seemed to walk hand in hand' (Reid 2002: 2). In these countries, where museums are understood as institutions which support the tourism industry, museology ('ilm al-mutahif') is rarely taught and the study of museums as a university discipline is still in its early stages of development. This becomes obvious in the case of Egypt, where museums form an important part of the tourist industry and function as key instruments for the formation of a national patriotic identity. Here museology is mainly taught as museum education ('at-tarbiya al-mathafiya') (Al-Gama'a al-qahira 2007). The positivist communication theory on which Egyptian museum education is based is described as having three pillars: the museum's object (sender), the museum guide (medium) and the child (recipient) (Al-Gama'a al-qahira 2007: 182–183, see also Nur Al-Din 2009).

There are, however, early signs of change. In 1994 the regional sub-organisation, ICOM Arab, was founded within the International Council of Museums (ICOM) which encompasses representatives from seventeen Arab countries. This organisation started out by discussing Arab museums along the themes of *Museum, Civilization, Development* (International Council of Museums 1994). At the same time, the regional sub-organisation started cooperating with the European organisation, ICOM Europe. Two meetings have taken place so far, in 2005 and 2006, on the subjects of *Children and Heritage* and *Bridging Cultures through Exhibitions*, respectively. Amongst others, the topics discussed included the use of educational concepts in museums.[11]

What is more, even if there is – as yet – no indigenous museum movement in Arab countries, museums that follow new museology approaches do exist. UNESCO's Nubia Museum in Aswan, Egypt, is one example. It can, in fact, be seen as a facilitator of the Marib Museum Project.

Research conducted in March 2008 (Kamel and Gerbich 2009) has also shown that the concept of the community museum or ecomuseum (Davis 1999, 2007) is successful in Aswan. In contrast to other Egyptian museums, Gerbich (2010) demonstrated that the Nubia Museum attracts its Egyptian and Nubian visitors many times over. In a survey conducted in 2008, 41 per cent of Egyptian visitors said that they had been to the Nubia Museum several times before, while this was the case for 20 per cent of Egyptian visitors to the Gayer-Anderson Museum and 17 per cent of visitors to the Coptic Museum (both in Cairo).

An inclusive planning process for Marib

What role has been ascribed to museums in Yemen in the past? Meynersen and Weber (1996) point to differences in the educational traditions of the northern and southern parts of the country which are linked to the opposing ideological regimes setting the political agenda. In their descriptions of museums in Yemen, they point out that the educational function of museums might have been rather more pronounced in the socialist southern part of the country where exhibitions were used to disseminate ideological ideas.

Apart from such regional differences which might still have an impact upon values and attitudes, the broader cultural dimension also invites a number of questions. For example, cultural differences between the Western and the Arab world in respect to learning styles and ways of perception are of interest to us. Although we are well aware of the risks of essentialising culturally determined differences, we do believe that such differences have to be taken into consideration when planning a museum. To give an example: whether we look at a painting from the right to the left or the other way around changes the way we interpret it and ascribe meanings.

But are we dealing only with cultural differences here? We know from our observations at Sana'a National Museum that the visitors' itinerary – their route through the museum – can be directed via an orientation system and this does not necessarily differ for Yemenis or foreigners. Nonetheless, different customs, attitudes and understandings need to be revealed, analysed and taken into account in the process of exhibition planning, not least because lack of funds might make it impossible to provide an elaborate educational programme once the exhibition opens its doors. Therefore, in planning the Marib Museum, emphasis was placed on an inclusive development process for the exhibition to provide the permanent displays with manifold stimulations for local audiences.

Although the past few years have seen an increase in the number of museums in Arab countries, we know little more about their visitors than their numbers (Doyon 2008). Even in countries with a long-standing tradition of museums, like Egypt, little is known about the composition or experience of audiences (Gerbich 2010). When we started the Marib Project, there was no information at all available on people who visit museums in Yemen. Therefore important steps towards creating a visitor-centred museum were (1) the study of museum audiences and (2) identifying special target groups in Sana'a and including them in the planning process in 2007 and 2009. Altogether, the research had three goals: to gain an understanding of existing museum audiences in Yemen; to enhance access to and acceptance of the museum for a greater diversity of people within Yemen; and to explicitly highlight the inclusive character of the museum by focusing on a variety of Yemeni voices during the exhibition-making process.

Procedures and results

Less than a handful of museums in the Yemeni capital could be considered for our survey: the Military Museum, the Ethnological Museum and the National Museum. We decided that the latter was a good place to conduct the survey because its collection resembles that of the planned museum. The National Museum displays objects from pre-Islamic times and the Islamic period in a chronological order on four floors. The upper floor hosts a *folklore* gallery, where life-sized dioramas display an idealised view of traditional life in the Yemen. In 2007, the museum was visited by approximately 18,000 Yemenis coming from all over the country.

(1) The survey was carried out in October and December of 2007. The questionnaire was developed through in-depth discussions by a team including German and Yemeni archaeologists, a museologist and a social scientist. The result was an instrument which asked for general information on visiting behaviour, a self-assessment of interest in archaeology as well as visitors' general opinion on the planned museum in Marib. Items to assess respondents' region of origin and socio-demographic background (age, gender, education) were also included.[12] Finally, we prepared versions for both face-to-face completion (with a researcher) as well as self-completion in order to avoid dropouts due to illiteracy (Plate 18.1a).

During the two phases of the survey, we managed to realise nearly 500 individual interviews, including 350 with Arabic-speaking people. The survey confirmed our assumptions regarding the differences between Yemeni and foreign audiences, especially in respect to socio-demographic factors. Neither were we surprised that the two groups differed in respect to their visiting behaviours and interests.

On average, the tourists in our sample were older. Twice as many tourists as Yemenis held a degree in higher education.[13] While the majority of tourists had visited a museum at least once in the previous year, two-thirds of Yemeni respondents had never been to a museum before. Foreigners knew the museum through the tourist infrastructure (tour guides, travel literature), while Yemenis mainly found out about the museum through informal sources like family, friends or colleagues as well as through school or university. Only a few differences were found between the two groups in respect to their self-reported use of information resources within the museum, although the survey did reveal that fewer local women than men made use of introduction panels and labels. This might be explained by the higher level of illiteracy among women, but also by the visiting behaviour of families who preferred to visit the exhibition as a group led by a male family member.

Since the new museum in Marib will mainly display archaeological finds, it was exciting to find out that many Yemenis reported a distinctive interest in archaeology, including technical details. However, when they were asked to express a preference for one of the museum's floors, it turned out that the dioramas in the folklore section were preferred over the classical presentation of archaeological objects.

(2) In addition to the survey we contacted different groups whose knowledge and expertise were considered of great value for the project. Among them were: a female and a male representative of the society for the blind; the head of the organisation of physically disabled women; school teachers; pupils (Plate 18.1b); professional tourist guides; artists who had been working in Yemen and Marib. As this part of the project develops in the future, it is hoped that diverse perspectives will be gathered including comments from Yemeni and foreign journalists, authors and curators.[14] These additional voices are considered a means to capture and hold the attention of the visitor as well as enabling a variety of perspectives on the presented objects. Studies have likewise convinced us that we will include contemporary art in the museum's representation of the cultural history of Yemen.[15]

This network-building was supplemented by a number of interviews to find out about the specific needs of certain target audiences. The storyline of the planned exhibition as it had been outlined by the archaeologists Iris Gerlach and Robert Arndt (Gerlach *et al.* 2010) was tested to see if its rationale was understood by local people. We started out asking people to give a general history of the Yemen to a good friend. The aim of this exercise was to identify what people saw as important themes and events in their country's history, but also to find out which historical periods should be mentioned. Except for one person, all of our interview partners faded out recent history but talked extensively about Yemen's ancient history, especially the mighty kingdoms of Saba, Hadramaut or Himyar. Only two respondents included the revolution of 1962, and only one mentioned the country's reunification in 1990. This might also be explained by the fact that Yemenis generally avoid talking about recent politics in public.

Personal meaning maps on relevant concepts like 'Bilqis' (the Queen of Sheba), 'Marib' and 'irrigation' were also done as part of this process. With these, we wanted to find out more about the extent of people's previous knowledge, but also to discover some of the 'hooks' that can be used to capture visitor interest in the exhibition.

Challenges to the community-centred approach

One of the challenges we encountered in the project was the lack of security in and around the region which made many of the communities[16] of Marib inaccessible to us. In July 2007 – two months before the start of our research – six Spanish tourists were killed and seven injured in a blast in Marib. This tragic incident has shaped our working conditions to this day. As a consequence, access to Yemeni participants was restricted to those living in the capital Sana'a. But the living conditions in the areas of Marib and Sana'a are quite different, both in terms of regional character and power relationships: the people of Marib live within a patrimonial tribal system which coexists with the official government in Sana'a. One can easily assume that our research could have had very different results if it had been conducted in cooperation with these tribal societies. For example, access to relevant stakeholders might have been more difficult.

Because we were committed to putting the concept of the museum as a social actor into practice as much as possible, we considered it a necessity to further expand our professional networks within Yemen. As newcomers to the country, we were happy to rely on the good reputation of the German Archaeological Institute and its networks to make relevant contacts in Sana'a. We started off by meeting two local archaeologists, Musleh al Qubati and Ahmad Shamsan, and we invited them to Germany to discuss the museological concept for Marib. A workshop was also held to introduce them to our social research methods and to introduce ourselves to the local conditions in Yemen. During this meeting, we also discussed visitor-friendly museum contexts. Our partners' intercultural work experience, their language skills and their knowledge of local networks were of immeasurable value for our common research.

Despite the considerable lessons we learned from these fruitful exchanges, the results of our research nevertheless suggested that cultural biases were sometimes at play. For example, we suspect the descriptions of respondents' leisure activities were influenced by a desire to present themselves as 'good' representatives of Yemen. Although religious practices like reading the holy Qur'an are important in Yemen's everyday life, ethnological research in Yemen has shown that other leisure activities, such as playing sports or watching the television, do play an important role (Linke 2009). However, only our juvenile respondents mentioned any leisure activities other than those related to religious practices. This clearly shows that in order to improve processes of communication and interpretation within the exhibition, we need to expand our local professional networks even further. The need for this becomes even clearer when we look at the content of the exhibition.

For example, many of the radical changes that were introduced in Yemen after the 1962 revolution are seen by Yemenis as a re-awakening of ancient traditions which extend to the pre-Islamic era. Many Yemenis also consider themselves the bearers of one of the oldest civilisations. This has been confirmed through interviews connected to the meaning maps: Bilquis, the Queen of Sheba, for instance, was named by some of our interview partners as the inventor of democracy, because she introduced the concept of 'Shura'[17] although this view is problematised by new research results (Nebes 2001) which suggest that migrants from the Levant into South Arabia were involved in the creation of the Sabaean civilisation. Our visitor-centred approach is also challenged by the fact that most Yemenis would deny that, during the Bronze Age, their culture was similar to that of east Africa and southern Arabia – despite archaeologists' claims to the contrary (Gerlach and Kamel forthcoming). Such taboos must be tackled sensitively but in line with new scientific research. It will also be important in the course of the project to develop fluid boundaries between the museum's departments on Islamic art and ethnography. Indeed, recent research has shown that the complex cartography of advanced civilizations and folk cultures and their many interrelationships must be drawn into focus.

With regard to its target audiences, one of the challenges will be for the planned exhibition to be gender-sensitive. In her report on gender and development in Yemen, Marta Colburn (2002) shows that mobility and education for women as well as the degree of segregation between the sexes varies not only regionally, but also with respect to socio-economic status. What women all over Yemen share, however, is the responsibility for family duties. Thus, an exhibition concept which strives to be accessible for women needs to serve family audiences and encourage cross-generational participation.

In this context, it is important to keep the issue of illiteracy in mind. Our observations revealed that Yemeni groups of visitors are very often led by one person who reads the labels and explains the contents. We have to think carefully about how we can support these mediators and how the exhibition's contents can most effectively be communicated to those who are unable to read – many of them being women. This has to be thought of and planned in advance because the exhibition design cannot rely on modern technologies due to poor local infrastructure and unresolved problems of maintenance.

More generally, when thinking about how the museum's contents are best communicated, the exhibition must strike the difficult balance of being both scientifically challenging and accessible for local visitors who are not familiar with the medium of the museum. For this, it is crucial to better understand what contents are meaningful to people as well as where and how learning takes place. What are the local teaching styles and who are the transmitters of knowledge? Besides through schools, is knowledge passed on through the Madrasas (Qur'an classes), the family or other social gatherings? What educational strategies are most appropriate within these contexts? As became clear to us during our observations of school groups (at a local school and during museum visits), pedagogical styles in Yemen tend to be restrictive rather than participatory and authoritarian rather than authoritative (see also Dwairy *et al.* 2006), in common with parenting styles in Yemen (ibid.). If we want the museum to function as a successful learning environment, it is crucial that we acknowledge these cultural differences. A constructivist learning approach – strongly favoured in Western museological practice – might be hindered by other cultural conventions that inhibit free-choice learning. However, this assumption might be refuted in the process of the formative evaluation.

New museologies are inclusive endeavours that demand some form of democracy. However, in Yemen, the tribal power of indigenous local leaders is confronted with the authority of a central government that seems to represent a multitude of interests. The success of the Marib Museum Project therefore depends not just on expertise and knowledge but also on diplomacy and the necessary sensitivity towards the region's needs.

Notes

1 It must be noted here that the discourse on 'inclusion' around the Marib museum project has taken place within the contemporary political and social limits of Yemen. Whilst some forms of inclusion can be openly explored, others remain challenging. Identities intersect ethnicity, race, gender, class, sexuality, health, religion, language and so on and whilst an individual might be excluded in relation to one of these identities they may be included by also belonging to another dominant identity (Mecheril *et al.* 2010: 15).

2 This chapter is based on work that was carried out before the Jasmine revolution swept over from Tunisia and Egypt to Yemen with many youth activists and opposition members demonstrating against the authoritarian government. At the time of writing, Yemen's political situation is more fragile than ever, the Marib Museum Project has come to a standstill and its future is dependent on the outcome of the current events.

3 For information on Yemen, see Kopp (2005).

4 On the conflict between the Universal Declaration of Human Rights and the Cairo Declaration, see Krämer (2007) and Littmann (1999, 2006). For the situation in Yemen, see Stiftl (1998). We would like to note here that we intentionally resist an understanding of the Declaration of Human Rights which emphasises a neat division between the 'West and the rest' – both spheres have always influenced each other. The political and social structures in 'Western' or 'Islamic' countries are more dependent on economic and social factors than on the Declarations themselves which have relatively limited authority.

5 Previously (1972–1990), Saleh had served as president of the Yemen Arab Republic (North Yemen).

6 A brief description of Yemeni museums and their collections is given by Meynersen and Weber (1996). For a list of museums in Yemen, see Nur Al-Din (2009: 446–449).

7 Here we would like to thank Iris Gerlach, project manager and head of the Sana'a DAI branch, and the Marib Museum team, namely Wolf-Dieter Thonhofer, Musleh al-Qubati, Robert C. Arndt, Sarah Japp, Holger Hitgen, Mike Schnelle, Ueli Brunner, Christian Weiß, Norbert Nebes, Désirée Heiden and Markus Wachowski. Our thanks also go to the SFD and Abdullah al-Dailami and Ahmad Haidarah.

8 The *Akhdam* are a marginalised group in Yemen, experiencing multiple forms of discrimination due to their African origin. For further information see Seif (2005).

9 We would like to stress here that we understand the terms *Arab* world and *Arab* country to mean 'Arabic-speaking world' and 'Arabic-speaking country' and we prefer these terms to *Islamic* world, *Islamic* country and so on. We are aware that when the issue of localisation is brought up, the 'naturalising imagery of geography' (Coronil 2002) is frequently called into question. This construes categories such as *west, occident, centre, east* or *orient* as naturally-given static areas on maps, outside the context of history. Maps and categorisations serve to subjugate other peoples and always enable the one or the other party to legitimise its world view: 'Maps can both predict and describe, both act and react' (Harwood 2007: 7). The division of the world in cultural areas stems from the nineteenth century and its encyclopaedic approach; see Coronil (2002), Rekacewicsz (2006) and Harwood (2007).

10 'Ilm al-muthaif al-gadida' is the Arabic term for new museology; see Gerlach *et al.* (2009: 10).

11 ICOM has also published a practical handbook and a trainers' manual for museum staff in Arabic.

12 The original English version of the questionnaire was translated and retranslated into German and Arabic to ensure that the different versions were largely functionally equivalent. As a result of our tests, this process was repeated for French and Italian.

13 The education sector in Yemen generally faces many challenges and the term 'higher education' must be understood in this context.

14 We also contacted well-known Yemenis living outside of Yemen like Yemeni-British film-maker Bader Ben Hirsi, whose film *A New Day in Old Sana'a* (2005) won the prize for best Arabic film at the International Film Festival in Cairo. Hirsi showed great interest in accompanying the development of the Marib Museum with his knowledge of Yemeni culture and aesthetics.

15 Contacts to Amna Nusairy, Fuad al-Futaih and Mazher Nizar were initiated and all of these artists have confirmed they will cooperate with the project.

16 In this context, it is also important to note that the term 'community' must be questioned and can no longer be taken for granted. For a critical view on the term, see Watson (2007). For Yemen, as Jones (2005) has found out, it is important to note that most of the time it is the Sheikh who speaks for the community.

17 Shura in Arabic means 'consultation' and is used to describe the group of people who gathers for decision-making processes or for the election of a leader.

References

Al-Gama'a al-qahira (2007) *Dalil Al-darasat al-'uliya. Kuliya al-athar*, Al-Giza: Al Gama'a al-qahira: 182–183.

Bawazir, A. (1994) 'Importance de la participation du peuple à la protection des villes historiques du Yémen', in International Council of Museums (ed.) *Actes de la Rencontre 'Musées, Civilisation et Développement' (Proceedings of the Encounter 'Museums, Civilization, and Development')*, Amman, Jordan, 26–30 April 1994: ICOM International Council of Museums, 359–361.

Ben Hirsi, B. (2005) *A New Day in Old Sana'a*. Producer: Abbas Abdali.

Colburn, M. (2002) *Gender and Development in Yemen*, Bonn: Friedrich Ebert Stiftung; Oxfam.

Coleridge, P. (2004) *The Social Fund for Development and Disabled People in Yemen*. Online. Available at: www.sfd-yemen.org/Arabic/working_for_inclusion.pdf (accessed 28 January 2011).

Coronil, F. (2002) 'Jenseits des Okzidentalismus. Unterwegs zu nichtimperialen geohistorischen Kategorien', in S. Conrad and S. Randeria (eds) *Jenseits des Eurozentrismus: Postkoloniale Perspektiven in den Geschichts- und Kulturwissenschaften*, Frankfurt/Main: Campus-Verlag, 177–218.

Davis, P. (1999) *Ecomuseums: A Sense of Place*, London: Leicester University Press.

Davis, P. (2007) 'Place exploration: museums, identity, community', in S. Watson (ed.) *Museums and their Communities*, London: Routledge, 53–75.

Dodd, J. and Sandell, R. (2001) *Including Museums: Perspectives on Museums, Galleries and Social Inclusion*, Leicester: RCMG.

Doyon, W. (2008) 'The poetics of Egyptian museum practice', *British Museum Studies in Ancient Egypt and Sudan* 10: 1–37.

Dwairy, M., Achoui, M., Abouserie, R., Farah, A., Sakhleh, A., Fayad, M. and Khan, H. (2006) 'Parenting styles in Arab societies: a first cross-regional research study', *Journal of Cross-Cultural Psychology* 37: 230–247.

European Community (2007) *Jemen –Europäische Gemeinschaft Strategiepapier für den Zeitraum 2007–2013*. Online. Available at: www.eeas.europa.eu/yemen/csp/07_13_de.pdf (accessed 10 January 2010).

Gerbich, C. (2010) 'Whom are they talking to? Egyptian museums and their visitors', in L. Guzy, R. Hatoum and S. Kamel (eds) *From Imperial Museum to Communication Centre? On the New Role of Museums as Mediators between Science and Non-Western Societies*, Würzburg: Königshausen & Neumann, 57–70.

Gerlach, I. and Kamel, S. (forthcoming) 'Das Marib Museum Projekt im Jemen: Ausstellungskonzept und Rahmenbedingungen', in M. Maischberger and B. Feller (eds) *Außenräume in Innenräumen: Die Musealen Raumkonzeptionen von Walter Andrae und Theodor Wiegand im Pergamonmuseum*.

Gerlach, I., Arndt, R. C. and Kamel, S. (2009) 'Inscha Mathaf Marib [The Marib Museum]', in General Organization of Antiquities and Museums in Yemen (ed.) *The Yemeni Museum*, Sana'a, 3–13.

Gerlach, I. Arndt, R. C. and Kamel, S. (2010) 'The establishment of the Marib Museum', in G. Katodrytis and S. Weiss (eds) *Museums in the Middle East, 2 A Architecture and Art Magazine* 13: 148–155.

Harwood, J. (2007) *Hundert Karten, die die Welt Veränderten*. Hamburg: National Geographic Deutschland.

Hein, G. E. (1998) *Learning in the Museum*, London: Routledge.

Hein, G. E. (2006) 'Museum education', in S. Macdonald (ed.) *A Companion to Museum Studies*, Oxford: Blackwell, 340–352.

Hitgen, H. (2005) *Marib: Archaeological Tourist Brochure,* Sana'a: Ministry of Culture and Tourism of the Republic of Yemen.

Hooper-Greenhill, E. (2006) 'Studying visitors', in S. Macdonald (ed.) *A Companion to Museum Studies*, Oxford: Blackwell, 362–376.

International Council of Museums (ed.) (1994) *Actes de la Rencontre 'Musées, Civilisation et Développement' (Proceedings of the Encounter 'Museums, Civilization, and Development')*.

Jones, A. M. E. (2005) 'Conflict, development and community participation in education: Pakistan and Yemen', *Internationales Asienforum* 3–4(36): 289–310.

Kamel, S. (2004) *Wege zur Vermittlung von Religionen in Berliner Museen: Black Kaaba meets White Cube*, Wiesbaden: VS Verlag für Sozialwissenschaften.

Kamel, S. (2009) 'Réprésentation de L'Ègypte', in L. Guzy, R. Hatoum and S. Kamel (eds) *Museumsinseln – Museum Islands,* Berlin: Panama Verlag, 139–205.

Kamel, S. (2010) 'Coming back from Egypt. Working on exhibitions and audience development in museums today', in L. Guzy, R. Hatoum and S. Kamel (eds) *From Imperial Museum to Communication Centre? On the New Role of Museums as Mediators between Science and Non-Western Societies,* Würzburg: Königshausen & Neumann, 35–56.

Kamel, S. and Gerbich, C. (2009) *Visiting Nubia: The Nubia Museum in the Focus of the New Museology*. Presentation at the UNESCO-Conference 'Lower Nubia: Revisiting Memories of the Past, Envisaging Perspectives for the Future' on 23 March 2009, Aswan (Egypt): Nubia Museum.

Karp, I., Kreamer, C. M. and Lavine, S. D. (eds) (1992) *Museums and Communities: The Politics of Public Culture,* Washington, DC: Smithsonian Books.

Kopp, H. (2005) *Länderkunde Jemen*, Wiesbaden: Reichert.

Krämer, G. (2007) *What's the Real Difference? Islam and the West*. Online. Available at: http://pierretristam.com/Bobst/0/wf012407.htm (accessed 3 January 2011).

Kreps, C. F. (2008) 'Appropriate museology in theory and practice', *Museum Management and Curatorship* 23(1): 23–41.

Linke, I. (2009) 'Women in Sanaa: public appearance and visual representation', *Forum Qualitative Sozialforschung/Forum: Qualitative Social Research* 10(2), Art. 15. Online. Available at: www.qualitative-research.net/index.php/fqs/article/view/1200/2746 (accessed 28 January 2011).

Littmann, D. G. (1999) 'Universal human rights and "human rights in Islam"', *Midstream* (February/March): 2–7. Online. Available at: www.dhimmitude.org/archive/universal_islam.html (accessed 11 January 2011).

Littmann, D. G. (2006) 'Human rights: universal or Islamic?', *American Thinker*, 25 August. Online. Available at: www.americanthinker.com/2006/08/human_rights_universal_or_isla.html (accessed 10 January 2011).

Macdonald, S. (ed.) (2006) *A Companion to Museum Studies*, Oxford: Blackwell.

Mackintosh-Smith, T. (2007) 'Faith, hope, love . . . and fish', *Guardian*, 24 February.

Mecheril, P. *et al.* (2010) *Einführung in die Migrationspädagogik*, Weinheim: Beltz.

Meijer-van Mensch, L. (2009) *Stadtmuseen und 'Social Inclusion': Die Positionierung des Stadtmuseums aus der 'New Museology'*, Paper presented at Berliner Stadtmuseen conference. Berlin, March.

Meynersen, S. F. and Weber, T. (1996) 'Kulturpaläste im weihrauchland: museen und archäologische Sammlungen des Yemen', *Antike Welt* 27(1): 25–36.

Nebes, N. (2001) 'Die genese der altsüdarabischen kultur: eine arbeitshypothese', in R. Eichmann and H. Parzinger (eds) *Migration und Kulturtransfer: der Wandel Vorder- und Zentralasiatischer Kulturen im Umbruch vom 2. zum 1. Vorchristlichen Jahrtausend. Akten des Internationalen Kolloquiums,* Berlin, 23. bis 26. November 1999. Bonn: Habelt, 427–435.

Necipoglu, G. (forthcoming) 'Islamic art: concepts and approaches', in B. Junod, G. Khalil and S. Weber (eds) *'Islamic Art and the Museum': Discussions on Scientific and Museological Approaches to Art and Archaeology of the Muslim World.*

Nur Al-Din, A.-a.-H. (2009) *Mutahif Al-Athar fi masr wa al-watan al-arabiy. Dirasata fig 'ilm al-mutahif,* Al-Qahira.

O'Neill, M. (2009) 'Welcome to Kelvingrove', in Gallery Curators of the Kelvingrove Art Gallery (ed.) *Kelvingrove Art Gallery and Museum: A Souvenir Guide*, Philip Wilson Publishers, 8–13.

Peers, L. and Brown, A. K. (2007) 'Museums and source communities', in S. Watson (ed.) *Museums and their Communities*, London: Routledge, 519–537.

Popp, H. (2004) 'Die arabische welt – was ist das eigentlich?', in G. Meyer (ed.) *Die Arabische Welt im Spiegel der Kulturgeographie*, Mainz: Zentrum für Forschung zur Arabischen Welt [u.a.], 8–29.

Reid, D. M. (2002) *Whose Pharaohs? Archaeology, Museums, and Egyptian National Identity from Napoleon to World War I*, Berkeley: University of California Press.

Rekacewicsz, P. (2006) 'Aus der werkstatt des kartographen', in Le Monde diplomatique (ed.) *Atlas der Globalisierung: Die Neuen Daten und Fakten zur Lage der Welt*, Berlin: taz Verlags-u. Vertriebs GmbH, 190.

Sandell, R. (ed.) (2002) *Museums, Society, Inequality*, London: Routledge.

Seif, H. (2005) 'The accursed minority: the ethno-cultural persecution of Al-Akhdam in the Republic of Yemen: a documentary & advocacy project', *Muslim World Journal of Human Rights* 2(1), Article 9.

Simon, N. (2010) *The Participatory Museum,* Santa Cruz: Museum 2.0.

Stiftl, L. (1998) *Politischer Islam und Pluralismus: Theoretische und Empirische Studie am Beispiel des Jemen,* Berlin: Hochschulschrift.

Torday, P. (2007) *Salmon Fishing in the Yemen*, London: Weidenfeld & Nicolson.

UNESCO (2008) 'Regional overview: Arab States', *Education for All Global Monitoring Report 2008.* Online. Available at: http://unesdoc.unesco.org/images/0015/001572/157267e.pdf (accessed 10 January 2011).

Watson, S. (ed.) (2007) *Museums and their Communities*, London: Routledge.

Weidnitzer, E. (1998) *Social Protection and Structural Adjustment in Yemen: Potential and Limitations of the Social Fund for Development*, Berlin: German Development Institute (Reports and working papers).

Wilk, C. and Humphrey, N. (eds) (2004) *Creating the British Galleries at the V & A: A Study in Museology*, London: V&A Publications.

Yousuf, N. (2006) 'Gallery interpretation', in R. Crill and T. Stanley (eds) *The Making of the Jameel Gallery of Islamic Art at the Victoria and Albert Museum*, London and New York: V&A Publications, 124–139.

19

EMBEDDING SHARED HERITAGE

Human rights discourse and the London Mayor's Commission on African and Asian Heritage

Janice Cheddie

Human rights and equality discourses, developed over the last three decades, increasingly sit alongside many of the theoretical and social analyses informing critical understandings of both the heritage and museum sectors. These discursive and social interventions have taken many guises (Sherman and Rogoff 1994; Duncan 1995; Weil 1988; Vergo 1989); they have sought to make known the structures, rituals and methodologies that inform relations between objects, bodies of expertise and knowledge and they have made transparent the ways that systems of power and privilege are enabled within these methodologies. Through this process of unveiling, the (often concealed) power relationships between the object, knowledge and institutional frameworks have provided a rich and fertile ground for intellectual inquiry.

Informed by post-structuralist theory and drawing upon museological discourses, this chapter seeks to locate the ways that human rights discourses were co-opted in order to posit the case for racial equality and the development of inclusive heritage narratives within London's museums and heritage institutions. I focus on a London-based initiative – the Mayor's Commission on African and Asian Heritage (MCAAH), Greater London Authority (GLA), 2003–2009 – and the deployment of human rights discourses within the Commission's publications, inquiry and implementation processes, particularly the report, *Delivering Shared Heritage* (Greater London Authority 2005), in order to articulate the case for cultural diversity. These discourses, outlined in the *Delivering Shared Heritage* report, announced the emergence of a lacuna whereby the intertwined histories of Britain and its African and Asian communities could be explored within a more open and invitational dialogue. My focus on international human rights discourses within the work of the Mayor's Commission on African and Asian Heritage highlights an aspect of the Commission's work which has generally been overlooked.

Furthermore, it is my contention that an understanding of the role that human rights discourses played within the work of the Commission, has the potential to inform future cultural diversity interventions concerned with broader principles of social justice and equality. Human rights discourses have the potential to provide a focus, not only for the issue of rights but also for related questions of justice, whilst also providing the basis for a broader national, international and theoretical dialogue. I make a distinction between cultural diversity work

– primarily focused on issues of visibility and the representation of individuals and communities of colour – and those concerned with wider issues of social justice and cultural democracy. I have argued elsewhere that equal access, participation and representation within museum and heritage institutions can only be progressed by placing, at the institution's core, a concern with underlying issues of structural inequality (Cheddie 2009) and moving away from an exclusive, singular focus on issues of visibility. Cultural democracy was a key theme explored by the Commission in its publications, symposia and subsequent international seminars. It was also explored within the final report of the Mayor's Commission on African and Asian Heritage, *Embedding Shared Heritage* (Coaston 2009).

Drawing upon Karp (1992), I define the Mayor's Commission on African and Asian Heritage as a political process engaged in intense discussions concerning the role and meaning of museums and heritage institutions. Thus, this chapter does not provide a historical account of the work of the Commission and neither does it seek to evaluate its successes and challenges (see Greater London Authority 2010; Coaston 2009). Rather it seeks to assess the legacy of the Commission within the local, national and global setting of London's heritage sector.

Local context

The work of the Mayor's Commission on African and Asian Heritage 2003–2009 should be understood as a structural policy response to a number of heritage sector-commissioned reports on inequity of provision in relationship to African and Asian communities within London's museum and heritage sector (Denniston 2003). The Commission, as part of the political process of London regional government, convened a body of individuals consisting of academics, museum professionals, community heritage practitioners, educators, writers and cultural theorists.[1] The Commission, sanctioned with the limited powers of the Mayor of London's office, provided a mechanism with which to initiate dialogue with London's museum and heritage sector on issues of human rights, accountability and representation.

The Commission was established by the left-of-centre politician Ken Livingstone, Mayor of London (2000–2008) and completed under his incumbent Boris Johnson (2008–). It formed part of the Mayor of London's Cultural Strategy (Greater London Authority 2003), which in turn informed London's successful bid to host the 2012 Olympic and Paralympic Games. The formation of the Commission was also framed by two overarching political and legislative developments. First, the election of a centrist Labour government in 1997 that was committed to delivering issues of greater participation and access to arts and culture within the publicly funded sphere.[2] Second, the passing of the Race Relations Amendment Act 2000 which required public authority heritage institutions, such as national and local authority museums, libraries and archives, to promote racial equality.[3]

The Commission, informed by these larger national and legislative changes, contextualized the work of cultural diversity within broader international debates on human rights, corporate responsibility, intellectual knowledge as well as UK equality law. The *Delivering Shared Heritage* (Greater London Authority 2005) report stated that there were six cases for diversity: *legal*; *ethical*; *human rights*; *intellectual*; *business*; and *corporate responsibility*. The aim of this categorization was to provide the legal, ethical and business basis for the work of the Commission, applying global and international frameworks to the local situation. The international language of human rights also provided the Commission with a vehicle to speak to the international obligations and commitments British governments had signed up to within the ratification of United Nations conventions. Many of these conventions also informed the work of professional museum and heritage bodies. Furthermore, by constructing the case for cultural diversity within these international, legal, business and discursive frameworks the Mayor's Commission was able to focus on the concept of the museum and of heritage organizations as a set of discursive practices (Sherman and Rogoff 1994).

Museums, public sphere and community

My unpacking of the work of the Mayor's Commission is informed by a theoretical position that understands museums and communities as part of the public sphere (Barrett 2011) and on Karp's analysis (1992: 14) of the relationship between museums, civil society and communities:

> The acknowledgement by museums of the existence of publics entails the idea that these entities should be asked about their own opinions and interests and about the effects of exhibitions on their sense of who they are. Inevitably we will discover that audiences have multiple opinions and multiple identities. As a result, the audience does not become a single commonality but many commonalities, called communities . . . On one side are the museums, who query their audience about its beliefs, opinions, and desires; on the other side is the changing mosaic of communities, which seek to influence and control how museums act, what they examine, what they represent, and how they represent it. This political process takes place in civil society.

By examining museums and heritage institutions within democratic societies as part of the public sphere, it is my assertion that they have civic responsibilities in relationship to their communities (Gaither 1992) and, more particularly, that they have particular responsibilities to communities whose histories and heritage have been under-represented within collections, institutional structures and modes of address. Furthermore I maintain that these responsibilities include equal access to heritage collections; nuanced and well researched interpretations of historically under-represented communities; and a stated commitment to equality within all aspects of the institution's operations and organizational infrastructure.

My argument draws upon critical theory that has sought to understand communities, not as groups of individuals defined within neatly defined sociological categories, but as communities 'imagined' into being through the construction of forms of commonality (Anderson 1983) and which views these communities as formed within the political and social contestations of power, authority and the use of public space.

Anderson's notion of 'imagined communities' can be productively coupled with Fish's concept of 'interpretive communities'. In his influential book, *Is There A Text in This Class? The Authority of Interpretive Communities* (1980), Fish reminds us of the link between the formation of the public sphere and the formation of communities when he states that:

> An interpretive community is not objective because as a bundle of interests of particular purposes and goals, its perspective is interested rather than neutral; but by the very same reasoning, the meanings and texts produced by an interpretive community are not subjective because they do not proceed from an isolated individual but from a public and conventional point of view.
>
> *1980: 14*

Drawing on this idea of interpretive communities I have situated the appointed Commissioners within the Mayor's Commission on African and Asian Heritage as interested, rather than objective neutral observers or experts, who had developed a perspective and critique of London's museums and heritage institutions based on scholarly knowledge and inquiry. I am positing the assemblage of the Mayor's Commissioners and the Commission's inquiry process as part of the development and articulation of a wider interpretive community. Thus, I locate the Commissioners and the Commission's two-year inquiry process as part of the development of a dialogue between two interpretive communities – the Black and Asian scholars and the community-based heritage practitioners on the one hand and the funded heritage and museum sectors on the other.

It is important to note that, in relation to the concept of interpretive communities, the Mayor's Commission went beyond previous policy initiatives in focusing on individuals and organizations who had made interventions to change the interpretation, collection and display of African and Asian heritage. This positioning of the Commissioners, as a community of experts, I would argue, challenges the marginalization of black and Asian scholarship within academia (Leatherwood *et al.* 2009; Painter 2006), and by implication within museological discourse. The under use of African and Asian heritage and museum scholarly knowledge, expertise and practice was noted in the *Delivering Shared Heritage* report (Greater London Authority 2005). The report also emphasized the centrality of the African and Asian expertise when seeking to develop a more nuanced and complex understanding of African and Asian histories:

> The use of African and Asian expertise and perspectives to interpret collections is critical to ensure that communities have ownership of their history and identity. Their voices can provide not only contextual grounding for collections, but can also help overcome challenges related to the interpretation of labeling of collections.
>
> *2005: 14*

An often ignored fact of the Commission's work is that not all of the experts identified in the *Delivering Shared Heritage* report were of African or Asian heritage, as witnessed by the inclusion of work by Italian-born Alda Terracciano and contributions by the white, English-born Sarah White.

The Commission's acknowledgement and recognition of the multi-racial character of knowledge about African and Asian heritage iterates much of the early work of black studies in the United States, as analysed by Noliwe Rooks (2006). In her study, Rooks locates the formation of black studies, initiated by funding from the Ford Foundation, as part of a multi-racial democratic imperative to change the nature of US higher educational institutions. The inclusion of white scholars and activists underscores the multi-racial and democratic desires of the work of the Mayor's Commission on African and Asian Heritage. Furthermore, the inclusion of scholars, such as Terracciano and White, redirects the focus onto an examination of how knowledge is acquired, negotiated and disseminated and away from the ethnic or racial identity of the scholar.

Drawing on the concepts of communities as both 'imagined' and 'interpretive' the formation of communities within the *Delivering Shared Heritage* report can be understood to play an active role in negotiating the construction, formation and contestation of cultural meaning; exploring how the museum as an institution enacts and stages the narratives, symbols and trope of national identity that inform the construction of meaning. This coupling of a relationship between communities, heritage and collective memory also echoes the UNESCO definitions of heritage employed within the body of the *Delivering Shared Heritage* report – away from a focus on materiality towards concepts of ritual, memory, transmission and orality (Chapter 13, this volume). *Delivering Shared Heritage* (Greater London Authority 2005: 46) articulates African and Asian communities as 'imagined communities' by underscoring the importance of collective memory: 'African and Asian organisations are repositories for their communities' collective memory, acting as a magnet that draws the knowledge base of their own communities and cultures.'

I have sought to expand this definition of community through an examination of the work of the feminist political theorist, Iris Marion Young, who stresses the significance of the structural character of inequality in understanding 'identity struggles':

> While they are often built upon and intersect with cultural differences, the social relations constituting gender, race, class, sexuality and ability are best understood as structural. The social movements motivated by such group-based experiences are largely attempts to politicize and protest structural inequalities that they perceive unfairly privilege some social segments and oppress others. Analysing structural difference and structural inequality, then, helps to show why these movements are not properly interpreted as 'identity politics'.
>
> *Young 2000: 92*

Young's work is important within the context of my examination of the work of the MCAAH because it activates an analysis that 'theorizes differentiated social segments struggling and engaging with each other across their differences rather than putting their differences aside to evoke the common good' (Young 2000: 18). Furthermore, analyses by Young and other feminist writers (Benhabib 2007) of the modern public sphere and processes of democratic inclusion provide a theoretical basis from which to explore the work of the Commission and critique recent accusations in the UK and elsewhere – that 'identity struggles' have weakened the basis of democracy and civil society.[4] Such critiques have attempted to dismiss the work of MCAAH and other initiatives focused on cultural diversity as socially divisive and/or 'box-ticking exercises' (Thomas and Dowell 2010). However, central to the work of MCAAH was a concern to democratize the heritage sector so that the Commission's work could be developed as a template for other communities: 'Whilst the Commission's focus was African and Asian diaspora communities, it also recognises that the principles that underpin the above recommendations may be applied to advance other diverse communities' (Greater London Authority 2005: 84).

The Mayor's Commission on African and Asian Heritage articulated a direct relationship between heritage institutions, the public sphere and representation, stating that:

> Representation and accountability emerge as central principles that have yet to be addressed in order to ensure equitable service provision for African and Asian communities. The two are intertwined by a process of interaction, by cause and effect. Increased representation is the key channel whereby cultural diversity can be embedded within institutional values and practices and begin to develop the sector's direction and identity. Adequate representation is the path along which greater accountability to diverse audiences can be forged.
>
> *Greater London Authority 2005: 20*

A focus on representation and accountability meant that the Commission was able to develop a more holistic approach to the question of cultural diversity. This macro approach meant that it interrogated the production of meaning within the physical space of the museum and heritage institution – exhibitions, collections, interpretation and so on, whilst also questioning the exisiting management and employment procedures and the governance structures of museum and heritage institutions.

Heritage definitions and the language of human rights

By mirroring discourses of human rights the *Delivering Shared Heritage* report was able to draw upon the international ethical and legal frameworks established within international law (see Chapters 14 and 15, this volume), whilst also formulating a discourse which assumed a relationship between the museum and heritage institution and the public sphere. Franceso Francioni and Martin Scheinin (2008: 7), alert us to the intersection between international law, human rights and the role of heritage in society:

> This incremental expansion of the concept of cultural heritage in the practice of international law has had the consequence of strengthening the conceptual link between heritage and cultural rights . . . However, it must be pointed out at the outset that in so far as cultural heritage represents the sum of practices, knowledges and representations that a community or group recognize as part of their history and identity, it is axiomatic that members of the group, individually and collectively, must be entitled to access, perform and enjoy such cultural heritage as a matter of right. Furthermore, the dynamic evolution of the concept of heritage from a mere historical–artistic object to intangible heritage entails that even cultural objects or places must be understood in the function and role they perform in a given society as indispensable tools for the exercise of certain fundamental rights and freedoms, such as the right of association or religious freedom.

The Commission's harnessing of the discourse of human rights, and its foregrounding of the relationship between museums and the public sphere, enabled the Commissioners to formulate a critique of the practices of London's museums and heritage institutions addressing both professional criteria and museological discourses. Furthermore, human rights discourse provided the means to challenge the still-strongly held conventional wisdom that the 'proper business' of museums is the collection, preservation and study of objects, thus creating, for Weil (1988), a false dichotomy between objects and audience; in this case London's communities of colour.

Delivering Shared Heritage's main areas of conceptual focus were drawn from the intersection between human rights, heritage and the museum. As a starting point the Mayor's Commission on African and Asian Heritage employed the International Council of Museums' (ICOM) 1974 definition of museums as guardians of heritage. Adopting this definition the *Delivering Shared Heritage* report (Greater London Authority 2005: 23) evoked the museum and heritage profession and institutions as 'guardians' of London's cultural heritage, a global city with a large ethnically diverse population. This expanded concept of guardianship allowed the Commission to construct a space and open up dialogue on the nature of heritage within an international setting and its role in contemporary Britain, building an argument based on national and international precedents for cultural diversity.

The use of human rights discourse was further supplemented throughout the report with references to the United Nations Declaration on Cultural Diversity (2001), and the UNESCO Convention on Intangible Cultural Heritage (2003):[5] 'Heritage lends immediate meaning and physical and spiritual nourishment to individual lives and communities at large' (Greater London Authority 2005: 10).

The report's citation of heritage as object and material culture tied to production of cultural meaning – both physical and spiritual – opened up heritage to a much wider conceptual framework. This approach also shifted the emphasis away from objects, artefacts and historical monuments towards an acknowledgement of the importance of intangible and communal forms of heritage coupled with a focus on ethical and equitable engagement with communities.[6] A more nuanced definition of heritage is explicitly conveyed in the *Delivering Shared Heritage* report's use of the concept 'shared' – rather than African and Asian – heritage. 'The heritage and history of London must be inclusive rather than exclusive, and that which must be investigated, understood, promoted and celebrated must be the heritage of us all' (2005: 76).

The contextualization of the museum and heritage sectors within the discourses of human rights created a space whereby the Commission was able to reach out to the museum and heritage sector and construct a common meeting point between Commissioners on the one hand and museum and heritage professionals on the other.

The emphasis on maintaining the language of human rights, equality and social justice refracted through the prism of national and international heritage professional ethics, debates and standards, provided a rich resource for dialogue, partnership and debate throughout the Commission process and its implementation body, the Heritage Diversity Task Force.

The work begun by the Mayor's Commission on African and Asian Heritage, emphasizes the need to focus on the globalized nature of Britain's history; the impact of this globalized network on all aspects of British heritage and culture and how these interconnected histories inform and impact on all of Britain's communities. Such challenges were addressed and explored in the *Revisiting Collections: Revealing Significance* project. *Revisiting Collections*, a collections management methodology, informed by the Commission's process, stated:

> Revisiting Collections starts from the premise that there can't be a generalist or specialist museum in London that doesn't in some way reflect the city's centuries' long position at the heart of a network of worldwide exploitation, trade (including the trade in human beings) and imperialism. The project seeks to explore how this impacted on every aspect of the capital's wealth and daily life, on science, aesthetics, technology and culture, and what that reveals about the intertwining histories.
>
> *Reed 2005: 5*

Thoughts on further development

The global economic downturn which began in 2008 and the election of a UK coalition government in 2010, have led to a sizeable reduction in funding for arts and cultural organizations. These developments will no doubt impact in many drastic and unforeseen ways on the cultural and heritage sector in the UK.

However, it is worth reiterating the importance museums and heritage institutions play in the cultural sphere not only in the formation of national identity. Museums and heritage institutions continue to play a key role in the acquisition and dissemination of cultural capital (Bennett 2010). Research conducted by Burke and McManus (2010) on the admissions procedures of Art and Design higher education instiutions in the UK highlights the continuing importance that access to knowledge of, and understanding of, museums and galleries plays in the selection process for entry into Art and Design college. It should be remembered that Art and Design education continues to be a key entrance route for many individuals working in the cultural and creative industries, including the heritage and museum sectors. Burke and McManus note that the 'ideal subject' of UK Art and Design higher education is seen as white and middle class. Furthermore, their findings assert that the black subject is often not seen as legitimate within the realm of higher education and black subject's spheres of influences or knowledge are drawn from sources that are often seen as 'invalid' (Burke and McManus 2010: 43). Their research highlights a case in which a young black woman applying for a fashion Bachelor of Arts is rejected, whilst the young white middle-class male student interviewed immediately after her, though less qualified, was offered a place.

Within the discourses of Art and Design education, as in the case cited, black popular culture is not seen as a valid point of reference for study. Burke and McManus' research reminds us of the important role that cultural capital plays within the cultural sphere and, in particular, the key contribution of museums and heritage in the development of educational and social opportunities of young people in the UK and the production and sanctioning of cultural knowledge and value. Thus, despite the criticisms of the Labour government's cultural policy (1997–2010), this research directs our attention to the continuing need to ensure that museums and heritage institutions have, at their core, principles of equal access and participation and the need to maintain the focus on the democratic potential of the 'new museum'.

In any formulation of cultural diversity policy or practice within the museum and heritage sector, emerging demographic trends will need to be taken into account and will no doubt impact on any future work. Sociologist Lucinda Platt (2009), analysing data from the UK Office of National Statistics, draws our attention to the growing presence of multiple heritage or 'mixed race'[7] individuals, who are forecasted to be the largest ethnic minority in the UK by 2020. These demographic shifts within the next decade demonstrate the urgency to develop complex definitions of cultural identity and ethnicity. New categories will no doubt impact on contemporary articulations of equality and identity within UK cultural, social and economic debates, and within the formations of political debates and struggles concerning heritage discourses within the UK and internationally.

But whilst this emerging ethnic diversity adds new layers of complexity within UK heritage, its emergence does not necessarily signal the necessity for new forms of visibility for individuals of colour. A number of provisos need to be taken into account when assessing the effect of the emerging demographic trend of the 'Multiple Heritage Community' and exploring how definitions of heritage may be drawn into this debate.

The complex nature of this rising demographic group does not constitute, by sheer numbers alone, the formation of community with articulated bonds of commonality (Anderson 1990). How this very diverse group of individuals – in terms of ethnicity, class, education, sexual orientation, geographical region, etc. – imagines itself into being in terms of collective narratives, tropes and visual signifiers, remains to be seen.

Such a demographic phenomenon should not be hailed as the end of racism or signalling the end of racial inequality and discrimination within the UK public sphere. In fact, a report by the Human Rights and Equality Commission, *How Fair is Britain?* (cited in Asthana 2010), highlights the continuing significance of structural inequality based on class, ethnicity and gender in contemporary Britain.

The formulation of nuanced analyses of race, ethnicity, class and migration should allow this emerging ethnic minority population and the UK at large to understand and make links with historic multiple heritage communities, past and present, in cities like Bristol, London, Liverpool and elsewhere. Despite these historic precedents, research on the nature of contemporary multiple heritage identity is only beginning to emerge. Little of this work has yet made the argument for cross-cultural research, or for exploration of this demographic phenomenon as the basis for the development of international co-operation and dialogue. Accelerating globalization will mean increasing creolization of communities, a phenomenon about which we can learn much from countries such as Brazil.

The rise of a multiple heritage population, far from lessening the need for multilayered and diverse histories of migration and settlement to the UK, I would argue, demonstrates a need for more multifaceted interpretations. These demographic trends call for multifarious formations of heritage, identity and history and an understanding of the links between structural inequality, class, gender and ethnicity. Young's (2000: 18) analyses remind us of the concept of social segments 'struggling and engaging with each other across their differences'. Within the context of heritage, an embracing of the discourse of human rights, which also prioritizes social justice, can provide a means to facilitate this much-needed dialogue.

The challenges of inequitable access to heritage will not go away and meaningful, transparent and equitable responses to these challenges need to be found, even (and perhaps especially) within strident economic times. A key way forward has been the development of equitable partnerships between heritage professionals, institutions, academics and community-based heritage organizations and practitioners. Such partnerships need to focus, not only on curation and collection, but on the role of heritage institutions in the public sphere and the importance of making them more accountable and transparent in their organizational and management structures (Chapter 3, this volume).

Engagement with human rights social justice discourses, as witnessed in the work of the Mayor's Commission on African and Asian Heritage, has the potential to open up a space for productive international and transnational exchange. Heritage, in the context of a more ethnically diverse Britain, has an important role to play in helping all audiences understand the intricacies of history, identity and nation, not only as means to understand the past, but also as a vehicle to create and envision the future.

Notes

1 A full list of the Commissioners is included with the Delivering Shared Heritage Report (Greater London Authority 2005).
2 It was this Labour government, led initially by Tony Blair, which established the new regional government for London, the Greater London Authority, headed by an elected Mayor in 2000.
3 The Race Relations Amendment Act 2000 embodied an emphasis on non-discriminatory practices by institutions and highlighted the importance of the inclusion of black and minority ethnic people in areas of employment, service delivery and partnerships. The Amendment to the previously existing law was in response to the recommendations of the Stephen Lawrence Inquiry Report (1999), produced after the murder of the black teenager Stephen Lawrence in 1993. The report summarises the duties of public institutions as being to monitor by racial group, staff in post, applicants for jobs, training and promotion; to monitor by racial group (for employers with more than 150 staff)

training, grievances, disciplinary procedures and benefit/detriments from performance appraisal, dismissals and other reasons for leaving; and to publish results of employment monitoring annually.

4 See Elshtain (1995: 74) cited in Young (2000: 84).

5 The Convention states, 'Culture takes diverse forms across time and space. This diversity is embodied in the uniqueness and plurality of the identities of the groups and societies making up humankind. As a source of exchange, innovation and creativity, cultural diversity is as necessary for humankind as biodiversity is for nature. In this sense, it is the common heritage of humanity and should be recognized and affirmed for the benefit of present and future generations' (Article 1, UNESCO Universal Declaration on Cultural Diversity, November, 2001).

6 See Lohman (2009).

7 The definitions used by the UK National Office of Statistics are: Mixed: White and Black Caribbean; Mixed White and Black African; White and Asian; Mixed Any Other Mixed Background. The term 'multiple heritage' allows for a different and more nuanced concept of complex identities.

References

Anderson, B. (1983) *Imagined Communities: Reflections on the Origin and Spread of Nationalism*, London: Verso.

Asthana, A. (2010) 'Britain's Divided Schools: A Disturbing Portrait of Inequality', *Observer*, 10 October: 10.

Barrett, J. (2011) *Museums and the Public Sphere*, Chichester: Wiley-Blackwell.

Benhabib, S. (2007) 'Is there a Human Right to Democracy? Beyond Intervention and Indifference?', *The Lindly Lecture*, Kansas: University of Kansas.

Burke, P. J. and McManus, J. (2010) *Art for a Few: Exclusion and Misrecognition in Art and Design Higher Education Admissions*, National Arts Learning Network.

Cheddie, J. (2009) 'Heritage and Cultural Democracy: A Work in Progress', in M. Coaston (ed.), *Embedding Shared Heritage*, Mayor's Commission on African and Asian Heritage, London: Greater London Authority: 74–79.

Coaston, M. (ed.) (2009) *Embedding Shared Heritage*, Mayor's Commission on African and Asian Heritage, London: Greater London Authority.

Denniston, H. (2003) *Holding Up the Mirror: Addressing Cultural Diversity in London's Museums*, London: London Museums Agency.

Duncan, C. (2005) *Civilizing Rituals: Inside Public Art Museums*, London and New York: Routledge.

Fish, S. (1980) *Is There a Text in This Class? The Authority of Interpretive Communities*, Cambridge, MA and London: Harvard University Press.

Francioni, F. and Scheinin, M. (eds) (2008) *Cultural Human Rights*, Leiden and Boston: Martinus Nijhoff Publishers.

Gaither, E. B. (1992) '"Hey! That's Mine": Thoughts on Pluralism and American Museums', in I. Karp, C. M. Kreamer and S. D. Lavine (eds), *Museums and Communities*, Washington, DC and London: Smithsonian Institution Press: 56–64.

Greater London Authority (2003) *London – Cultural Capital: Realising the Potential of a World Class City*, The Mayor's Draft Cultural Strategy, London: GLA.

Greater London Authority (2005) *Delivering Shared Heritage* report, Mayor's Commission on African and Asian Heritage, London: Greater London Authority.

Greater London Authority (2010) *Cultural Metropolis*, London: Greater London Authority.

Karp, I. (1992) 'Museums and Communities: The Politics of Public Culture', in I. Karp, C. M. Kreamer and S. D. Lavine (eds), *Museums and Communities*, Washington, DC and London: Smithsonian Institution Press: 1–17.

Leatherwood, C., Maylor, U. and Moreau, M. (2009) *The Experience of Black and Ethnic Minority Staff Working in Higher Education*, Bath: Equality Challenge Unit. Online. Available at: www.bath.ac.uk/universitysecretary/equalities/ethnicity/experienceofbmestaffinhe.pdf (accessed 9 September 2011).

Lohman, J. (2009) 'Equitable Partnerships: A View from London', in M. Coaston (ed.), *Embedding Shared Heritage: The Heritage Diversity Task Force Report*, London: Greater London Authority.

Painter, N. I. (2006) 'Black Studies, Black Professors and the Struggles of Perception', in L. R. Gordon and J. A. Gordon (eds), *A Companion to African-American Studies*, Oxford: Blackwell Publishing: 136–141.

Platt, L. (2009) *Ethnicity and Family: Relationships Within and Between Ethnic Groups: An Analysis using the Labour Force Survey*, London: Equality and Human Rights Commission.

Reed, R. (2005) *Revisiting Collections: Revealing Significance: An ALM Project,* London: London Archives, Libraries, Museums.

Rooks, N. (2006) *White Money/Black Power: The Surprising History of African American Studies*, Boston: Beacon Books.

Sherman, D. J. and Rogoff, I. (eds) (1994) *Museum Culture: Histories, Discourses, Spectacles*, London and New York, Routledge.

Thomas, L. and Dowell, B. (2010) 'Arts Organisations Can't Rely on Using Women and Ethnic Minorities to Win Public Cash', *Daily Mail*. Online. Available at: www.dailymail.co.uk/news/article-1310585/Arts-organisations-rely-using-women-ethnic-minorities-win-public-cash.html#ixzz1XSDptLvK (accessed 9 September 2011).

Vergo, P. (ed.) (1989) *The New Museology*, London: Reaktion Press.

Weil, S. (1988) 'The Proper Business of the Museum: Ideas or Things?', in S. Weil (ed.), *Rethinking the Museum and Other Meditations*, Washington, DC and London: Smithsonian Institution Press: 43–56.

Young, I. M. (2000) *Inclusion and Democracy*, Oxford: Oxford University Press.

20

SOCIAL MEDIA TOWARDS SOCIAL CHANGE

Potential and challenges for museums

Amelia Wong

Whether with words of love, hate, curiosity or indifference, the museum world is talking about social media. These technologies appeal on bases both practical and philosophical. In the face of declining budgets, social media offer new channels for audience outreach (as well as internal communication) that require relatively low set-up costs and little to no technical training to use and support. As museums face questions of definition and relevance in the so-called 'digital' or 'information' age, the explosive popularity and increasing accessibility of social media represent ways to make traditional-seeming institutions less intimidating and more regularly present in everyday life. Facing the continuing need to address and correct the historical role museums have played in the oppression and exclusion of disenfranchised populations, social media even offer museums potential to democratize their practices. Their myriad forms and promising reach may help expand and diversify audiences, make museums more responsive and transparent, and acknowledge and incorporate the knowledge of audiences into practice.

Social media inspire such visions because, in the early twenty-first century Western zeitgeist, they strongly suggest potential for democratizing media and thus provoking social change. Because the rise of networked digital media decentralized and proliferated producers of information, this technology has long intrigued popular and scholarly commentators for the ways it foments novel social, political and economic behaviors that trouble established practices and industries. The emergence of online social media has caused further disruption, posing challenges to professions like journalism and entertainment, and signaling potential and – in Tunisia and Egypt – realized threats to long-standing governments. Meanwhile, collaborative projects like Wikipedia and Linux attest to the power of diverse, distant and anonymous contributors to produce (overall) quality results (Giles 2005). Amidst these conditions, and undergirded by long-held assumptions that networked digital media in general are inherently democratic, speculation abounds about how social media might shape a more democratic and just world.

This chapter explores how social media might affect democratic change in museums and society in terms of their potential for nurturing methods, conditions and institutional changes that advance the democratic values of equality, diversity and social justice. Extending the wave of democratizing reforms that began among their ranks in the mid-twentieth century, some museums have explored the capacity of social media to increase accessibility, openness, transparency, accountability and responsiveness; to attend to diversity; and to manifest 'shared authority' with audiences, such as by validating various models of knowledge-building and nurturing collaborations.

As data about social media is notoriously hard to collect and interpret, and as these tools and culture are still quite new, I do not attempt a comprehensive discussion about my subject. Rather, by drawing on international examples as well as my own experiences of managing social media outreach at the United States Holocaust Memorial Museum (Holocaust Museum) in Washington, DC, I aim to offer a panoramic perspective that expresses the range of manners and purposes of museums' social media efforts in the pursuit of democratic values.[1] Acknowledging that their abilities to affect democratic change are complex, ambiguous and inchoate, I argue that social media best supports equality, diversity and social justice in museum practice if implemented with a critical mindset that understands that ambiguity, is conscientious about evaluation and ethical practice, and, nevertheless, experiments with (and is open to) the potential of social media for affecting change within institutions. Towards this end, it is important to understand what I mean by social media, so I begin with a definition.

Defining social media

Social media refers to a culture and subset of networked digital media. As a term, it came into vogue in the past few years to refer to a suite of technologies – including commenting, tagging and syndication – and the culture that shapes (and is shaped by) their development and use. That culture celebrates openness, frequent communication, participation, customization, collaboration and the visible articulation of identity and networks. The term became popular to describe these tools and culture amidst a media environment of shifting understandings of networked digital media, converging media types, and blurring relationships between producers and audiences of information.

Social media indicates these changes, as the term speaks to the remediation of networked digital media. J. David Bolter and Richard Grusin describe remediation as the mutual process by which a society and new technology adapt to each other (2000). In this case, people's understanding of the capacity of networked computing reformulated their uses and approach to it. The norm is no longer to question the Internet's ability to support social relationships; the norm is no longer to build websites as if setting down type. Instead, people accept networked digital media as useful and convenient means of maintaining social connections, while developers and designers exploit the dynamic and flexible nature of this media to convey information.

Expanding perceptions about networked computing influenced the convergence of media. Convergence does not simply describe how modern computers, mobile phones and televisions now perform the same functions; as media scholar Henry Jenkins writes, it signifies a cultural shift in how people produce and consume media. It represents 'the flow of content across multiple media platforms, the cooperation between multiple media industries, and the migratory behavior of media audiences who will go almost anywhere in search of the kinds of entertainment experiences they want' (2006: 2).

These occurrences nurture the idea that networked digital media serve what Pierre Lévy calls 'collective intelligence'. Faced with a glut of information, people turn to others to help sort and filter it; in the process, they can manifest collective intelligence, which is 'based on the notion of a universally distributed intelligence. No one knows everything, everyone knows something, all knowledge resides in humanity' (1999: 13–14). With our remediating understanding of networked digital media saturated by such ideas, our perception of their democratizing potential has only grown. Social media is a product of that growth.

Shaped by these ideas, social media carry connotations of democratizing the media landscape and societies in various ways. These include advancing the democratic notions that all people are equal and should have equal access to participate in public discourse. Following that increase in access, they feasibly allow the diversification of contributors, backgrounds and opinions that circulate in that discourse. And, by manifesting more equal access and diverse participation in society, they may further social justice. These, of course, are ideal scenarios for how social media might affect society. Although there is an absence of data that can prove they can accomplish these vaunted goals, it is still useful, I would argue, to explore their potential in order to understand their benefits and limitations. Such learnings can help direct their use into the future. I turn now to consider the potential that social media might play in relation to equality, diversity and social justice.

Social media towards equality

Equality was a founding value of the modern museum; its archetype – the Louvre – was a king's palace claimed by revolutionaries for 'the people' of France. Yet, this history bequeathed a twisted legacy. The Louvre was a political and civic symbol of the new equality of French citizens before the state, but class and gender circumscribed those ideal citizens (Duncan 1995). In the early twenty-first century, museums continue to struggle with the challenge of being 'public' institutions – open to all comers – while in actuality still attracting the highly-educated middle class and upper middle class as their regular audience (Falk 1998). Therefore, exploring how social media might advance equality means considering their potential to broaden access and the appeal of museums to larger and more diverse audiences.

The intention of extending access has long motivated museums to use digital technology. They now turn to external social media platforms (in contrast to in-house tools or projects) with this goal clearly in mind. Blogs, social networking, social bookmarking, social review, media-sharing and micro-blogging sites have exploded in popularity over the past decade, attracting millions of users and quickly becoming aspects of many people's daily lives (van Grove 2010; Zickuhr 2010). Museums create profiles on sites like Jumo, Flickr and Tumblr in order to expand their digital footprints; in the words of the trailblazing Brooklyn Museum, 'why should we expect them to come to us?' (Caruth and Bernstein 2007). Uploading content to sites like Facebook, which enjoys over 500 million users around the world, and YouTube, which streams two billion video views a day, means greater exposure to audiences larger than any entering any museum's doors each day (Zuckerberg 2010; Parr 2010). Further, as Google, the world's most popular search engine, indexes Facebook and other social media sites, these efforts make museums' content easier to find. They also make it easier to share, facilitating the spread of information between museum-lovers and non-museum-goers. Through channels likes these, museums ideally make themselves known to new audiences.

Accessibility means making museums more open to more people, but not simply as a resource. Social media also may change how people think about museums, fuelling a conceptual shift that could encourage visitation from people who find museums irrelevant or intimidating and typically spend their leisure time elsewhere. Museums may come to be seen as more 'everyday' than 'event' as they make daily appearances within a user's broader news-stream of updates from friends, family, national newspapers and the corner bakery. These outlets also may help museums seem more accessible because the culture of social media champions transparency, casual tone and first-person voice. The field of public relations celebrates their ability to 'humanize' organizations by depicting them as less bureaucratic: blogs written by individuals *as* individuals with personalities encourage consumers to identify with companies and foster trust and empathy (Kent 2008). Hence, museums typically identify staff authors on institutional blogs and Twitter feeds to show a 'human face', which also helps represent them more as peers and facilitators in education rather than anonymous purveyors of authority. Social media's informality also provokes museums to use them to engage audiences through play, such as by offering scavenger hunts or trivia questions through Facebook or Twitter, and to give 'friendly' designs to in-house projects. For example, the Indianapolis Museum of Art's *Art Babble*, a site for sharing and discussing video about art, uses slang (its tagline reads 'Play Art Loud'), warm pastels, and rounded, 'handwritten' fonts to convey the idea that art and art museums can make for casual encounters.

[handwritten margin note: access more everyday people]

Social media towards diversity

Conceptually, equality 'implies similarity rather than "sameness"' (Gosepath 2009). In other words, diversity is built into the concept of equality. But, as debates over multiculturalism within democracies illustrate, these concepts often chafe against each other in practice (Delanty 2003: 92–110). Museums wrestle with the representation of diversity because, while conceived as institutions of universal public education, they operate with finite space, resources and reach. Nevertheless, the inclusion of diversity within museums, and the contests it sparks, is imperative for telling accurate narratives about human experiences.

Concerns about diversity in museums encompass revising the traditional composition of audiences, content and staff. Social media have potential to make museums more fairly representative of difference in each of these areas. Currently, evidence that social media helps diversify audiences is largely anecdotal (Vaughan 2010), but their potential for helping to enlarge audiences is significant. While the user demographics of social media sites vary and these sites can be monopolized by specific populations (boyd and Ellison 2007), they feasibly may diversify the traditional demographics of museum visitors because they enjoy massive audiences. Similarly, social media's casual and friendly culture may be more inviting to audiences who traditionally have felt unwelcome at museums.

In contrast, the capacity of social media to allow people to represent themselves in all their diversity is already highly apparent. It is standard practice now in museums to strive to share authority with constituencies being represented in exhibits, and with the general public. Such activities pay deference to the notion of collective intelligence, which is founded on the idea that people add value to collaborative projects by opening them to diverse voices, opinions and experiences. Social media facilitate audience feedback and bring the public into museum practice. The in-construction Museum of the History of Polish Jews launched the *Virtual Shtetl* to act as a portal and eventual social forum for people to contribute text, photographs, audio, and video of Jewish life in Poland. The blog aspect of *Science Buzz*, a project of the Science Museum of Minnesota, encourages people to see themselves as scientists and to share scientific topics that are of interest to them. The Australian Museum used a blog and a

Facebook group to conduct front-end evaluation for an exhibition (Jensen and Kelly 2009), while visitors to the Mattress Factory can use YouTube's Quick Capture feature to record and broadcast their feelings on what the Mattress Factory means to them. Further, the *Flickr Commons*, a project started by the Library of Congress and now including over forty institutions in Australia, Europe, and North America, lets the public tag, annotate and comment on historical photographs. In some cases, this 'crowd-sourcing' revealed information about photographs, which has been integrated into collection metadata (Springer *et al.* 2008). Additionally, the Indianapolis Museum of Art incorporates commenting directly into its website so users can remark on its collections, an option that will likely become more frequent as museums redesign their websites and become more comfortable with the commingling of curatorial and audience voices.

[handwritten margin note: direct feedback]

Social media also support the representation of diversity in museums by providing more 'floorspace' to display the scope and variety of their collections. As with digital media generally, museums can approach external social media sites as a form of open storage or extra exhibition space. At the Holocaust Museum, we use the social storytelling platform *VoiceThread* to highlight artifacts from the vast permanent collection. The project lets us share behind-the-scenes information about artifacts with audiences, and also lets us give each object more attention than it receives as part of any exhibition.

Finally, social media can help diversify the ways museums present and order content, capitalizing on their digital nature to create alternatives to traditional methods of depicting knowledge. Mainstream museums tend to exhibit artifacts and ideas according to the epistemological lens of the Enlightenment, which privileged reason over emotion, observation over immersion, and order over chaos; it also supported the development of display conventions that expressed knowledge as a hierarchy with Western white men at the pinnacle. The material nature of museums and their collections made this version of knowledge even more convincing as it seemed to solidify 'truth' and certainty (Porter 2003), as well as put finite boundaries on what could be presented and how often it could be changed.

The culture and digital nature of social media nurture more dynamic methods of presenting knowledge. By always offering avenues for audience feedback and often having ways to overtly represent revisions, they present conversation and the delivery of information as open-ended, processual and even argumentative, such as how every Wikipedia entry displays the record of its edits and has a 'Discussion' tab that shows debates over its definition. While examples of museums using wikis with audience input are still relatively rare,[2] they more frequently experiment with 'tagging'. Sometimes called 'social' or 'folksonomic tagging', this activity produces a form of classification particularly useful for describing and filtering digital information (Weinberger 2007). Where classification in the West developed as a practice based on a rigid set of terms that follow an equally rigid hierarchy, tagging is a free-form and idiosyncratic venture that lets individuals describe content based on whatever they deem important. The results are messy, as well as often obtuse, but such qualities are also what make them valuable – a multitude of descriptive terms means they more broadly encompass people's various systems of interpretation. Art museums are at the forefront of experimentation with tagging. A host of major North American art museums launched the *Steve* tagging experiment (Steve Project 2011) to gauge the benefits of opening up the description of art to the public. Their findings showed differences between the way art historians described art (based on context) and the way laypeople did (based on content). The project hopes incorporating both methods into collection metadata may improve searches by the general public (Trant 2006). Finally, tags also present new means of visually representing the knowledge of classification. Tag clouds and maps like that on the National Museum of African American History & Culture's website convey knowledge as networks of conceptual associations, rather than imposing value through hierarchy.

Social media towards social justice

When museums try to advance equality and diversity in their work, they implicitly suggest they seek to advance these values in society in general. When museums explicitly take on such an agenda, they are generally interested in directly furthering social justice. This concept is defined in various ways, but in the contemporary context involves a platform of equality, human rights, and the reforming of structures that maintain iniquities in societies, such as by the redistribution of resources. In terms of museum practice, social justice intrinsically includes advancing equality and diversity, just not as ends in and of themselves. Museums that adopt missions of social justice embrace their political nature and strive to use their social, cultural and financial capital to cultivate critical thinking, empathy and appreciation for equality and diversity in visitors, as well as generally encourage transformation towards a more just society. They may even act as direct advocates, as the District Six Museum has done for land reclamation in South Africa (Layne 2008).

Much has been said, both positively and negatively, about social media's potential to advance democracy and aid activism. A modest view allows that they can help promote political activism, and attributes their potency to their ability to organize large numbers of people towards common action (Shirky 2008: 186–187). A more ambitious view argues that social media can serve social justice in general thanks to their participatory nature and because they provide alternatives to mass media. For instance, legal scholar Yochai Benkler's work concentrates on the effects of the development of an information economy fed by both non-market 'peer production' and traditional market production and he proposes that this situation (which includes social media) may serve justice since they expose the potential benefits of universal accessibility (2003). Similarly, information scientists Jennifer Preece and Ben Shneiderman hold that '[responses] to many of the world's difficult challenges could be dramatically more successful if social participation could be made more consistently effective' (2009: 15). Further, Benkler and Nissenbaum pose:

> that the emergence of peer production offers an opportunity for more people to engage in practices that permit them to exhibit and experience virtuous behavior. We posit: (a) that a society that provides opportunities for virtuous behavior is one that is more conducive to virtuous individuals; and (b) that the practice of effective virtuous behavior may lead to more people adopting virtues as their own, or as attributes of what they see as their self-definition.
>
> *2006: 394*

Finally, Lévy's principle of collective intelligence is actually conceived as a social justice movement. He sees networked digital media as opening an opportunity for the general reconceptualization of the 'other' through constant interaction with different and dynamic people who are not restricted to static identities:

Far from merging individual intelligence into some indistinguishable magma, collective intelligence is a process of growth, differentiation, and the mutual revival of singularities. The shifting image that emerges from such skills and projects, and from the relations among members in the knowledge space, constitutes, for a community, a new mode of identification, one that is open, dynamic, and positive. New forms of democracy, better suited to the complexity of contemporary problems than conventional forms of representation, could then come into being.

1999: 17

Museums bring similarly hopeful stances to their applications of social media for social justice. A modest use of social media for this purpose is to alert people to social injustice. To make the invisible visible, they create opportunities for the public to contribute information about their experiences to historical archives. The website for the Canadian Museum for Human Rights, currently under construction, asks visitors: 'Do you have a personal story related to human rights? Have members of your family, your ancestors, or people in your community had an experience of discrimination, freedom, or opportunity that needs to be shared?' Submitted stories will become part of the museum's oral history collection and may influence their future exhibits and programs. Similarly, the digital archive *Soweto '76*, from the Hektor Pieterson Memorial and Museum in South Africa and the Maryland Institute for Technology in the Humanities, collects accounts of the tragic 1976 student uprising.

Museums also strive to make the invisible visible by infiltrating what social scientists call people's 'ambient' or 'peripheral social awareness' – their awareness of events and others' activities – with enduring problems, like those of human trafficking, sexism and institutionalized racism. For instance, following the signing into law of a controversial immigration bill in Arizona that allows police officers to detain people suspected of being in the United States illegally, the social media team at the Lower East Side Tenement Museum used Twitter to stage its response. Acting according to the museum's mission to 'promote tolerance and historical perspective', they published 'tweets' culled from John F. Kennedy's *A Nation of Immigrants* in the hopes that these historical tidbits would provide context to the public dialogue and critical perspective on immigration generally.

In addition, museums use social media to promote online discussion about social justice issues in order to raise awareness, spark critical thinking and engender empathy. They often use blogs for this purpose since these tools developed in the last decade with strong associations to conversation; scholars argue they enact a kind of 'secondary orality' that mixes conventions of literacy with those of dialogue, including informality and immediate revision (Rettberg 2008; Barlow 2008). Hence, the National Underground Railroad Freedom Center keeps a *Freedom Blog*, while the International Museum of Women, a 'groundbreaking social change museum', runs *Her Blueprint: The I.M.O.W Blog* to share behind-the-scenes news, interviews and to 'learn more about issues close to our heart as activists for women's human rights'. Museum Victoria, Melbourne, Australia used a blog to 'begin our conversation' as part of its online media project, *Talking Difference*, which is 'dedicated to sparking dialogue about cultural difference'. Similarly, Te Papa's *Mixing Room* project, which shares the viewpoints of young refugees in New Zealand, uses a blog to present their experiences through text, photography and video.

Moving forward

Currently, museums employ a variety of social media in a variety of ways to serve equality, diversity and social justice. But, it is an open question as to how well these efforts work. Like museum experiences in general, trying to evaluate the benefits and detriments of social media is difficult (Falk *et al.* 2006). The collection of useful data about museums' use of networked digital media generally and defining criteria to analyze that data pose ongoing challenges. Furthermore, the democratizing and transformative effects of social media are ambiguous. In general, divides in access and skills to use and manipulate networked digital media remain 'resilient because the bar of technological sophistication continues to rise' (Ito 2008: 7).[3] As Lisa Nakamura cautions, the 'dream of a flat, democratic, media landscape in which every-one is an equal participant and social inequalities can be eliminated or at least ignored is an extremely utopian perspective' (2010: 338). Meanwhile, social media do not inherently serve the interests of 'the people', nor protect them from prejudice or threat. Research shows that everything from chat rooms to digital games to social network sites replicate and reinforce social bias (Nakamura 2010; boyd 2011). And, while Twitter, Facebook, and YouTube help protesters organize and record injustices, they may also be used to spread misinformation and to identify dissidents for arrest. Further, while social media have shaken up the Goliaths of corporate capitalism, they have not fallen. Corporations morph their business models and utilize social media for free labor – enlisting individuals as 'viral marketers' – and to increase their information about consumers and citizens. This situation benefits consumer electronics and social media companies, prompting Lev Manovich to ask:

> does this mean that people's identities and imagination are now even more firmly col-onized by commercial media than in the twentieth century? In other words, is the replacement of the mass consumption of commercial culture by users' mass production of cultural objects a progressive development?

> *2008: 71*

Critics of social media also posit that the ability to customize and filter our daily exposure to information through 'social news' sites like Digg or right- or left-leaning blogs creates an 'echo chamber effect'. Rather than feeding democratic deliberation in the public sphere, social media may encourage self-segregation and, as people face fewer 'others' that challenge their opinions, may diminish rather than enhance the critical thinking skills and empathy that are necessary for building a more just world (Sunstein 2007; Farrell *et al.* 2008).

In this context, museums using social media to engender equality, diversity and social justice must consider the ambiguous returns of this media and the ethical questions they raise for practice. Social media may help serve equality by expanding access, but the persistence of digital divides means Ross Parry's admonition that 'to use the Web medium is not to reach out to the entire community' (2007: 98) still holds true. Similarly, using social media does not guarantee that content will find larger audiences. Social media's affordances for public participation means the possible diversification and enrichment of general knowledge, but, as is the case with including visitor voices in physical galleries, they also mean dealing with misinformed and even hateful opinions (Witcomb 2003: 79–101). Further, social media's capacity to support productive discussion is, as yet, underwhelming. Their open nature, often experienced under conditions of anonymity and only through text, seem to provoke polarized rather than productive discussions (Kolko and Reid 1998); in these conditions, antagonist cultures sometimes breed (Lange 2007). In their physical spaces, museums can create 'safe spaces' for discussion, utilizing facilitators and rules for civil discussion that produce promising results in promoting critical thinking, empathy and appreciation for different views (Abram 2007). But, currently social media interfaces usually make it difficult to institute similar conditions. For instance, I have been involved in trying to foster discussion about anti-Semitism and hatred on the Holocaust Museum's Facebook page, but the platform's interface and frequent alterations make it difficult to shape a productive space for dialogue about emotional and political issues. Finally, social media's emphasis on 'real-time' and 'most recent' information seems to favor immediate response rather than to encourage the contemplative, substantive reaction museums typically value.

This critical perspective may read like fuel for social media's naysayers, but I offer it only to acknowledge social media's complexity. Recognizing that social media do not inherently or instantly realize museums' democratizing goals need not prevent their use or inhibit experimentation. Rather, it begins to take very seriously the potential of social media to advance democratic practices both in and outside of museums and to consider how museums may best utilize them. While using social media requires that museums are mindful of their flexibility, it also requires heeding the old adage of Voltaire's that has so greatly informed the development of modern digital technology: 'The perfect is the enemy of the good.'

At this formative stage, then, museums can do many things to support equality, diversity and social justice. First, they must employ social media with a critically informed understanding of their constraints and potential. Oftentimes museums regard social media as inherently democratizing forces and assume they have instantly achieved more democratic practice simply by using these technologies. But, affording the public more opportunities to encounter and comment on museums and their content does not equate with change in institutional structures, practices or relations with audiences. Museums often open these channels of communication and participation without a sense of what they will do with the publics' comments and contributions, how they will respond to them, or how they may serve visitor research. They also often use them to encourage publicly visible participation, forgetting that the majority of online users often prefer to observe (Shirky 2008).

Museums using social media with a critical perspective do not take for granted their democratizing potential. Ideally, they utilize these technologies with explicit goals that guide implementation and evaluation. For instance, rather than soliciting user-generated content for the sake of doing so, museums should consider when seeking comments or user contributions actually serves a particular goal in a project. If the public's participation is deemed necessary and appropriate, then staff should consider how social media should be optimized to encourage their contributions. Rather than providing only public opportunities to participate and converse, they should consider if private and anonymous ways are also (or more) appropriate. Further, because museums often judge the public's comments on social media to be vague, inane or idiosyncratic – just as they are when written in exhibit comment books – they frequently dismiss them as useful sources of visitor research and neither collect nor assess them. Yet, visitor comment books can offer evidence for audience research, and the Library of Congress' recent acquisition of Twitter's archives similarly exposes how social media data are beneficial for research due to their sheer breadth (Macdonald 2005; Nys 2009; Liberman 2010). Although time-consuming at this point, it would be helpful for museums to strategically collect visitor contributions to their social media efforts in order to use them for visitor research and shaping their work. Finally, a critical approach towards social media would influence museums to implement them with more pointed structures of evaluation. For example, if a museum seeks to use social media to grow and diversify its online audience, it should set up evaluative criteria according to what data it can collect, such as by trying to assess how many more people social media serve on a daily basis in comparison to those visiting physically or to the institution's website. It could also conduct surveys to collect demographic information, or study comments by coding them to consider the range of viewpoints being represented.

Museums may also serve democratizing goals by being mindful that social media involve ethical implications in practice. Museums often venture into social media because an intrepid and energetic staff member allocates time to take them there. Standards for web content can be forgotten under such ad hoc circumstances, leading museums to overlook obligations of access that such standards help serve. Whenever possible, staff should not forget to enter descriptive text for images into *alt tags* so that people using screen readers or text browsers can hear descriptions of the images. Similarly, transcripts or caption files should be provided for all videos released on social media platforms, whether uploaded as caption files or added as comments when captioning is not possible.

Finally, museums striving to use social media for democratizing interests should consider how actively and widely their staff contribute to those efforts. Practitioners involved in crafting more democratic museums observe that infusing democratic values into institutional culture is important to their success (Tchen 1992). Often museums allocate social media outreach to the young or to one department; they task interns or twenty-something staff (who are assumed to be 'naturally' more familiar with such things) with exploring social media, or limit participation to staff in the marketing department. But, social media as conduits of information are richest if filled with the diverse expertise that museums possess. Audiences are also excited to get direct access to experts, who may be celebrities in their field of interest. To exploit social media's capacity to reach new audiences and engage people in novel ways, museums might reassess how they operate in their organizations and consider enlisting more diverse staff to enrich the content they offer. By creating more opportunities for more staff to mix with audiences, museums may also find that these interactions also serve their democratizing goals by exposing staff to people and experiences they may not deal with on a daily basis.

Conclusions

The remediative process of networked digital media is ongoing. Over time, interface designs will change, new features will arise, new devices will emerge, and people's attitudes and uses of social media will continue to evolve. In this process, how museums best advance equality, diversity, and social justice through social media remains ambiguous, but also promising. Social media alter how we share and get information, how we coordinate and organize, how we socialize and consume, and they are as available to traditional preserves of power as they are to the average person. While social media may affect change towards more open, equitable and just societies, whether they will – and to what extent – remains up to us. Thus, to figure out how they can do so at all requires continued experimentation informed by critical understanding of the media, strategic and ethical frameworks of implementation and evaluation, and participation from diverse staff.

Moving these efforts forward also requires more research. A global survey of museum uses of social media towards the goals of equality, diversity and social justice might help all institutions understand the landscape better in order to share data and compare and contrast stories of success and failure. This knowledge could help museums form collaborations to jointly pursue goals, creating networks that disseminate the values of equality, diversity and social justice through wide-scale redundancy and through translation at local levels. At this point, museums tend to use social media as bulwarks of their physical brands, creating digital versions of their institutions and not always taking advantage of the opportunities social media present to combine efforts, expertise and resources with other museums. Collaborative projects like *Steve* and *Art Babble*, as well as the *Flickr Commons*, provide models for combining resources. To expand and diversify their audiences, as well as to facilitate deeper engagement with audiences, museums should take advantage of social media to cross-pollinate with their brethren and create networked museums that can add value to each other. Such an attitude approaches social media with an appreciation not only for how these technologies serve one museum's brand and mission, but also for how they overcome the challenges of being physical institutions with finite staff, space and resources and allow museums to exponentially increase their power to serve democratizing goals in general.

Notes

1 The assertions, opinions and conclusions in this chapter are those of the author and do not necessarily reflect those of the United States Holocaust Memorial Museum.
2 An example of a museum making a wiki open to public contribution was the Walker Art Center which included a wiki to develop a lexicon of terms related to suburbia as part of the website for the exhibit, *Worlds Away: New Suburban Landscapes* (February 16 – August 17, 2008).
3 For further discussion on this issue see Witte and Mannon (2010).

References

Abram, R. J. (2007) 'Kitchen Conversations: Democracy in Action at the Lower East Side Tenement Museum', *The Public Historian* 29 (1f): 59–76.

Barlow, A. (2008) *Blogging America: The New Public Sphere*, Westport: Praeger Publishers.

Benkler, Y. (2003) 'Freedom in the Commons: Towards a Political Economy of Information', *Duke Law Journal* 52: 1245–1275.

Benkler, Y. and Nissenbaum, H. (2006) 'Commons-based Peer Production and Virtue', *The Journal of Political Philosophy* 14 (4): 394–419.

Bolter, J. D. and Grusin, R. (2000) *Remediation: Understanding New Media*, Cambridge, MA: The MIT Press.

boyd, d. (2011) 'White Flight in Networked Publics? How Race and Class Shaped American Teen Engagement with MySpace and Facebook', in L. Nakamura and P. Chow-White (eds) *Race After the Internet,* London and New York: Routledge: 203–222.

boyd, d. and Ellison, N. (2007) 'Social Network Sites: Definition, History, and Scholarship', *Journal of Computer-Mediated Communication* 13 (1): article 11. Online. Available at: http://jcmc.indiana.edu/vol13/issue1/boyd.ellison.html (accessed 26 June 2010).

Canadian Museum for Human Rights (2011) 'Share Your Story', *Canadian Museum for Human Rights*. Online. Available at: http://humanrightsmuseum.ca/share-your-story (accessed 1 May 2011).

Caruth, N. and Bernstein, S. (2007) 'Building an On-line Community at the Brooklyn Museum: A Timeline', in J. Trant and D. Bearman (eds) *Museums and the Web 2007: Proceedings*, Toronto: Archives & Museum Informatics. Online. Available at: www.archimuse.com/mw2007/papers/caruth/caruth.html (accessed 17 February 2008).

Delanty, G. (2003) *Community*, London: Routledge.

Duncan, C. (1995) *Civilizing Rituals: Inside Public Art Museums*, London: Routledge.

Falk, J. H. (1998) 'Visitors: Who Does, Who Doesn't, and Why', *Museum News* 77: 38–43.

Falk, J. H., Dierking, L. D. and Adams, M. (2006) 'Living in a Learning Society: Museums and Free-choice Learning', in S. Macdonald (ed.) *A Companion to Museum Studies*, Malden, MA: Blackwell Publishing: 323–339.

Farrell, H., Lawrence, E. and Sides, J. (2008) 'Self-Segregation or Deliberation? Blog Readership, Participation and Polarization in American Politics', *Social Science Research Network*. Online. Available at: http://ssrn.com/abstract=1151490 (accessed 7 May 2010).

Giles, J. (2005) 'Internet Encyclopaedias Go Head to Head', *Nature* 438: 900–901.

Gosepath, S. (2009) 'Equality', in E. Zalta (ed.) *The Stanford Encyclopedia of Philosophy,* Winter 2009 edn. Online. Available at: http://plato.stanford.edu/archives/win2009/entries/equality (accessed 31 January 2011).

Hektor Pieterson Memorial and Maryland Institute for Technology in the Humanities. *Soweto '76.* Online. Available at: www.soweto76archive.org (accessed 1 May 2011).

Indianapolis Museum of Art (2011) *Art Babble*. Online. Available at: www.artbabble.org (accessed 3 May 2011).

International Museum of Women. *Her Blueprint: The I.M.O.W. Blog*. Online. Available at: http://imowblog.blogspot.com (accessed 31 January 2011).

Ito, M. (2008) 'Introduction', in K. Varnelis (ed.) *Networked Publics,* Cambridge, MA: The MIT Press: 1–14.

Jenkins, H. (2006) *Convergence Culture: Where Old and New Media Collide,* New York: New York University Press.

Jensen, B. and Kelly, L. (2009) 'Exploring Social Media for Front-End Evaluation', *Exhibitionist*: 19–25.

Kent, M. L. (2008) 'Critical Analysis of Blogging in Public Relations', *Public Relations Review* 34: 32–40.

Kolko, B. E. and Reid, E. (1998) 'Dissolution and Fragmentation: Problems in Online Communities', in S. Jones (ed.) *Cybersociety 2.0*, Thousand Oaks, CA: Sage Press: 212–229.

Lange, P. G. (2007) 'Commenting on Comments: Investigating Reponses to Antagonism on YouTube', Paper presented at the Society for Applied Anthropology Conference. Tampa, Florida.

Layne, V. (2008) 'The District Six Museum: An Ordinary People's Place', *The Public Historian* 30 (1): 53–62.

Lévy, P. (1999) *Collective Intelligence: Mankind's Emerging World in Cyberspace*, Cambridge, MA: Perseus Books.

Liberman, M. (2010) 'Mapping the Demographics of American English with Twitter', *Language Log*. Online. Available at: http://languagelog.ldc.upenn.edu/nll/?p=2334 (accessed 20 May 2011).

Library of Congress and Flickr (2011) *Flickr Commons*. Online. Available at: www.flickr.com/commons (accessed 10 April 2011).

Macdonald, S. (2005) 'Accessing Audiences: Visiting Visitor Books', *Museum and Society* 3 (3): 119–136.

Manovich, L. (2008) 'Art after Web 2.0.', in R. Frieling (ed.) *The Art of Participation: 1950 to Now*, New York: Thames & Hudson: 67–80.

Mattress Factory (2011) 'MF iConfess', *YouTube*. Online. Available at: www.youtube.com/user/MFiConfess (accessed 1 May 2011).

Museum of the History of Polish Jews (2011) *Virtual Shtetl*. Online. Available at: www.sztetl.org.pl/en (accessed 3 May 2011).

Museum Victoria (2011) 'Talking Difference', *Museum Victoria*. Online. Available at: http://museumvictoria.com.au/discoverycentre/websites-mini/talking-difference (accessed 1 May 2011).

Nakamura, L. (2010) 'Race and Identity in Digital Media', in J. Curran (ed.) *Media and Society*, 5th edn, London and New York: Bloomsbury Academic: 336–347.

National Underground Railroad Freedom Center (2011) *Freedom Blog*. Online. Available at: www.freedomcenter.org/freedom-forum (accessed 7 May 2011).

Nys, L. (2009) 'The Public's Signatures: Visitors' Books in Nineteenth-Century Museums', *Museum History Journal* 2 (2): 143–162.

Parr, B. (2010) 'YouTube Surpasses Two Billion Video Views Daily', *Mashable*. Online. Available at: http://mashable.com/2010/05/17/youtube-2-billion-views (accessed 28 February 2011).

Parry, R. (2007) *Recoding the Museum: Digital Heritage and the Technologies of Change*, London and New York: Routledge.

Porter, G. (2003) 'Seeing Through Solidity: A Feminist Perspective on Museums', in B. Carbonell (ed.) *Museum Studies: An Anthology of Contexts*, Malden, MA: Blackwell Publishing: 104–116.

Preece, J. and Shneiderman, B. (2009) 'The Reader-to-Leader Framework: Motivating Technology-Mediated Social Participation', *Transactions on Human-Computer Interaction* 1 (1): 13–32.

Rettberg, J. W. (2008) *Blogging*, Cambridge: Polity.

Science Museum of Minnesota (2011) *Science Buzz*. Online. Available at: www.sciencebuzz.org (accessed 10 April 2011).

Shirky, C. (2008) *Here Comes Everybody: The Power of Organizing Without Organizations*, New York: Penguin.

Springer, M., Dulabhan, B., Michel, P., Natanson, B., Reser, D., Woodward, D. and Zinkham, H. (2008) 'For the Common Good: The Library of Congress Flickr Pilot Project'. Online. Available at: www.loc.gov/rr/print/flickr_pilot.html (accessed 22 December 2008).

Steve Project (2011) *Steve: The Museum Social Tagging Project*. Online. Available at: www.steve.muscum (accessed 7 May 2011).

Sunstein, C. R. (2007) *Republic.com 2.0*, Princeton: Princeton University Press.

Tchen, J. (1992) 'Creating a Dialogic Museum: The Chinatown History Museum Experiment', in I. Karp, C. M. Kreamer and S. D. Lavine (eds) *Museums and Communities: The Politics of Public Culture*, Washington, DC: Smithsonian Institution Press: 286–326.

Te Papa (2011) 'The Mixing Room', *Te Papa*. Online. Available at: http://sites.tepapa.govt.nz/refugeesblog (accessed 1 May 2011).

Trant, J. (2006) 'Social Classification and Folksonomy in Art Museums: Early Data from the Steve. Museum Tagger Prototype'. A paper for the ASIST-CR Social Classification Workshop.

Van Grove, J. (2010) 'Social Networking Usage Surges Globally [STATS]', *Mashable*. Online. Available at: http://mashable.com/2010/03/19/global-social-media-usage (accessed 28 February 2011).

Vaughan, J. (2010) 'Insights Into The Commons on Flickr', *Portal: Libraries and the Academy* 10 (2): 185–214.

Walker Art Center (2011) 'Worlds Away: New Suburban Landscapes', *Walker Art Center*, Online. Available at: http://design.walkerart.org/worldsaway (accessed 30 April 2011).

Weinberger, D. (2007) *Everything is Miscellaneous: The Power of the New Digital Disorder*, New York: Times Books.

Witcomb, A. (2003) *Re-Imagining the Museum: Beyond the Mausoleum*, London and New York: Routledge.

Witte, J. C. and Mannon, S. E. (2010) *The Internet and Social Inequalities*, New York: Routledge.

Zickuhr, K. (2010) 'Generations 2010', *Pew Internet and American Life Project*. Online. Available at: www.pewinternet.org/Reports/2010/Generations-2010.aspx (accessed 29 April 2011).

Zuckerberg, M. (2010) '500 Million Stories', *The Facebook Blog*. Online. Available at: http://blog.facebook.com/blog.php?post=409753352130 (accessed 31 January 2011).

21

MUSEUMS, AFRICAN COLLECTIONS AND SOCIAL JUSTICE

Helen Mears and Wayne Modest

Over the past few decades museums have been undergoing significant changes in how they relate to their numerous publics. From monologue (producing narratives *for*) to dialogue (producing narratives *with*); from mono-vocal to poly-vocal, these changes in thinking and practice can be seen to coincide with (and to, in some ways, result from) increasing demands from museum publics to have a say in how 'their' museums function to serve them, as well as a critical reflection on museum practice from academics and museum practitioners alike.

Arguably, this has been especially true for ethnographic museums – or museums with ethnographic ('world art', 'world cultures') collections. Indeed, recent years have seen a mushrooming in claims from former colonised peoples, indigenous rights groups and other marginalised communities to have a say in how their cultural heritage is acquired and cared for and how they are portrayed within museums (Peers and Brown 2003; Simpson 1996). These claims coincide with the refiguring of national polities resulting from, among other factors, large scale movements of peoples from the former colonised world towards colonial centres of power, some of whom are claiming a place in their 'new home' and demanding a say in how their heritage is represented. Not to be ignored as well is the reflexive turn in anthropology as an academic discipline during this period and with it the emergence of a critical museology that has also served to challenge older modes of museum practice.

These developments have had significant effects on policy and practice. Some museums have sought to adopt more inclusive and participatory models for exhibition planning, public programming and even research and, at the same time, notions of social inclusion, poly-vocality, shared authority, and even social justice have found a place on many museums' agendas. All of this is already a well-rehearsed story and one which has attracted increasing attention within museum studies (Sandell 2002; Watson 2007).

In this chapter the authors seek to take up the issue of social justice and museums. More specifically, we are interested to explore how museums with African collections can utilise these to promote issues of social justice. While such an endeavour can easily fall into racial or ethnic reductionism and simplistic identity claims the authors attempt a more nuanced approach to try and tease out the various issues of justice that a circumscribed collection (area) raises for broader museum publics and propose some preliminary ideas on how these issues can be addressed. In doing so we draw on the work of the late political theorist Iris Marion Young. We explore Young's ambition to 'expand the idea of a heterogeneous public . . . by arguing for a principle of representation for oppressed groups in democratic decisionmaking bodies' (Young 1990: 158). We consider what this might mean for museums with African collections and examine specific curatorial strategies employed by UK institutions in recent years and assess their effectiveness in this respect.

African collections in museums, including those in the UK, did not come about spontaneously or independently. The 'boom' in holdings of material from the African continent in the collections of British museums in the late nineteenth and twentieth century was a direct consequence of the significant social, political, cultural and economic changes brought to that continent by the experience of colonialism. This, as many in the UK's Black and minority ethnic community rightly insist, must be accounted for by any museum using African collections to address issues of social justice. Thus we begin this chapter by acknowledging the particular circumstances, as well as the power relations, which enabled the creation of African museum collections and which continue to colour our perceptions of this material.

social justice yet not acquired ethically

We will then present some theoretical concerns about social justice within the multicultural present. Finally we will bring these two strands together to suggest some ways in which African collections might be deployed to promote issues of social justice.

A crude history (or unhidden histories)

It is a well known fact, but perhaps one worth drawing attention to here, that few museum collections of African material in the UK were formed by African people.[1] Indeed, outside the national museums where the creation of large field collections required the assistance, if not the consent, of members of the communities from which they were extracted, African objects in UK museum collections were acquired largely independently by British people for their personal gratification or for the entertainment and edification of other British people via display in British museums. The process through which these collections developed and were displayed was in many ways informed – indeed structured – by the racialisation that informed the colonial endeavour (Coombes 1997a). For much of the late nineteenth and early twentieth centuries the narrative through which collections of 'African' material culture were presented to British audiences served to reinforce the distance and presumed difference between those regarded as British and others regarded as Africans. Africans were presented as 'barbarous' and 'savage'; their material culture regarded as, among other things, 'fetishes' and 'ju-jus' (Shelton 1995).

Much as the British Empire asserted itself over its colonial subjects, creating new geographical boundaries and divisions, British museums participated in the categorisation, stratification and definition of Africa and Africans through an edited sample of their material culture. British collecting was rarely representative: certain kinds of objects were preferred to others just as certain ethnic groups were more likely to form the focus of collecting activities than others. Favoured groups included those embroiled in imperial conflict who provided popular subjects for museum display. Exhibitions such as those at the South Kensington Museum following the Abyssinian 'Expedition' of 1868 and the punitive raid on Kumasi in 1874 confidently reflected the imperialist tone of the popular press (Barringer 1998). Many museum acquisitions during this period carried uncritical associations with imperial conquests and, even in the absence of material directly relating to imperial confrontation, displays of African material in British museums made extensive use of weaponry, with spears, bows and arrows laid out in trophy-like fans to suggest imperial triumph over the warmongering native (Edwards 2001).

Some of these tropes persisted in museum displays throughout the twentieth century, despite the many changes that took place on the African continent most notably from the 1960s (including significant demographic changes within the national community described as 'British', with a growing population of people of African descent), as well as the voluminous academic critique of the negative portrayal of Africa within academic and popular discourse (Coombes 1997b; Hall 1997). UK museum displays were also slow to change their display aesthetic or interpretative framework. Ethnographic displays such as that at Brighton Museum & Art Gallery (Figure 21.1) – which typically featured static displays of nineteenth-century African material culture organised by 'ethnic group' (the 'Asante'; the 'Sande'; the 'Baluba') in a darkened room, in cases backed with faux-snakeskin or leopard-skin wallpaper – seemingly resisted the protracted struggles of black British people against the negative stereotypes that these displays often posited or reinforced, and remained undisturbed until the 1990s.

Black resistance to outright racism within British society resulted in several riots across Britain in the mid to late twentieth century, such as the Brixton riots of 1981. Arguably still an unfinished process, this ongoing struggle has contributed significantly to forcing government to implement policies and establish initiatives addressing issues of inequality and social exclusion.[2] These initiatives also had an impact on the way museums in the UK worked. Indeed, the election of 'New Labour' in 1997 resulted in policies that required that culture 'do some work', especially in terms of promoting social cohesion (Department for Culture, Media and Sport (DCMS) 2000). One consequence of these changes was that museums with significant ethnographic collections began to question the ways in which these collections were displayed, as well as the role that they could play more generally in the museum and beyond. With the support of public funders willing to invest in those organisations prepared to raise their game in this respect, the late 1990s and early 2000s witnessed a flowering of new museum display projects which included African material. Notable examples include the African Worlds Gallery at the Horniman Museum (discussed below), which opened in 1999, and the Sainsbury Africa Gallery at the British Museum, which opened in 2001.

As the landscape has changed over time, so too have museums, at least at the level of the mission statement. Social outcomes, including ones clumsily targeting issues of 'race', have become a standard feature of museum work and of the organisations, public and charitable, which fund them. At first, many of these initiatives were delivered by peripheral elements of the museum; by the education and then freshly-formed outreach teams, but increasingly they have moved closer to the core of museum business and utilised collections in achieving these outcomes.

In what follows, we consider the results of these changes for issues of social justice. Also, we will reflect on how thinking about new social purposes for historic African museum collections can promote or prohibit social justice.

Collections and the politics of difference

That (African) collections within museums can be used to serve social justice agendas is neither self-evident, nor straightforward. Indeed, formulating such an agenda can risk reproducing reductionist identitarian politics that serve only to continue the racialised thinking – *raciology* according to Paul Gilroy (2004) – that is the bequest of our colonial past. It also

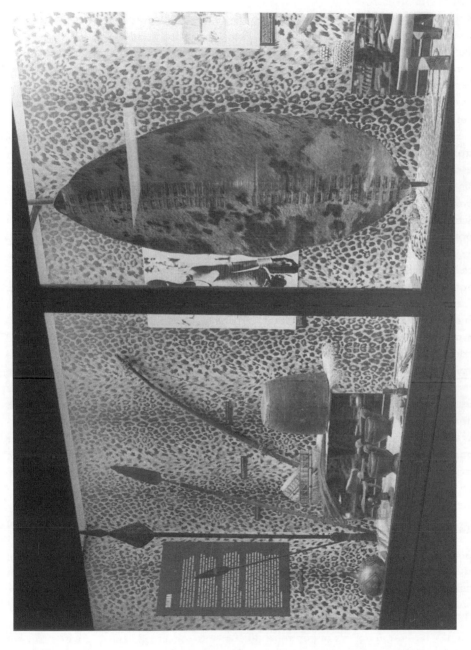

FIGURE 21.1 Displays of ethnographic material, in this case from the 'Baluba' and 'Zulu', as they appeared at Brighton Museum & Art Gallery until the early 1990s. © Royal Pavilion & Museums, Brighton & Hove.

stands the risk of generating symbolic political gestures that effect little change in the status quo. Using collections in ways that reduce the barriers to inclusion as well as addressing some of the negative images within a society about one particular group or community is, however, possible, if not urgent.

Recent attempts by museums to develop multicultural and social justice agendas have been set against the uncertainty circulating amongst academics, politicians and the general public alike about the nature of multiculturalism, the importance of associated concepts such as identity and difference, and the role of these in constructing the national polity (Keith 2005). Indeed, if we were to take the recent pronouncement by British Prime Minister, David Cameron – which reflects a general sentiment sweeping across several European countries – multiculturalism has failed (Doward 2011). An important question to ask, then, is whether museums can successfully adopt policies of inclusion and social justice within a political environment that is less than supportive of such endeavours.

As a way into thinking about how such policies might function, we locate our discussion within a now long-standing debate on justice and the politics of difference, and particularly the work of Iris Marion Young. Young's political theory employs a mix of theoretical strands from feminist theory to Marxism to better understand issues of justice within a framework of the politics of difference. In *Justice and the Politics of Difference* (1990), for example, Young challenges conventional conceptions of equality which seek the transcendence of group difference in the pursuit of a common humanity. She draws attention to how this position implicitly supports the appropriation of the universal subject position by socially privileged groups and notes how, accordingly, 'the achievement of formal equality [has] not eliminate[d] social differences'. Indeed, she continues, a 'rhetorical commitment to the sameness of persons [has made it] impossible even to name how those differences presently structure privilege and oppression' (1990: 164). For these reasons she argues that 'groups cannot be socially equal unless their specific experience, culture, and social contributions are publicly affirmed and recognised' (1990: 174).

In contrast to this commitment to sameness – what she describes as liberal humanist ideals – Young argues for 'democratic cultural pluralism'; 'in this vision the good society does not eliminate or transcend group difference. Rather, there is equality among socially and culturally differentiated groups, who mutually respect one another and affirm one another in their differences' (1990: 163). For multicultural societies, following Young, it is in acknowledging difference and addressing the social, cultural and economic limitations that such difference creates, that will lead to more just societies.

Politics of positional difference

In conceptualising difference Young distinguishes between the politics of *cultural* difference and the politics of *positional* difference, highlighting the ways in which the two frame current political thought around social justice, especially within multicultural societies. Young argues that in current political debates too much emphasis is placed on cultural difference instead of positional difference which, for her, stands the risk of obscuring important issues of justice. In Young's terms, the politics of positional difference is concerned primarily with 'issues of justice concerning structural inequality' (1990: 82):

> Persons suffer injustice by virtue of structural inequality when their group social positioning means that the operation of diverse institutions and practices conspire to limit

their opportunities to achieve well being. Persons suffer specifically culture-based injustice when they are not free to express themselves as they wish, associate with others with whom they share forms of expression and practices, or to socialize their children in the cultural ways they value, or when their group situation is such that they bear significant economic or political cost in trying to pursue a distinctive way of life.

Ibid.

A politics of positional difference, then, struggles against difference-blind approaches which tend to interpret equality as 'sameness for all' and therefore fail to comprehend structural barriers. Young identifies disability as central to issues of positional difference, suggesting that we 'can learn much about social justice generally as concerning issues of structural inequality, normalization, and stigmatization' if we utilise disability and draw on the experiences and perspectives of disabled people (Young 2007: 86). Drawing on debates at the heart of disability studies, Young argues that disability is not a shortcoming of the disabled person, as was the historic perception, but rather an example of the 'lack of fit' between the certain attributes of some persons and structures and practices (for example, at the workplace or in public places), that have become normalised.[3] Addressing these issues for Young, therefore, cannot be achieved by denying or overlooking difference.

Within positional difference, Young addresses the issue of racial inequality:

Racism consists in structural processes that normalize body aesthetic, determine that physical, dirty or servile work is most appropriate for members of certain groups, produces and reproduces segregation of members of these racialized groups, and renders deviant the comportments and habits of these segregated persons in relation to dominant norms.

Young 2007: 89

To effectively address such structural inequality, then, a society must *notice* the processes of racial differentiation around which these inequalities are founded and 'call them out' before it can correct them. A difference-blind approach, in Young's account, cannot go far enough in redressing social inequalities.

Politics of cultural difference

Young's analysis poses a central question to museums and other public institutions:

Given that a political society consists of two or more societal cultures, what does justice require in the way of their mutual accommodation to one another's practices and forms of cultural expression, and to what extent can and should a liberal society give public recognition to these cultural diversities?

1990: 97

For her, a politics of cultural difference argues for the freedom of particular groups within a multi (as in more than one) cultural polity to be able to express cultural expressions that they believe are important to them, whether being religious difference, stylistic choices or the freedom to congregate to celebrate particular events or occasions.

Museums, particularly those with African and 'world cultures' collections, are then well-placed to facilitate the process of public recognition for cultural difference that Young endorses. While the possibility to falter into essentialism remains close, for Young this process of *recognising* difference is the first step towards identifying – and beginning to work to unpick – the ways in which 'those differences presently structure privilege and oppression' (1990: 164).

Much of the British museums sector is clearly in agreement with Young's suggestion and does much in terms of identifying – some might say reifying – difference. Through programming, displays, exhibitions, web projects and learning resources, museums across the UK have done much to raise the profile (and publicly affirm) the specific experience, cultural practices and social contributions of distinctive social groups. It may even be fair to ask if they have not taken this too far, adopting simplistic approaches based on what are seen as fixed cultural markers for historically-unchanging, visibly 'different' homogeneous groups; the kinds of groups curators can find historically 'described' by groups of material culture and their documentation in museum collections.

A more serious concern is that these projects seldom go further than that. Rarely are participants given the opportunity to challenge the dominant narratives of the museum and museum work with 'cultural' groups, outside of programming activities – to consider collecting policies, marketing schemes, mission statements, for example – is even rarer.

Accommodating difference: curatorial strategies

While acknowledging that some of the efforts already taken by some museums have been successful, in what follows we want to propose a rereading of Young's ideas towards a more nuanced, if not speculative, understanding of the ways that African collections can be employed within a social justice agenda. These strategies, we suggest, do not deny difference but seek to use them to remove the barriers to inclusion. We explore three case examples where distinctive curatorial strategies were employed to promote public access to 'African' material culture in the pursuit of social justice.

The dialogic paradigm: developing African Worlds

Regarded as an import milestone in increasing poly-vocality in museums, the *African Worlds* gallery at the Horniman Museum opened in March 1999 as one of the first galleries dedicated to Africa in the UK (Phillips 2003; Shelton 2003). With a curatorial and advisory team drawn from Africa, the Caribbean and the UK as well as drawing on the input of members of London's African Diaspora, the gallery addressed some of the trenchant circulating myths and misunderstandings about the African continent. Moreover, it established connections with (and included the participation of) persons from Africa and the African Diaspora living in the UK. Misconceptions, perhaps unbelievable today, as simple as 'Africa is one country', to more complex concerns such as redressing ideas that Africa has no history, whether Egypt is part of the African continent, or exploring gender relationships in West Africa, were addressed in the gallery (Shelton 2003).

The development of the *African Worlds* gallery was intended to not just address the racialised histories that produced skewed narratives of Africa and the African Diaspora, but also to acknowledge the multi-ethnic difference that constituted the city of London and to give voice, through the African collections, to different forms of African cultural expressions.

Indeed, in Young's terms, it was allowing 'public recognition of the cultural diversity' (1990: 97) of the city. At the same time the inclusion of 'African voices' in the exhibition itself was an attempt to give over some of the decision-making about how objects from Africa were to be interpreted while allowing people from Africa and the African Diaspora to have a voice in articulating their own histories (Figure 21.2).

By taking a stand against the ways in which Africa was framed within contemporary discourse the exhibition made a stand against the some of the racialisation that the museum itself was implicated in creating. Moreover, the consultation process and the inclusion of people from Africa and the African Diaspora in the curatorial project team, as well as in the exhibition interpretation itself, was intended both to address diversity as well as give voice to the specific 'community' from whom the objects were understood to have come. In this way, the exhibition project employed models for justice based on both *cultural* and *positional* difference.

Revealing hidden histories: the Museum of London and the V&A Museum

The recovery of 'hidden histories' has been one curatorial strategy applied by a number of UK institutions in order to secure recognition for historically marginalised groups. This approach recognises that museum collections were established on terms which privilege certain aspects of class, gender and race but remains optimistic in its belief that these same collections can be 'mined' – to use Fred Wilson's evocative term – for evidence of other, divergent histories. This was the approach taken by the Museum of London in its 2004–6 project, *Re-assessing What We Collect*, which resulted in an online resource currently featuring over 800 objects linked to 42 'communities'.

At the V&A, the African Diaspora Research Project set out to disprove the assumption that the V&A had never collected 'African' objects (these, considered 'ethnography' rather than decorative art, had been presumed to be the exclusive preserve of the British Museum). The wide terms of the research project – which included Africa's Diasporas and so the UK's own 'Black History' – ensured that a rich seam of material could be identified, from eighteenth-century European prints with their ubiquitous Black child servant to works by diasporic artists such as Aubrey Williams (Figure 21.3), Frank Bowling and Chris Ofili (Figure 21.4 and Plate 21.1), as well as the usual nineteenth-century African ethnography. By locating more than 4,000 objects of relevance, the project inadvertently highlighted the institutional racism which had, in the twentieth century, blinded the organisation to this material. In 1999, the then director Alan Borg, was reported as saying at the landmark *Whose Heritage?* conference that:

> [The V&A] was seriously impeded by its own 'skewed' collection . . . [N]othing had been collected from Africa . . . The collection resembled an encyclopaedia with several volumes missing. Replacing those now would make no sense, in his view: better that other organisations should do that job.
>
> *Arts Council of England 1999: 21*

The hidden histories model – in raising the profile of collections material that speaks to and of the experiences of marginalised communities – seems at one level to draw on Young's assertion that 'groups cannot be socially equal unless their specific experience, culture, and social contributions are publicly affirmed and recognised' (1990: 174). Museums – as organisations concerned with the promotion of culture and heritage – are uniquely well-placed to facilitate

FIGURE 21.2   Display case showing Yoruba maternity figure and Ibejis twin figures. The display label includes curatorial description and interpretation from an artist and teacher from Africa living in the UK. Courtesy of the Horniman Museum and Gardens.

FIGURE 21.3 Aubrey Williams, *Untitled*, 1958–64. Given by Mrs Eve Williams, widow of the artist. With permission of the Victoria and Albert Museum, London.

FIGURE 21.4 Chris Ofili, *Tibidabo*. Plate from the suite of ten entitled To T from B with L., 1992. With permission of the Victoria and Albert Museum, London.

this public affirmation, even if doing so also entails recognising the extent to which they have historically been informed by 'dominant norms which claim universality and neutrality' (ibid.: 167).

And yet in practice the model is often flawed. A central challenge of the approach, which seeks to privilege the previously marginal, is the same challenge of 'cultural diversity', which looks for 'culture' and 'diversity' only outside of the mainstream. While these 'hidden histories' are, for the length of the project, privileged, they are rarely given the opportunity to move into, or fundamentally unsettle, the mainstream. In Young's terms there is little opportunity for 'transformational assimilation'; for the learning to flow from group to institution and for both to be changed by the experience. In the case of the V&A project, the research was externally funded (and therefore tightly time- and output-bound) and subject to limited resources. Unlike the museum's core work on 'Asia', with its devoted team of curatorial staff, the African Diaspora research project was conducted by one part-time, fixed-term researcher. Moreover, the project outputs were all web-based meaning the main museum interface – its exhibitions and displays – remained largely undisturbed by the project findings. Therefore, identifying and formulating specific projects around difference is not necessarily the solution to issues of exclusion.

Addressing absences: The West Indian Front Room

In a discussion about the range of activities organised by UK museums to commemorate the Bicentenary of the Parliamentary Abolition of Slavery in 2007, Katherine Prior remarks on the striking absence of post-Columbian Caribbean material in the collections of British museums;

> a situation arising from persistent colonial and racist attitudes to the societies that emerged from slavery. For generations British colonial officers and scholars viewed these societies as culturally impure, as 'creole' or 'bastard' cultures, that, being neither wholly African nor wholly European, had not produced anything distinctive or worth collecting.
>
> *2007: 208*

Through highlighting this absence, Prior reminds us of the subjectivities implicit in our historic collections, which, over time and through the cycles of exhibitionary and academic discourse, have become normalised; those biases and omissions which are too rarely interrogated. Indeed, the ideologies that subtended nineteenth-century collecting practices resulted in the material culture of the modern Caribbean being excluded from British museum collections. As new cultural subjects formed out of colonial contact, Caribbean peoples did not fall within the category of objects to be salvaged through fear of a disappearing culture – salvage anthropology – nor did they represent a people with sufficiently important 'history' or 'culture' – a great civilisation – to make collecting them important for museums. Not surprisingly, on the whole, Caribbean collections in Britain are significantly weighted towards the indigenous population of the region (who have in fact, in most cases, disappeared).[4]

Prior notes that this has resulted in the region 'mostly [being] featured in museums only when slavery has been on the agenda' (ibid.: 208). However, another consequence is that, as museums try to address Caribbean audiences through their programming, they intentionally or unintentionally (perhaps even simplistically) choose objects from Africa as representative of the region. In some instances, Indian objects are also mobilised. While not denying the importance of Africa or India to Caribbean formation, this practice can result in simplistic originary claims without accounting for the complexities of Caribbean identity formation.

Prior points us to an 'outstanding recent exception' that addressed the Caribbean. The exhibition, *The West Indian Front Room: Memories and Impressions of Black British Homes,* was presented at the Geffrye Museum, London, October 2005–February 2006 (Plate 21.2). The show, which had been in development since 1999, used a range of artefacts and home decorations to imaginatively reconstruct the front room of a family of West Indian immigrants living in Britain in the 1960s. Even to give the exhibition this description is, perhaps, to assign it with too fixed a meaning because what this installation revealed was the fluid, hybrid, contradictory and contested nature of what is regarded as Caribbean identities in Britain. In contrast to other museum projects, which so often peddle ideas of cultural fixity, the West Indian front room was presented as a personal, creative response to the processes of colonialism and migration. While its origins were colonial – 'This was the idealized parlor that the colonial elite in the Caribbean attempted to imitate as a romantic reinvention of an English home in a "tropical" climate' (McMillan 2009: 138) – the incarnation presented to museum visitors was a product of diasporic imagination. It was British as much as it was Caribbean.

The installation provoked humour – the kitsch paintings; the ubiquitous sculpted, starched, crocheted dollies; the eye-aching carpets – it provoked nostalgia and it demanded respect for the experiences and aspirations of its imagined inhabitants. Its sensory accessibility invited all visitors to engage with it (and during its five-month display, 35,000 visitors did) and evoked 'emotional responses through sensorial recognition, identification, even ambivalence for visitors about what they saw, touched, heard, and even smelled that triggered a kaleidoscopic body of memories' (McMillan 2009: 142).

Curated by a museum 'outsider', the writer and artist Michael McMillan, who describes himself as 'a second-generation, Black British person from an aspirant working-class family of Vincentian parentage' (ibid.: 137), it is interesting to consider whether there is a museum which could have 'self-generated' this display. For as much as the installation generated an emotional, sensory response, it also made no secret of its ambitions to attend to 'some of these erasures and mis(sed) representations in the Caribbean and diasporic context' (2009: 136). In evoking and questioning ideas of home and belonging it also;

> raised questions about diasporic identities, intergenerational identifications, and disavowal; gendered practices in the domestic domain. Institutionally it also raised issues about mis(sed) representations, struggles over meaning, and authenticity in museum/gallery culture about the legitimization and policing of representations of the black British experience.
>
> *Ibid.: 138*

More than the hidden histories approach, where objects are typically brought out of storage in an acknowledgement both that the museum had these collections and that they have value, the *West Indian Front Room* addressed a group for whom no real collection existed. The museum, therefore, had to examine its own exhibition policy and collections to consider the ways in which they did not facilitate inclusion of a large group of people living in its vicinity.

Conclusions

In her report to the V&A at the end of the grant-aided scheme which had funded her research project, the African Diaspora Research Fellow drew attention to the richness and diversity of the 'Africa'-related objects and images in its possession (Mears 2010). She also noted the institutional disinterest, which, until the 1990s, had blinded the organisation to these riches. Now made aware of them she urged the organisation to let itself be transformed by these objects; to find mechanisms for changing its core position on the collecting and display of African objects and images. For the museum to fulfil its self-appointed role as 'the world's greatest museum of art and design', it was essential that it saw itself as a natural home for African art and design.

To its credit, the V&A has taken its first steps towards this curatorial ambition. It has revised its collecting policy as well as developed a temporary exhibition, new gallery interpretation and education programmes which have sought to expose historic and contemporary objects and images from Africa and the African Diaspora in its collection to new audiences. However only time will tell how much of this work becomes organisationally embedded. Indeed, more critical reflection and structural changes might need to occur, not only at the V&A but in museums in general, if they are to fulfil their potential to promote social justice. Nowhere was the researcher at the V&A able to record the small frustrations of her days – the curators still found to be using the (now legally-actionable) term 'Kaffir' in updated catalogue records for South African material; the discovery that every photographic image of a *Black Hair & Nails* event had been catalogued with the keyword 'Negro'; the fact that the only Nigerian she met at the museum during her tenure was the woman who cleaned her office – those details which, while unsubstantiated and apparently trivial in themselves, add up to something which requires further reflection on the potential of African museum collections to effect social justice.

Young, as we have sought to highlight here, makes a useful distinction between cultural and positional difference in developing a framework for the promotion of social justice. The eruption of cultural diversity work by museums in recent years – with greater or lesser relevance to their historic collections – suggests we are very good at identifying cultural difference. And yet, as Young has shown us, by over-emphasising *cultural* difference, we often overlook other forms of difference with which cultural difference is articulated and interdependent. Differences in health, housing, education and access to life opportunities also function to structure inequality. African collections in British museums offer unique entry points into developing understanding of how history informs the racialised discourses that framed our multicultural present. However, understanding may no longer be enough: museums need to begin to dismantle those internal structures that structure contemporary racialisation.

Many cultural diversity initiatives in museums, including some of those discussed in this chapter, adopt a relatively noncomplex methodology – a one-on-one mapping of African collections onto people of African and African Diaspora origins which potentially sets up dangerous presumptions on the basis that content equals audience. Indeed, such initiatives run the risk of eliding the very complexity of identities and of neglecting academic work, produced over the past two decades, that has tried to complicate originary identity discourses.

Yet these strategies also provide other under-explored possibilities that potentially disrupt the manufacturing of difference. The question is whether it is possible for museums to avoid making reductive parallels between the 'communities' described in their collections (and their documentation) and their target audiences in terms of display, exhibition, educational and outreach programmes? What if, instead of seeing difference as a structuring force for our public projects and programmes (this event for Africans, that event for Asians), we see difference as a tool through which to undo the prohibitions to inclusion? Instead of seeing the categories of colonial formation as fixed and unchangeable, we see them as categories to undo through our programmes.

By this we suggest that it may be possible that the work of museums is not so much to target (visible) difference itself and formulate programmes addressed at these groups, but rather to target the ways that museums – through their catalogues, the *voice*, language or positionality they adopt – continue to reinscribe the categories of colonial formation that informed their practices. The question is how to address 'communities' without continuing race thinking. This may seem only to produce a small change in the institution. Yet the targeting of communities through specific programmes is often not enough to change the underlying issues of exclusion that exist within an institution. Moreover, many of these programmes are very often dependent on the politics (and therefore the funding regime) of the day. Using African collections to address people from Africa or African Diaspora may go some way in giving that 'community' a sense of place and a feeling of control over their cultural heritage. However, this may not help to reduce general stereotypes and misconceptions about Africa that exist within the wider population. The approach with the *African Worlds* gallery at the Horniman Museum sought to address both the African community *and* broader museum going publics as it tried to reinterpret its collections.

What we suggest therefore is that, in looking forwards from this point, identifying the structures that discourage the inclusion of diverse populations and removing those from the museum organisation; asking how collections can be used to combat societal prejudices and facilitate a better way of living with diversity; could serve as a more meaningful and impactful way to address the injustices embedded in society.

Notes

1 Of note, in this respect, is research being conducted by Zachary Kingdon into African donors to the collections of what is now Liverpool World Museum. Findings from this research are as yet unpublished but background is given in Kingdon (2008) and Kingdon and van den Bersselaar (2008). It would probably also be useful to note that very few people from Africa or of African descent currently work in curatorial positions within museums with African collections in the UK.
2 For discussions of racial struggle within the context of multicultural Britain see Amin (2002), Gilroy (2004) and Keith (2005).
3 For recent work on museums and disability see Sandell *et al.* (2010) and Walters (2009).
4 See Modest (forthcoming) for a discussion of how this collecting of the material culture of the Tainos in Jamaica help to frame the island as a 'natural' as opposed to a 'cultural' place. Also how this practice served to displace interest in the Black population of Jamaica. This practice was also seen within museums in the Caribbean.

References

Amin, A. (2002) 'Ethnicity and the multicultural city: living with diversity', *Environment and Planning A* 34(6): 959–980.

Arts Council of England (1999) 'Notes on Alan Borg's introductory address', *The Impact of Cultural Diversity on Britain's Living Heritage*, Report of National Conference at G-Mex, Manchester 1–3 November 1999, London: Arts Council of England.

Barringer, T. (1998) 'The South Kensington Museum and the colonial project', in T. Barringer and T. Flynn (eds) *Colonialism and the Object: Empire, Material Culture and the Museum*, London and New York: Routledge, 11–26.

Coombes, A. (1997a) *Reinventing Africa: Museums, Material Culture and Popular Imagination in Late Victorian and Edwardian England*, New Haven: Yale University Press.

Coombes, A. (1997b) 'Material culture at the crossroads of knowledge: the case of the Benin Bronzes', in S. Hall (ed.) *Representation: Cultural Representations and Signifying Practices*, London, Thousand Oaks and New Delhi: Sage Publications Limited: 219–222.

DCMS (2000) *Centres for Social Change: Museums, Galleries and Archives for All: Policy Guidance on Social Inclusion for DCMS Funded and Local Authority Museums, Galleries and Archives in England*, London: Department for Culture Media and Sport.

Doward, J. (2011) 'David Cameron's attack on multiculturalism divides the coalition', *Observer*, 6 February: 8.

Edwards, E. (2001) 'Photographing objects', in E. Edwards, *Raw Histories: Photographs, Anthropology and Museums*, Oxford and New York: Berg, 51–81.

Gilroy, P. (2004) *After Empire: Multiculture or Postcolonial Melancholia*, London and New York: Routledge.

Hall, S. (ed.) (1997) *Representation: Cultural Representations and Signifying Practices*, London, Thousand Oaks, CA and New Delhi: Sage Publications Limited.

Keith, M. (2005) *After the Cosmopolitan? Multicultural Cities and the Future of Racism*, Oxford and New York: Routledge.

Kingdon, Z. (2008) 'Reinterpreting the African collections of the World Museum Liverpool', *Critical Interventions* 1(2): 31–41.

Kingdon, Z. and van den Bersselaar, D. (2008) 'Collecting empire? African objects, West African trade, and a Liverpool museum', in S. Haggerty, A. Webster and N. J. White (eds) *The Empire in One City? Liverpool's Inconvenient Imperial Past*, Manchester: Manchester University Press, 100–122.

Mears, H. (2010) 'Locating Africa at the V&A: reflecting on the outcomes of the African Diaspora research project', in E. Nightingale (ed.) *Capacity Building and Cultural Ownership: Working with Culturally Diverse Communities*, London: V&A Publications, 118–124.

McMillan, M. (2009) 'The West Indian Front Room: reflections on a diasporic phenomenon', *small axe* 28: 135–156.

Modest, W. (Forthcoming) 'We've always been modern: museums, collections and modernity in the Caribbean', *Museum Anthropology*.

Peers, L. and Brown, A. K. (eds) (2003) *Museums and Source Communities: A Routledge Reader*, London and New York: Routledge.

Phillips, R. B. (2003) 'Community collaboration in exhibitions: towards a dialogic paradigm: introduction', in L. Peers and A. K. Brown (eds) *Museums and Source Communities: A Routledge Reader*, London and New York: Routledge, 155–170.

Prior, K. (2007) 'Commemorating slavery 2007: a personal view from inside the museums', *History Workshop Journal* 64: 200–210.

Sandell, R. (ed.) (2002) *Museums, Society, Inequality*, London and New York: Routledge.

Sandell, R., Dodd, J. and Garland-Thomson, R. (eds) (2010) *Re-Presenting Disability: Activism and Agency in the Museum*, London and New York: Routledge.

Shelton, A. (1995) *Fetishism: Visualising Power and Desire*, London: Lund Humphries.

Shelton, A. (2003) 'Curating African Worlds', in L. Peers and A. K. Brown (eds) *Museums and Source Communities: A Routledge Reader*, London and New York: Routledge, 181–193.

Simpson, M. G. (1996) *Making Representations: Museums in the Post-colonial Era*, London and New York: Routledge.

Walters, D. (2009) 'Approaches in museums towards disability in the United Kingdom and the United States', *Museum Management and Curatorship* 24(1): 29–46.

Watson, S. (ed.) (2007) *Museums and their Communities*, London and New York: Routledge.

Young, I. M. (1990) *Justice and the Politics of Difference*, Princeton: Princeton University Press.

Young, I. M. (2007) 'Structural injustice and the politics of difference' in *Justice, Governance, Cosmopolitanism, and the Politics of Difference Reconfigurations in a Transnational World: Distinguished W.E.B. Du Bois Lectures 2004/2005*. 79–116. Online. Available at: www.newschool.edu/uploadedfiles/tcds/democracy_and_diversity_institutes/young_structural%20injustice%20and%20politics.pdf (accessed 29 July 2011).

INDEX

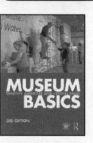

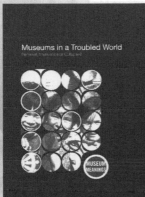